$1.00
411
CG

# Shakespeare's

# Names

## A New Pronouncing Dictionary

# Shakespeare's Names

## Names

A New Pronouncing Dictionary

Louis Colaianni

DRAMA PUBLISHERS
an imprint of
Quite Specific Media Group Ltd.
New York

For information address:
Quite Specific Media Group Ltd.
260 Fifth Avenue
New York, NY 10001


ISBN 0-89676-215-7


(212) 725-5377  v.  (212) 725-8506  f.
web: www.quitespecificmedia.com
email:  info@quitespecificmedia.com


Quite Specific Media Group Ltd. imprints:
Costume & Fashion Press
Drama Publishers
By Design Press
Jade Rabbit
EntertainmentPro


Printed in Canada

"... Then shall our NAMES,
Familiar in his mouth as household words—
Harry the King, Bedford and Exeter,
Warwick and Talbot, Salisbury and Gloucester—
Be in their flowing cups freshly remembered."

*Henry The Fifth*, IV iii

*This book is dedicated to my parents,*
*James Francis Colaianni, and Patricia Kelly Colaianni*

# Table of contents

# Acknowledgments

I would like to thank the team at Quite Specific Media Group Ltd., my editor, Ina Kohler, and Ralph Pine, Editor in Chief, who, to my good fortune, believe in me; David Golston, who is my constant source of support, and encouragement; Claudia Anderson, Speech Teacher, California Institute of the Arts, who made so many useful suggestions throughout this project; My colleagues at University of Missouri-Kansas City, particularly, Cal Pritner, Chair, Department of Theatre, who has shared his wisdom, and given me every possible assistance in completing this project; Dale AJ Rose, Director of Performance Training, with whom I have discussed every conceivable pronunciation for Shakespeare's names in the many projects on which we have collaborated; Jennifer Martin, mentor and fellow coach who shares my quest for the embodiment of language; Theodore Swetz, who teaches Shakespeare through the example of his acting, and the traditions of his teachers; Felicia Londre, who first encouraged me to write; John Ezell, whose Charrette program made it possible for me to interview Fiona Shaw; George Keathley, Artistic Director, Missouri Repertory Theater, who has given me so many opportunities to share my work in the professional theater; Marilyn Carbonell, Librarian, who first gave me the idea for this dictionary.

I would also like to thank Jeanette Nelson, speech coach, The National Theater, London, for her views on contemporary British speech training; Fiona Shaw, who so generously and patiently answered my questions, and read my lists of names; Mike King, Windows 95 Support Specialist, who was always there to help when I was having computer trouble; Marc Plowman, Macintosh Technical Support Specialist, who opened his office to me and my staff, and so generously gave of his time and expertise. Peggy Loft, whose lively and challenging discussions of 'standard speech' were an inspiration; My brother, James Colaianni Jr, who always drops what he's doing to answer my computer and editing questions; My student and Editorial Assistant Kelly MacAndrew; My technical assistant Sean Harman; My students Rick Wasserman, Carrie Vujcec, Jimmy Augustine, Nguyen Cao Huynh, Ian Borden, Anthony Hubert, Robert Morgan, Sarah Peters, Cecilia Saunders, Nicholas Toren, and Dana Vranic, who helped me prepare the manuscript; Robert Leibacher, who taught me phonetics and Shakespeare at the Boston Conservatory; Tina Packer and the faculty of Shakespeare & Company, for many unforgettable, enriching experiences with the words of Shakespeare; and finally, my teacher Kristin Linklater, who has spoken and written so eloquently on the subject of 'good speaking.'

# Preface

This dictionary provides actors, students, and scholars with pronunciations of the names in Shakespeare's plays and poems which are both aesthetically suitable to the texts in which they occur, and mindful of the current trends in American and British pronunciation. It is my intent to bring the sound of Shakespeare's names into the 21st century, reflecting the vitality and ever-evolving nature of the English language. This is, for the most part, a descriptive dictionary; that is, it sets out to *describe* authentic speaking patterns in current use, rather than to *prescribe* idealized, 'standard' pronunciations. Two types of pronunciation are documented here: 1) 'general American,' which encompasses the current, common speech patterns of US English, and 2) Received Pronunciation, or, RP, the speech standard for southern England, in its most current form. These pronunciations usually agree with the models for 'general American,' and 'British RP' speech outlined in Longman's Pronunciation Dictionary, JC Wells, 1990; (the transcription style, however, differs from Wells in many ways; see an explanation of the symbols page 335). Wells documents trends in American and British speech, which in the scope of older pronunciation dictionaries had not yet evolved, or were considered sub-standard (Jones, Kenyon and Knott). Like Wells, the present work reflects a shifting attitude toward conservative forms of 'good speech' in the US and England. In the US, the prescriptive speech pattern variously known as,'Theater Standard,' 'Transatlantic,' (Hobbs), 'Eastern Standard,'(Kenyon and Knott) and 'good speech for classic texts' (Skinner), which was the preferred speaking style for 'classic texts' in the

1920s, 30s and 40s, has lost popularity in recent years (Hobbs). This erstwhile requisite for American Shakespeare performance, has both a vowel scheme, and an R-drop which are reminiscent of southern British speech (Knight). The use of 'Theater Standard' speech in classic plays in the US presents a dilemma of cultural identity. It has been characterized as "an accent we can't quite place, except to say that it is not of this world—British-sounding but not British, American but not American-sounding" (Mufson). Today, many American actors and speech teachers prefer the more familiar-sounding, colloquial style of 'general American' speech (Mufson). In England, meanwhile, attitudes toward RP have become increasingly democratic (Wells, 1990). The parameters of RP have been broadened to include recent innovations in British common speech, such as: a shift in vowel formation in words such as BOWL, and COLD; the replacement of the 'liquid U' sound in words such as SUIT, and LUNAR, with the 'long U' sound of words such as MOON; the disappearance of the aspirated 'WH' sound, in words such as WHERE, and WHICH, once fastidiously insisted upon as a mark of 'good speech' and now considered 'incorrect.' Additionally, the class-crossing 'Estuary Accent,' is responsible for a general lowering of the vowels; and a weakened, or dropped final l, in words such as WHEEL, in the speech of many Londoners, irrespective of class (Ezard).

Shifting attitudes toward pronunciation, determine the life-span of a pronunciation manual. It is folly to adhere to old-fashioned, or pretentious-sounding pronunciations just because they have been written down. The style in which Shakespeare's words are pronounced changes and adapts to suit the tastes and style of each region, and of each generation. "Unlike Chaucer, whose poetry is unintelligible unless one adopts a reconstructed style of speech with the help of phonemic transcriptions, Shakespeare will always be read in the more or less natural pronunciation of the reader or actor" (Cercignani). It is therefore, necessary to periodically update pronunciation resources for Shakespeare.

The two previously published pronunciation dictionaries of Shakespeare's names, Irvine, 1919, and, Kokeritz 1959, both fine works of scholarship, each contain many antiquated pronunciations. Today, Irvine is more an artifact of post-Victorian elocution than a practical manual in pronunciation. Published in the US, Irvine cautions readers not to sound affected, yet, follows a British vowel scheme and prescribes the now archaic practice of R-trilling. Kokeritz remains an invaluable resource for insights into Shakespeare's intended use of rhyme, pun and verse patterns, as well as reconstructions of Elizabethan pronunciations of the names. Like Irvine, however, Kokeritz's vowel scheme is basically British. Kokeritz's primary reference for US pronunciation was 'Eastern Standard' speech (see above) as outlined in Kenyon and Knott, 1944, revised, 1953. Kokeritz's primary reference for British RP pronunciation, was Jones, 1917, revised, 1958. Although both Kenyon and Knott, and Jones, are standard references in the field of speech, they offer a more conservative view of contemporary pronunciation than Wells, even in their most recent editions. As a case in point, the pronunciation of nearly one hundred words in Wells have been determined through an Opinion Poll of two hundred seventy five native speakers of British English (Wells, 1990).

The present work differs from its two predecessors in many respects: First, a newly compiled data base adds approximately one hundred names which were overlooked in the previous dictionaries. Furthermore, the pronunciation schemes of the previous dictionaries have been largely rejected. Pronunciations found in Kokeritz and Irvine which disagree with those of present-day general American and RP have not been included. Whenever possible, the viability of pronunciations has been verified through comparison with recent descriptive references, such as Wells 1990 and Bollard. In cases where no documentation of current pronunciation is available, pronunciations given in Kokeritz and Irvine have been reinterpreted to reflect current usage. But even in cases where pronunciations given in the previous works are considered viable, they are transcribed in a significantly different style in the present work.

The present dictionary employs two transcription styles for each entry: A form of International Phonetic Alphabet transcription which combines elements of broad and narrow transcription and avoids the use of diacritic markings, and Simplified Phonics transcription which follows simplistic rules of spelling and pronunciation which are easily accessible to the layman. This is done to achieve maximum accessibility for the user. Kokeritz and Irvine each employed only one transcription style. Kokeritz used a form of International Phonetic Alphabet transcription which is somewhat narrower than the IPA transcriptions of the present work. Irvine used a combination of Roman alphabet symbols and dictionary diacritics, which is significantly different from the Simplified Phonics transcriptions of the present work. Furthermore, in the present work, the entire lexicon of names mentioned in the Shakespeare canon is catalogued according to the individual play or poem in which it occurs. In Kokeritz, the names are arranged in one alphabetical sequence. In Irvine an appendix of the *Dramatis Personae* (which accounts for a small fraction of the total number of names which appear in the canon) catalogues the names of characters according to the play in which they occur, but the dictionary proper, as in Kokeritz, is arranged in a single alphabetical sequence.

The advantages of the present work are: User-friendly transcriptions; the capability for a quick overview of name-pronunciations in each individual work; And, above all, pronunciations which are in step with current usage.

The non-prescriptive, democratic tone of modern speech training is evident in the words of renowned voice teacher Kristin Linklater: "If *'holding the mirror up to nature'* means that there is a diversity of sounds on stage, then, standardization of speech for Shakespeare is codswallop; if the way a person speaks obscures the content of the scene or the fullness of the character then, clearly, that it is a limitation, but if the person is really a good actor, why should you dock him of his pay because he has an accent of a certain sort?" Linklater argues that "as the plays [of Shakespeare] are universal, and reflect life, they should reflect the diversity of life, and there is no standardization of speech in life. Nor is it likely that the actors in Shakespeare's companies spoke alike, coming as they did from different parts of England." She observes that "elocution flourished in the nineteenth century, at a time when the unacceptable realities of emotional and psychological turmoil were well hidden under the guise of manners and social style." Linklater has " entered into almost killing arguments with directors who insist that they must have a homogenized sound on stage. Homogenizing the sounds that happen on stage will bring about the death of the art of speaking, and the death of the art of speaking Shakespeare."

Many recent stage and film productions bear witness to a trend for speaking Shakespeare in indigenous varieties of English. On the US stage, noted productions, such as, Ron Daniel's 1991 *Hamlet,* and Steven Berkoff's 1988 *Coriolanus,* continue an American tradition of indigenously pronounced Shakespeare which began with the New York Shakespeare Festival (Mufson). London has seen recent productions of *King Lear,* and *Titus Andronicus* which were infused with the vitality of regional accents. Classical stage actors such as Fiona Shaw, whose Irish vowels and rhoticity place her well outside the pale of British RP, prove *clarity,* not conformity, to be the by-word of well-spoken English. Furthermore, such films as Brannagh's *Much Ado About Nothing,* McKellen's *Richard III,* and Parker's *Othello* have brought a refreshing array of regional and national accents to an international audience.

As the future of live-Shakespeare performance depends upon audience development, many theater companies conduct Shakespeare-in-the-schools programs in which the actors speak in their native accents. One such program at the Market Theater in Johannesburg, brought Shakespeare's words into full accessibility for Black South African students who found British stage-pronunciation unintelligible (Lane-Plescia).

It is urgent that we enter the new millennium with the treasures of our language accessible to all. This dictionary is a plea that Shakespeare's plays not become museum curiosities, but remain a vital part of our living language. Raymond Williams wrote that a language such as English could not be engineered by a committee of individuals seeking to define 'good speech;' but, rather, the natural course of evolution, which can never be predetermined or second-guessed, would steer the path of the language's future. "There will doubtless always be people and groups who are anxious to show that they are not as other men, but the deep processes of the growth of a great international language will not be much affected by them, though they may for a time be blurred. We want to speak as ourselves, and . . . at the same time in an extending community, we want to speak with each other, reserving our actual differences but reducing those that we find irrelevant. We are almost past the stage of difficulties of meaning, in ordinary discourse . . . The [remaining] problems [surrounding speech] are of emotional tension, and these, while certain to continue, can be much reduced if we learn to look at them openly and rationally, with the rich and continuing history of English as our basis of understanding. History did not end around 1800, or in the 1920s. The living language offers its deciding witnesses."

The pronunciations in this dictionary are considerably different from those which, four hundred years ago,

Shakespeare is said to have used. These pronunciations, witnesses to contemporary speech, remain, forevermore, open to revision.

Louis Colaianni
Kansas City, 1998

# Introduction

## The Organization of the Names

The names in this dictionary are catalogued according to the play or poem in which they occur (see table of contents). It is the aim of this dictionary to provide actors, students, and scholars with a quick comprehensive reference with which to study the names of a single play or poem. The plays and poems are arranged in alphabetical order and within each play or poem the names are arranged in alphabetical order. For entries where portions of a name are contained within brackets, it is the unbracketed portion of the name which is alphabetized. For example the name [de la] Pole is found under P, and cross listed in its unbracketed form, de la Pole, under D.

## The Phonetic Alphabets Used in This Dictionary

Each entry in this dictionary is given in two different types of phonetic transcription: the International Phonetic Alphabet, and the Simplified Phonics Alphabet. The International Phonetic Alphabet provides a more detailed analysis of spoken sounds, than the Simplified Phonics Alphabet. In some cases where more than one pronunciation of a name is given, an ellipsis [ ... ] will appear in place of the Simplified Phonics Alphabet transcription. This indicates that the pronunciation variance is too subtle for transcription in Simplified Phonics Alphabet transcription and the user is referred to the International Phonetic Alphabet transcription of that entry.

## The Transcription Styles Used In This Dictionary

In the explanatory material below, all International

Phonetic Alphabet Symbols will appear within slash marks / /. This is done in order to separate them from the Roman alphabet text. In the dictionary proper, the International Phonetic Alphabet Symbols will appear without the use of slash marks.

As stated in the preface, this dictionary documents the pronunciation of Shakespeare's names in two speaking styles: 'general American' speech, and 'British received pronunciation' (RP). The first entry, or series of entries for each name is given in 'general American' transcription. 'General American' entries are unmarked except in cases of unusual variant pronunciations (see Variant Pronunciations, below). 'British RP' pronunciations are identified by a diamond symbol, ◊ which appears to the right of the transcription. For example, the first transcription of the name Antonio is 'general American,' the second, identified by the diamond symbol, is 'British RP,' (see Antonio entry on page 30).

The diamond symbol does not appear in entries where 'general American' and 'British RP' are in agreement. For example, a single transcription of the name Iris, applies to both 'general American' and 'British RP' pronunciation, (see Iris entry on page 25).

## Variant Pronunciations

In many cases there is no difference between the 'general American' and 'British RP' pronunciation. In these cases either a single pronunciation, or, a series of variant pronunciations which apply to both speaking styles is given. For example the two pronunciations of the name Amiens, /'æ miənz/, and /'eɪ miənz/, are current in both 'general American,' and 'British RP' speech.

In some cases, a single pronunciation which is current in both 'general American,' and 'British RP' speech is given, followed by an exclusively American, or, British variant. In these cases, the *common* pronunciation is not identified as such, but the subsequent 'general American,' or, 'British RP' *variant* will be followed by the notation: [gen Am var], or, [Brit RP var]. In the case of the name Cadwal, the first pronunciation applies to both 'general American,' and 'British RP' speech: /kæd wɔl/ but, the second pronunciation is identified as applying exclusively to 'general American' speech: /kæd wɑl/ [gen Am var]. In the case of the name Ralph, the first pronunciation applies to both 'general American,' and 'British RP' speech: /rælf/ but, the second pronunciation is identifed as applying exclusively to 'British RP' speech: /reɪf/ [Brit RP var].

## *Pronunciation of Foreign Names*

As stated in the preface, the pronunciations given in this dictionary are those which are commonly heard in 'general American' and 'British RP' speech. Foreign names are therefore transcribed in a more or less Anglicized form. This is in keeping with Shakespeare's own tendancy to Anglicize foreign names, as evidenced by spellings, scansion, and rhymes found in the plays (Kokeritz). The reader is advised to interpret foreign names creatively; giving them the flavor of Anglicised, or, foreign pronunciation as suits the purpose. For instance, English characters might pronounce the name Orleans in a typically Anglicized way, while French characters might pronounce it in the French manner. Guidelines for authentic foreign pronunciations can be found in a diction manual, such as Diction, by John Moriarty (see Bibliography). Consulting such a resource will broaden the options for pronunciation of French, Italian, German, and Latin names found in the Shakespeare canon.

A pronunciation key footnote appears at the beginning of each play and poem. For a detailed explanation of the symbols used in this dictionary see pages 335–358.

## All's Well That Ends Well

| NAME | INTERNATIONAL PHONETIC ALPHABET* | SIMPLIFIED PHONICS** |
|---|---|---|
| **Antonio** | æn ˈtoʊ nio<br>æn ˈtəʊ niəʊ ◊ | an to nee o<br>... ◊ |
| **Austria** | ˈɔ striə<br>ˈɔs tʃriə | aw stree uh<br>aws chree uh |
| **Bajazet** | bæ ʤə ˈzɛt<br>bæ ʤə ˈzet ◊ | ba juh zet<br>... ◊ |
| **Bentii** | ˈbɛn ʃi aɪ<br>ˈben ʃi aɪ ◊ | ben shee ai<br>... ◊ |
| **Bertram** | ˈbɝ trəm<br>ˈbɝ tʃrəm<br>ˈbɜ trəm ◊ | bər truhm<br>bər chruhm<br>bə truhm ◊ |
| **Caesar** | ˈsi zɚ<br>ˈsi zə ◊ | see zər<br>see zə ◊ |
| **Capilet** | ˈkæ pə lɪt | ka puh lit |
| **Charbon** | ˈʃɑr bɑn<br>ˈʃɑ bɒn ◊ | shahr bahn<br>shah bon ◊ |
| **Charlemain** | ˈʃɑr lə meɪn<br>ˈʃɑ lə meɪn ◊ | shahr luh mein<br>shah luh mein ◊ |
| **Chitopher** | ˈtʃɪ tə fɚ<br>ˈkɪ tə fɚ<br>ˈtʃɪ tə fə ◊<br>ˈkɪ tə fə ◊ | chi tuh fər<br>ki tuh fər<br>chi tuh fə ◊<br>ki tuh fə ◊ |
| **Christendom** | ˈkrɪ sən dəm | kri suhn duhm |

*International Phonetic Alphabet Pronunciation Key: (General American) i-see, happy, Juliet; ɪ-sit; eɪ-say; ɛ-set; æ-sat; ɑ-father; ʌ-sun; ə-about; ɔ-saw; oʊ-so; o-hero; ʊ-shook; u-soon; aɪ-sigh; ɔɪ-soy; aʊ-south; ju-cube; ɚ-supper; ɛr-fair; ɝ-bird; k-cut, kite; g-go; ʤ-joy; j-yes; ŋ-sing; ʃ-shoe; tʃ-chop; ð-that; θ-thin; ʒ-measure; (Additional symbols for British RP) e-set; ɛə-fair; ə-supper; ɜ-bird; ɒ-stop; əʊ-so, hero; o-(followed by l) pole.

**Simplified Phonics Pronunciation Key: (General American) ee-see, happy; i-sit; ei-say; e-set; a-sat; ah-father; uh-sun, about; aw-saw; o-so; oo-shook; oo-soon; ai-sigh; oy-soy; ow-south; yoo-cube; ər-bird, supper; k-cut, kite; g-go; j-joy; ng-sing; kw-quick; sh-shoe; ch-chop; th-that; th-thin; zh-measure; (Additional symbols for British RP) ə-bird; ə-supper; o-stop; ... indicates pronunciation variance too subtle for Simplified Phonics transcription see International Phonetic Alphabet transcription.

◊ British RP pronunciation-see Introduction.

| NAME | INTERNATIONAL PHONETIC ALPHABET* | SIMPLIFIED PHONICS** |
|------|----------------------------------|----------------------|
| **Christian** | 'krɪs tʃən | kris chuhn |
| **Corambus** | kə 'ræm bəs | kuh ram buhs |
| **Cosmo** | 'kɑz mo<br>'kɒz məʊ ◊ | kahz mo<br>koz mo ◊ |
| **Cox** | 'kɑks<br>'kɒks ◊ | kahks<br>koks ◊ |
| **Cressid** | 'krɛ sɪd<br>'kre sɪd ◊ | kre sid<br>... ◊ |
| **Cupid** | 'kju pɪd | kyoo pid |
| **Curtal** | 'kɝ təl<br>'kɜ təl ◊ | kər tuhl<br>kə tuhl ◊ |
| **Dane** | 'deɪn | dein |
| **de Narbon** | də 'nɑr bən<br>də 'nɑ bən ◊ | duh nahr buhn<br>duh nah buhn ◊ |
| **Dian** | 'daɪ ən<br>'daɪ æn | dai uhn<br>dai an |
| **Diana** | daɪ 'æ nə | dai a nuh |
| **Drum** | 'drʌm<br>'dʒrʌm | druhm<br>jruhm |
| **Dumain** | du 'meɪn<br>dju 'meɪn ◊ | doo mein<br>dyoo mein ◊ |
| **Dutch** | 'dʌtʃ | duhch |
| **English** | 'ɪŋ glɪʃ | ing glish |
| **Escalus** | 'ɛs kə ləs<br>'es kə ləs ◊ | es kuh luhs<br>... ◊ |

| NAME | INTERNATIONAL PHONETIC ALPHABET* | SIMPLIFIED PHONICS** |
|---|---|---|
| **Florence** | 'flɔ rɪns<br>'flɑ rɪns<br>'flɒ rɪns ◊ | flaw rins<br>flah rins<br>flo rins ◊ |
| **Florentine** | 'flɔ rən tin<br>'flɑ rən tin<br>'flɒ rən taɪn ◊ | flaw ruhn teen<br>flah ruhn teen<br>flo ruhn tain ◊ |
| **Fontibel** | 'fɑn tɪ bɛl<br>'fɒn tɪ bel ◊ | fahn ti bel<br>font ti bel ◊ |
| **France** | 'fræns<br>'frɑns ◊ | frans<br>frahns ◊ |
| **[Saint] Francis** | [seɪnt] 'fræn sɪs<br>[sɪnt] 'frɑn sɪs ◊ | [seint] fran sis<br>[sint] frahn sis ◊ |
| **French** | 'frɛntʃ<br>'frentʃ ◊ | french<br>… ◊ |
| **Galen** | 'geɪ lən | gei luhn |
| **Gerard** | 'dʒe rɚd<br>dʒə 'rɑrd<br>'dʒɜ rəd ◊<br>dʒə 'rɑd ◊ | je rərd<br>juh rahrd<br>jə ruhd ◊<br>juh rahd ◊ |
| **German** | 'dʒɚ mən<br>'dʒɜ mən ◊ | jər muhn<br>jə muhn ◊ |
| **[le] Grand** | lə grænd<br>lə grɑn | luh grand<br>luh grahn |
| **Gratii** | 'greɪ ʃi aɪ | grei shee ai |
| **Grecian** | 'gri ʃən | gree shuhn |
| **Guiltian** | 'gɪl tiən<br>'gɪl ʃiən | gil tee uhn<br>gil shee uhn |

| NAME | INTERNATIONAL PHONETIC ALPHABET* | SIMPLIFIED PHONICS** |
|------|------|------|
| Helen | 'hɛ lən | he luhn |
| | 'hɛ lɪn | he lin |
| | 'he lɪn ◊ | ... ◊ |
| Helena | 'hɛl ə nə | hel uh nuh |
| | 'hel ə nə ◊ | ... ◊ |
| Hercules | 'hɝ kjə liz | hər kyuh leez |
| | 'hɝ kju liz | hər kyoo leez |
| | 'hɝ kjʊ liz ◊ | hə kyoo leez ◊ |
| Hesperus | 'hɛs pə rəs | hes puh ruhs |
| | 'hes pə rəs ◊ | ... ◊ |
| Indian | 'ɪn diən | in dee uhn |
| Iris | 'aɪ rɪs | ai ris |
| Isabel | 'ɪz ə bɛl | i zuh bel |
| | 'ɪz ə bel ◊ | ... ◊ |
| Isbel | 'ɪz bɛl | iz bel |
| | 'ɪz bel ◊ | ... ◊ |
| Italian | ɪ 'tæl jən | i tal yuhn |
| Italy | 'ɪ tə li | i tuh lee |
| Jack | 'ʤæk | jak |
| [Saint] Jaques | [seɪnt] 'ʤeɪ kwiz | [seint] jei kweez |
| | [seɪnt] 'ʒɑk | [seint] zhahk |
| | [sɪnt] 'ʤeɪ kwiz ◊ | [sint] jei kweez ◊ |
| | [sɪnt] 'ʒɑk ◊ | [sint] zhahk ◊ |
| John | 'ʤɑn | jahn |
| | 'ʤɒn ◊ | jon ◊ |
| Jove | 'ʤoʊv | jov |
| | 'ʤəʊv ◊ | ... ◊ |

| NAME | INTERNATIONAL PHONETIC ALPHABET* | SIMPLIFIED PHONICS** |
|------|----------------------------------|----------------------|
| June | 'ʤun | joon |
| Juno | 'ʤu no<br>'ʤu nəʊ ◊ | joo no<br>… ◊ |
| Lafeu/Lafew | lə 'fju | luh fyoo |
| Lavache/Lavatch | lə 'væʧ<br>lə 'vɑʧ | luh vach<br>luh vahch |
| le Grand | lə grænd<br>lə grɑn | luh grand<br>luh grahn |
| Limbo | 'lɪm bo<br>'lɪm bəʊ ◊ | lim bo<br>… ◊ |
| Lodowick | 'loʊ də wɪk<br>'lɒ də wɪk ◊ | lo duh wik<br>lo duh wik ◊ |
| Mariana | mɛ ri 'æ nə<br>mæ ri 'æ nə<br>mɛə ri 'ɑ nə ◊<br>mæ ri 'ɑ nə ◊ | me ree a nuh<br>ma ree a nuh<br>meə ree ah nuh ◊<br>ma ree ah nuh ◊ |
| Mars | 'mɑrz<br>'mɑz ◊ | mahrz<br>mahz ◊ |
| Marseilles | mɑr 'seɪ<br>mɑ 'seɪ ◊ | mahr sei<br>mah sei ◊ |
| Maudlin | 'mɔd lɪn | mawd lin |
| May-Day | 'meɪ deɪ | mei dei |
| Mile End Green | 'maɪl 'ɛnd 'grin<br>'maɪl 'end 'grin ◊ | mail end green<br>… ◊ |
| Morgan | 'mɔr gən<br>'mɔ gən ◊ | mawr gin<br>maw gin ◊ |

| NAME | INTERNATIONAL PHONETIC ALPHABET* | SIMPLIFIED PHONICS** |
|------|------|------|
| **Muskos** | ˈmʌs koz<br>ˈmʌs kəʊz ◊ | muhs koz<br>… ◊ |
| **[de] Narbon** | də ˈnɑr bən<br>də ˈnɑ bən ◊ | duh nahr buhn<br>duh nah buhn ◊ |
| **Nebuchadnezzar** | nɛ bə kəd ˈnɛ zɚ<br>ne bə kjʊd ˈne zə ◊ | ne buh kuhd ne zər<br>ne buh kyood ne zə ◊ |
| **Nessus** | ˈnɛ səs<br>ˈne səs ◊ | ne suhs<br>… ◊ |
| **Pandarus** | ˈpæn də rəs | pan duh ruhs |
| **Paracelsus** | pæ rə ˈsɛl səs<br>pæ rə ˈsel səs ◊ | pa ruh sel suhs<br>… ◊ |
| **Paris** | ˈpæ rɪs | pa ris |
| **Parolles** | pə ˈroʊ liz<br>pə ˈrɒ liz ◊ | puh ro leez<br>puh ro leez ◊ |
| **Pepin** | ˈpɛ pɪn<br>ˈpɪ pɪn<br>ˈpe pɪn ◊ | pe pin<br>pi pin<br>… ◊ |
| **Phoenix** | ˈfi nɪks | fee niks |
| **Plutus** | ˈplu təs | ploo tuhs |
| **Poysam** | ˈpɔɪ səm | poy suhm |
| **Priam** | ˈpraɪ əm | prai uhm |
| **Pythagorus** | pə ˈθæ gə rəs<br>paɪ ˈθæ gə rəs ◊ | puh *th*a guh ruhs<br>pai *th*a guh ruhs ◊ |
| **Rinaldo** | rɪ ˈnæl doʊ<br>rɪ ˈnɑl do<br>rɪ ˈnæl dəʊ ◊ | ri nal do<br>ri nahl do<br>… ◊ |

| NAME | INTERNATIONAL PHONETIC ALPHABET* | SIMPLIFIED PHONICS** |
|------|------|------|
| Rousillon | rə 'sɪl jən<br>rɒ 'sɪl jən ◊ | ruh sil yuhn<br>ro sil yuhn ◊ |
| Satan | 'seɪ tən | sei tuhn |
| Sebastian | sə 'bæs ʧən<br>sə 'bæs tiən ◊ | suh bas chuhn<br>suh bas tee uhn ◊ |
| Senoys | 'sɛ nɔɪz<br>'se nɔɪz ◊ | se noyz<br>… ◊ |
| Shrove Tuesday | ʃroʊv 'tuz deɪ<br>ʃrəʊv 'tjuz di ◊ | shrov tooz dei<br>shrov tyooz dee ◊ |
| Spanish | 'spæ nɪʃ | spa nish |
| Spinii | 'spɪ ni aɪ | spi nee ai |
| Spurio | 'spjʊ rio<br>'spjʊ riəʊ ◊ | spyoo ree o<br>… ◊ |
| Tartar | 'tɑr tə˞<br>'tɑ tə ◊ | tahr tər<br>tah tə ◊ |
| Tib | 'tɪb | tib |
| Tom | 'tɑm<br>'tɒm ◊ | tahm<br>tom ◊ |
| Troy | 'trɔɪ<br>'ʧrɔɪ | troy<br>chroy |
| Tuesday | 'tuz deɪ<br>'tjuz di ◊ | tooz dei<br>tyooz dee ◊ |
| Tuscan | 'tʌs kən | tuhs kuhn |
| Vaumond | 'vɔ mənd | vaw muhnd |
| Violenta | vaɪ ə 'len tə | vai uh len tuh |

| NAME | INTERNATIONAL PHONETIC ALPHABET* | SIMPLIFIED PHONICS** |
|------|----------------------------------|----------------------|
| **Actium** | 'æk tiəm | ak tee uhm |
| **Adallas** -folio **Adullas** | ə 'dæ ləs | uh dal uhs |
| **Aemilius** | i 'mi liəs<br>i 'mil jəs | ee mee lee uhs<br>ee meel yuhs |
| **Aeneas** | ɪ 'ni əs<br>i 'ni əs | i nee uhs<br>ee nee uhs |
| **Agrippa** | ə 'grɪ pə | uh gri puh |
| **Ajax** | 'eɪ dʒæks | ei jaks |
| **Alcides** | æl 'saɪ diz | al sai deez |
| **Alexander** | æ lɪg 'zæn dɚ<br>æ lɪg 'zɑn də ◊ | a lig zan dər<br>a lig zahn də ◊ |
| **Alexandria** | æ lɪg 'zæn driə<br>æ lɪg 'zæn dʒriə<br>æ lɪg 'zɑn driə ◊ | a lig zan dree uh<br>a lig zan jree uh<br>a lig zahn dree uh ◊ |
| **Alexas** | ə 'lɛk sɪs<br>ə 'lek sɪs ◊ | uh lek sis<br>… ◊ |
| **Alps** | 'ælps | alps |
| **Amintas/ Amyntas** | ə 'mɪn təs | uh min tuhs |

*International Phonetic Alphabet Pronunciation Key: (General American) i-s<u>ee</u>, happ<u>y</u>, J<u>u</u>liet; ɪ-s<u>i</u>t; eɪ-s<u>ay</u>; ɛ-s<u>e</u>t; æ-s<u>a</u>t; ɑ-f<u>a</u>ther; ʌ-s<u>u</u>n; ə-<u>a</u>bout; ɔ-s<u>aw</u>; oʊ-s<u>o</u>; o-her<u>o</u>; ʊ-sh<u>oo</u>k; u-s<u>oo</u>n; aɪ-s<u>igh</u>; ɔɪ-s<u>oy</u>; aʊ-s<u>ou</u>th; ju-c<u>u</u>be; ɚ-s<u>upp</u>er; ɛr-f<u>air</u>; ɝ-b<u>ir</u>d; k-<u>c</u>ut, <u>k</u>ite; g-go; dʒ-joy; j-<u>y</u>es; ŋ-si<u>ng</u>; ʃ-<u>sh</u>oe; tʃ-<u>ch</u>op; ð-<u>th</u>at; θ-<u>th</u>in; ʒ-mea<u>s</u>ure; (Additional symbols for British RP) e-s<u>e</u>t; ɛə-f<u>air</u>; ə-s<u>upp</u>er; ɜ-b<u>ir</u>d; ɒ-st<u>o</u>p; əʊ-s<u>o</u>, her<u>o</u>; o-(followed by l) p<u>o</u>le.

**Simplified Phonics Pronunciation Key: (General American) ee-s<u>ee</u>, happ<u>y</u>; i-s<u>i</u>t; ei-s<u>ay</u>; e-s<u>e</u>t; a-s<u>a</u>t; ah-f<u>a</u>ther; uh-s<u>u</u>n, <u>a</u>bout; aw-s<u>aw</u>; o-s<u>o</u>; oo-sh<u>oo</u>k; oo-s<u>oo</u>n; ai-s<u>igh</u>; oy-s<u>oy</u>; ow-s<u>ou</u>th; yoo-c<u>u</u>be; ər-b<u>ir</u>d, s<u>upp</u>er; k-<u>c</u>ut, <u>k</u>ite; g-go; j-joy; ng-si<u>ng</u>; kw-<u>qu</u>ick; sh-<u>sh</u>oe; ch-<u>ch</u>op; th-<u>th</u>at; th-<u>th</u>in; zh-mea<u>s</u>ure; (Additional symbols for British RP) ə-b<u>ir</u>d; ə-s<u>upp</u>er; <u>o</u>-st<u>o</u>p; … indicates pronunciation variance too subtle for Simplified Phonics transcription see International Phonetic Alphabet transcription.

◊ British RP pronunciation-see Introduction.

| NAME | INTERNATIONAL PHONETIC ALPHABET* | SIMPLIFIED PHONICS** |
|---|---|---|
| **Antoniad** | æn 'toʊ niæd<br>æn 'təʊ niæd ◊ | an to nee ad<br>... ◊ |
| **Antonio** | æn 'toʊ nio<br>æn 'təʊ niəʊ ◊ | an to nee o<br>... ◊ |
| **Antonius** | æn 'toʊ niəs<br>æn təʊ niəs ◊ | an to nee uhs<br>... ◊ |
| **Anthony** | 'æn θə ni | an *th*uh nee |
| **Antony** | 'æn tə ni | an tuh nee |
| **Apollodorus** | ə pɑ lə 'dɔ rəs<br>ə pɒ lə 'dɔ rəs ◊ | uh pah luh daw ruhs<br>uh p*o* luh daw ruhs ◊ |
| **April** | 'eɪ prəl | ei pruhl |
| **Arabia** | ə 'reɪ biə | uh rei bee uh |
| **Arabian** | ə 'reɪ biən | uh rei bee uhn |
| **Archelaus** | ɑr kə 'leɪ əs<br>ɑ kə 'leɪ əs ◊ | ahr kuh lei uhs<br>ah kuh lei uhs ◊ |
| **Armenia** | ɑr 'mi niə<br>ɑ 'mi niə ◊ | ahr mee nee uh<br>ah mee nee uh ◊ |
| **Asia** | 'eɪ ʒə<br>'eɪ ʃə ◊ | ei zhuh<br>ei shuh ◊ |
| **Athens** | 'æ θɪnz<br>'æ θənz | a *th*inz<br>a *th*uhnz |
| **Atlas** | 'æt ləs | at luhs |
| **Bacchanal** | bæ kə 'næl<br>'bæ kə næl<br>bɑ kə 'næl<br>  [gen Am var] | ba kuh nal<br>...<br>bah kuh nal<br>  [gen Am var] |

| NAME | INTERNATIONAL PHONETIC ALPHABET* | SIMPLIFIED PHONICS** |
|------|-----------------------------------|----------------------|
| Bacchus | 'bæ kəs<br>'bɑ kəs | ba kuhs<br>bah kuhs |
| Basan | 'beɪ sən<br>'beɪ sæn ◊ | bei suhn<br>bei san ◊ |
| Bocchus | 'bɑ kəs<br>'bɒ kəs ◊ | bah kuhs<br>bo kuhs ◊ |
| Brundusium | brʌn 'du ziəm<br><br>brʌn 'dju ʒiəm ◊ | bruhn doo zee uhm<br><br>bruhn dyoo zhee uhm ◊ |
| Caelius/Coelius<br>folio- Celius | 'si liəs<br>'sil jəs | see lee uhs<br>seel yuhs |
| Caesar | 'si zɚ<br>'si zə ◊ | see zər<br>see zə ◊ |
| Caesarion | sə 'zɛ riən<br>sə 'zɛə riən ◊ | se ze ree uhn<br>se zeə ree uhn ◊ |
| Caius | 'kaɪ əs<br>'kei əs | kai uhs<br>kei uhs |
| Canidius | kə 'nɪ diəs | kuh ni dee uhs |
| Capitol | 'kæ pɪ təl | ka pi tuhl |
| Cappadocia | kæ pə 'doʊ ʃiə<br>kæ pə 'doʊ ʧə<br>kæ pə 'dəʊ siə ◊ | ka puh do shee uh<br>ka puh do chuh<br>ka puh do see uh ◊ |
| Cassius | 'kæ ʃəs<br>'kæ siəs | ka shuhs<br>ka see uhs |

| NAME | INTERNATIONAL PHONETIC ALPHABET* | SIMPLIFIED PHONICS** |
|------|----------------------------------|----------------------|
| **Charmian** | 'tʃɑr miən | chahr mee uhn |
| | 'ʃɑr miən | shahr mee uhn |
| | 'kɑr miən | kahr mee uhn |
| | 'tʃɑ miən ◊ | chah mee uhn ◊ |
| | 'ʃɑ miən ◊ | shah mee uhn ◊ |
| | 'kɑ miən ◊ | kah mee uhn ◊ |
| **Cilicia** | sə 'lɪ ʃə | suh li shuh |
| | saɪ 'lɪ siə ◊ | sai li see uh ◊ |
| **Cleopatra** | kliə 'pæ trə | klee uh pa truh |
| | kliə 'pæ tʃrə | klee uh pa chruh |
| | kliə 'pɑ trə | klee uh pah truh |
| | [Brit RP var] | [Brit RP var] |
| **Cneius** | 'ni əs | nee uhs |
| **Comagene** | 'kɑ mə ʤin | kah muh jeen |
| | 'kɒ mə ʤin ◊ | k*o* muh jeen ◊ |
| **Crassus** | 'kræ səs | kra suhs |
| **Cupid** | 'kju pɪd | kyoo pid |
| **Cydnus** | 'sɪd nəs | sid nuhs |
| **Cyprus** | 'saɪ prəs | sai pruhs |
| **Demetrius** | də 'mi triəs | duh mee tree uhs |
| | də 'mi tʃriəs | duh mee chree uhs |
| **Dercetas** | dɚ 'sɪ təs | dər si tuhs |
| | 'dɝ sɪ təs | … |
| | də 'sɪ təs ◊ | də si tuhs ◊ |
| | 'dɜ sɪ təs ◊ | də si tuhs ◊ |
| **Dido** | 'daɪ do | dai do |
| | 'daɪ dəʊ ◊ | … ◊ |
| **Diomed** | 'daɪ ə məd | dai uh muhd |

| NAME | INTERNATIONAL PHONETIC ALPHABET* | SIMPLIFIED PHONICS** |
|------|----------------------------------|----------------------|
| Diomedes | daɪ ə 'mi diz | dai uh mee deez |
| Dolabella | dɑ lə 'bɛ lə<br>dɒ lə 'be lə ◊ | dah luh be luh<br>do luh be luh ◊ |
| Domitius | də 'mɪ ʃəs<br>doʊ 'mɪ ʃəs<br>dəʊ 'mɪ ʃəs ◊ | duh mi shuhs<br>do mi shus<br>... ◊ |
| Egypt | 'i ʤɪpt | ee jipt |
| Egyptian | i 'ʤɪp ʃən | ee jip shuhn |
| Enobarb | 'i nə bɑrb<br>'i nɔ bab ◊ | ee nuh bahrb<br>ee nuh bahb ◊ |
| Enobarbus | i nə 'bɑr bəs<br>i nə 'bɑ bəs ◊ | ee nuh bahr buhs<br>ee nuh bah buhs ◊ |
| Epicurian | ɛ pɪ 'ku riən<br>ɛ pɪ kju 'riən<br>ɐ pɪ kju 'riɔn ◊ | e pi kyoo ree uhn<br>...<br>... ◊ |
| Eros | 'ɛ rɑs<br>'ɛ ros<br>'ɪə rɒs ◊ | e rahs<br>e ros<br>iə ros ◊ |
| Euphrates | ju 'freɪ tiz<br>'ju frə tiz | yoo frei teez<br>yoo fruh teez |
| Euphroneus | ju 'froʊ niəs<br>ju 'frəʊ niəs ◊ | yoo fro nee uhs<br>... ◊ |
| Fulvia | 'fʌl viə | fuhl vee uh |
| Gallus | 'gæ ləs | ga luhs |
| Gorgon | 'gɔr gən<br>'gɔ gən ◊ | gawr guhn<br>gaw guhn ◊ |

| NAME | INTERNATIONAL PHONETIC ALPHABET* | SIMPLIFIED PHONICS** |
|---|---|---|
| Hector | ˈhɛk tɚ | hek tər |
| | ˈhek tə ◊ | hek tə ◊ |
| Hercules | ˈhɝ kjə liz | hər kyuh leez |
| | ˈhɝ kju liz | hər kyoo leez |
| | ˈhɝ kjʊ liz ◊ | hə ky*oo* leez ◊ |
| Herod | ˈhɛ rəd | he ruhd |
| | ˈhe rəd ◊ | ... ◊ |
| Hipparchus | hɪ ˈpɑr kəs | hi pahr kuhs |
| | hɪ ˈpɑ kəs ◊ | hi pah kuhs ◊ |
| Hirtius | ˈhɝ ʃəs | hər shuhs |
| | ˈhɝ ʃəs ◊ | hə shuhs ◊ |
| Ionia | aɪ ˈoʊ niə | ai o nuee uh |
| | aɪ ˈəʊ niə ◊ | ... ◊ |
| Ionian | aɪ ˈoʊ niən | ai o nee uhn |
| | aɪ ˈəʊ niən ◊ | ... ◊ |
| Iras | ˈaɪ rəs | ai ruhs |
| Isis | ˈaɪ sɪs | ai sis |
| Italy | ˈɪ tə li | i tuh lee |
| Jack | ˈdʒæk | jak |
| Jewry | ˈdʒu ri | joo ree |
| Jove | ˈdʒoʊv | jov |
| | ˈdʒəʊv ◊ | ... ◊ |
| Julius | ˈdʒu liəs | joo lee uhs |
| | ˈdʒul jəs | jool yuhs |
| June | ˈdʒun | joon |

| NAME | INTERNATIONAL PHONETIC ALPHABET* | SIMPLIFIED PHONICS** |
|------|-----------------------------------|----------------------|
| **Juno** | 'ʤu no<br>'ʤu nəʊ ◊ | joo no<br>... ◊ |
| **Jupiter** | 'ʤu pɪ tɚ<br>'ʤu pɪ tə ◊ | joo pi tər<br>joo pi tə ◊ |
| **Justeius**<br>folio-**Justeus** | ʤə 'sti əs | juh stee uhs |
| **Labienus** | læ bi 'i nɪs | la bee ee nis |
| **Lepidus** | 'lɛ pɪ dəs<br>'le pɪ dəs ◊ | le pi duhs<br>... ◊ |
| **Lethe** | 'li θi | lee *th*ee |
| **Libya** | 'lɪ biə | li bee uh |
| **Lichas** | 'laɪ kəs | lai kuhs |
| **Livia** | 'lɪ viə | li vee uh |
| **Lucius** | 'lu ʃəs | loo shuhs |
| **Lycaonia** | laɪ keɪ 'oʊ niə<br>laɪ keɪ 'əʊ niə ◊ | lai kei o nee uh<br>... ◊ |
| **Lydia** | 'lɪ diə | li dee uh |
| **Maecanas/**<br>**Mecaenas**<br>folio **Mecana** | mɪ 'si nəs<br>mi 'si nəs<br>maɪ 'si næs | mi see nuhs<br>mee see nuhs<br>mai see nas |
| **Malchus** -folio<br>**Mauchus** | 'mæl kəs | mal kuhs |
| **Marcellus** | mɑr 'sɛ ləs<br>mɑ 'se ləs ◊ | mahr se luhs<br>mah se luhs ◊ |
| **Marcus** | 'mɑr kəs<br>'mɑ kəs ◊ | mahr kuhs<br>mah kuhs ◊ |

| NAME | INTERNATIONAL PHONETIC ALPHABET* | SIMPLIFIED PHONICS** |
|------|----------------------------------|----------------------|
| **Mardian** | 'mɑr diən<br>'mɑ diən ◊ | mahr dee uhn<br>mah dee uhn ◊ |
| **Mark** | 'mɑrk<br>'mɑk ◊ | mahrk<br>mahk ◊ |
| **Mars** | 'mɑrz<br>'mɑz ◊ | mahrz<br>mahz ◊ |
| **Mecaenas/<br>Maecanas**<br>folio **Mecana** | mɪ 'si nəs<br>mi 'si nəs<br>maɪ 'si næs | mi see nuhs<br>mee see nuhs<br>mai see nas |
| **Mede** | 'mid | meed |
| **Media** | 'mi diə | mee dee uh |
| **Menas** | 'mi nəs | mee nuhs |
| **Menecrates** | mə 'nɛ krə tiz<br>mə 'ne krə tiz ◊ | muh ne kruh teez<br>... ◊ |
| **Mercury** | 'mɝ kjə ri<br>'mɜ kjʊ ri ◊ | mər kyuh ree<br>mə ky*oo* ree ◊ |
| **Mesopotamia** | mɛ sə pə 'teɪ miə<br><br>me sə pə 'teɪ miə ◊ | me suh puh tei<br>  mee uh<br>... ◊ |
| **Misena** | mɪ 'si nə | mi see nuh |
| **Misenum/<br>Misenium** | mɪ 'si nəm<br>mɪ 'si niəm | mi see nuhm<br>mi see nee uhm |
| **Mithradates** | mɪ θrə 'deɪ tiz | mi *th*ruh dei teez |
| **Modena** | moʊ 'deɪ nə<br>moʊ 'di nə<br>məʊ 'deɪ nə ◊<br>məʊ 'di nə ◊ | mo dei nuh<br>mo dee nuh<br>... ◊<br>... ◊ |

| NAME | INTERNATIONAL PHONETIC ALPHABET* | SIMPLIFIED PHONICS** |
|------|----------------------------------|----------------------|
| Narcissus | nɑr ˈsɪ səs<br>nɑ ˈsɪ səs ◊ | nahr si suhs<br>nah si suhs ◊ |
| Neptune | ˈnɛp tun<br>ˈnep tjun ◊ | nep toon<br>nep tyoon ◊ |
| Nereid | ˈnɪ ri ɪd<br>ˈnɪə ri ɪd ◊ | ni ree id<br>niə ree id ◊ |
| Nessus | ˈnɛ səs<br>ˈne səs ◊ | ne suhs<br>… ◊ |
| Nile | ˈnaɪl | nail |
| Nilus | ˈnaɪ ləs | nai luhs |
| Octavia | ɑk ˈteɪ viə<br>ɒk ˈteɪ viə ◊ | ahk tei vee uh<br>ok tei vee uh ◊ |
| Octavius | ɑk ˈteɪ viəs<br>ɒk ˈteɪ viəs ◊ | ahk tei vee uhs<br>ok tei vee uhs ◊ |
| Orodes<br>  -folio Orades | ə ˈroʊ diz<br>ɒ ˈrəʊ diz ◊ | uh ro deez<br>o ro deez ◊ |
| Pacorus | ˈpæ kə rəs | pa kuh ruhs |
| Pansa | ˈpæn zə<br>ˈpæn sə | pan zuh<br>pan suh |
| Paphlagonia | pæf lə ˈgoʊ niə<br>pæ flə ˈgəʊ niə ◊ | paf luh go nee uh<br>… ◊ |
| Parthia | ˈpɑr θiə<br>ˈpɑ θiə ◊ | pahr *th*ee uh<br>pah *th*ee uh ◊ |
| Parthian | ˈpɑr θiən<br>ˈpɑ θiən ◊ | pahr *th*ee uhn<br>pah *th*ee uhn ◊ |

| NAME | INTERNATIONAL PHONETIC ALPHABET* | SIMPLIFIED PHONICS** |
|---|---|---|
| **Peloponnesus** | pɛ lə pə 'ni səs | pe luh puh nee suhs |
| | pe lə pə 'ni səs ◊ | ... ◊ |
| **Pharsalia** | fɑr 'seɪl jə | fahr seil yuh |
| | fɑ 'seɪl jə ◊ | fah seil yuh ◊ |
| **Philadelphos** | fɪ lə 'dɛl fəs | fi luh del fuhs |
| | fɪ lə 'del fəs ◊ | ... ◊ |
| **Phillipan** | 'fɪ lɪ pən | fi li puhn |
| | fɪ 'lɪ pən | ... |
| **Phillipi** | 'fɪ lɪ paɪ | fi li pai |
| | fɪ 'lɪ paɪ | ... |
| **Philo** | 'faɪ loʊ | fai lo |
| | 'faɪ ləʊ ◊ | ... ◊ |
| **Phoebus** | 'fi bəs | fee buhs |
| **Phoenecia** | fə 'ni ʃə | fuh nee shuh |
| | fə 'nɪ ʃə | fuh ni shuh |
| **Phoenician** | fə 'ni ʃən | fuh nee shuhn |
| | fə 'nɪ ʃən | fuh ni shuhn |
| **Photinus** | 'foʊ tɪ nəs | fo ti nuhs |
| | 'fɒ tɪ nəs ◊ | *fo* ti nuhs ◊ |
| **Polemon** -folio | pə 'lɛ mən | puh le muhn |
| **Polemen** | pə 'li mən | puh lee muhn |
| | pə 'le mən ◊ | ... ◊ |
| **Pompeius/** | 'pɑm piəs | pahm pee uhs |
| **Pompey** | 'pɒm piəs ◊ | p*o*m pee uhs ◊ |
| **Pompey** | 'pɑm pi | pahm pee |
| | 'pɒm pi ◊ | p*o*m pee ◊ |

| NAME | INTERNATIONAL PHONETIC ALPHABET* | SIMPLIFIED PHONICS** |
|------|------|------|
| Pont | 'pɑnt<br>'pɒnt ◊ | pahnt<br>pont ◊ |
| Proculeius | proʊ kju 'li əs<br>prəʊ kju 'li əs ◊ | pro kyoo lee uhs<br>... ◊ |
| Ptolemy | 'tɑ lə mi<br>'tɒ lə mi ◊ | tah luh mee<br>to luh mee ◊ |
| Publicola | pəb 'lɪ kə lə | puhb li kuh luh |
| Roman | 'roʊ mən<br>'rəʊ mən ◊ | ro muhn<br>... ◊ |
| Rome | 'roʊm<br>'rəʊm ◊ | rom<br>... ◊ |
| Sardinia | sɑr 'dɪ niə<br>sɑ 'dɪ niə ◊ | sahr di nee uh<br>sah di nee uh ◊ |
| Scarus | 'skɛ rəs<br>'skɛə rəs ◊ | ske ruhs<br>skeə ruhs ◊ |
| Seleucus | sə 'lu kəs | suh loo kuhs |
| Sextus | 'sɛks təs<br>'seks təs ◊ | seks tuhs<br>... ◊ |
| Sicily | 'sɪ sə li | si suh lee |
| Sicyon | 'sɪ ʃiən<br>'sɪ siən | si shee uhn<br>si see uhn |
| Silius | 'sɪ liəs | si lee uhs |
| Silvius | 'sɪl viəs | sil vee uhs |
| Soothsayer | 'suθ seɪ ɚ<br>'suθ seɪ ə ◊ | sooth sei ər<br>sooth sei ə ◊ |

| NAME | INTERNATIONAL PHONETIC ALPHABET* | SIMPLIFIED PHONICS** |
|------|------|------|
| Sossius | 'soʊ ʃiəs<br>'səʊ ʃiəs ◊ | so shee uhs<br>... ◊ |
| Syria | 'sɪ riə | si ree uh |
| Tarentum | tə 'rɛn təm<br>tə 'ren təm ◊ | tuh ren tuhm<br>... ◊ |
| Taurus<br>  -folio, **Towrus** | 'tɔ rəs<br>'tɑ rəs<br>  [gen Am var] | taw ruhs<br>tah ruhs<br>  [gen Am var] |
| Telamon | 'tɛ lə mən<br>'te lə mən ◊ | te luh muhn<br>... ◊ |
| Termagant | 'tɝ mə gənt<br>'tɜ mə gənt ◊ | tər muh guhnt<br>tə muh guhnt ◊ |
| Thessaly | 'θɛ sə li<br>'θe sə li ◊ | *the* suh lee<br>... ◊ |
| Thetis | 'θi tɪs<br>'θɛ tɪs<br>'θe tɪs ◊ | *the*e tis<br>*the* tis<br>... ◊ |
| Thracian | 'θreɪ ʃən | *the*i shuhn |
| Thyreus<br>  -folio, **Thidias** | 'θaɪ riəs | *tha*i ree uhs |
| Tiber | 'taɪ bɚ | tai bər |
| Toryne<br>  -folio, **Troine** | 'tɔ rɪn | taw rin |
| Varrius | 'væ riəs | va ree uhs |
| Ventidius | vɛn 'tɪ diəs<br>ven 'tɪ diəs ◊ | ven ti dee uhs<br>... ◊ |
| Venus | 'vi nəs | vee nuhs |

| NAME | INTERNATIONAL PHONETIC ALPHABET* | SIMPLIFIED PHONICS** |
|------|----------------------------------|----------------------|
| **Adam** | 'æd əm | a duhm |
| **Aliena** | eɪ li 'i nə<br>eɪ li 'ɛ nə | ei lee ee nuh<br>ei lee e nuh |
| **Amiens** | 'æ miənz<br>'eɪm iənz | a mee uhnz<br>ei mee uhnz |
| **April** | 'eɪ prəl | ei pruhl |
| **Arden** | 'ɑr dən<br>'ɑ dən ◊ | ahr duhn<br>ah duhn ◊ |
| **Atalanta** | æ tə 'læn tə | a tuh lan tuh |
| **Audrey** | 'ɔ dri<br>'ɔ ʤri | aw dree<br>aw jree |
| **Barbary** | 'bɑr bə ri<br>'bɑ bə ri | bahr buh ree<br>bah buh ree ◊ |
| **[le] Beau** | lə 'boʊ<br>lə 'bəʊ ◊ | luh bo<br>... ◊ |
| **[de] Bois/Boys** | də 'bɔɪz | duh boyz |
| **Caesar** | 'si zɚ<br>'si zə ◊ | see zər<br>see zə ◊ |
| **Celia** | 'si liə<br>'sil jə | see lee uh<br>seel yuh |

*International Phonetic Alphabet Pronunciation Key: (General American) i-see, happy, Juliet; ɪ-sit; eɪ-say; ɛ-set; æ-sat; ɑ-father; ʌ-sun; ə-about; ɔ-saw; oʊ-so; o-hero; ʊ-shook; u-soon; aɪ-sigh; ɔɪ-soy; aʊ-south; ju-cube; ɚ-supper; ɛr-fair; ɝ-bird; k-cut, kite; g-go; ʤ-joy; j-yes; ŋ-sing; ʃ-shoe; ʧ-chop; ð-that; θ-thin; ʒ-measure; (Additional symbols for British RP) e-set; ɛə-fair; ə-supper; ɜ-bird; ɒ-stop; əʊ-so, hero; o-(followed by l) pole.

**Simplified Phonics Pronunciation Key: (General American) ee-see, happy, i-sit; ei-say; e-set; a-sat; ah-father; uh-sun, about; aw-saw; o-so; oo-shook; oo-soon; ow-south; yoo-cube; ər-bird, supper; k-cut, kite; g-go; j-joy; ng-sing; kw-quick; sh-shoe; ch-chop; th-that; th-thin; zh-measure; (Additional symbols for British RP) ə-bird; ə-supper; o-stop; ... indicates pronunciation variance too subtle for Simplified Phonics transcription see International Phonetic Alphabet transcription.

◊ British RP pronunciation-see Introduction.

| NAME | INTERNATIONAL PHONETIC ALPHABET* | SIMPLIFIED PHONICS** |
|---|---|---|
| **Charles** | 'tʃɑrlz<br>'tʃalz ◊ | chahrlz<br>chahlz ◊ |
| **Christian** | 'krɪs tʃən | kris chuhn |
| **Cleopatra** | kliə 'pæ trə<br>kliə 'pæ tʃrə<br>kliə 'pɑ trə<br>　[Brit RP var] | klee uh pa truh<br>klee uh pa chruh<br>klee uh pah truh<br>　[Brit RP var] |
| **Corin** | 'kɔ rɪn<br>'kɒ rɪn ◊ | kaw rin<br>ko rin ◊ |
| **Cupid** | 'kju pɪd | kyoo pid |
| **de Bois/Boys** | də 'bɔɪz | duh boyz |
| **December** | di 'sɛm bɚ<br>dɪ 'sem bə ◊ | dee sem bər<br>di sem bə ◊ |
| **Dennis** | 'dɛ nɪs<br>'de nɪs ◊ | de nis<br>… ◊ |
| **Diana** | daɪ 'æ nə | dai a nuh |
| **Egypt** | 'i ʤɪpt | ee jipt |
| **England** | 'ɪŋ glənd | ing gluhnd |
| **Ethiop** | 'i θiɑp<br>'i θiɒp ◊ | ee *the*e ahp<br>ee *the*e *o*p ◊ |
| **Ethiope** | 'i θiop<br>'i θiəʊp ◊ | ee *the*e op<br>… ◊ |
| **France** | 'fræns<br>'frɑns ◊ | frans<br>frahns ◊ |
| **Frederick** | 'frɛd rɪk<br>'frɛ də rɪk<br>'fred rɪk ◊<br>'fre də rɪk ◊ | fred rik<br>fre duh rik<br>… ◊<br>… ◊ |

42

| NAME | INTERNATIONAL PHONETIC ALPHABET* | SIMPLIFIED PHONICS** |
|---|---|---|
| Friday | 'fraɪ deɪ<br>'fraɪ di ◊ | frai dei<br>frai dee ◊ |
| Ganymede | 'gæ nə mid | ga nuh meed |
| Gargantua/<br>  Garagantua | gɑr 'gæn tʃuə<br>gɑ 'gæn tjuə ◊ | gahr gan choo uh<br>gah gan tyoo uh ◊ |
| Goth | 'gɑθ<br>'gɒθ ◊ | gahth<br>goth ◊ |
| Grecian | 'gri ʃən | gree shuhn |
| Greek | 'grik | greek |
| Helen | 'hɛ lən<br>'hɛ lɪn<br>'he lɪn ◊ | he luhn<br>he lin<br>… ◊ |
| Hellespont | 'hɛ ləs pɑnt<br>'he lɪs pɒnt ◊ | he luhs pahnt<br>he lis pont ◊ |
| Hercules | 'hɝ kjə liz<br>'hɝ kju liz<br>'hɜ kjʊ liz ◊ | hər kyuh leez<br>hər kyoo leez<br>hə kyoo leez ◊ |
| Hero | 'hi roʊ<br>'hɪə rəʊ ◊ | hee ro<br>hiə ro ◊ |
| Hesperia | hɛs 'pɪ riə<br>hes 'pɪə riə ◊ | hes pi ree uh<br>hes piə ree uh ◊ |
| Hood | 'hʊd | hood |
| Hymen | 'haɪ mən | hai muhn |
| Ind/Inde | 'ɪnd<br>'aɪnd | ind<br>aind |
| Irish | 'aɪ rɪʃ | ai rish |

| NAME | INTERNATIONAL PHONETIC ALPHABET* | SIMPLIFIED PHONICS** |
|------|----------------------------------|----------------------|
| Jane | 'dʒeɪn | jein |
| Jaques/Jacques | 'dʒeɪk wiz<br>'ʒɑk (for<br>    Jacques de Boys) | jei kweez<br>zhahk (for<br>    Jacques de Boys) |
| Jove | 'dʒoʊv<br>'dʒəʊv ◊ | jov<br>… ◊ |
| Judas | 'dʒu dəs | joo duhs |
| Juno | 'dʒu noʊ<br>'dʒu nəʊ ◊ | joo no<br>… ◊ |
| Jupiter | 'dʒu pɪ tɚ<br>'dʒu pɪ tə ◊ | joo pi tər<br>joo pi tə ◊ |
| Latin | 'læ tən<br>'læ tɪn | la tuhn<br>la tin |
| Leander | li 'æn dɚ<br>li 'æn də ◊ | lee an dər<br>lee an də ◊ |
| le Beau | lə 'boʊ<br>lə 'bəʊ ◊ | luh bo<br>… ◊ |
| Lucretia | lu 'kri ʃə | loo kree shuh |
| May | 'meɪ | mei |
| Martext | 'mɑr tɛkst<br>'mɑ tɛkst ◊ | mahr tekst<br>mah tekst ◊ |
| Oliver | 'ɑ lɪ vɚ<br>'ɒ lɪ və ◊ | ah li vər<br>*o* li vuh ◊ |
| Orlando | ɔr 'læn do<br>ɔ 'læn dəʊ ◊ | awr lan do<br>aw lan do ◊ |
| Ovid | 'ɑ vɪd<br>'ɒ vɪd ◊ | ah vid<br>*o* vid ◊ |

| NAME | INTERNATIONAL PHONETIC ALPHABET* | SIMPLIFIED PHONICS** |
|---|---|---|
| Phebe | 'fi bi | fee bee |
| Phoenix | 'fi nɪks | fee niks |
| Portugal | 'pɔr ʧə gəl <br> 'pɔ tjʊ gəl ◊ | pawr chuh guhl <br> paw ty*oo* guhl ◊ |
| Pythagorus | pə 'θæ gə rəs <br> paɪ 'θæ gə rəs ◊ | puh *tha* guh ruhs <br> pai *tha* guh ruhs ◊ |
| Robin Hood | 'rɑ bɪn 'hʊd <br> 'rɒ bɪn 'hʊd ◊ | rah bin h*oo*d <br> r*o* bin h*oo*d ◊ |
| Roman | 'roʊ mən <br> 'rəʊ mən ◊ | ro muhn <br> ... ◊ |
| Rosalind | 'rɑ zə lɪnd <br> 'rɒ zə lɪnd ◊ | rah zuh lind <br> r*o* zuh lind ◊ |
| Rosalinda | rɑ zə 'lɪndə <br> rɒ zə 'lɪndə ◊ | rah zuh lin duhh <br> r*o* zuh lin duh ◊ |
| Rose | 'roʊz <br> 'rəʊz ◊ | roz <br> ... ◊ |
| Rowland <br> -folio **Roland** | 'roʊ lənd <br> 'ro lənd ◊ | ro luhnd <br> ... ◊ |
| Saturday | 'sæ tɚ deɪ <br> 'sæ tə di ◊ | sa tər dei <br> sa tuh dee ◊ |
| Sestos | 'sɛs təs <br> 'sɛs tos <br> 'ses təs ◊ | ses tuhs <br> ses tos <br> ... ◊ |
| Silvius | 'sɪl viəs | sil vee uhs |
| Smile | 'smaɪl | smail |
| Touchstone | 'tʌʧ ston <br> 'tʌʧ stəʊn ◊ | tuhch ston <br> ... ◊ |

| NAME | INTERNATIONAL PHONETIC ALPHABET* | SIMPLIFIED PHONICS** |
|------|-----------------------------------|----------------------|
| **Turk** | 'tɜ·k<br>'tɜk ◊ | tərk<br>tək ◊ |
| **Venus** | 'vi nəs | vee nuhs |
| **William** | 'wɪl jəm | wil yuhm |

# The Comedy of Errors

| NAME | INTERNATIONAL PHONETIC ALPHABET* | SIMPLIFIED PHONICS** |
|------|------|------|
| **Adam** | 'æ dəm | a duhm |
| **Adriana** | eɪ dri 'æ nə | ei dree a nuh |
| | eɪ dʒri 'æ nə | ei jree a nuh |
| | eɪ dri 'ɑ nə | ei dree ah nuh |
| | eɪ dʒri 'ɑ nə | ei jree ah nuh |
| **Aegeon/Egeon** | i 'dʒi ən | ee jee uhn |
| **Aemilia** | ɪ 'mi liə | i mee lee uh |
| | ɪ 'mil jə | i meel yuh |
| **America** | ə 'mɛ rɪ kə | uh me rik uh |
| | ə 'mɛə rɪ kə ◊ | uh meə rik uh ◊ |
| **Angelo** | 'æn dʒə lo | an juh lo |
| | 'æn dʒə ləʊ ◊ | ... ◊ |
| **Antipholus** | æn 'tɪ fə ləs | an ti fuh luhs |
| **Asia** | 'eɪ ʒə | ei zhuh |
| | 'eɪ ʃə ◊ | ei shuh ◊ |
| **Balthasar/ Balthazar** | bæl θə 'zɑr | bal *th*uh zahr |
| | 'bæl θə zɑr | ... |
| | bæl θə 'zɑ ◊ | bal *th*uh zah ◊ |
| **Belgia** | 'bɛl dʒə | bel juh |
| | 'bɛl dʒiə | bel jee uh |
| | 'bel dʒiə ◊ | ... ◊ |
| **Bridget** | 'brɪ dʒɪt | bri jit |

*International Phonetic Alphabet Pronunciation Key: (General American) i-s_ee, happy, Jul_iet; ɪ-s_it; eɪ-s_ay; ɛ-s_et; æ-s_at; ɑ-f_ather; ʌ-s_un; ə-_about; ɔ-s_aw; oʊ-s_o; ʊ-sh_ook; u-s_oon; aɪ-s_igh; ɔɪ-s_oy; aʊ-s_outh; ju-c_ube; ə-s_upper; ɛr-f_air; ɜ-b_ird; k-_cut, k_ite; g-_go; dʒ-_joy; j-_yes; ŋ-si_ng; ʃ-_shoe; ʧ-_chop; ð-_that; θ-_thin; ʒ-mea_sure; (Additional symbols for British RP) e-s_et; ɛə-f_air; ə-s_upper; ɜ-b_ird; ɒ-st_op; əʊ-s_o, hero; o-(followed by l) p_ole.

**Simplified Phonics Pronunciation Key: (General American) ee-s_ee, happy; i-s_it; ei-s_ay; e-s_et; a-s_at; ah-f_ather; uh-s_un, _about; aw-s_aw; o-s_o; oo-sh_ook; oo-s_oon; ai-s_igh; oy-s_oy; ow-s_outh; yoo-c_ube; ar-b_ird; supper; k-_cut, k_ite; g-_go; j-_joy; ng-si_ng; kw-_quick; sh-_shoe; ch-_chop; th-_that; *th*-_thin; zh-mea_sure; (Additional symbols for British RP) ə-b_ird; ə-s_upper; o-st_op; ... indicates pronunciation variance too subtle for Simplified Phonics transcription see International Phonetic Alphabet transcription.

◊ British RP pronunciation-see Introduction.

| NAME | INTERNATIONAL PHONETIC ALPHABET* | SIMPLIFIED PHONICS** |
|------|-----------------------------------|----------------------|
| Centaur | 'sɛn tɔr<br>'sentɔ ◊ | sen tawr<br>sen taw ◊ |
| Christian | 'krɪs tʃən | kris chuhn |
| Cicely | 'sɪ sə li<br>'sɪs li | si suh lee<br>sis lee |
| Circe | 'sɝ si<br>'sɜ si ◊ | sər see<br>sə see ◊ |
| Corinth | 'kɔ rɪnθ<br>'kɒ rɪnθ ◊ | kaw rinth<br>ko rinth ◊ |
| Courtezan/<br>  Courtesan<br>  -folio **Curtizan** | 'kɔr tə zən<br>'kɔ tə zən ◊ | kawr tuh zuhn<br>kaw tuh zuhn ◊ |
| Delay | də 'leɪ<br>dɪ 'leɪ<br>di 'leɪ | duh lei<br>di lei<br>dee lei |
| Dowsabel | 'daʊ sə bɛl<br>'daʊ sə bel ◊ | dow suh bel<br>… ◊ |
| Dromio | 'droʊ mio<br>'dʒroʊ mio<br>'drəʊ mi əʊ ◊ | dro mee o<br>jro mee o<br>dro mee o ◊ |
| Egeon | i 'dʒi ən | ee jee uhn |
| Emilia | ɪ 'mi liə<br>ɪ 'mil jə | i mee lee uh<br>i meel yuh |
| England | 'ɪŋ glənd | ing gluhnd |
| Ephesus | 'ɛ fɪ səs<br>'e fɪ səs ◊ | e fi suhs<br>… ◊ |

| NAME | INTERNATIONAL PHONETIC ALPHABET* | SIMPLIFIED PHONICS** |
|------|----------------------------------|----------------------|
| **Epidamnum** | ɛ pɪ 'dæm nəm | e pi dam nuhm |
| -folio | e pɪ 'dæm nəm ◊ | ... ◊ |
| **Epidamium** | | |
| **Epidaurus** | ɛ pɪ 'dɔ rəs | e pi daw ruhs |
| | e pɪ 'dɔ rəs ◊ | ... ◊ |
| **Expedition** | ɛk spə 'dɪ ʃən | ek spuh di shuhn |
| | ek spə 'dɪ ʃən ◊ | ... ◊ |
| **France** | 'fræns | frans |
| | 'frɑns ◊ | frahns ◊ |
| **Gillian** | 'ʤɪ liən | ji lee uhn |
| **Ginn/Jen** | 'ʤɛn | jen |
| | 'ʤɪn | jin |
| | 'ʤen ◊ | ... ◊ |
| **Greece** | 'gris | grees |
| **Indies** | 'ɪn diz | in deez |
| **Ireland** | 'aɪ ɚ lənd | ai ər luhnd |
| | 'aɪ ə lənd ◊ | ai ə luhnd ◊ |
| **Jen/Ginn** | 'ʤɛn | jen |
| | 'ʤɪn | jin |
| | 'ʤen ◊ | ... ◊ |
| **Jew** | 'ʤu | joo |
| **Lapland** | 'læp lænd | lap land |
| **Lictor** | 'lɪk tɚ | lik tər |
| | 'lɪk tə ◊ | lik tə ◊ |
| **Limbo** | 'lɪm boʊ | lim bo |
| | 'lɪm bəʊ ◊ | ... ◊ |
| **Luce** | 'lus | loos |

| NAME | INTERNATIONAL PHONETIC ALPHABET* | SIMPLIFIED PHONICS** |
|---|---|---|
| Luciana<br>  -folio **Iuliana** | lu ˈʧi ˈɑ nə<br>lu ˈʃi ˈɑ nə<br>lu si ˈɑ nə | loo chee ah nuh<br>loo shee ah nuh<br>loo see ah nuh |
| Marian | ˈmɛ riən<br>ˈmɛə riən ◊ | me ree uhn<br>… ◊ |
| Maud | ˈmɔd | mawd |
| Menaphon | ˈmɛ nə fən<br>ˈme nə fən ◊ | me nuh fuhn<br>… ◊ |
| Nell | ˈnɛl<br>ˈnel ◊ | nel<br>… ◊ |
| Netherlands | ˈnɛ ðɚ ləndz<br>ˈne ðə ləndz ◊ | ne thər luhndz<br>ne thə luhndz ◊ |
| Noah | ˈnoʊ ə<br>ˈnəʊ ə ◊ | no uh<br>… ◊ |
| Pentecost | ˈpɛn tə kɔst<br>ˈpɛn tə kɑst<br>ˈpen tə kɒst ◊ | pen tuh kawst<br>pen tuh kahst<br>pen tuh kost ◊ |
| Persia | ˈpɝ ʒə<br>ˈpɜ ʃə ◊ | pər zha<br>pə shuh ◊ |
| Phoenix | ˈfi nɪks | fee niks |
| Pinch | ˈpɪnʧ | pinch |
| Poland | ˈpoʊ lənd<br>ˈpo lənd ◊ | po luhnd<br>… ◊ |
| Porpentine | ˈpɔr pən taɪn<br>ˈpɔ pən taɪn ◊ | pawr puhn tain<br>paw puhn tain ◊ |
| Satan -folio<br>  **Sathan** | ˈseɪ tən | sei tuhn |

| NAME | INTERNATIONAL PHONETIC ALPHABET* | SIMPLIFIED PHONICS** |
|------|----------------------------------|----------------------|
| **Scotland** | 'skɑt lənd<br>'skɒt lənd ◊ | skaht luhnd<br>skot luhnd ◊ |
| **Sicily/Cicely** | 'sɪ sə li | si suh lee |
| **Solinus** | sə 'laɪ nəs<br>sə 'li nəs | suh lai nuhs<br>suh lee nuhs |
| **Spain** | 'speɪn | spein |
| **Syracusa** | sɪ rə 'kju sə<br>saɪ rə 'kju zə | si ruh kyoo suh<br>sai ruh kyoo zuh |
| **Syracusan** | sɪ rə 'kju zən<br>saɪ rə 'kju zən | si ruh kyoo zuhn<br>sai ruh kyoo zuhn |
| **Syracuse** | 'sɪ rə kjus<br>'saɪ rə kjuz | si ruh kyoos<br>sai ruh kyooz |
| **Tartar** | 'tɑr tɚ<br>'tɑ tə ◊ | tahr tər<br>tah tə ◊ |
| **Tiger** | 'taɪ gɚ<br>'taɪ gə ◊ | tai gər<br>tai gə ◊ |
| **Turkish** | 'tɝ kɪʃ<br>'tɜ kɪʃ | tər kish<br>tə kish |
| **Wednesday** | 'wɛnz deɪ<br>'wenz di ◊ | wenz dei<br>wenz dee ◊ |

# Coriolanus

| NAME | INTERNATIONAL PHONETIC ALPHABET* | SIMPLIFIED PHONICS** |
|------|----------------------------------|----------------------|
| **Adrian** | 'eɪ driən<br>'eɪ ʤriən | ei dree uhn<br>ei jree uhn |
| **Afric** | 'æ frɪk | a frik |
| **Agrippa** | ə 'grɪ pə | uh gri puh |
| **Alexander** | æ lɪg 'zæn dɚ<br>æ lɪg 'zɑn də ◊ | al ig zan dər<br>al ig zahn də ◊ |
| **Amazonian** | æ mə 'zoʊ niən<br>æ mə 'zəʊ niən ◊ | a muh zo nee uhn<br>… ◊ |
| **Ancus** | 'æŋ kəs | ang kuhs |
| **Antiates** | 'æn ʃi eɪts | an shee eits |
| **Antium** | 'æn tiəm | an tee uhm |
| **Arabia** | ə 'reɪ biə | uh rei bee uh |
| **Aufidius** -folio<br>**Auffidius,**<br>**Auffidious** | ɔ 'fɪ diəs | aw fi dee uhs |
| **Brutus** | 'bru təs | broo tuhs |
| **Caius** | 'kaɪ əs<br>'keɪ əs | kai uhs<br>kei uhs |
| **Capitol** | 'kæ pɪ təl | ka pi tuhl |
| **Cato** -folio<br>also **Calves** | 'keɪ to<br>'keɪ təʊ ◊ | kei to<br>… ◊ |

*International Phonetic Alphabet Pronunciation Key: (General American) i-see, happy, Juliet; ɪ-sit; eɪ-say; ɛ-set; æ-sat; ɑ-father; ʌ-sun; ə-about; ɔ-saw; oʊ-so; o-hero; ʊ-shook; u-soon; aɪ-sigh; ɔɪ-soy; aʊ-south; ju-cube; ɚ-supper; ɛr-fair; ɝ-bird; k-cut, kite; g-go; ʤ-joy; j-yes; ŋ-sing; ʃ-shoe; ʧ-chop; ð-that; θ-thin; ʒ-measure; (Additional symbols for British RP) e-set; ɛə-fair; ə-supper; ɜ-bird; ɒ-stop; əʊ-so, hero; o-(followed by l) pole.

**Simplified Phonics Pronunciation Key: (General American) ee-see, happy; i-sit; ei-say; e-set; a-sat; ah-father; uh-sun, about; aw-saw; o-so; oo-shook; oo-soon; ai-sigh; oy-soy; ow-south; yoo-cube; ər-bird, supper; k-cut, kite; g-go; j-joy; ng-sing; kw-quick; sh-shoe; ch-chop; th-that; th-thin; zh-measure; (Additional symbols for British RP) ə-bird; ə-supper; o-stop; … indicates pronunciation variance too subtle for Simplified Phonics transcription see International Phonetic Alphabet transcription.

◊ British RP pronunciation-see Introduction.

| NAME | INTERNATIONAL PHONETIC ALPHABET* | SIMPLIFIED PHONICS** |
|------|----------------------------------|----------------------|
| **Censorinus** | sɛn sə 'raɪ nəs<br>sen sə 'raɪ nəs ◊ | sen suh rai nuhs<br>…◊ |
| **Cominius** | kə 'mɪ niəs | kuh mi nee uhs |
| **Coriolanus** | kɔ ri ə 'leɪ nəs | kaw ree uh lei nuhs |
| **Corioli** | kə 'raɪ ə laɪ<br>kə 'ri ə li | kuh rai uh lai<br>kuh ree uh lee |
| **Cotus** | 'koʊ təs<br>'kəʊ təs ◊ | ko tuhs<br>… ◊ |
| **Cyprus** | 'saɪ prəs | sai pruhs |
| **Deucalion** | du 'keɪ liən<br>du 'keɪl jən<br>dju 'keɪ liən ◊ | doo kei lee uhn<br>doo keil yuhn<br>dyoo kei lee uhn ◊ |
| **Dian** | 'daɪ ən<br>'daɪ æn | dai uhn<br>dai an |
| **Dick** | 'dɪk | dik |
| **Galen** | 'geɪ lən | gei luhn |
| **Greece** | 'gris | grees |
| **Grecian** | 'gri ʃən | gree shuhn |
| **Hector** | 'hɛk tɚ<br>'hek tə ◊ | hek tər<br>hek tə ◊ |
| **Hecuba** | 'hɛ kju bə<br>'he kjʊ bə ◊ | he kyoo buh<br>he ky*oo* buh ◊ |
| **Hercules** | 'hɝ kjə liz<br>'hɝ kju liz<br>'hɜ kjʊ liz ◊ | hər kyuh leez<br>hər kyoo leez<br>hə ky*oo* leez ◊ |

| NAME | INTERNATIONAL PHONETIC ALPHABET* | SIMPLIFIED PHONICS** |
|---|---|---|
| Hob | 'hɑb<br>'hɒb ◊ | hahb<br>hob ◊ |
| Hostilius | hɑ 'stɪ liəs<br>hɑ 'stɪl jəs<br>hɒ 'stɪ liəs ◊ | hah sti lee uhs<br>hah stil yuhs<br>ho sti lee uhs ◊ |
| Hydra | 'haɪ drə<br>'haɪ ʤrə | hai druh<br>hai jruh |
| Italy | 'ɪ tə li | i tuh lee |
| Ithaca<br>  -folio **Athica** | 'ɪ θə kə | i *th*uh kuh |
| Jove | 'ʤoʊv<br>'ʤəʊv ◊ | jov<br>… ◊ |
| Junius | 'ʤu niəs | joo nee uhs |
| Juno | 'ʤu noʊ<br>'ʤu nəʊ ◊ | joo no<br>… ◊ |
| Jupiter | 'ʤu pɪ tɚ<br>'ʤu pɪ tə ◊ | joo pi tər<br>joo pi tə ◊ |
| Lartius | 'lɑr ʃəs<br>'lɑ ʃəs ◊ | lahr shuhs<br>lah shuhs ◊ |
| Lycurgus | laɪ 'kɝ gəs<br>laɪ 'kɜ gəs ◊ | lai kər guhs<br>lai kə guhs ◊ |
| Marcian | 'mɑr ʃən<br>'mɑ ʃən ◊ | mahr shuhn<br>mah shuhn ◊ |
| Marcius<br>  -folio **Martius** | 'mɑr ʃiəs<br>'mɑr ʃəs<br>'mɑ ʃiəs ◊<br>'mɑ ʃəs ◊ | mahr shee uhs<br>mahr shuhs<br>mah shee uhs ◊<br>mah shuhs ◊ |

54

| NAME | INTERNATIONAL PHONETIC ALPHABET* | SIMPLIFIED PHONICS** |
|------|----------------------------------|----------------------|
| **Marcus** | 'mɑr kəs<br>'mɑ kəs ◊ | mahr kuhs<br>mah kuhs ◊ |
| **Mars** | 'mɑrz<br>'mɑz ◊ | mahrz<br>mahz ◊ |
| **Menenius** | mɛ 'ni niəs<br>me 'ni niəs ◊ | me nee nee uhs<br>... ◊ |
| **Neptune** | 'nɛp tun<br>'nep tjun ◊ | nep toon<br>nep tyoon ◊ |
| **Nicanor** | nɪ 'keɪ nɚ<br>naɪ 'keɪ nɚ<br>naɪ 'keɪ nə ◊ | ni kei nər<br>nai kei nər<br>nai kei nə ◊ |
| **Numa** | 'nu mə<br>'nju mə ◊ | noo muh<br>nyoo muh ◊ |
| **Olympus** | o 'lɪm pəs<br>ə 'lɪm pəs | o lim puhs<br>uh lim puhs |
| **Penelope** | pə 'nɛ lə pi<br>pə 'ne lə pi ◊ | puh ne luh pee<br>... ◊ |
| **Phoebus** | 'fi bəs | fee buhs |
| **Pluto** | 'plu to<br>'plu təʊ ◊ | ploo to<br>... ◊ |
| **Publicola** | pə 'blɪ kə lə | puh bli kuh luh |
| **Publius** | 'pʌ bliəs | puh blee uhs |
| **Quintus** | 'kwɪn təs | kwin tuhs |
| **Roman** | 'roʊ mən<br>'rəʊ mən ◊ | ro muhn<br>... ◊ |
| **Rome** | 'roʊm<br>'rəʊm ◊ | rom<br>...◊ |

| NAME | INTERNATIONAL PHONETIC ALPHABET* | SIMPLIFIED PHONICS** |
|------|-----------------------------------|----------------------|
| Sicinius | sɪ 'sɪ niəs | si si nee uhs |
| Tarpeian | tɑr 'piən<br>tɑ 'piən ◊ | tahr pee uhn<br>tah pee uhn ◊ |
| Tarquin | 'tɑr kwɪn<br>'tɑ kwɪn ◊ | tahr kwin<br>tah kwin ◊ |
| Tiber | 'taɪ bɚ<br>'taɪ bə ◊ | tai bər<br>tai bə ◊ |
| Titus | 'taɪ təs | tai tuhs |
| Triton | 'traɪ tən<br>'tʃraɪ tən | trai tuhn<br>chrai tuhn |
| Tullus | 'tʌ ləs | tuh luhs |
| Ulysses<br>-folio **Ulises** | ju 'lɪ siz | yoo li seez |
| Velaria | və 'lɪ riə<br>və 'lɪə riə | vuh li ree uh<br>vuh liə ree uh |
| Velutus | və 'lu təs | vuh loo tuhs |
| Virgilia | vɚ 'dʒɪ liə<br>vɚ 'dʒɪl jə<br>və 'dʒɪ liə ◊ | vər ji lee uh<br>vər jil yuh<br>və ji lee uh ◊ |
| Volscian | 'vɑls skiən<br>'vɒl skiən ◊ | vahl skee uhn<br>vol skee uhn ◊ |
| Volsce | 'vɑls<br>'vɒls ◊ | vahls<br>vols ◊ |
| Volumnia | və 'lʌm niə | vuh luhm nee uh |
| Wednesday | 'wɛnz deɪ<br>'wenz di ◊ | wenz dei<br>wenz dee ◊ |

56

| NAME | INTERNATIONAL PHONETIC ALPHABET* | SIMPLIFIED PHONICS** |
|---|---|---|
| **Aeneas** | ɪ 'ni əs | i nee uhs |
| | i 'ni əs | ee nee uhs |
| **Afric** | 'æ frɪk | a frik |
| **Ajax** | 'eɪ ʤæks | ei jaks |
| **Arabian** | ə 'reɪ biən | uh rei bee uhn |
| **Arviragus** | ɑr vɪ 'ræ gəs | ahr vi ra guhs |
| | ɑr 'vɪ rə gəs | ahr vee ruh guhs |
| | ɑ vɪ 'ræ gəs ◊ | ah vi ra guhs ◊ |
| | ɑ 'vɪ rə gəs ◊ | ah vee ruh guhs ◊ |
| **Augustus** | ɔ 'gʌs təs | aw guh stuhs |
| | ə 'gʌs təs | uh guh stuhs |
| **Belarius** | bə 'læ riəs | buh la ree uhs |
| | bə 'lɛə riəs ◊ | buh lea ree uhs ◊ |
| **Britain** | 'brɪ tən | bri tuhn |
| **British** | 'brɪ tɪʃ | bri tish |
| **Briton** | 'brɪ tən | bri tuhn |
| **Cadwal** | 'kæd wɔl | kad wawl |
| | 'kæd wɑl | kad wahl |
| | [gen Am var] | [gen Am var] |
| **Caesar** | 'si zɚ | see zər |
| | 'si zə ◊ | see zə ◊ |

*International Phonetic Alphabet Pronunciation Key: (General American) i-see, happy, Juliet; ɪ-sit; eɪ-say; ɛ-set; æ-sat; ɑ-father; ʌ-sun; ə-about; ɔ-saw; oʊ-so; o-hero; ʊ-shook; u-soon; aɪ-sigh; ɔɪ-soy; aʊ-south; ju-cube; ə-supper; ɛr-fair; ɚ-bird; k-cut, kite; g-go; ʤ-joy; j-yes; ŋ-sing; ʃ-shoe; ʧ-chop; ð-that; θ-thin; ʒ-measure; (Additional symbols for British RP) e-set; ɛə-fair; ə-supper; ɜ-bird; ɒ-stop; əʊ-so, hero; o-(followed by l) pole.

**Simplified Phonics Pronunciation Key: (General American) ee-see, happy, i-sit; ei-say; e-set; a-sat; ah-father; uh-sun, about; aw-saw; o-so; oo-shook; oo-soon; ai-sigh; oy-soy; ow-south; yoo-cube; ər-bird, supper; k-cut, kite; g-go; j-joy; ng-sing; kw-quick; sh-shoe; ch-chop; th-that; th-thin; zh-measure; (Additional symbols for British RP) ə-bird; ə-supper; o-stop; ... indicates pronunciation variance too subtle for Simplified Phonics transcription see International Phonetic Alphabet transcription.

◊ British RP pronunciation-see Introduction.

| NAME | INTERNATIONAL PHONETIC ALPHABET* | SIMPLIFIED PHONICS** |
|---|---|---|
| Caius | 'kaɪ əs<br>'keɪ əs | kai uhs<br>kei uhs |
| Cambria | 'kæm briə | kam bree uh |
| Capitol | 'kæ pɪ təl | ka pi tuhl |
| Cassibelan | kæ 'sɪ bə lən | ka si buh luhn |
| du Champ | du 'ʃamp<br>dju 'ʃamp ◊ | doo shahmp<br>dyoo shahmp ◊ |
| Cleopatra | kliə 'pæ trə<br>kliə 'pæ tʃrə<br>kliə 'pɑ trə<br>   [Brit RP var] | klee uh pa truh<br>klee uh pa chruh<br>klee uh pah truh<br>   [Brit RP var] |
| Cloten | 'kloʊ tən<br>'kləʊ tən ◊ | klo tuhn<br>… ◊ |
| Cornelius | kɔr 'ni liəs<br>kɔr 'nil jəs<br>kɔ 'ni liəs ◊ | kawr nee lee uhs<br>kawr neel yuhs<br>kaw nee lee uhs ◊ |
| Cupid | 'kju pɪd | kyoo pid |
| Cydnus -folio<br>   Sidnis, Cidrus,<br>   Sidnus | 'sɪd nəs | sid nuhs |
| Cymbelline | 'sɪm bə lin | sim buh leen |
| Cytherea | sɪ θə 'ri ə | si *th*uh ree uh |
| Dalmatian | dæl 'meɪ ʃən | dal mei shuhn |
| December | di 'sɛm bɚ<br>dɪ 'sem bə ◊ | dee sem bər<br>di sem bə ◊ |
| Dian | 'daɪ ən<br>'daɪ æn | dai uhn<br>dai an |

| NAME | INTERNATIONAL PHONETIC ALPHABET* | SIMPLIFIED PHONICS** |
|------|----------------------------------|----------------------|
| **Diana** | daɪ ˈæ·nə | dai a nuh |
| **Dorothy** | ˈdɔ rə θi | daw ruh *th*ee |
| | ˈdɑ rə θ | dah ruh *th*ee |
| | ˈdɒ rə θi ◊ | d*o* ruh *th*ee ◊ |
| **du Champ** | du ˈʃamp | doo shahmp |
| | dju ˈʃamp ◊ | dyoo shahmp ◊ |
| **Elysium** | ɪ ˈlɪ ziəm | i li zee uhm |
|   -folio **Elizium** | ɪ ˈlɪ ʒiəm | i li zhee uhm |
| **Euriphile** | ju ˈrɪ fə li | yoo ri fuh lee |
| **Europe** | ˈjʊ rəp | *y*oo ruhp |
| | ˈjʊə rəp ◊ | *y*ooə ruhp ◊ |
| **Fidele** | fɪ ˈdi li | fi dee lee |
| **French** | ˈfrɛntʃ | french |
| | ˈfrentʃ ◊ | … ◊ |
| **Gallia** | ˈgæ liə | ga lee uh |
| **Gallian** | ˈgæ liən | ga lee uhn |
| **German** | ˈdʒɝ mən | jər muhn |
|   -folio **Iarman** | ˈdʒɜ mən ◊ | jə muhn ◊ |
| **Gordian** | ˈgɔr diən | gawr dee uhn |
| | ˈgɔ diən ◊ | gaw dee uhn ◊ |
| **Greek** | ˈgrik | greek |
| **Guiderius** | gwɪ ˈdɪ riəs | gwi di ree uhs |
| **Hecuba** | ˈhɛ kju bə | he kyoo buh |
| | ˈhe kjʊ bə ◊ | he ky*oo* buh ◊ |

| NAME | INTERNATIONAL PHONETIC ALPHABET* | SIMPLIFIED PHONICS** |
|------|----------------------------------|---------------------|
| **Helen** | 'hɛ lɪn | he lin |
| -folio **Helene** | 'hɛ lən | he luhn |
| | 'he lən ◊ | ... ◊ |
| **Hercules** | 'hɝ kjə liz | hər kyuh leez |
| | 'hɝ kju liz | hər kyoo leez |
| | 'hɜ kjʊ liz ◊ | hə ky*oo* leez ◊ |
| **Iachimo** | 'jɑ kɪ moʊ | yah ki mo |
| | 'ʤɑ kɪ moʊ | jah ki mo |
| | 'jɑ kɪ məʊ ◊ | ... ◊ |
| | 'ʤɑ kɪ məʊ ◊ | ... ◊ |
| **Imogen** | 'ɪ mə ʤən | i muh juhn |
| **Italian** | ɪ 'tæl jən | i tal yuhn |
| **Italy** | 'ɪ tə li | i tuh lee |
| **Jack** | 'ʤæk | jak |
| **Jove** | 'ʤoʊv | jov |
| | 'ʤəʊv ◊ | ... ◊ |
| **Julius** | 'ʤu liəs | joo lee uhs |
| | 'ʤul jəs | jool yuhs |
| **Juno** | 'ʤu noʊ | joo no |
| | 'ʤu nəʊ ◊ | ... ◊ |
| **Jupiter** | 'ʤu pɪ tɚ | joo pi tər |
| | 'ʤu pɪ tə ◊ | joo pi tə ◊ |
| **Leonati** | li ə 'nɑ ti | lee uh nah tee |
| | li ə 'neɪ taɪ | lee uh nei tai |
| **Leonato** | li ə 'nɑ to | lee uh nah to |
| | li ə 'neɪ to | lee uh nei to |
| | li ə 'nɑ təʊ ◊ | ...◊ |
| | li ə neɪ təʊ ◊ | ...◊ |

| NAME | INTERNATIONAL PHONETIC ALPHABET* | SIMPLIFIED PHONICS** |
| --- | --- | --- |
| **Leonatus** | li ə 'neɪ təs | lee uh nei tuhs |
| **Lucina** | lu 'si nə | loo see nuh |
| | lu 'ʧi nə | loo chee nuh |
| | lu 'saɪ nə | loo sai nuh |
| **Lucius** | 'lu ʃəs | loo shuhs |
| **Lud** | 'lʌd | luhd |
| **Mars** | 'mɑrz | mahrz |
| | 'mɑz ◊ | mahz ◊ |
| **Milford Haven** | 'mɪl fɚd 'heɪ vən | mil fərd hei vuhn |
| | 'mɪl fəd 'heɪ vən ◊ | mil fəd hei vuhn ◊ |
| **Minerva** | mɪ 'nɚ və | mi nər vuh |
| | mɪ 'nɜ və ◊ | mi nə vuh ◊ |
| **Morgan** | 'mɔr gən | mawr guhn |
| | 'mɔ gən ◊ | maw guhn ◊ |
| **Mulmutius** | məl 'mju ʃəs | muhl myoo shuhs |
| **Neptune** | 'nɛp tun | nep toon |
| | 'nɛp tjun ◊ | nep tyoon ◊ |
| **Nile** | 'naɪl | nail |
| **Orleans** | 'ɔr liənz | awr lee uhnz |
| -folio **Orleance** | ɔr 'liənz | awr lee uhnz |
| | 'ɔ liənz ◊ | aw lee uhnz ◊ |
| | ɔ 'li ənz ◊ | aw lee uhnz ◊ |
| **Pannonian** | pə 'noʊ niən | puh no nee uhn |
| | pə 'nəʊ niən ◊ | ... ◊ |
| **Parthian** | 'pɑr θiən | pahr *th*ee uhn |
| | 'pɑ θiən ◊ | pah *th*ee uhn ◊ |

| NAME | INTERNATIONAL PHONETIC ALPHABET* | SIMPLIFIED PHONICS** |
|------|----------------------------------|----------------------|
| **Philario** | fɪ 'lɑ ri o<br>fɪ 'lɑ ri əʊ ◊ | fi lah ree o<br>… ◊ |
| **Philarmonous** | fi lɚ 'moʊ nəs<br>fi lə 'məʊ nəs ◊ | fi lər mo nuhs<br>fi lə mo nuhs ◊ |
| **Philomel** | 'fɪ lə mɛl<br>'fɪ lə mel ◊ | fi luh mel<br>… ◊ |
| **Phoebus** | 'fi bəs | fee buhs |
| **Pisanio** | pɪ 'zɑ nioʊ<br>pɪ 'zɑ niəʊ ◊ | pi zah nee o<br>… ◊ |
| **Polydore** | 'pɑ li dɔr<br>'pɒ li dɔ ◊ | pah lee dawr<br>po lee daw ◊ |
| **Posthumous** | pɑs 'tʃu məs<br>'pɑs tʃu məs<br>pɒst 'hju məs ◊<br>'pɒst hju məs ◊ | pahs choo muhs<br>…<br>post hyoo muhs ◊<br>… ◊ |
| **Richard** | 'rɪ tʃɚd<br>'rɪ tʃəd ◊ | ri chərd<br>ri chəd ◊ |
| **Roman** | 'roʊ mən<br>'rəʊ mən ◊ | ro muhn<br>…◊ |
| **Rome** | 'roʊm<br>'rəʊm ◊ | rom<br>… ◊ |
| **Romish** | 'roʊ mɪʃ<br>'rəʊ mɪʃ ◊ | ro mish<br>… ◊ |
| **Saturn** | 'sæ tɚn<br>'sæ tən ◊ | sa tərn<br>sa tən ◊ |
| **Severn** | 'sɛ vɚn<br>'se vən ◊ | se vərn<br>se vən ◊ |

| NAME | INTERNATIONAL PHONETIC ALPHABET* | SIMPLIFIED PHONICS** |
|---|---|---|
| **Sicilius** | sɪ 'sɪ liəs | si si lee uhs |
| -folio **Sicillius** | sɪ 'sɪl jəs | si sil yuhs |
| **Sienna/Syenna** | si 'ɛ nə | see e nuh |
| | si 'e nə ◊ | … ◊ |
| **Sinon** | 'saɪ nən | sai nuhn |
| **Spaniard** | 'spæn jɚd | span yərd |
| | 'spæn jəd ◊ | span yəd ◊ |
| **Tarquin** | 'tɑr kwɪn | tahr kwin |
| | 'tɑ kwɪn ◊ | tah kwin ◊ |
| **Tenantius** | tə 'næn ʃəs | tuh nan shuhs |
| **Tereus** | 'ti rus | tee roos |
| **Thersites** | θɚ 'saɪ tiz | *th*ər sai teez |
| | θə 'saɪ tiz ◊ | *th*ə sai teez ◊ |
| **Titan** | 'taɪ tən | tai tuhn |
| **Venus** | 'vi nəs | vee nuhs |
| **Wales** | 'weɪlz | weilz |

# *Hamlet*

| NAME | INTERNATIONAL PHONETIC ALPHABET* | SIMPLIFIED PHONICS** |
|---|---|---|
| **Adam** | 'æ dəm | a duhm |
| **Aeneas** | ɪ 'ni əs<br>i 'ni əs | i nee uhs<br>ee nee uhs |
| **Alexander** | æ lɪg 'zæn dɚ<br>æ lɪg 'zan də ◊ | al ig zan dər<br>al ig zahn də ◊ |
| **Baptista** | bæp 'tɪstə<br>bæp 'tistə | bap tis tuh<br>bap tees tuh |
| **Barbary** | 'bɑr bə ri<br>'ba bə ri ◊ | bahr buh ree<br>bah buh ree ◊ |
| **Bernardo** | bɚ 'nɑr do<br>bə 'na dəʊ ◊ | bər nahr do<br>bə nah do ◊ |
| **Briton** | 'brɪ tən | bri tuhn |
| **Caesar** | 'si zɚ<br>'si zə ◊ | see zər<br>see zə ◊ |
| **Cain** | 'keɪn | kein |
| **Capitol** | 'kæ pɪ təl | ka pi tuhl |
| **[Saint] Charity** | [seɪnt] 'ʧæ rə ti<br>[sɪnt] 'ʧæ rə ti ◊ | [seint] cha ruh tee<br>[sint] cha ruh tee ◊ |
| **Christian** | 'krɪs ʧən | kris chuhn |
| **Claudio** | 'klɔ dio<br>'klɔ diəʊ ◊ | klaw dee o<br>… ◊ |

*International Phonetic Alphabet Pronunciation Key: (General American) i-s<u>ee</u>, happ<u>y</u>, Jul<u>i</u>et; ɪ-s<u>i</u>t; eɪ-s<u>ay</u>; ɛ-s<u>e</u>t; æ-s<u>a</u>t; ɑ-f<u>a</u>ther; ʌ-s<u>u</u>n; ə-<u>a</u>bout; ɔ-s<u>aw</u>; oʊ-s<u>o</u>; o-h<u>e</u>ro; ʊ-sh<u>oo</u>k; u-s<u>oo</u>n; aɪ-s<u>igh</u>; ɔɪ-s<u>oy</u>; aʊ-s<u>ou</u>th; ju-c<u>u</u>be; ɚ-s<u>upper</u>; er-f<u>air</u>; ɝ-b<u>ir</u>d; k-<u>c</u>ut, <u>k</u>ite; g-<u>g</u>o; ʤ-<u>j</u>oy; j-<u>y</u>es; ŋ-si<u>ng</u>; ʃ-<u>sh</u>oe; ʧ-<u>ch</u>op; ð-<u>th</u>at; θ-<u>th</u>in; ʒ-mea<u>s</u>ure; (Additional symbols for British RP) e-s<u>e</u>t; ɛə-f<u>air</u>; ə-s<u>upper</u>; ɜ-b<u>ir</u>d; ɒ-st<u>o</u>p; əʊ-s<u>o</u>, h<u>e</u>ro; o-(followed by l) p<u>o</u>le.

**Simplified Phonics Pronunciation Key: (General American) ee-s<u>ee</u>, happ<u>y</u>; i-s<u>i</u>t; ei-s<u>ay</u>; e-s<u>e</u>t; a-s<u>a</u>t; ah-f<u>a</u>ther; uh-s<u>u</u>n, ab<u>ou</u>t; aw-s<u>aw</u>; o-s<u>o</u>; oo-sh<u>oo</u>k; oo-s<u>oo</u>n; ai-s<u>igh</u>; oy-s<u>oy</u>; ow-s<u>ou</u>th; yoo-c<u>u</u>be; ər-b<u>ir</u>d, s<u>upper</u>; k-<u>c</u>ut, <u>k</u>ite; g-<u>g</u>o; j-<u>j</u>oy; ng-si<u>ng</u>; kw-<u>q</u>uick; sh-<u>sh</u>oe; ch-<u>ch</u>op; th-<u>th</u>at; *th*-<u>th</u>in; zh-mea<u>s</u>ure; (Additional symbols for British RP) ə-b<u>ir</u>d; ə-s<u>upper</u>; <u>o</u>-st<u>o</u>p; … indicates pronunciation variance too subtle for Simplified Phonics transcription see International Phonetic Alphabet transcription.

◊ British RP pronunciation-see Introduction.

| NAME | INTERNATIONAL PHONETIC ALPHABET* | SIMPLIFIED PHONICS** |
|---|---|---|
| Claudius | 'klɔ diəs | klaw dee uhs |
| Cornelius | kɔr 'ni liəs<br>kɔr nil jəs<br>kɔ 'ni liəs ◊ | kawr nee lee uhs<br>kawr neel yuhs<br>kaw nee lee uhs ◊ |
| Cyclops | 'saɪ klɑps<br>'saɪ klɒps ◊ | sai klahps<br>sai klops ◊ |
| Damon | 'deɪ mən | dei muhn |
| Dane | 'deɪn | dein |
| Danish | 'deɪ nɪʃ | dei nish |
| Dansker | 'dæn skɚ<br>'dæn skə ◊ | dan skər<br>dan skə ◊ |
| Denmark | 'dɛn mɑrk<br>'den mɑk ◊ | den mahrk<br>den mahk ◊ |
| Dido | 'daɪ do<br>'daɪ dəʊ ◊ | dai do<br>... ◊ |
| Elsinore | 'ɛl sə nɔr<br>'el sɪ nɔ ◊ | el suh nawr<br>el si naw ◊ |
| England | 'ɪŋ glənd | ing gluhnd |
| Fortinbras | 'fɔr tɪn bræs<br>'fɔ tɪn bræs ◊ | fawr tin bras<br>faw tin bras ◊ |
| Francisco | fræn 'sɪs ko<br>fræn 'sɪs kəʊ ◊ | fran sis ko<br>... ◊ |
| French | 'frɛnʧ<br>'frɛnʧ ◊ | french<br>... ◊ |
| Gertrude | 'gɚ trud<br>'gɚ ʧrud<br>'gɜ trud ◊ | gər trood<br>gər chrood<br>gə trood ◊ |

| NAME | INTERNATIONAL PHONETIC ALPHABET* | SIMPLIFIED PHONICS** |
|---|---|---|
| Gis | 'ʤiz | jeez |
| Gonzago | gən 'zɑ goʊ<br>gən 'zɑ gəʊ ◊ | guhn zah go<br>… ◊ |
| Greek | 'grik | greek |
| Guildenstern | 'gɪl dən stɚn<br>'gɪl dən stən ◊ | gil duhn stərn<br>gil duhn stən ◊ |
| Hamlet | 'hæm lɪt | ham lit |
| Hecate | 'hɛ kɪt<br>'he kɪt ◊ | he kit<br>… ◊ |
| Hecuba | 'hɛ kju bə<br>'he kjʊ bə ◊ | he kyoo buh<br>he ky*oo* buh ◊ |
| Hercules | 'hɝ kjə liz<br>'hɝ kju liz<br>'hɜ kjʊ liz ◊ | hər kyuh leez<br>hər kyoo leez<br>hə ky*oo* leez ◊ |
| Herod | 'hɛ rəd<br>'he rəd ◊ | he ruhd<br>…◊ |
| Horatio | hə 'reɪ ʃio<br>hə 'reɪ ʃiəʊ ◊ | huh rei shee o<br>… ◊ |
| Hymen | 'haɪ mən | hai muhn |
| Hyperion | haɪ 'pɪ riən | hai pi ree uhn |
| Hyrcania | hɝ 'keɪ niə<br>hɜ 'keɪ niə ◊ | hər kei nee uh<br>hə kei nee uh ◊ |
| Hyrcanian | hɝ 'keɪ niən<br>hɜ 'keɪ niən ◊ | hər kei nee uhn<br>hə kei nee uhn ◊ |
| Illium | 'ɪ liəm<br>'ɪl jəm<br>'aɪ liəm ◊ | i lee uhm<br>il yuhm<br>ai lee uhm ◊ |

| NAME | INTERNATIONAL PHONETIC ALPHABET* | SIMPLIFIED PHONICS** |
|---|---|---|
| Israel | 'ɪz ri əl<br>'ɪz reɪ əl | iz ree uhl<br>iz rei uhl |
| Italian | ɪ 'tæl jən | i tal yuhn |
| Jephthah | 'ʤɛf θə<br>'ʤɛp θə<br>'ʤef θə ◊ | jef *th*uh<br>jep *th*uh<br>... ◊ |
| John | 'ʤɑn<br>'ʤɒn ◊ | jahn<br>j*o*n ◊ |
| Jove | 'ʤoʊv<br>'ʤəʊv ◊ | jov<br>... ◊ |
| Julius | 'ʤu liəs<br>'ʤul jəs | joo lee uhs<br>jool yuhs |
| Laertes | leɪ 'ɛr tiz<br>li 'ɝ tiz<br>leɪ 'ɜ tiz ◊ | lei er teez<br>lee ər teez<br>lci ə teez ◊ |
| Lamond | lə 'mɑnd<br>lə 'mɒnd ◊ | luh mahnd<br>luh m*o*nd ◊ |
| Lethe | 'li θi | lee *th*ee |
| Lucianus | lu ʧi 'ɑ nəs<br>lu ʃi 'æ nəs<br>lu si 'ɑ nəs ◊ | loo chee ah nuhs<br>loo shee an uhs<br>loo see ah nuhs ◊ |
| Marcellus | mɑr 'sɛ ləs<br>mɑ 'se ləs ◊ | mahr se luhs<br>mah se luhs ◊ |
| Mars | 'mɑrz<br>'mɑz ◊ | mahrz<br>mahz ◊ |
| May | 'meɪ | mei |
| Mercury | 'mɝ kjə ri<br>'mɜ kjʊ ri ◊ | mər kyuh ree<br>mə ky*oo* ree ◊ |

67

| NAME | INTERNATIONAL PHONETIC ALPHABET* | SIMPLIFIED PHONICS** |
|------|----------------------------------|----------------------|
| Monday | 'mʌn deɪ <br> 'mʌn di ◊ | muhn dei <br> muhn dee ◊ |
| Nemean | 'ni miən <br> nɪ 'miən | nee mee uhn <br> ni mee uhn |
| Neptune | 'nɛp tun <br> 'nep tjun ◊ | nep toon <br> nep tyoon ◊ |
| Nero | 'ni ro <br> 'nɪə rəʊ ◊ | nee ro <br> ni ro ◊ |
| Niobe | 'naɪ ə bi | nai uh bee |
| Norman | 'nɔr mən <br> 'nɔ mən ◊ | nawr muhn <br> naw muhn ◊ |
| Normandy | 'nɔr mən di <br> 'nɔ mən di ◊ | nawr muhn dee <br> naw muhn dee ◊ |
| Norway | 'nɔr weɪ <br> 'nɔ weɪ ◊ | nawr wei <br> naw wei ◊ |
| Olympus | o 'lɪm pəs <br> ə 'lɪm pəs | o lim puhs <br> uh lim puhs |
| Ophelia | o 'fil jə <br> o 'fi liə <br> əʊ 'fi liə ◊ | o feel yuh <br> o fee lee uh <br> … ◊ |
| Osric/Osrick <br> -folio **Osricke** | 'ɑz rɪk <br> 'ɒz rɪk ◊ | ahz rik <br> *o*z rik ◊ |
| Ossa | 'ɑ sə <br> 'ɒ sə ◊ | ah suh <br> *o* suh ◊ |
| Paris | 'pæ rɪs | pa ris |
| Patrick | 'pæ trɪk <br> 'pæ tʃrɪk | pa trik <br> pa chrik |

| NAME | INTERNATIONAL PHONETIC ALPHABET* | SIMPLIFIED PHONICS** |
|---|---|---|
| **Pelion** | 'pil jən<br>'pi liən | peel yuhn<br>pee lee uhn |
| **Phoebus** | 'fi bəs | fee buhs |
| **Plautus** | 'plɔ təs | plaw tuhs |
| **Polack** -folio<br>   **Poleak, Pollax** | 'poʊ lak<br>'poʊ læk<br>'po lak ◊<br>'po læk ◊ | po lahk<br>po lak<br>… ◊<br>… ◊ |
| **Poland** | 'poʊ lənd<br>'po lənd ◊ | po luhnd<br>… ◊ |
| **Pole** | 'poʊl<br>'pol ◊ | pol<br>…◊ |
| **Polonius** | pə 'loʊ niəs<br>pə 'ləʊ niəs ◊ | puh lo nee uhs<br>… ◊ |
| **Priam** | 'praɪ əm | prai uhm |
| **Provencial** | prɑ vɑn 'sal<br>prɒ vɒn 'sal ◊<br>prə 'vɛn ʃəl<br>prə 'ven ʃəl ◊ | prah vahn sahl<br>pro von sahl<br>pruh ven shuhl<br>… ◊ |
| **Pyrrhus** | 'pɪ rəs | pi ruhs |
| **Reynaldo** | rɪ 'nɑl do<br>rɪ 'nældo<br>rɪ 'næl dəʊ ◊ | ri nahl do<br>ri nal do<br>… ◊ |
| **Rhenish** | 'rɛ nɪʃ<br>'re nɪʃ ◊ | re nish<br>… ◊ |
| **Robin** | 'rɑ bɪn<br>'rɒ bɪn ◊ | rah bin<br>ro bin ◊ |

| NAME | INTERNATIONAL PHONETIC ALPHABET* | SIMPLIFIED PHONICS** |
|------|----------------------------------|----------------------|
| **Roman** | 'roʊ mən<br>'rəʊ mən ◊ | ro muhn<br>... ◊ |
| **Rome** | 'roʊm<br>'rəʊm ◊ | rom<br>... ◊ |
| **Roscius** | 'rɑ ʃiəs<br>'rɒ ʃiəs ◊ | rah shee uhs<br>ro shee uhs ◊ |
| **Rosencrantz** | 'roʊ zən krænts<br>'rəʊ zən krænts ◊ | ro zuhn krants<br>... ◊ |
| **Seneca** | 'sɛ nɪ kə<br>'se nɪ kə ◊ | se ni kuh<br>... ◊ |
| **Sunday** | 'sʌn deɪ<br>'sʌn di ◊ | suhn dei<br>suhn dee ◊ |
| **Switzer** | 'swɪt sɚ<br>'swɪtsə ◊ | swit sər<br>swit sə ◊ |
| **Tellus** | 'tɛ ləs<br>'te ləs ◊ | te luhs<br>...◊ |
| **Termagent** | 'tɝ mə gənt<br>'tɜ mə gənt ◊ | tər muh guhnt<br>tə muh guhnt ◊ |
| **Turk** | 'tɝk<br>'tɜk ◊ | tərk<br>tək ◊ |
| **[Saint] Valentine** | [seɪnt] 'væ lən taɪn<br>[sɪnt] 'væ lən taɪn ◊ | [seint] va luhn tain<br>[sint] va luhn tain ◊ |
| **Vienna** | vi 'ɛ nə<br>vi 'e nə ◊ | vee e nuh<br>... ◊ |
| **Voltimand** | 'vɑl tə mænd<br>'vɒl tə mænd ◊ | vahl tuh mand<br>vol tuh mand ◊ |
| **Vulcan** | 'vʌl kən | vuhl kuhn |

| NAME | INTERNATIONAL PHONETIC ALPHABET* | SIMPLIFIED PHONICS** |
|------|----------------------------------|----------------------|
| **Wittenberg** | 'wɪ tən bɚg<br>'wɪ tən bəg ◊ | wi tuhn bərg<br>wi tuhn bəg ◊ |
| **Yaughan** | 'jɔn | yawn |
| **Yorick** | 'jɔ rɪk<br>'jɒ rɪk ◊ | yaw rik<br>yo rik ◊ |

| NAME | INTERNATIONAL PHONETIC ALPHABET* | SIMPLIFIED PHONICS** |
|---|---|---|
| **Adam** | 'æd əm | a duhm |
| **[Saint] Alban** -folio **Albon, Albone** | [seɪnt] 'ɔl bən<br>[sɪnt] 'ɒl bən ◊ | [seint] awl buhn<br>[sint] *o*l buhn ◊ |
| **All Hallown** | 'ɔl 'hæ lon<br>'ɔl 'hæ ləʊn ◊ | awl ha lon<br>... ◊ |
| **Amaimon/ Amamon** | ə 'meɪ mɑn<br>ə 'meɪ mən<br>ə 'meɪ mɒn ◊ | uh mei mahn<br>uh mei muhn<br>uh mei m*o*n ◊ |
| **Angus** | 'æŋ gəs | ang guhs |
| **Archibald** | 'ɑr tʃɪ bɔld<br>'ɑ tʃɪ bɔld ◊ | ahr chi bawld<br>ah chi bawld ◊ |
| **Athol** | 'æ θəl | a *th*uhl |
| **Bangor** | 'bæŋ gɔr<br>'bæŋ gɚ<br>'bæŋ gə ◊ | bang gawr<br>bang gər<br>bang gə ◊ |
| **Barbary** | 'bɑr bə ri<br>'bɑ bə ri ◊ | bahr buh ree<br>bahr buh ree ◊ |
| **Bardolph** | 'bɑr dɑlf<br>'bɑr dɔlf<br>'bɑ dɒlf ◊ | bahr dahlf<br>bahr dawlf<br>bah d*o*lf ◊ |

*International Phonetic Alphabet Pronunciation Key: (General American) i-s<u>ee</u>, happ<u>y</u>, Jul<u>ie</u>t; ɪ-s<u>i</u>t; eɪ-s<u>ay</u>; ɛ-s<u>e</u>t; æ-s<u>a</u>t; ɑ-f<u>a</u>ther; ʌ-s<u>u</u>n; ə-<u>a</u>bout; ɔ-s<u>aw</u>; oʊ-s<u>o</u>; o-h<u>e</u>ro; ʊ-sh<u>oo</u>k; u-s<u>oo</u>n; aɪ-s<u>igh</u>; ɔɪ-s<u>oy</u>; aʊ-s<u>ou</u>th; ju-c<u>u</u>be; ɚ-supp<u>er</u>; ɛr-f<u>air</u>; ɝ-b<u>ir</u>d; k-<u>c</u>ut, <u>k</u>ite; g-<u>g</u>o; ʤ-<u>j</u>oy; j-<u>y</u>es; ŋ-si<u>ng</u>; ʃ-<u>sh</u>oe; tʃ-<u>ch</u>op; ð-<u>th</u>at; θ-<u>th</u>in; ʒ-mea<u>s</u>ure; (Additional symbols for British RP) e-s<u>e</u>t; ɛə-f<u>air</u>; ə-supp<u>er</u>; ɜ-b<u>ir</u>d; ɒ-st<u>o</u>p; əʊ-s<u>o</u>, h<u>e</u>ro; o-(followed by l) p<u>o</u>le.

**Simplified Phonics Pronunciation Key: (General American) ee-s<u>ee</u>, happ<u>y</u>; i-s<u>i</u>t; ei-s<u>ay</u>; e-s<u>e</u>t; a-s<u>a</u>t; ah-f<u>a</u>ther; uh-s<u>u</u>n, ab<u>ou</u>t; aw-s<u>aw</u>; o-s<u>o</u>; *oo*-sh<u>oo</u>k; oo-s<u>oo</u>n; ai-s<u>igh</u>; oy-s<u>oy</u>; ow-s<u>ou</u>th; yoo-c<u>u</u>be; ər-b<u>ir</u>d, supp<u>er</u>; k-<u>c</u>ut, <u>k</u>ite; g-<u>g</u>o; j-<u>j</u>oy; ng-si<u>ng</u>; kw-<u>qu</u>ick; sh-<u>sh</u>oe; ch-<u>ch</u>op; th-<u>th</u>at; *th*-<u>th</u>in; zh-mea<u>s</u>ure; (Additional symbols for British RP) ə-b<u>ir</u>d; ə-supp<u>er</u>; *o*-st<u>o</u>p; ... indicates pronunciation variance too subtle for Simplified Phonics transcription see International Phonetic Alphabet transcription.

◊ British RP pronunciation-see Introduction.

| NAME | INTERNATIONAL PHONETIC ALPHABET* | SIMPLIFIED PHONICS** |
|------|------|------|
| **Berkeley/Berkley** folio **Barkely, Barkley, Berkley** | 'bɑrk li 'bɝk li [gen Am var] 'bɑk li ◊ | bahrk lee bərk lee [gen Am var] bahk lee ◊ |
| **Blunt** | 'blʌnt | bluhnt |
| **Boar's Head** | 'bɔrz 'hɛd 'bɔz 'hed ◊ | bawrz hed bawz hed ◊ |
| **Bolingbroke** -folio **also Bullingbrooke, Bollingbrooke** | 'bɑ lɪŋ brʊk 'boʊ lɪŋ brʊk 'bʊ lɪŋ brʊk ◊ 'bɒ lɪŋ brʊk ◊ | bah ling brook bo ling brook boo ling brook ◊ bo ling brook ◊ |
| **Bracy** | 'breɪ si | brei si |
| **Bridgenorth** | 'brɪdʒ nɔrθ 'brɪdʒ nɔθ ◊ | brij nawrth brij nawth ◊ |
| **Bristol** | 'brɪ stəl | bri stuhl |
| **Bullcalf** | 'bʊl kæf 'bʊl kɑf ◊ | bool kaf bool kahf |
| **Burton** | 'bɝ tən 'bɜ tən ◊ | bər tuhn bə tuhn ◊ |
| **Cambyses** | kæm 'bai siz | kam bai seez |
| **Canterbury** | 'kæn tɚ bɛ ri 'kæn tə bə ri ◊ | kan tər be ree kan tə buh ree ◊ |
| **Charing [Cross]** | 'tʃæ rɪŋ | cha ring |
| **Charles** | 'tʃɑrlz 'tʃɑlz ◊ | chahrlz chahlz ◊ |
| **Christ** | 'kraɪst | kraist |
| **Christendom** | 'krɪ sən dəm | kri suhn duhm |

| NAME | INTERNATIONAL PHONETIC ALPHABET* | SIMPLIFIED PHONICS** |
|---|---|---|
| **Christian** | 'krɪs tʃən | kris chuhn |
| **Clifton** | 'klɪf tən | klif tuhn |
| **Col'fil'/Coldfield** | 'koʊl fil<br>'kol fil ◊ | kol feel<br>… ◊ |
| **Colossus** | kə 'lɑ səs<br>kə 'lɒ səs ◊ | kuh lah suhs<br>kuh lo suhs ◊ |
| **Corinthian** | kə 'rɪn θiən | kuh rin *thee* uhn |
| **Coventry** | 'kʌ vən tri<br>'kʌ vən tʃri<br>'kɒ vən tri ◊ | kuh vuhn tree<br>kuh vuhn chree<br>ko vuhn tree ◊ |
| **Cross** | 'krɔs<br>'krɑs<br>'krɒs ◊ | kraws<br>krahs<br>kro s ◊ |
| **Cut** | 'kʌt | kuht |
| **Daventry** | 'deɪn tri<br>'deɪn tʃri<br>'dæ vən tri<br>'dæ vən tʃri | dein tree<br>dein chree<br>da vuhn tree<br>da vuhn chree |
| **Diana** | daɪ 'æ nə | dai a nuh |
| **Dick** | 'dɪk | dik |
| **Dives** | 'daɪ viz | dai veez |
| **Doncaster** | 'dɑn kæ stɚ<br>'dɑŋ kæ stɚ<br>'dɒŋ kə stə ◊ | dahn ka stər<br>dahng ka stər<br>dong kuh stə ◊ |
| **Douglas** | 'dʌg ləs | duh gluhs |
| **Eastcheap** | 'is tʃip | ees cheep |

74

| NAME | INTERNATIONAL PHONETIC ALPHABET* | SIMPLIFIED PHONICS** |
|------|----------------------------------|----------------------|
| 'Ebrew | 'i bru | ee broo |
| Edmund | 'ɛd mənd<br>'ed mənd ◊ | ed muhnd<br>... ◊ |
| England | 'ɪŋ glənd | ing gluhnd |
| English | 'ɪŋ glɪʃ | ing glish |
| Europe | 'jʊ rəp<br>'jʊə rəp ◊ | yoo ruhp<br>... ◊ |
| Falstaff | 'fɔl stæf<br>'fɔl stɑf ◊ | fawl staf<br>fawl stahf ◊ |
| Fife | 'faɪf | faif |
| Finsbury | 'fɪnz bɛ ri<br>'fɪnz bə ri ◊ | finz be ree<br>finz buh ree ◊ |
| Francis | 'fræn sɪs<br>'frɑn sɪs ◊ | fran sis<br>frahn sis ◊ |
| Gadshill | 'gædz hɪl | gadz hil |
| Gaunt | 'gɔnt | gawnt |
| Gawsey | 'gɔ zi<br>'gɔ si ◊ | gaw zee<br>gaw see ◊ |
| Gilliams | 'gɪl jəmz | gil yuhmz |
| Glendower | 'glɛn daʊɚ<br>glɛn 'daʊɚ<br>'glɛn daʊ ə ◊<br>glɛn 'daʊ ə ◊ | glen dow ər<br>...<br>glen dow ə ◊<br>... ◊ |
| Gloucestershire | 'glɑ stɚ ʃɚ<br>'glɔ stɚ ʃɚ<br>'glɒ stə ʃə ◊ | glah stər shər<br>glaw stər shər<br>glo stə shə ◊ |

| NAME | INTERNATIONAL PHONETIC ALPHABET* | SIMPLIFIED PHONICS** |
|------|------|------|
| Gregory | 'grɛ gə ri<br>'gre gə ri ◊ | gre guh ree<br>… ◊ |
| Hal | 'hæl | hal |
| Halfmoon | 'hæf 'mun<br>'hɑf 'mun ◊ | haf moon<br>hahf moon ◊ |
| Harry | 'hæ ri | ha ree |
| Harvey -folio only, spelled Haruey | 'hɑr vi<br>'hɑ vi ◊ | hahr vee<br>hah vee ◊ |
| Henry | 'hɛn ri<br>'hen ri ◊ | hen ree<br>… ◊ |
| Hercules | 'hɝ kjə liz<br>'hɝ kju liz<br>'hɜ kjʊ liz ◊ | hər kyuh leez<br>hər kyoo leez<br>hə ky*oo* leez ◊ |
| Herefordshire | 'hɛ rɪ fə·d ʃə·<br>'hɝ fə·d ʃə·<br>'he rɪ fəd ʃə ◊ | he ri fərd shər<br>hər fərd shər<br>he ri fəd shə ◊ |
| Holland | 'hɑ lənd<br>'hɒ lənd ◊ | hah luhnd<br>h*o* luhnd ◊ |
| Holmedon -folio also Holmeden | 'hoʊm dən<br>'hom dən ◊ | hom duhn<br>… ◊ |
| Holy Rood Day | 'hoʊ li 'rud 'deɪ<br>'ho li 'rud 'deɪ ◊ | ho lee rood dei<br>… ◊ |
| Hotspur | 'hɑt spə·<br>'hɒt spə ◊ | haht spər<br>h*o*t spə ◊ |
| Hybla -folio Hibla | 'haɪ blə | hai bluh |
| Hydra | 'haɪ drə<br>'haɪ ʤrə | hai druh<br>hai jruh |

| NAME | INTERNATIONAL PHONETIC ALPHABET* | SIMPLIFIED PHONICS** |
|------|----------------------------------|----------------------|
| **India** | 'ɪn diə | in dee uh |
| **Irish** | 'aɪ rɪʃ | ai rish |
| **Jack** | 'ʤæk | jak |
| **Jerusalem** | ʤə 'ru sə ləm | juh roo suh luhm |
| **Jesu** | 'ʤi zu<br>'ʤi su<br>'ʤi zju ◊ | jee zoo<br>jee soo<br>jee zyoo ◊ |
| **Jesus** | 'ʤi zəs | jee zuhs |
| **Jew** | 'ʤu | joo |
| **John** | 'ʤɑn<br>'ʤɒn ◊ | jahn<br>jon ◊ |
| **June** | 'ʤun | joon |
| **Kate** | 'keɪt | keit |
| **Kendal** | 'kɛn dəl<br>'ken dəl ◊ | ken duhl<br>… ◊ |
| **Lancaster** | 'læŋ kə stɚ<br>'læŋ kæ stɚ<br>'læŋ kə stə ◊ | lang kuh stər<br>lang ka stər<br>lang kuh stə ◊ |
| **Lazarus** | 'læ zə rəs | la zuh ruhs |
| **Lincolnshire** | 'lɪŋ kən ʃɚ<br>'lɪŋ kən ʃə ◊ | ling kuhn shər<br>ling kuhn shə ◊ |
| **London** | 'lʌn dən | luhn duhn |
| **Lucifer** | 'lu sɪ fɚ<br>'lu sɪ fə ◊ | loo si fər<br>loo si fə ◊ |

| NAME | INTERNATIONAL PHONETIC ALPHABET* | SIMPLIFIED PHONICS** |
|---|---|---|
| Madeira/ Maderia | mə 'dɪ rə<br>mə 'dɪə rə ◊ | muh di ruh<br>muh diə ruh |
| Manningtree | 'mænɪŋ tri<br>'mæ nɪŋ ʧri | ma ning tree<br>ma ning chree |
| March | 'mɑrʧ<br>'mɑʧ ◊ | mahrch<br>mahch ◊ |
| Marian | 'mɛ riən<br>'mæ riən<br>'mɛə riən ◊ | me ree uhn<br>ma ree uhn<br>meə ree uhn ◊ |
| Mars | 'mɑrz<br>'mɑz ◊ | mahrz<br>mahz ◊ |
| Menteith | mɛn 'tiθ<br>men 'tiθ ◊ | men tee*th*<br>… ◊ |
| Mercury | 'mɝ kjə ri<br>'mɜ kjʊ ri ◊ | mər kyuh ree<br>mə ky*oo* ree ◊ |
| Merlin | 'mɝ lɪn<br>'mɜ lɪn ◊ | mər lin<br>mə lin ◊ |
| Michael | 'maɪ kəl | mai kuhl |
| Michaelmas | 'mɪ kəl məs | mi kuhl muhs |
| Monday | 'mʌn deɪ<br>'mʌn di ◊ | muhn dei<br>muhn dee ◊ |
| Monmouth | 'mɑn məθ<br>'mɒn məθ ◊<br>'mʌn məθ ◊ | mahn muh*th*<br>m*o*n muh*th* ◊<br>muhn muh*th* ◊ |
| Moorditch | 'mur dɪʧ<br>'muə dɪʧ ◊ | moor dich<br>mooə dich ◊ |
| Moredake | 'mɝ dɑk<br>'mɜ dɒk ◊ | mər dahk<br>mə d*o*k ◊ |

| NAME | INTERNATIONAL PHONETIC ALPHABET* | SIMPLIFIED PHONICS** |
|------|----------------------------------|----------------------|
| Mortimer | 'mɔr tə mɚ<br>'mɔ tɪ mə ◊ | mawr ti mər<br>mawr ti mə ◊ |
| Mugs -folio<br>  Mugges | 'mʌgz | muhgz |
| Murray | 'mɝi<br>'mʌri | məree<br>muh ree |
| Ned | 'nɛd<br>'ned ◊ | ned<br>... ◊ |
| Newgate | 'nu geɪt<br>'nju geɪt ◊ | noo geit<br>nyoo geit ◊ |
| [Saint] Nicholas | [seɪnt] 'nɪ kə ləs<br>[sɪnt] 'nɪ kə ləs ◊ | [seint] ni kuh luhs<br>[sint] ni kuh luhs ◊ |
| Nothumberland | nɔr 'θʌm bɚ lənd<br><br>nɔ 'θʌm bə lənd ◊ | nawr thuhm bər<br>   luhnd<br>naw thuhm bə<br>   luhnd ◊ |
| Oldcastle | 'oʊld kæ səl<br>'old kɑ səl ◊ | old ka suhl<br>old kah suhl ◊ |
| Owen | 'oʊ ɪn<br>'oʊ ən<br>'əʊ ɪn ◊ | o in<br>o uhn<br>... ◊ |
| Partlet | 'pɑrt lɪt<br>'pɑt lɪt ◊ | pahrt lit<br>paht lit ◊ |
| [Saint] Paul | [seɪnt] 'pɔl<br>[sɪnt] 'pɔl ◊ | [seint] pawl<br>[sint] pawl ◊ |
| Paunch | 'pɔnʧ | pawnch |
| Pegasus | 'pɛ gə səs<br>'pe gə səs ◊ | pe guh suhs<br>... ◊ |

| NAME | INTERNATIONAL PHONETIC ALPHABET* | SIMPLIFIED PHONICS** |
|------|----------------------------------|----------------------|
| **Percy** | 'pɝ si<br>'pɜ si ◊ | pər see<br>pə see ◊ |
| **Peto** | 'pi to<br>'pi təʊ ◊ | pee to<br>… ◊ |
| **Pharoah** | 'fɛ ro<br>'fɛə rəʊ ◊ | fe ro<br>… ◊ |
| **Phoebus** | 'fi bəs | fee buhs |
| **Plantagenet** | plæn 'tæ ʤə nɪt<br>plæn 'tæ ʤɪ nɪt | plan ta juh nit<br>plan ta ji nit |
| **Poins/Poines** | 'pɔɪnz | poynz |
| **Pomgarnet** | 'pɑm gɑr nət<br>'pɒm gɑ nɪt ◊<br>'pʌm gɑ nɪt ◊ | pahm gahr nuht<br>pom gah nit ◊<br>puhm gah nit ◊ |
| **Quickly** | 'kwɪk li | kwik lee |
| **Ralph** -folio **Rafe** | 'rælf<br>'reɪf ◊ | ralf<br>reif ◊ |
| **Ravenspurgh** | 'reɪ vənz pɝg<br>'reɪnz pɚ<br>'reɪ vənz pəg ◊<br>'reɪnz pə ◊ | rei vuhnz pərg<br>reinz pər<br>rei vuhnz pəg ◊<br>reinz pə ◊ |
| **Richard** | 'rɪ tʃɚd<br>'rɪ tʃəd ◊ | ri chərd<br>ri chəd ◊ |
| **Robin** | 'rɑ bɪn<br>'rɒ bɪn ◊ | rah bin<br>ro bin ◊ |
| **Rochester** | 'rɑ tʃɛ stɚ<br>'rɒ tʃɪ stə ◊ | rah che stər<br>ro chi stə ◊ |

| NAME | INTERNATIONAL PHONETIC ALPHABET* | SIMPLIFIED PHONICS** |
|---|---|---|
| **Rossill** | ˈrɔ səl<br>ˈrɑ səl<br>ˈrɒ səl ◊ | raw suhl<br>rah suhl<br>ro suhl ◊ |
| **Satan** | ˈseɪ tən | sei tuhn |
| **Scot** | ˈskɑt<br>ˈskɒt ◊ | skaht<br>skot ◊ |
| **Scotland** | ˈskɑt lənd<br>ˈskɒt lənd ◊ | skaht luhnd<br>skot luhnd ◊ |
| **Scroop** | ˈskrup | skroop |
| **Severn** | ˈsɛ vɚn<br>ˈse vən ◊ | se vərn<br>se vən ◊ |
| **Shirley** | ˈʃɚ li<br>ˈʃɜ li ◊ | shər lee<br>shə lee ◊ |
| **Shrewsbury** | ˈʃruz bɛ ri<br>ˈʃrəʊz bə ri ◊ | shrooz be ree<br>shroz buh ree ◊ |
| **Spanish** | ˈspæ nɪʃ | spa nish |
| **Stafford** | ˈstæ fɚd<br>ˈstæ fəd ◊ | sta fərd<br>sta fəd ◊ |
| **Sunday** | ˈsʌn deɪ<br>ˈsʌn di ◊ | suhn dei<br>suhn dee ◊ |
| **Sutton Col'fil'**<br>   -folio<br>  **Sutton-cop-hill** | ˈsʌ tən ˈkoʊl fil<br>ˈsʌ tən ˈkol fil ◊ | suh tuhn kol fil<br>… ◊ |
| **Termagant** | ˈtɚ mə gənt<br>ˈtɜ mə gənt | tər muh guhnt<br>tə muh guhnt |
| **Thursday** | ˈθɚz deɪ<br>ˈθɜz di ◊ | *th*ərz dei<br>*th*əz dee ◊ |

| NAME | INTERNATIONAL PHONETIC ALPHABET* | SIMPLIFIED PHONICS** |
|------|----------------------------------|----------------------|
| **Titan** | 'taɪ tən | tai tuhn |
| **Tom** | 'tɑm | tahm |
| | 'tɒm ◊ | tom ◊ |
| **Trent** | 'ʧrɛnt | chrent |
| | 'trɛnt | trent |
| | 'trent ◊ | … ◊ |
| **Trojan/Troyan** | 'ʧroʊ ʤən | chro juhn |
| | 'troʊ ʤən | tro juhn |
| | 'trəʊ ʤən ◊ | … ◊ |
| **Tuesday** | 'tuz deɪ | tooz dei |
| | 'tjuz di ◊ | tyooz dee ◊ |
| **Turk** | 'tɝk | tərk |
| | 'tɜk ◊ | tək ◊ |
| **Vernon** | 'vɝ nən | vər nuhn |
| | 'vɜ nən ◊ | və nuhn ◊ |
| **Wales** | 'weɪlz | weilz |
| **Walter** | 'wɔl tɚ | wawl tər |
| | 'wɔl tə ◊ | wawl tə ◊ |
| **Warkworth [Castle]** | 'wɔrk wɚθ ['kæ səl] | wawrk wərth [ka suhl] |
| | 'wɔk wəθ ['kɑ səl] ◊ | wawk wəth [kah suhl] ◊ |
| **Warwickshire** | 'wɔ rɪk ʃɚ | war rik shər |
| | 'wɒ rɪk ʃə ◊ | wo rik shə ◊ |
| **Wednesday** | 'wɛnz deɪ | wenz dei |
| | 'wenz di ◊ | wenz dee ◊ |
| **Welsh** | 'wɛlʃ | welsh |
| | 'welʃ ◊ | … ◊ |

| NAME | INTERNATIONAL PHONETIC ALPHABET* | SIMPLIFIED PHONICS** |
|---|---|---|
| **Westmoreland**<br>-folio<br>**Westmerland** | 'wɛst mɚ lənd<br>'wɛst mə lənd ◊ | west mər luhnd<br>west mə luhnd ◊ |
| **Windsor** | 'wɪn zɚ<br>'wɪn zə ◊ | win zər<br>win zə ◊ |
| **Whitsun/**<br>**Wheeson** | 'wɪtsən | wit suhn |
| **Worcester** | 'wʊ stɚ<br>'wʊ stə ◊ | woo stər<br>woo stə ◊ |
| **Wye** | 'waɪ | wai |
| **Yedward** | 'jɛd wɚd<br>'jed wəd ◊ | yed wərd<br>yed wəd ◊ |
| **York** | 'jɔrk<br>'jɔk ◊ | yawrk<br>yawk ◊ |

| NAME | INTERNATIONAL PHONETIC ALPHABET* | SIMPLIFIED PHONICS** |
|---|---|---|
| **Achitophel** | ə ˈkɪ tə fɛl<br>ə ˈkɪ tə fel ◊ | uh ki tuh fel<br>… ◊ |
| **Africa** | ˈæ frɪ kə | a fri kuh |
| **Agamemnon** | æ gə ˈmɛm nɑn<br>æ gə ˈmem nɒn ◊<br>æ gə ˈmɛm nən<br>æ gə ˈmem nən ◊ | a guh mem nahn<br>a guh mem non ◊<br>a guh mem nuhn<br>… ◊ |
| **[Saint] Alban**<br>-folio **Albon,**<br>**Albone** | [seɪnt] ˈɔl bən<br>[seɪnt] ˈal bən<br>[sɪnt] ˈɔl bən ◊ | [seint] awl buhn<br>[seint] ahl buhn<br>[sint] awl buhn ◊ |
| **Alecto** | ə ˈlɛk to<br>ə ˈlek təʊ ◊ | uh lek to<br>… ◊ |
| **Althaea/Althea** | æl ˈθi ə<br>ˈæl θiə | al *th*ee uh<br>… |
| **Amaimon/**<br>**Amamon** | ə ˈmeɪ mɑn<br>ə ˈmeɪ mɒn ◊ | uh mei mahn<br>uh mei mon ◊ |
| **Amurath** | ɑ mu ˈrat<br>ˈæ mu ræt | ah moo raht<br>a mu rat |
| **Arthur** | ˈɑr θɚ<br>ˈɑ θə ◊ | ahr *th*ər<br>ah *th*ə ◊ |
| **Asia** | ˈeɪ ʒə<br>ˈeɪ ʃə ◊ | ei zhuh<br>ei shuh ◊ |
| **Assyrian** | ə ˈsɪ riən | uh si ree uhn |

| NAME | INTERNATIONAL PHONETIC ALPHABET* | SIMPLIFIED PHONICS** |
|---|---|---|
| Atrophus/ Atropos | 'æ trə pɑs<br>'æ tʃrə pɑs<br>'æ trə pɒs ◊ | a truh pahs<br>a chruh pahs<br>a truh pos ◊ |
| Barbary | 'bɑr bə ri<br>'bɑ bə ri ◊ | bahr buh ree<br>bah buh ree ◊ |
| Bardolph | 'bɑr dɑlf<br>'bɑr dɔlf<br>'bɑ dɒlf ◊ | bahr dahlf<br>bahr dawlf<br>bah dolf ◊ |
| Barnes | 'bɑrnz<br>'bɑnz ◊ | bahrnz<br>bahnz ◊ |
| Barson | 'bɑr sən<br>'bɑ sən ◊ | bahr suhn<br>bah suhn ◊ |
| Bartholemew | bɑr 'θɑ lə mju<br><br>bɑ 'θɒ lə mju ◊ | bahr thah luh myoo<br>bah tho luh myoo ◊ |
| Basingstoke | 'beɪ zɪŋ stoʊk<br>'beɪ zɪŋ stəʊk ◊ | bei zing stok<br>... ◊ |
| Besonian/ Bezonian | 'bə zoʊ niən<br>'bɪ zəʊ niən ◊ | buh zo nee uhn<br>bi zo nee uhn ◊ |
| Billingsgate | 'bɪ lɪŋz geɪt | bi lingz geit |
| Blunt | 'blʌnt | bluhnt |
| Boar's Head | 'bɔrz hɛd<br>'bɔz hed ◊ | bawrz hed<br>bawz hed ◊ |
| Bourdeaux/ Bordeaux | 'bɔr do<br>bɔr 'doʊ<br>'bɔ dəʊ ◊<br>bɔ 'dəʊ ◊ | bawr do<br>...<br>baw do ◊<br>... ◊ |

85

| NAME | INTERNATIONAL PHONETIC ALPHABET* | SIMPLIFIED PHONICS** |
|------|------|------|
| **Bullcalf** | ˈbʊl kæf<br>ˈbʊl kɑf ◊ | bool kaf<br>bool kahf ◊ |
| **Butler** | ˈbʌt lɚ<br>ˈbʌt lə ◊ | buht lər<br>buht lə ◊ |
| **Caesar** | ˈsi zɚ<br>ˈsi zə ◊ | see zər<br>see zə ◊ |
| **Cain** | ˈkeɪn | kein |
| **Calipolis** | kə ˈlɪ pə lɪs | kuh li puh lis |
| **Cerberus** | ˈsɝ bə rəs<br>ˈsɜ bə rəs ◊ | sər buh ruhs<br>sə buh ruhs ◊ |
| **Chester** | ˈtʃɛ stɚ<br>ˈtʃe stə ◊ | che stər<br>che stə ◊ |
| **Christian** | ˈkrɪs tʃən | kris chuhn |
| **Clarence** | ˈklæ rəns<br>ˈklæ rɪns | kla ruhns<br>kla rins |
| **Clement** | ˈklɛ mənt<br>ˈkle mənt ◊ | kle muhnt<br>… ◊ |
| **Clifford** | ˈklɪ fɚd<br>ˈklɪ fəd ◊ | kli fərd<br>kli fəd ◊ |
| **Coldspur** | ˈkoʊld spɚ<br>ˈkold spə ◊ | kold spər<br>kold spə ◊ |
| **Coleville** | ˈkoʊl vɪl<br>ˈkol vɪl ◊ | kol vil<br>… ◊ |
| **Cophetua** | kə ˈfɛ tʃu ə<br>kəʊ ˈfe tju ə ◊ | kuh fe choo uh<br>ko fe tyoo uh ◊ |
| **Cotsale/Cotsall** | ˈkɑt səl<br>ˈkɒt səl ◊ | kaht suhl<br>kot suhl ◊ |

| NAME | INTERNATIONAL PHONETIC ALPHABET* | SIMPLIFIED PHONICS** |
|------|------|------|
| Cotswold | 'kɑts wold<br>'kɒts wold ◊ | kahts wold<br>kots wold ◊ |
| Coventry | 'kʌ vən tri<br>'kʌ vən tʃri<br>'kɒ vən tri ◊ | kuh vuhn tree<br>kuh vuhn chree<br>ko vuhn tree ◊ |
| Dagonet | 'dæ gə nɛt<br>'dæ gəʊ net ◊ | da guh net<br>da go net ◊ |
| Davy | 'deɪ vi | dei vee |
| Doit | 'dɔɪt | doyt |
| Doll -folio Dol | 'dɑl<br>'dɒl ◊ | dahl<br>dol ◊ |
| Dombledon/<br>Dumbledon | 'dʌm bəl dən | duhm buhl duhn |
| Dorothy | 'dɔ rə θi<br>'dɑ rə θi<br>'dɒ rə θi ◊ | daw ruh *thee*<br>dah ruh *thee*<br>do ruh *thee* ◊ |
| Double | 'dʌ bəl | duh buhl |
| Douglas -folio<br>also Dowglas | 'dʌ gləs | duh gluhs |
| Dumb/Dumbe | 'dʌm | duhm |
| Eastcheap | 'is tʃip | ees cheep |
| Edward | 'ɛd wɚd,<br>'ed wəd ◊ | ed wərd<br>ed wəd ◊ |
| Ellen | 'ɛ lən<br>'e lən ◊ | e luhn<br>... ◊ |
| England | 'ɪŋ glənd | ing gluhnd |
| English | 'ɪŋ glɪʃ | ing glish |

| NAME | INTERNATIONAL PHONETIC ALPHABET* | SIMPLIFIED PHONICS** |
|------|----------------------------------|----------------------|
| **Ephesians** | ɪ ˈfi ʒənz<br>ɪ ˈfi ʒiənz | i fee zhuhnz<br>i fee zhee uhnz |
| **Erebus** | ˈɛ rəbəs<br>ˈe rɪ bəs ◊ | e ruh buhs<br>e ri buhs ◊ |
| **Europe** | ˈjʊ rəp<br>ˈjʊə rəp ◊ | yóo ruhp<br>... ◊ |
| **Falstaff** | ˈfɔl stæf<br>ˈfɔl stɑf ◊ | fawl staf<br>fawl stahf ◊ |
| **Fang** | ˈfæŋ | fang |
| **Feeble** | ˈfi bəl | fee buhl |
| **Fleet** | ˈflit | fleet |
| **Francis** | ˈfræn sɪs<br>ˈfrɑn sɪs ◊ | fran sis<br>frahn sis ◊ |
| **French** | ˈfrɛntʃ<br>ˈfrɛntʃ ◊ | french<br>... ◊ |
| **Gadshill** | ˈgædz hɪl | gadz hil |
| **Galen** | ˈgeɪ lən | gei luhn |
| **Galloway** | ˈgæ lə weɪ | ga luh wei |
| **Gaultree** | ˈgɔl tri<br>ˈgɔl tʃri | gawl tree<br>gawl chree |
| **Gaunt** | ˈgɔnt | gawnt |
| **[Saint] George** | [seɪnt] ˈdʒɔrdʒ<br>[sɪnt] ˈdʒɔdʒ ◊ | [seint] jawrj<br>[sint] jawj ◊ |
| **German** | ˈdʒɝ mən<br>ˈdʒɜ mən ◊ | jər muhn<br>jə muhn ◊ |

| NAME | INTERNATIONAL PHONETIC ALPHABET* | SIMPLIFIED PHONICS** |
|------|----------------------------------|----------------------|
| **Glendower** -folio<br>**Glendoure** | 'glɛn daʊ ɚ<br>glɛn 'daʊ ɚ<br>'glɛn daʊ ə ◊<br>glɛn 'daʊ ə ◊ | glen dow ər<br>...<br>glen dow ə ◊<br>... ◊ |
| **Gloucester** | 'glɑ stɚ<br>'glɔ stɚ<br>'glɒ stə ◊ | glah stər<br>glaw stər<br>glo stə ◊ |
| **Gloucestershire** | 'glɑ stɚ ʃɚ<br>'glɔ stɚ ʃɚ<br>'glɒ stə ʃə ◊ | glah stər shər<br>glaw stər shər<br>glo stə shə ◊ |
| **Gower** | 'gaʊ ɚ<br>'gaʊ ə ◊ | gow ər<br>gow ə ◊ |
| **Gray** | 'greɪ | grei |
| **Greek** | 'grik | greek |
| **Hal** | 'hæl | hal |
| **Hannibal** | 'hæ nə bəl<br>'hæ nɪ bəl ◊ | ha nuh buhl<br>ha ni buhl ◊ |
| **Harcourt** -folio<br>**Harecourt** | 'hɑr kɔrt<br>'hɑr kɚt<br>'hɑ kɔt ◊<br>'hɑ kət ◊ | hahr kawrt<br>hahr kərt<br>hah kawt ◊<br>hah kət ◊ |
| **Harry** | 'hæ ri | ha ree |
| **Hastings** | 'heɪ stɪŋz | hei stingz |
| **Hector** | 'hɛk tɚ<br>'hek tə ◊ | hek tər<br>hek tə ◊ |
| **Helen** | 'hɛ lən<br>'hɛ lɪn<br>'he lɪn ◊ | he luhn<br>he lin<br>... ◊ |

| NAME | INTERNATIONAL PHONETIC ALPHABET* | SIMPLIFIED PHONICS** |
|------|-----------------------------------|----------------------|
| **Helicon** | 'hɛ lɪ kɑn<br>'he lɪ kɒn ◊<br>'hɛlɪ kən<br>'he lɪ kən ◊ | he li kahn<br>he li kon ◊<br>he li kuhn<br>... ◊ |
| **Henry** | 'hɛn ri<br>'hen ri ◊ | hen ree<br>... ◊ |
| **Hereford** | 'hɛ rɪ fɚd<br>'he rɪ fəd ◊ | he ri fərd<br>he ri fəd ◊ |
| **Hinkley** | 'hɪŋ kli | hing klee |
| **Hiren** | 'haɪ rən | hai ruhn |
| **Holland** | 'hɑ lənd<br>'hɒ lənd ◊ | hah luhnd<br>ho luhnd ◊ |
| **Hood** | 'hʊd | hood |
| **Hotspur** | 'hɑt spɚ<br>'hɒt spə ◊ | haht spər<br>hot spə ◊ |
| **Humphrey** -folio<br>  **Humfrey** | 'hʌm fri<br>'hʌmp fri | huhm free<br>huhmp free |
| **Hydra** | 'haɪ drə<br>'haɪ ʤrə | hai druh<br>hai jruh |
| **Jane** | 'ʤeɪn | jein |
| **Japhet** | 'ʤeɪ fɪt<br>'ʤeɪ fet ◊ | jei fit<br>jei fet ◊ |
| **Jerusalem** | ʤə 'ru sə ləm | juh roo suh luhm |
| **Jesu** | 'ʤi zu<br>'ʤi su<br>'ʤi zju ◊ | jee zoo<br>jee soo<br>jee zyoo ◊ |

| NAME | INTERNATIONAL PHONETIC ALPHABET* | SIMPLIFIED PHONICS** |
|---|---|---|
| Job | 'ʤoʊb <br> 'ʤəʊb ◊ | job <br> ... ◊ |
| John | 'ʤɑn <br> 'ʤɒn ◊ | jahn <br> jon ◊ |
| John a Gaunt | 'ʤɑn ə gɔnt <br> 'ʤɒn ə gɔnt ◊ | jahn uh gawnt <br> jon uh gawnt ◊ |
| Jove | 'ʤoʊv <br> 'ʤəʊv ◊ | jov <br> ... ◊ |
| Katherine | 'kæ θrɪn <br> 'kæ θə rɪn | ka *th*rin <br> ka *th*uh rin |
| Keech | 'kitʃ | keech |
| Lancaster | 'læŋ kæ stɚ <br> 'læŋ kə stɚ <br> 'læŋ kə stə ◊ | lang ka stər <br> lang kuh stər <br> lang kuh stə ◊ |
| Lent | 'lɛnt <br> 'lent ◊ | lent <br> ... ◊ |
| Lethe | 'li θi | lee *th*ee |
| Lombard | 'lɑm bɑrd <br> 'lʌm bɑrd <br> 'lɒm bəd ◊ | lahm bahrd <br> luhm bahrd <br> lom buhd ◊ |
| Lubbar/Lubber | 'lʌ bɚ <br> 'lʌ bə ◊ | luh bər <br> luh bə ◊ |
| Lucifer | 'lu sɪ fɚ <br> 'lu sɪ fə ◊ | loo si fər <br> loo si fə ◊ |
| Lumbert | 'lʌm bɚt <br> 'lʌm bət ◊ | luhm bərt <br> luhm bət ◊ |
| Mile End Green | 'maɪl 'ɛnd ' grin <br> 'maɪl 'end ' grin ◊ | mail end green <br> ... ◊ |

| NAME | INTERNATIONAL PHONETIC ALPHABET* | SIMPLIFIED PHONICS** |
|------|----------------------------------|----------------------|
| **Monmouth** | ˈmɑn məθ | mahn muhth |
| | ˈmɒn məθ ◊ | mon muhth ◊ |
| | ˈmʌn məθ ◊ | muhn muhth ◊ |
| **Mortimer** | ˈmɔr tə mɚ | mawr tuh mər |
| | ˈmɔ tɪ mə ◊ | maw ti mə ◊ |
| **Morton** | ˈmɔr tən | mawr tuhn |
| | ˈmɔ tən ◊ | maw tuhn ◊ |
| **Mouldy** -folio | ˈmoʊl di | mol dee |
| **Mouldie** | ˈmol di ◊ | ... ◊ |
| **Mowbray** | ˈmoʊ bri | mo bree |
| | ˈməʊ bri ◊ | ... ◊ |
| | ˈməʊ breɪ ◊ | mo brei ◊ |
| **Ned** | ˈnɛd | ned |
| | ˈned ◊ | ... ◊ |
| **Nell** | ˈnɛl | nel |
| | ˈnel ◊ | ... ◊ |
| **Neptune** | ˈnɛp tun | nep toon |
| | ˈnep tjun ◊ | nep tyoon ◊ |
| **Nevil** | ˈnɛ vəl | ne vuhl |
| | ˈne vɪl ◊ | ne vil ◊ |
| **Nightwork** | ˈnaɪt wɚk | nait wərk |
| | ˈnaɪt wək ◊ | nait wək ◊ |
| **Norfolk** | ˈnɔr fək | nawr fuhk |
| | ˈnɔ fək ◊ | naw fuhk ◊ |
| **Northumberland** | nɔr ˈθʌm bɚ lənd | nawr *th*uhm bər luhnd |
| | nɔ ˈθʌm bə lənd ◊ | naw *th*uhm bə luhnd ◊ |

| NAME | INTERNATIONAL PHONETIC ALPHABET* | SIMPLIFIED PHONICS** |
|------|----------------------------------|----------------------|
| Oldcastle | ˈoʊld kæ səl<br>ˈold kɑ səl ◊ | old ka suhl<br>old kah suhl ◊ |
| Orleans | ˈɔr liənz<br>ɔr ˈliənz<br>ˈɔ liənz ◊<br>ɔ ˈliənz ◊ | awr lee uhnz<br>…<br>aw lee uhnz ◊<br>… ◊ |
| Oxford | ˈɑks fərd<br>ˈɒks fəd ◊ | ahks fərd<br>oks fəd ◊ |
| [Saint] Paul | [seɪnt] ˈpɔl<br>[sɪnt] ˈpɔl ◊ | [seint] pawl<br>[sint] pawl ◊ |
| Peesel | ˈpi səl | pee suhl |
| Percy | ˈpɚ si<br>ˈpɜ si ◊ | pər see<br>pə see ◊ |
| Perkes/Parks | ˈpɑrks<br>ˈpɑks ◊ | pahrks<br>pahks ◊ |
| Peter | ˈpi tɚ<br>ˈpi tə ◊ | pee tər<br>pee tə ◊ |
| Peto | ˈpi toʊ<br>ˈpi təʊ ◊ | pee to<br>… ◊ |
| Pickbone | ˈpɪk bon<br>ˈpɪk bəʊn ◊ | pik bon<br>… ◊ |
| Pie Corner | ˈpaɪ ˈkɔr nɚ<br>ˈpaɪ ˈkɔ nə ◊ | pai kawr nər<br>pai kaw nə ◊ |
| Pistol | ˈpɪ stəl | pi stuhl |
| Pluto | ˈplu to<br>ˈplu təʊ ◊ | ploo to<br>… ◊ |
| Poins/Poines | ˈpɔɪnz | poynz |

| NAME | INTERNATIONAL PHONETIC ALPHABET* | SIMPLIFIED PHONICS** |
|------|------|------|
| **Pomfret** | 'pʌm frɪt<br>'pɑm frɪt<br>  [gen Am var]<br>'pɒm frɪt<br>  [Brit RP var] | puhm frit<br>pahm frit<br>  [gen Am var]<br>pom frit<br>  [Brit RP var] |
| **Priam** | 'praɪ əm | prai uhm |
| **Puff** | 'pʌf | puhf |
| **Quickly** | 'kwɪk li | kwik lee |
| **Ralph** | 'rælf<br>'reɪf [Brit RP var] | ralf<br>reif [Brit RP var] |
| **Richard** | 'rɪ tʃɚd<br>'rɪ tʃəd ◊ | ri chərd<br>ri chəd ◊ |
| **Robert** | 'rɑ bɚt<br>'rɒ bət ◊ | rah bərt<br>ro bət ◊ |
| **Robin** | 'rɑ bɪn<br>'rɒ bɪn ◊ | rah bin<br>ro bin ◊ |
| **Roman** | 'roʊ mən<br>'rəʊ mən ◊ | ro muhn<br>... ◊ |
| **Rome** | 'roʊm<br>'rəʊm ◊ | rom<br>... ◊ |
| **Rumor/Rumour** | 'ru mɚ<br>'ru mə ◊ | roo mər<br>roo mə ◊ |
| **Samingo** | sə 'mɪŋ go<br>sə 'mɪŋ gəʊ ◊ | suh ming go<br>... ◊ |
| **Sampson** | 'sæmp sən | samp suhn |
| **Saturn** | 'sæ tɚn<br>'sæ tən ◊ | sa tərn<br>sa tən ◊ |

| NAME | INTERNATIONAL PHONETIC ALPHABET* | SIMPLIFIED PHONICS** |
|---|---|---|
| **Scarlet** | 'skɑr lɪt<br>'skɑ lɪt ◊ | skahr lit<br>skah lit ◊ |
| **Scot** | 'skɑt<br>'skɒt ◊ | skaht<br>skot ◊ |
| **Scotland** | 'skɑt lənd<br>'skɒt lənd ◊ | skaht luhnd<br>skot luhnd ◊ |
| **Scroop** | 'skrup | skroop |
| **Shadow** | 'ʃæ do<br>'ʃæ dəʊ ◊ | sha do<br>... ◊ |
| **Shallow** | 'ʃæ lo<br>'ʃæ ləʊ ◊ | sha lo<br>... ◊ |
| **Shrewsbury** | 'ʃruz bɛ ri<br>'ʃrəʊz bə ri ◊ | shrooz be ree<br>shroz bə ree ◊ |
| **Shrove-tide** | 'ʃroʊv taid<br>'ʃrəʊv taɪd ◊ | shrov taid<br>... ◊ |
| **Silence** | 'sai ləns | sai luhns |
| **Simon** | 'saɪ mən | sai muhn |
| **Skogan** -folio<br>  **Scoggan** | 'skɑ gən<br>'skɒ gən ◊ | skah guhn<br>sko guhn ◊ |
| **Smithfield** | 'smɪθ fild | smith feeld |
| **Smooth** | 'smuð | smooth |
| **Snare** | 'snɛr<br>'snɛə ◊ | sner<br>sneə ◊ |
| **Spaniard** | 'spæn jɚd<br>'spæn jəd ◊ | span yərd<br>span yəd ◊ |
| **Squele** | 'skwil | skweel |

| NAME | INTERNATIONAL PHONETIC ALPHABET* | SIMPLIFIED PHONICS** |
|------|----------------------------------|----------------------|
| **Stafford** | 'stæ fɚd<br>'stæ fəd ◊ | sta fərd<br>sta fəd ◊ |
| **Staffordshire** | 'stæ fɚd ʃɚ<br>'stæ fəd ʃə ◊ | sta fərd shər<br>sta fəd shə ◊ |
| **Stamford** | 'stæm fɚd<br>'stæm fəd ◊ | stam fərd<br>stam fəd ◊ |
| **Stockfish** | 'stɑk fɪʃ<br>'stɒk fɪʃ ◊ | stahk fish<br>stok fish ◊ |
| **Surecard** | 'ʃʊr kɑrd<br>'ʃʊə kad ◊ | shoor kahrd<br>shooə kahd ◊ |
| **Surrey** | 'sɝi<br>'sɜ ri | səree<br>sə ree |
| **Tearsheet** -folio<br>**Teare-Sheet,**<br>**Teare Sheete** | 'tɛr ʃit<br>'tɛə ʃit ◊ | ter sheet<br>teə sheet ◊ |
| **Tewksbury** | 'tuks bɛ ri<br>'tjuks bə ri ◊ | tooks be ree<br>tyooks buh ree ◊ |
| **Thomas** | 'tɑ məs<br>'tɒ məs ◊ | tah muhs<br>to muhs ◊ |
| **Thursday** | 'θɝz deɪ<br>'θɜz di ◊ | *th*ərz dei<br>*th*əz dee ◊ |
| **Tisick** | 'tɪ zɪk | ti zik |
| **Travers** | 'træ vɚz<br>'tʃræ vɚz<br>'træ vəz ◊ | tra vərz<br>chra vərz<br>tra vəz ◊ |
| **Trojan** | 'tʃroʊ ʤən<br>'troʊ ʤən<br>'trəʊ ʤən ◊ | chro juhn<br>tro juhn<br>... ◊ |

96

| NAME | INTERNATIONAL PHONETIC ALPHABET* | SIMPLIFIED PHONICS** |
|------|----------------------------------|----------------------|
| Troy | 'trɔɪ | troy |
| | 'tʃrɔɪ | chroy |
| Tuesday | 'tuz deɪ | tooz dei |
| | 'tjuz di ◊ | tyooz dee ◊ |
| Turk | 'tɜ˞k | tərk |
| | 'tɜk ◊ | tək ◊ |
| Turkish | 'tɜ˞ kɪʃ | tər kish |
| | 'tɜ kɪʃ ◊ | tə kish |
| Turnbull | 'tɜ˞n bʊl | tərn bool |
| | 'tɜn bʊl ◊ | tən bool ◊ |
| Umpreville | 'ʌm frə vɪl | uhm fruh vil |
| Ursula | 'ɚ sə lə | ər suh luh |
| | 'ɜ sə lə ◊ | ə suh luh ◊ |
| Venus | 'vi nəs | vee nuhs |
| Vice | 'vaɪs | vais |
| Visor | 'vaɪ zɚ | vai zər |
| | 'vaɪ zə ◊ | vai zə ◊ |
| Wales | 'weɪlz | weilz |
| Warkworth | 'wɑrk wɚθ | wahrk wərth |
| | 'wɔrk wɚθ | wawrk wərth |
| | 'wɔk wəθ ◊ | wawk wəth ◊ |
| Wart | 'wɑrt | wahrt |
| | 'wɔrt | wawrt |
| | 'wɔt ◊ | wawt ◊ |
| Warwick | 'wɑ rɪk | wah rik |
| | 'wɔ rɪk | waw rik |
| | 'wɔr wɪk | wawr wik |
| | 'wɒ rɪk ◊ | wo rik ◊ |

| NAME | INTERNATIONAL PHONETIC ALPHABET* | SIMPLIFIED PHONICS** |
|---|---|---|
| Wednesday | ˈwɛnz deɪ <br> ˈwenz di ◊ | wenz dei <br> wenz dee ◊ |
| Welsh | ˈwɛlʃ <br> ˈwelʃ ◊ | welsh <br> … ◊ |
| Westminster | ˈwɛst mɪn stɚ <br> ˈwest mɪn stə ◊ | west min stər <br> west min stə ◊ |
| Westmoreland | ˈwɛst mɔr lənd <br> ˈwest mə lənd ◊ | west mawr luhnd <br> west mə luhnd ◊ |
| Whitsun/ <br> Wheeson | ˈwɪt sən | wit suhn |
| Will | ˈwɪl | wil |
| William | ˈwɪl jəm | wil yuhm |
| Wincot/ <br> Wilnecote | ˈwɪŋ kət | wing kuht |
| Windsor | ˈwɪn zɚ <br> ˈwɪn zə ◊ | win zər <br> win zə ◊ |
| Woncot | ˈwɑŋ kət <br> ˈwʊŋ kət <br> ˈwɒŋ kət ◊ | wahng kuht <br> woong kuht <br> wong kuht ◊ |
| Worcester | ˈwʊ stɚ <br> ˈwʊ stə ◊ | woo stər <br> woo stə ◊ |
| York | ˈjɔrk <br> ˈjɔk ◊ | yawrk <br> yawk ◊ |
| Yorkshire | ˈjɔrk ʃɚ <br> ˈjɔk ʃə ◊ | yawrk shər <br> yawk shə ◊ |

| NAME | INTERNATIONAL PHONETIC ALPHABET* | SIMPLIFIED PHONICS** |
|------|----------------------------------|----------------------|
| **Adam** | 'æ dəm | a duhm |
| **Agamemnon** | æ gə 'mɛm nɑn<br>æ gə 'mem nɒn ◊<br>æ gə 'mɛm nən<br>æ gə 'mem nən ◊ | a guh mem nuhn<br>a guh mem non ◊<br>a guh mem nahn<br>... ◊ |
| **Agincourt** | 'æ ʤɪn kɔrt<br>'æ ʤɪn kɔt ◊ | a jin kawrt<br>a jin kawt ◊ |
| **Albion** | 'æl biən | al bee uhn |
| **Alençon** | æ lən 'soun<br>ə 'lɛn sən<br>'æ lən sɒn ◊<br>ə 'len sɒn ◊ | a luhn son<br>uh len suhn<br>a luhn son ◊<br>uh len son ◊ |
| **Alexander** | æ lɪg 'zæn dɚ<br>æ lɪg 'zɑn də ◊ | a lig zan dər<br>a lig zahn də ◊ |
| **Alice** | 'æ lɪs | a lis |
| **Angleterre** | æŋ glə 'tɛr<br>æŋ glə 'tɛə ◊ | ang gluh ter<br>ang gluh teə ◊ |
| **Angliae** | 'æŋ gli eɪ | ang glee ei |
| **Anglish** | 'æŋ glɪʃ | ang glish |
| **Anthony** | 'æn θə ni | an *th*uh nee |
| **Antony** | 'æn tə ni | an tuh nee |

*International Phonetic Alphabet Pronunciation Key: (General American) i-s<u>ee</u>, happ<u>y</u>, Jul<u>i</u>et; ɪ-s<u>i</u>t; eɪ-s<u>ay</u>; e-s<u>e</u>t; æ-s<u>a</u>t; ɑ-f<u>a</u>ther; ʌ-s<u>u</u>n; ə-<u>a</u>bout; ɔ-s<u>aw</u>; oʊ-s<u>o</u>; o-h<u>e</u>ro; ʊ-sh<u>oo</u>k; u-s<u>oo</u>n; aɪ-s<u>igh</u>; ɔɪ-s<u>oy</u>; aʊ-s<u>ou</u>th; ju-c<u>u</u>be; ɚ-s<u>upp</u>er; ɛr-f<u>air</u>; ɝ-b<u>ir</u>d; k-<u>c</u>ut, <u>k</u>ite; g-<u>g</u>o; ʤ-<u>j</u>oy; j-<u>y</u>es; ŋ-si<u>ng</u>; ʃ-<u>sh</u>oe; ʧ-<u>ch</u>op; ð-<u>th</u>at; θ-<u>th</u>in; ʒ-mea<u>s</u>ure; (Additional symbols for British RP) e-s<u>e</u>t; ɛə-f<u>air</u>; ə-s<u>upp</u>er; ɜ-b<u>ir</u>d; ɒ-st<u>o</u>p; əʊ-s<u>o</u>, her<u>o</u>; o-(followed by l) p<u>o</u>le.

**Simplified Phonics Pronunciation Key: (General American) ee-s<u>ee</u>, happ<u>y</u>; i-s<u>i</u>t; ei-s<u>ay</u>; e-s<u>e</u>t; a-s<u>a</u>t; ah-f<u>a</u>ther; uh-s<u>u</u>n, <u>a</u>bout; aw-s<u>aw</u>; o-s<u>o</u>; oo-sh<u>oo</u>k; oo-s<u>oo</u>n; ai-s<u>igh</u>; oy-s<u>oy</u>; ow-s<u>ou</u>th; yoo-c<u>u</u>be; ər-b<u>ir</u>d, supp<u>er</u>; k-<u>c</u>ut, <u>k</u>ite; g-<u>g</u>o; j-<u>j</u>oy; ng-si<u>ng</u>; kw-<u>qu</u>ick; sh-<u>sh</u>oe; ch-<u>ch</u>op; th-<u>th</u>at; *th*-<u>th</u>in; zh-mea<u>s</u>ure; (Additional symbols for British RP) ə-b<u>ir</u>d; ə-s<u>upp</u>er; <u>o</u>-st<u>o</u>p; ... indicates pronunciation variance too subtle for Simplified Phonics transcription see International Phonetic Alphabet transcription.

◊ British RP pronunciation-see Introduction.

| NAME | INTERNATIONAL PHONETIC ALPHABET* | SIMPLIFIED PHONICS** |
|---|---|---|
| Arthur | 'ɑr θɚ<br>'ɑ θə ◊ | ahr *th*ər<br>ah *th*ə ◊ |
| Assyrian | ə 'sɪ riən | uh si ree uhn |
| Babylon | 'bæ bɪ lən<br>'bæ bə lɑn<br>    [gen Am var] | ba bi luhn<br>ba buh lahn<br>    [gen Am var] |
| Bar | 'bɑr<br>'bɑ ◊ | bahr<br>bah ◊ |
| Barbason | 'bɑr bə sən<br>'bɑ bə sən ◊ | bahr buh suhn<br>bah buh suhn ◊ |
| Bardolph | 'bɑr dɑlf<br>'bɑr dɔlf<br>'bɑ dɒlf ◊ | bahr dahlf<br>bahr dawlf<br>bah dolf ◊ |
| Bartholomew | bɑr 'θɑ lə mju<br><br>bɑ 'θɒ lə mju ◊ | bahr *th*ah luh<br>    myoo<br>bah *th*o luh<br>    myoo ◊ |
| Bates | 'beɪts | beits |
| Beaufort | 'boʊ fɚt<br>'bəʊ fət ◊ | bo fərt<br>bo fət ◊ |
| Beaumont | 'boʊ mɑnt<br>'bəʊ mɒnt ◊<br>'bəʊ mənt ◊ | bo mahnt<br>bo mont ◊<br>bo muhnt ◊ |
| Bedford | 'bɛd fɚd<br>'bed fəd ◊ | bed fərd<br>bed fəd ◊ |
| Berri/Berry | 'bɛ ri<br>'be ri ◊ | be ree<br>… ◊ |
| Blackheath | 'blæk hiθ | blak hee*th* |

| NAME | INTERNATIONAL PHONETIC ALPHABET* | SIMPLIFIED PHONICS** |
|------|----------------------------------|---------------------|
| **Blithild** | 'blɪ θɪld | bli *th*ild |
| **Bouciqualt** -folio<br>**Bouciquall,**<br>**Bouchiquald** | 'bu sɪ kɔlt | boo si kawlt |
| **Bourbon** -folio<br>**Burbon** | 'bɝ bən<br>'bʊə bən ◊ | bər buhn<br>b*oo*ə buhn ◊ |
| **Brabant** | 'brɑ bənt<br>brə 'bænt | brah buhnt<br>bruh bant |
| **Bretagne** | 'brɪ tən<br>brə 'tæŋ | bri tuhn<br>bruh tang |
| **Brutus** | 'bru təs | broo tuhs |
| **Burgundy** | 'bɝ gən di<br>'bɜ gən di ◊ | bər guhn dee<br>bə guhn dee ◊ |
| **Cadwaller** | 'kæd wɑ lɚ<br>'kæd wɒ lə ◊ | kad wah lər<br>kad w*o* lə ◊ |
| **Caesar** | 'si zɚ<br>'si zə ◊ | see zər<br>see zə ◊ |
| **Calais** | 'kæ leɪ<br>kə 'leɪ<br>[gen Am var] | ka lei<br>kuh lei<br>[gen Am var] |
| **Cambridge** | 'keɪm brɪʤ | keim brij |
| **Canterbury** | 'kæn tɚ bɛ ri<br>'kæn tə bə ri ◊ | kan tər be ree<br>kan tə buh ree ◊ |
| **Capet** | 'keɪ pɪt<br>'kæ pɪt | kei pit<br>ka pit |
| **Caveto** | kə 'vi to<br>kə 'vi təʊ ◊ | kuh vee to<br>… ◊ |

| NAME | INTERNATIONAL PHONETIC ALPHABET* | SIMPLIFIED PHONICS** |
|------|----------------------------------|----------------------|
| **Charlemain** | ˈʃɑr lə meɪn<br>ˈʃɑ lə meɪn ◊ | shahr luh mein<br>shah luh mein ◊ |
| **Charles** | ˈtʃɑrlz<br>ˈtʃɑlz ◊ | chahrlz<br>chahlz ◊ |
| **Charolois** -folio<br>**Charoloyes** | ˈʃɑ rə lɔɪz | shah ruh loyz |
| **Chatillon** | ʃə ˈtɪl jən<br>ʃə ˈtɪ lən | shuh til yuhn<br>shuh ti luhn |
| **Chesu** | ˈtʃi zu<br>ˈtʃi zju ◊ | jee zoo<br>jee zyoo ◊ |
| **Childeric/**<br>**Childerick** | ˈtʃɪl də rɪk | chil duh rik |
| **Chrish** | ˈkraɪʃ | kraish |
| **Christ** | ˈkraɪst | kraist |
| **Christian** | ˈkrɪs tʃən | kris chuhn |
| **Clarence** | ˈklæ rəns | kla ruhns |
| **Cleitus/Clitus/**<br>**Clytus** | ˈklaɪ təs | klai tuhs |
| **Clothair** | ˈkloʊ tɛr<br>ˈkləʊ tɛə ◊ | klo ter<br>klo teə ◊ |
| **Constantinople** | kɑn stæn tɪ ˈnoʊ pəl<br>kɒn stæn tɪ ˈnəʊ pəl ◊ | kahn stan ti no puhl<br>kon stan ti no puhl ◊ |
| **Cornish** | ˈkɔr nɪʃ<br>ˈkɔ nɪʃ ◊ | kawr nish<br>kaw nish ◊ |

| NAME | INTERNATIONAL PHONETIC ALPHABET* | SIMPLIFIED PHONICS** |
|---|---|---|
| **Court** | 'kɔrt<br>'kɔt ◊ | kawrt<br>kawt ◊ |
| **Cressid** | 'krɛ sɪd<br>'kre sɪd ◊ | kre sid<br>... ◊ |
| **Cressy** | 'krɛ si<br>'kre si ◊ | kre see<br>... ◊ |
| **Crete** | 'krit | kreet |
| **Crispian** | 'krɪ spiən | kri spee uhn |
| **Crispianus** | krɪ spi 'ɑ nəs | kri spee ah nuhs |
| **Crispin** | 'krɪ spɪn | kri spin |
| **Dauphin** -folio<br>**Dolphin**<br>(see below) | 'dɔ fɪn<br>do 'fæn | daw fin<br>do fan |
| **Davy** | 'deɪ vi | dei vee |
| **Delabreth** | dɛ lə 'brɛθ<br>de lə 'breθ ◊ | de luh bre*th*<br>... ◊ |
| **Denis/Dennis** | 'dɛ nɪs<br>'de nɪs ◊ | de nis<br>... ◊ |
| **Dieu** | 'dju | dyoo |
| **Dolphin/**<br>**Dauphin**<br>(see above) | 'dɑl fɪn<br>'dɒl fɪn ◊ | dahl fin<br>d*o*l fin ◊ |
| **Doll** | 'dɑl<br>'dɒl ◊ | dahl<br>d*o*l ◊ |
| **Dover** | 'doʊ vɚ<br>'dəʊ və ◊ | do vər<br>do və ◊ |

| NAME | INTERNATIONAL PHONETIC ALPHABET* | SIMPLIFIED PHONICS** |
|------|----------------------------------|----------------------|
| Edward | 'ɛd wə˞d<br>'ed wəd ◊ | ed wərd<br>ed wəd ◊ |
| Elbe | 'ɛlb<br>'elb ◊ | elb<br>... ◊ |
| Ely | 'i li | ee lee |
| Elyzium -folio<br>    Elizium | ɪ 'lɪ ziəm<br>ɪ 'lɪ ʒiəm | i li zee uhm<br>i li zhee uhm |
| England | 'ɪŋ glənd | ing gluhnd |
| English | 'ɪŋ glɪʃ | ing glish |
| Ermengare | 'ɝ mɪn gɑr<br>'ɝ mɪn gɑrd<br>'ɜ mɪn gɑ ◊<br>'ɜ mɪn gɑd ◊ | ər min gahr<br>ər min gahrd<br>ə min gah ◊<br>ə min gahd ◊ |
| Erpingham | 'ɝ pɪŋ hæm<br>'ɜ pɪŋ əm ◊ | ər ping ham<br>ə ping uhm ◊ |
| Europe | 'jʊ rəp<br>'jʊə rəp ◊ | yoo ruhp<br>... ◊ |
| Exeter | 'ɛk sɪ tə˞<br>'ɛk sɪ tə ◊ | ek si tər<br>ek si tə ◊ |
| Falstaff | 'fɔl stæf<br>'fɔl staf ◊ | fawl staf<br>fawl stahf ◊ |
| Fauconberg<br>    -folio also<br>    **Faulconbridge** | 'fɔ kən bɚg<br>'fɔ kən bəg ◊ | faw kuhn bərg<br>faw kuhn bəg ◊ |
| Faulconbridge | 'fɔ kən brɪʤ<br>'fɔl kən brɪʤ<br>'fæl kən brɪʤ<br>    [gen Am var] | faw kuhn brij<br>fawl kuhn brij<br>fal kuhn brij<br>    [gen Am var] |

| NAME | INTERNATIONAL PHONETIC ALPHABET* | SIMPLIFIED PHONICS** |
|------|----------------------------------|----------------------|
| le Fer | lə 'fɛr<br>lə 'fɛə ◊ | luh fer<br>luh feə ◊ |
| Fluellen | flu 'ɛ lɪn<br>flu 'e lɪn ◊ | floo e lin<br>... ◊ |
| Foix -folio<br>  Loys, Foyes | 'fɔɪz | foyz |
| France | 'fræns<br>'frɑns ◊ | frans<br>frahns ◊ |
| Franciae | 'fræn ki aɪ | fran kee ai |
| Francois | fræn 'swɑ | fran swah |
| French | 'frɛntʃ<br>'frɛntʃ ◊ | french<br>... ◊ |
| Gallia | 'gæ liə | ga lee uh |
| Gam | 'gæm | gam |
| George | 'dʒɔrdʒ<br>'dʒɔdʒ ◊ | jawrj<br>jawj ◊ |
| German | 'dʒɚ mən<br>'dʒɜ mən ◊ | jər muhn<br>jə muhn ◊ |
| Germany | 'dʒɚ mə ni<br>'dʒɜ mə ni ◊ | jər muh nee<br>jə muh nee ◊ |
| Gloucester | 'glɑ stɚ<br>'glɔ stɚ<br>'glɒ stə ◊ | glah stər<br>glaw stər<br>glo stə ◊ |
| Gordian | 'gɔr diən<br>'gɔ diən ◊ | gawr dee uhn<br>gaw dee uhn ◊ |
| Gower | 'gaʊ ɚ<br>'gaʊ ə ◊ | gow ər<br>gow ə ◊ |

| NAME | INTERNATIONAL PHONETIC ALPHABET* | SIMPLIFIED PHONICS** |
|------|----------------------------------|----------------------|
| **Grandpre** | grɑnd ˈpreɪ<br>grɑnd ˈpri | grahnd prei<br>grahnd pree |
| **Grey** | ˈgreɪ | grei |
| **Guichard** | ˈgɪ tʃɚd<br>ˈgɪ tʃəd ◊ | gi chərd<br>gi chəd ◊ |
| **Hampton** | ˈhæmp tən<br>ˈhæm tən | hamp tuhn<br>ham tuhn |
| **Harfleur** | ˈhɑr flɚ<br>ˈhɑ flə ◊ | hahr flər<br>hah flə ◊ |
| **Harry** | ˈhæ ri | ha ree |
| **Henricus** | ˈhɛn rɪ kəs<br>ˈhen rɪ kəs ◊ | hen ri kuhs<br>… ◊ |
| **Henry** | ˈhɛn ri<br>ˈhen ri ◊ | hen ree<br>… ◊ |
| **Hermes** | ˈhɚ miz<br>ˈhɜ miz ◊ | hər meez<br>hə meez ◊ |
| **Herod** | ˈhɛ rəd<br>ˈhe rəd ◊ | he ruhd<br>… ◊ |
| **Holland** | ˈhɑ lənd<br>ˈhɒ lənd ◊ | hah luhnd<br>ho luhnd ◊ |
| **Hugh** | ˈhju | hyoo |
| **Humphrey** -folio<br>  **Humfrey** | ˈhʌm fri<br>ˈhʌmp fri | huhm free<br>huhmp free |
| **Huntington** | ˈhʌn tɪŋ tən | huhn ting tuhn |
| **Hydra** | ˈhaɪ drə<br>ˈhaɪ dʒrə | hai druh<br>hai jruh |

| NAME | INTERNATIONAL PHONETIC ALPHABET* | SIMPLIFIED PHONICS** |
|------|----------------------------------|----------------------|
| **Hyperion** ◊ | haɪ ˈpɪ riən<br>haɪ ˈpɪə riən ◊ | hai pi ree uhn<br>hai piə ree uhn |
| **Iceland** -folio **Island** | ˈaɪs lənd | ais luhnd |
| **Ireland** | ˈaɪ ɚ lənd<br>ˈaɪ ə lənd ◊ | ai ər luhnd<br>ai ə luhnd ◊ |
| **Irish** | ˈaɪ rɪʃ | ai rish |
| **Isabel** | ˈɪ zə bɛl<br>ˈɪ zə bel ◊ | i zuh bel<br>... ◊ |
| **Jack** | ˈdʒæk | jak |
| **Jacques/Jaques** | ˈʒɑk<br>ˈdʒæk<br>ˈdʒeɪ kwiz | zhahk<br>jak<br>jei kweez |
| **James** | ˈdʒeɪmz | jeimz |
| **Jamy** | ˈdʒeɪ mi | jei mee |
| **Jaques/Jacques** | ˈʒɑk<br>ˈdʒæk<br>ˈdʒeɪ kwiz | zhahk<br>jak<br>jei kweez |
| **Jeshu** | ˈdʒi ʃu<br>ˈdʒi ʒu | jee shoo<br>jee zhoo |
| **John** | ˈdʒɑn<br>ˈdʒɒn ◊ | jahn<br>jon ◊ |
| **Jove** | ˈdʒoʊv<br>ˈdʒəʊv ◊ | jov<br>... ◊ |
| **Kate** | ˈkeɪt | keit |

| NAME | INTERNATIONAL PHONETIC ALPHABET* | SIMPLIFIED PHONICS** |
|------|----------------------------------|----------------------|
| **Katherine** | 'kæ θrɪn<br>'kæ θə rɪn | ka *th*rin<br>ka *th*uh rin |
| **Ketely/Ketly** | 'kɛt li<br>'ket li ◊ | ket lee<br>… ◊ |
| **le Roy** | lə 'rɔɪ | luh roy |
| **Lestrale** | lɛ 'strɑl<br>le 'strɑl ◊ | le strahl<br>… ◊ |
| **Lewis** | 'lu ɪs | loo is |
| **Lingard/Lingare** | 'lɪŋ gɑr<br>'lɪŋ gɑrd<br>'lɪŋ gɑ ◊<br>'lɪŋ gɑd ◊ | ling gahr<br>ling gahrd<br>ling gah ◊<br>ling gahd ◊ |
| **London** | 'lʌn dən | luhn duhn |
| **Lorain/Lorraine** | lə 'reɪn | luh rein |
| **Louvre** | 'luv<br>'luvrə | loov<br>loovruh |
| **Lucifer** | 'lu sɪ fɚ<br>'lu sɪ fə ◊ | loo si fər<br>loo si fə ◊ |
| **Macedon** | 'mæ sə dɑn<br>'mæ sɪ dən ◊ | ma suh dahn<br>ma si duhn ◊ |
| **MacMorris** | mək 'mɔ rɪs<br>mæk 'mɔ rɪs | muhk maw ris<br>mak maw ris |
| **Mark** | 'mɑrk<br>'mɑk ◊ | mahrk<br>mahk ◊ |
| **Marle** | 'mɑrl<br>'mɑl ◊ | mahrl<br>mahl ◊ |

| NAME | INTERNATIONAL PHONETIC ALPHABET* | SIMPLIFIED PHONICS** |
|------|------|------|
| **Mars** | ˈmɑrz <br> ˈmɑz ◊ | mahrz <br> mahz ◊ |
| **Masham** | ˈmæ səm <br> ˈmæ ʃəm | ma suhm <br> ma shuhm |
| **May** | ˈmeɪ | mei |
| **Meissen** | ˈmaɪ sən | mai suhn |
| **Mercury** | ˈmɝ kjə ri <br> ˈmɜ kjʊ ri ◊ | mər kyuh ree <br> mə ky*oo* ree ◊ |
| **Monmouth** | ˈman məθ <br> ˈmʌn məθ ◊ <br> ˈmɒn məθ ◊ | mahn muh*th* <br> muhn muh*th* ◊ <br> m*o*n muh*th* ◊ |
| **Montjoy** -folio <br> **Mountjoy,** <br> **Monjoy** | ˈmant ʤɔɪ <br> mant ˈʤɔɪ <br> ˈmɒnt ʤɔɪ ◊ <br> mɒnt ˈʤɔɪ ◊ | mahnt joy <br> mahnt joy <br> m*o*nt joy ◊ <br> m*o*nt joy ◊ |
| **Nell** | ˈnɛl <br> ˈnel ◊ | nel <br> ... ◊ |
| **Norman** | ˈnɔr mən <br> ˈnɔ mən ◊ | nawr muhn <br> naw muhn ◊ |
| **Northumberland** | nɔr ˈθʌm bɚ lənd <br><br> nɔ ˈθʌm bə lənd ◊ | nawr *th*uhm bər luhnd <br><br> naw *th*uhm bə luhnd ◊ |
| **Nym** -folio **also** <br> **Nim, Nymme** | ˈnɪm | nim |
| **Orleans** | ˈɔr liənz <br> ɔr ˈli ənz <br> ˈɔ liənz ◊ <br> ɔ ˈli ənz ◊ | awr lee uhnz <br> ... <br> aw lee uhnz ◊ <br> ... ◊ |

109

| NAME | INTERNATIONAL PHONETIC ALPHABET* | SIMPLIFIED PHONICS** |
|---|---|---|
| **Parca** | 'pɑr kə<br>'pɑ kə ◊ | pahr kuh<br>pah kuh ◊ |
| **Paris** | 'pæ rɪs | pa ris |
| **Pegasus** | 'pɛ gə səs<br>'pe gə səs ◊ | pe guh suhs<br>... ◊ |
| **Pepin** | 'pɛ pɪn<br>'pɪ pɪn<br>'pe pɪn ◊ | pe pin<br>pi pin<br>... ◊ |
| **Perseus** | 'pɝ sus<br>'pɝ siəs<br>'pɜ sjus ◊<br>'pɜ siəs ◊ | pər soos<br>pər see uhs<br>pə syoos ◊<br>pə see uhs ◊ |
| **Pharamond** | 'fæ rə mɑnd<br>'fæ rə mənd<br>'fæ rə mɒnd ◊ | fa ruh mahnd<br>fa ruh muhnd<br>fa ruh mond ◊ |
| **Phillip** | 'fɪ lɪp | fi lip |
| **Phoebus** | 'fi bəs | fee buhs |
| **Picardy** | 'pɪ kɚ di<br>'pɪ kə di ◊ | pi kər dee<br>pi kə dee ◊ |
| **Pistol** | 'pɪ stəl | pi stuhl |
| **Plantagenet** | plæn 'tæ ʤə nɪt<br>plæn 'tæ ʤɪ nɪt | plan ta juh nit<br>plan ta ji nit |
| **Pompey** | 'pɑm pi<br>'pɒm pi ◊ | pahm pee<br>pom pee ◊ |
| **Quickly** | 'kwɪk li | kwik lee |
| **Rambures** | ræm 'bjurz<br>ræm 'bjuəz ◊ | ram byoorz<br>ram byoo əz ◊ |

| NAME | INTERNATIONAL PHONETIC ALPHABET* | SIMPLIFIED PHONICS** |
|------|------|------|
| **Richard** | 'rɪ tʃɚd | ri chərd |
| | 'rɪ tʃəd ◊ | ri chəd ◊ |
| **Roman** | 'roʊ mən | ro muhn |
| | 'rəʊ mən ◊ | ... ◊ |
| **Rome** | 'roʊm | rom |
| | 'rəʊm ◊ | ... ◊ |
| **Rouen** | ru 'ɑŋ | roo ahng |
| | 'ru ɑŋ | roo ahng |
| **Roussi/Rousie** | 'ru si | roo see |
| | ru 'si | roo see |
| **Sala** | 'seɪ lə | sei luh |
| | 'sæ lə | sa luh |
| **Salicam** | 'sæ lɪ kəm | sa li kuhm |
| **Salique** | 'sæ lɪk | sa lik |
| | 'seɪ lɪk | sei lik |
| **Salisbury** | 'sɔlz bɛ ri | sawlz be ree |
| | 'sælz bɛ ri | salz be ree |
| | 'sɔlz bə ri ◊ | sawlz buh ree ◊ |
| **Saxon** | 'sæk sən | sak suhn |
| **Scot** | 'skɑt | skaht |
| | 'skɒt ◊ | skot ◊ |
| **Scotland** | 'skɑt lənd | skaht luhnd |
| | 'skɒt lənd ◊ | skot luhnd ◊ |
| **Scroop** | 'skrup | skroop |
| **Somme** | 'sʌm | suhm |
| | 'sɑm | sahm |
| | 'sɒm ◊ | som ◊ |

111

| NAME | INTERNATIONAL PHONETIC ALPHABET* | SIMPLIFIED PHONICS** |
|------|------|------|
| **Southampton** | saʊθ 'hæmp tən<br>saʊ 'θæm tən | sow*th* hamp tuhn<br>sow *th*am tuhn |
| **Spain** | 'speɪn | spein |
| **Staines** | 'steɪnz | steinz |
| **Suffolk** | 'sʌ fək | suh fuhk |
| **Talbot** | 'tɔl bət<br>'tæl bət | tawl buht<br>tal buht |
| **Tartar** | 'tɑr tɚ<br>'tɑ tə ◊ | tahr tər<br>tah tə ◊ |
| **Tavy** | 'teɪ vi | tei vee |
| **Tearsheet** | 'tɛr ʃit<br>'teə ʃit ◊ | ter sheet<br>teə sheet ◊ |
| **Thames** | 'tɛmz<br>'temz ◊ | temz<br>... ◊ |
| **Thomas** | 'tɑ məs<br>'tɒ məs ◊ | tah muhs<br>t*o* muhs ◊ |
| **Trojan** | 'tʃroʊ ʤən<br>'troʊ ʤən<br>'trəʊ ʤən ◊ | chro juhn<br>tro juhn<br>... ◊ |
| **Turk** | 'tɝk<br>'tɜk ◊ | tərk<br>tək ◊ |
| **Turkish** | 'tɝ kɪʃ<br>'tɜ kɪʃ ◊ | tər kish<br>tə kish ◊ |
| **Vaudemont** | 'voʊd mɑnt<br>'vəʊd mɒnt ◊ | vod mahnt<br>vod mont ◊ |
| **Wales** | 'weɪlz | weilz |

| NAME | INTERNATIONAL PHONETIC ALPHABET* | SIMPLIFIED PHONICS** |
|------|----------------------------------|----------------------|
| **Warwick** | 'wɑ rɪk<br>'wɔ rɪk<br>'wɔr wɪk<br>'wɒ rɪk ◊ | wah rik<br>waw rik<br>wawr wik<br>wo rik ◊ |
| **Welsh/Welch** | 'wɛlʃ<br>'welʃ | welsh<br>… |
| **Westmoreland** luhnd | 'wɛst mɔr lənd<br><br>'west mə lənd ◊ | west mawr<br><br>west mə luhnd ◊ |
| **Whitsun** | 'wɪt sən | wit suhn |
| **Williams** | 'wɪl jəmz | wil yuhmz |
| **Wye** | 'waɪ | wai |
| **York** | 'jɔrk<br>'jɔk ◊ | yawrk<br>yawk ◊ |

113

| NAME | INTERNATIONAL PHONETIC ALPHABET* | SIMPLIFIED PHONICS** |
|---|---|---|
| **Abel** | 'ei bəl | ei buhl |
| **Adonis** | ə 'dɑ nɪs | uh dah nis |
| | ə 'doʊ nɪs | uh do nis |
| | ə 'dəʊ nɪs ◊ | … ◊ |
| **Ajax** | 'eɪ dʒæks | ei jaks |
| **Alcides** | æl 'saɪ diz | al sai deez |
| **Alençon** | æ lən 'soʊn | a luhn son |
| | ə 'lɛn sən | uh len suhn |
| | 'æ lən sɒn ◊ | a luhn son ◊ |
| | ə 'len sɒn ◊ | uh len son ◊ |
| **Alton** | 'ɔl tən | awl tuhn |
| **Amazon** | 'æ mə zɑn | a muh zahn |
| | 'æ mə zɒn ◊ | a muh zon ◊ |
| **Anjou** | ɑn 'dʒu | ahn joo |
| | ɑn 'ʒu | ahn zhoo |
| **Armagnac** | 'ɑr mən jæk | ahr muhn yak |
| | 'ɑ mən jæk ◊ | ah muhn yak ◊ |
| **Artois** -folio | ɑr 'twɑ | ahr twah |
| **Artoys** | ɑ 'twɑ ◊ | ah twah ◊ |
| **Astraea** | æ 'stri ə | a stree uh |
| | æs 'tʃri ə | as chree uh |
| **August** | 'ɔ gəst | aw guhst |

*International Phonetic Alphabet Pronunciation Key: (General American) i-see, happy, Juliet; ɪ-sit; eɪ-say; ɛ-set; æ-sat; ɑ-father; ʌ-sun; ə-about; ɔ-saw; oʊ-so; o-hero; ʊ-shook; u-soon; aɪ-sigh; ɔɪ-soy; aʊ-south; ju-cube; ɚ-supper; ɛr-fair; ɝ-bird; k-cut, kite; g-go; dʒ-joy; j-yes; ŋ-sing; ʃ-shoe; tʃ-chop; ð-that; θ-thin; ʒ-measure; (Additional symbols for British RP) e-set; ɛə-fair; ə-supper; ɜ-bird; ɒ-stop; əʊ-so, hero; o-(followed by l) pole.

**Simplified Phonics Pronunciation Key: (General American) ee-see, happy; i-sit; ei-say; e-set; a-sat; ah-father; uh-sun, about; aw-saw; o-so; oo-shook; oo-soon; ai-sigh; oy-soy; ow-south; yoo-cube; ar-bird, supper; k-cut, kite; g-go; j-joy; ng-sing; kw-quick; sh-shoe; ch-chop; th-that; th-thin; zh-measure; (Additional symbols for British RP) ə-bird; ə-supper; o-stop; … indicates pronunciation variance too subtle for Simplified Phonics transcription see International Phonetic Alphabet transcription.

◊ British RP pronunciation-see Introduction.

| NAME | INTERNATIONAL PHONETIC ALPHABET* | SIMPLIFIED PHONICS** |
|---|---|---|
| **Auvergne** | o ˈvɜ·n<br>əu ˈvɛən ◊ | o vərn<br>o veən ◊ |
| **Basset** | ˈbæ sɪt | ba sit |
| **Beaufort** | ˈbou fə·t<br>ˈbəu fət ◊ | bo fərt<br>bo fət ◊ |
| **Bedford** | ˈbɛd fə·d<br>ˈbed fəd ◊ | bed fərd<br>bed fəd ◊ |
| **Blackmere** | ˈblæk mɪr<br>ˈblæk mɪə ◊ | blak mir<br>blak miə ◊ |
| **Blois** | ˈblwɑ | blwah |
| **Bourdeaux/<br>Bordeaux** | ˈbɔr do<br>bɔr ˈdou<br>ˈbɔ dəu ◊<br>bɔ ˈdəu ◊ | bawr do<br>…<br>baw do ◊<br>… ◊ |
| **Bolingbroke** | ˈbɑ lɪŋ brʊk<br>ˈbou lɪŋ brʊk<br>ˈbʊ lɪŋ brʊk ◊<br>ˈbɒ lɪŋ brʊk ◊ | bah ling brook<br>bo ling brook<br>boo ling brook ◊<br>bo ling brook ◊ |
| **Bracy** | ˈbreɪ si | brei see |
| **Bridgenorth** | ˈbrɪʤ nɔrθ<br>ˈbrɪʤ nɔθ ◊ | brij nawrth<br>brij nawth ◊ |
| **Burgundy** | ˈbɜ· gən di<br>ˈbɜ gən di ◊ | bər guhn dee<br>bə guhn dee ◊ |
| **Caesar** | ˈsi zə·<br>ˈsi zə ◊ | see zər<br>see zə ◊ |
| **Cain** | ˈkeɪn | kein |

| NAME | INTERNATIONAL PHONETIC ALPHABET* | SIMPLIFIED PHONICS** |
|---|---|---|
| **Calais** | 'kæ leɪ | ka lei |
| | kə 'leɪ | kuh lei |
| | [gen Am var] | [gen Am var] |
| **Cambridge** | 'keɪm brɪʤ | keim brij |
| **Champagne/ Champaigne** | ʃæm 'peɪn | sham pein |
| **Charles** | 'tʃɑrlz | chahrlz |
| | 'tʃɑlz ◊ | chahlz ◊ |
| **Christ** | 'kraɪst | kraist |
| **Christendom** | 'krɪ sən dəm | kri suhn duhm |
| **Christian** | 'krɪs tʃən | kris chuhn |
| **Circe** | 'sɝ si | sər see |
| | 'sɜ si ◊ | sə see ◊ |
| **Clarence** | 'klæ rəns | kla ruhns |
| **Coeur de Lion** | kɝ də 'li ɑn | kər duh lee ahn |
| | kɜ də 'li ɒn ◊ | kə duh lee on ◊ |
| **Constantine** | 'kɑn stən tin | kahn stuhn teen |
| | 'kɑn stən taɪn | kahn stuhn tain |
| | 'kɒn stən tin ◊ | kon stuhn teen ◊ |
| | 'kɒn stən taɪn ◊ | kon stuhn tain ◊ |
| **Crete** | 'krit | kreet |
| **Cromwell** | 'krɑm wɛl | krahm wel |
| | 'krɑm wəl | krahm wuhl |
| | 'krɒm wel ◊ | krom wel ◊ |
| | 'krɒm wəl ◊ | krom wuhl ◊ |
| **Cyrus** | 'saɪ rəs | sai ruhs |
| **Damascus** | də 'mæ skəs | duh ma skuhs |

| NAME | INTERNATIONAL PHONETIC ALPHABET* | SIMPLIFIED PHONICS** |
|---|---|---|
| **Darius** | də 'raɪ əs | duh rai uhs |
| **Dartford** | 'dɑrt fɚd<br>'dɑt fəd ◊ | dahrt fərd<br>daht fəd ◊ |
| **Dauphin** -folio<br>**Dolphin**<br>(see below) | 'dɔ fɪn<br>do 'fæn<br>   [gen Am var] | daw fin<br>do fan<br>   [gen Am var] |
| **Deborah** | 'dɛ bə rə<br>'de bə rə ◊ | de buh ruh<br>... ◊ |
| **de la Pole** | dɛ lə 'poʊl<br>de lə 'pol ◊ | de luh pol<br>... ◊ |
| **Dennis** | 'dɛ nɪs<br>'de nɪs ◊ | de nis<br>... ◊ |
| **Dolphin/**<br>**Dauphin**<br>(see above) | 'dɑl fɪn<br>'dɒl fɪn ◊ | dahl fin<br>dol fin ◊ |
| **Dover** | 'doʊ vɚ<br>'dəʊ və ◊ | do vər<br>do və ◊ |
| **Edmund** | 'ɛd mənd<br>'ed mənd ◊ | ed muhnd<br>... ◊ |
| **Edward** | 'ɛd wɚd<br>'ed wəd ◊ | ed wərd<br>ed wəd ◊ |
| **Eltham** -folio<br>   **Eltam** | 'ɛl təm<br>'ɛl θəm<br>'el təm ◊ | el tuhm<br>el *th*uhm<br>... ◊ |
| **England** | 'ɪŋ glənd | ing gluhnd |
| **English** | 'ɪŋ glɪʃ | ing glish |
| **Europe** | 'jʊ rəp<br>'jʊə rəp ◊ | *y*oo ruhp<br>... ◊ |

117

| NAME | INTERNATIONAL PHONETIC ALPHABET* | SIMPLIFIED PHONICS** |
|---|---|---|
| Exeter | 'ɛk sɪ tɚ<br>'ɛk sə tə ◊ | ek si tər<br>ek si tə ◊ |
| Fastolfe | 'fæ stɑlf<br>'fæ stɔlf<br>'fæ stɒlf ◊ | fa stahlf<br>fa stawlf<br>fa stolf ◊ |
| Faulconbridge/<br>    Falconbridge | 'fɔ kən brɪʤ<br>'fɔl kən brɪʤ<br>'fæl kən brɪʤ<br>    [gen Am var] | faw kuhn brij<br>fawl kuhn brij<br>fal kuhn brij<br>    [gen Am var] |
| French | 'frɛnʧ<br>'frɛnʧ ◊ | french<br>… ◊ |
| Froissart -folio<br>    Froysard | 'frɔɪ sɑrt<br>'frɔɪ sɑt ◊ | froy sahrt<br>froy saht ◊ |
| Furnival | 'fɚ nə vəl<br>'fɜ nɪ vəl ◊ | fər nuh vuhl<br>fə nuh vuhl ◊ |
| Gallia | 'gæ liə | ga lee uh |
| Gallian | 'gæ liən | ga lee uhn |
| Gargrave | 'gɑr greɪv<br>'gɑ greɪv ◊ | gahr greiv<br>gah greiv ◊ |
| Gascony | 'gæs kə ni | gas kuh nee |
| Gaunt | 'gɔnt | gawnt |
| George | 'ʤɔrʤ<br>'ʤɔʤ ◊ | jawrj<br>jawj ◊ |
| Glansdale | 'glænz deɪl<br>'glænz dəl ◊ | glanz deil<br>glanz duhl ◊ |
| Gloucester | 'glɑ stɚ<br>'glɔ stɚ<br>'glɒ stə ◊ | glah stər<br>glaw stər<br>glo stə ◊ |

| NAME | INTERNATIONAL PHONETIC ALPHABET* | SIMPLIFIED PHONICS** |
|---|---|---|
| Goliases/ Goliasses | gə 'laɪ ə sɪz | guh lai uh siz |
| Goodrig/ Goodricke | 'gʊd rɪg | good rig |
| Greece | 'gris | grees |
| Guienne | gi 'ɛn<br>gi 'en ◊ | gee en<br>... ◊ |
| Guysors | ʤi 'zɔrz<br>ʤi 'zɔz ◊ | jee zawrz<br>jee zawz ◊ |
| Hannibal | 'hæ nə bəl<br>'hæ nɪ bəl | ha nuh buhl<br>ha ni buhl |
| Hecate | 'hɛ kɪt<br>'hɛ kə ti<br>'he kɪt ◊<br>'he kə ti ◊ | he kit<br>he kuh tee<br>... ◊<br>... ◊ |
| Hector | 'hɛk tɚ<br>'hek tə ◊ | hek tər<br>hek tə ◊ |
| Helen | 'hɛ lən<br>'hɛ lɪn<br>'he lən ◊ | he luhn<br>he lin<br>... ◊ |
| Henry | 'hɛn ri<br>'hen ri ◊ | hen ree<br>... ◊ |
| Hercules | 'hɝ kjə liz<br>'hɝ kju liz<br>'hɜ kjʊ liz ◊ | hər kyuh leez<br>hər kyoo leez<br>hə kyoo leez ◊ |
| Humphrey | 'hʌm fri<br>'hʌmp fri | huhm free<br>huhmp free |
| Hungerford | 'hʌŋ gɚ fəd<br>'hʌŋ gə fəd ◊ | huhng gər fərd<br>huhng gə fəd ◊ |

| NAME | INTERNATIONAL PHONETIC ALPHABET* | SIMPLIFIED PHONICS** |
|------|-----------------------------------|----------------------|
| **Icarus** | 'ɪ kə rəs<br>'aɪ kə rəs<br>　[Brit RP var] | i kuh ruhs<br>ai kuh ruhs<br>　[Brit RP var] |
| **Jack** | 'ʤæk | jak |
| **Jerusalem** | ʤə 'ru sə ləm | juh roo suh luhm |
| **Joan** -folio **Ioane** | 'ʤoʊn<br>'ʤəʊn ◊ | jon<br>... ◊ |
| **John** | 'ʤɑn<br>'ʤɒn ◊ | jahn<br>jon ◊ |
| **Julius** | 'ʤu liəs<br>'ʤul jəs | joo lee uhs<br>jool yuhs |
| **Katherine** | 'kæ θrɪn<br>'kæ θə rɪn | ka *th*rin<br>ka *th*uh rin |
| **la Pucelle** -folio<br>　**Puzel, Pucell,**<br>　**Pussel** | lə pju 'sɛl<br>lə pju 'sel ◊ | luh pyoo sel<br>... ◊ |
| **Lancaster** | 'læŋ kə stɚ<br>'læŋ kæ stɚ<br>'læŋ kə stə ◊ | lang kuh stər<br>lang ka stər<br>lang kuh stə ◊ |
| **Langley** | 'læŋ li | lang lee |
| **Lionel** | 'laɪ ə nəl | lai uh nuhl |
| **London** | 'lʌn dən | luhn duhn |
| **Lucy** | 'lu si | lu see |
| **Machiavel** | 'mæ kjə vɛl<br>mæ kiə 'vɛl<br>mæ kiə 'vel ◊ | ma kyuh vel<br>ma kee uh vel<br>... ◊ |

| NAME | INTERNATIONAL PHONETIC ALPHABET* | SIMPLIFIED PHONICS** |
|------|-----------------------------------|----------------------|
| **Mahomet** | mə 'hɑ mət<br>mə 'hɒ mɪt ◊ | muh hah muht<br>muh ho muht ◊ |
| **Maine** | 'meɪn | mein |
| **March** | 'mɑrtʃ<br>'mɑtʃ ◊ | mahrch<br>mahch ◊ |
| **Margeret** | 'mɑr grɪt<br>'mɑr gə rɪt<br>'mɑ grɪt ◊<br>'mɑ gə rɪt ◊ | mahr grit<br>mahr guh rit<br>mah grit ◊<br>mah guh rit ◊ |
| **Mars** | 'mɑrz<br>'mɑz ◊ | mahrz<br>mahz ◊ |
| **Martin** | 'mɑr tɪn<br>'mɑr tən<br>'mɑ tɪn ◊ | mahr tin<br>mahr tuhn<br>mah tin ◊ |
| **May** | 'meɪ | mei |
| **Memphis** | 'mɛm fɪs<br>'mɪm fɪs<br>   [gen Am var]<br>'mem fɪs ◊ | mem fis<br>mim fis<br>   [gen Am var]<br>... ◊ |
| **[Saint] Michael** | [seɪnt] 'maɪ kəl<br>[sɪnt] 'maɪ kəl ◊ | [seint] mai kuhl<br>[sint] mai kuhl ◊ |
| **Minotaur** | 'mɪ nə tɔr<br>'maɪ nə tɔ ◊ | mi nuh tawr<br>mai nuh taw ◊ |
| **Monmouth** | 'mʌn məθ<br>'mɑn məθ<br>   [gen Am var]<br>'mɒn məθ<br>   [Brit RP var] | muhn muhth<br>mahn muhth<br>   [gen Am var]<br>mon muhth<br>   [Brit RP var] |
| **Mortimer** | 'mɔr tə mɚ<br>'mɔ tɪ mə ◊ | mawr tuh mər<br>maw ti mə ◊ |

| NAME | INTERNATIONAL PHONETIC ALPHABET* | SIMPLIFIED PHONICS** |
| --- | --- | --- |
| Naples | ˈneɪ pəlz | nei puhlz |
| Nemesis | ˈnɛ mə sɪs<br>ˈnɛ mɪ sɪs<br>ˈne mə sɪs ◊ | ne muh sis<br>ne mi sis<br>… ◊ |
| Nero | ˈni ro<br>ˈnɪə rəʊ ◊ | nee ro<br>niə ro ◊ |
| Nestor | ˈnɛs tɚ<br>ˈnes tə ◊ | nes tər<br>nes tə ◊ |
| Oliver | ˈɑ lɪ vɚ<br>ˈɒ lɪ və ◊ | ah li vər<br>o li və ◊ |
| Orleans -folio<br>  Orleance | ˈɔr liənz<br>ɔr ˈliənz<br>ˈɔ liənz ◊<br>ɔ ˈli ənz ◊ | awr lee uhnz<br>…<br>aw lee uhnz ◊<br>… ◊ |
| Ostler | ˈɑ slɚ<br>ˈɒ slə ◊ | ah slər<br>o slə ◊ |
| Paris | ˈpæ rɪs | pa ris |
| Parisian | pə ˈri ʒən | puh ree zhuhn |
| Patay -folio<br>  Poictiers<br>  (see below) | pæ ˈteɪ | pa tei |
| Pendragon | pɛn ˈdʒræ gən<br>pɛn ˈdræ gən<br>pen ˈdræ gən ◊ | pen jra guhn<br>pen dra guhn<br>… ◊ |
| Percy | ˈpɚ si<br>ˈpɜ si ◊ | pər see<br>pə see ◊ |
| [Saint] Phillip | [seɪnt] ˈfɪ lɪp<br>[sɪnt] ˈfɪ lɪp ◊ | [seint] fi lip<br>[sint] fi lip ◊ |

| NAME | INTERNATIONAL PHONETIC ALPHABET* | SIMPLIFIED PHONICS** |
|---|---|---|
| Phoenix | 'fi nɪks | fee niks |
| Picardy | 'pɪ kɚ di<br>'pɪ kə di ◊ | pi kər dee<br>pi kə dee ◊ |
| Plantagenet | plæn 'tæ ʤə nɪt<br>plæn 'tæ ʤɪ nɪt | plan ta juh nit<br>plan ta ji nit |
| Poictiers/Patay<br>(see above) | pwɑ ti 'eɪ<br>pɔɪ 'ti ɚz<br>  [Ang. Gen Am]<br>pɔɪ 'ti əz<br>  [Ang. Brit RP] | pwah tee ei<br>poy tee ərz<br>  [Ang. Gen Am]<br>poy tee əz<br>  [Ang. Brit RP] |
| [de la] Pole/<br>  Poole | dɛ lə 'poʊl<br>de lə 'pol ◊ | de luh pol<br>... ◊ |
| Ponton<br>  [de Santrailles] | 'pɑn tən<br>'pɒn tən ◊ | pahn tuhn<br>pon tuhn ◊ |
| [la] Pucelle -folio<br>  Puzel, Pucell,<br>  Pussel | lə pju 'sɛl<br>lə pju 'sel ◊ | luh pyoo sel<br>... ◊ |
| Reignier | 'reɪn jei<br>reɪn 'jei | *rein* yei<br>rein *yei* |
| Rheims -folio<br>  Rheimes | 'rimz | reemz |
| Rhodope | 'roʊ də pi<br>ro 'doʊ pi<br>'rəʊ də pi ◊<br>rəʊ 'dəʊ pi ◊ | ro duh pee<br>ro do pee<br>... ◊<br>... ◊ |
| Richard | 'rɪ ʧɚd<br>'rɪ ʧəd ◊ | ri chərd<br>ri chəd ◊ |
| Robin | 'rɑ bɪn<br>'rɒ bɪn ◊ | rah bin<br>r*o* bin ◊ |

123

| NAME | INTERNATIONAL PHONETIC ALPHABET* | SIMPLIFIED PHONICS** |
|---|---|---|
| **Rome** | 'roʊm<br>'rəʊm ◊ | rom<br>… ◊ |
| **Rouen** | ru 'ɑŋ<br>'ru ɑŋ | roo ahng<br>roo ahng |
| **Rowland** | 'roʊ lənd<br>'ro lənd ◊ | ro luhnd<br>… ◊ |
| **Salisbury** | 'sɔlz bɛ ri<br>'sælz bɛ ri<br>'sɔlz bə ri ◊ | sawlz be ree<br>salz be ree<br>sawlz buh ree ◊ |
| **[de] Santrailles/ Santrayles** | də sæn 'treɪl | duh san treil |
| **Sampson** | 'sæm sən<br>'sæmp sən | sam suhn<br>samp suhn |
| **Scales** | 'skeɪlz | skeilz |
| **Scot** | 'skɑt<br>'skɒt ◊ | skaht<br>skot ◊ |
| **Scythian** | 'sɪ θiən<br>'sɪ ðiən | si *th*ee uhn<br>si thee uhn |
| **Sheffield** | 'ʃɛ fild<br>'ʃe fild ◊ | she feeld<br>… ◊ |
| **Shrewsbury** | 'ʃruz bɛ ri<br>'ʃrəʊz bə ri ◊ | shrooz be ree<br>shroz buh ree ◊ |
| **Sibyl/Sybil** | 'sɪ bəl<br>'sɪ bɪl | si buhl<br>si bil |
| **Somerset** | 'sʌ mɚ sɛt<br>'sʌ mə sɪt ◊<br>'sʌ mə set ◊ | suh mər set<br>suh mə sit ◊<br>suh mə set ◊ |
| **Strange** | 'streɪnʤ | streinj |

| NAME | INTERNATIONAL PHONETIC ALPHABET* | SIMPLIFIED PHONICS** |
|---|---|---|
| **Suffolk** | 'sʌ fək | suh fuhk |
| **Talbot** | 'tɔl bət | tawl buht |
| | 'tæl bət | tal buht |
| **Talbotites** -folio | 'tɔl bə taɪts | tawl buh taits |
| **Talbonites** | 'tæl bə taɪts | tal buh taits |
| **Telemon** | 'tɛ lə mən | te luh muhn |
| | 'tɛ lə mɑn | te luh mahn |
| | 'te lə mɒn ◊ | te luh mon ◊ |
| **Temple** | 'tɛm pəl | tem puhl |
| | 'tem pəl ◊ | ... ◊ |
| **Thomas** | 'tɑ məs | tah muhs |
| | 'tɒ məs ◊ | to muhs ◊ |
| **Tomyris/** | 'tɑ mɪ rɪs | tah mi ris |
| **Thomyris** | 'tɒ mɪ rɪs ◊ | to mi ris ◊ |
| **Touraine** -folio | 'tu reɪn | too rein |
| **Torayne** | tʊ 'reɪn | too rein |
| **Tours** | 'tuɚ | tooər |
| | 'tʊə ◊ | tooə ◊ |
| **Trojan** | 'tʃroʊ ʤən | chro juhn |
| | 'troʊ ʤən | tro juhn |
| | 'trəʊ ʤən ◊ | ... ◊ |
| **Turk** | 'tɝk | tərk |
| | 'tɜk ◊ | tək ◊ |
| **Urchinfield** | 'ɝ tʃɪn fild | ər chin feeld |
| | 'ɜ tʃɪn fild ◊ | ə chin feeld ◊ |
| **Valence** | 'væ ləns | va luhns |
| **Venus** | 'vi nəs | vee nuhs |

| NAME | INTERNATIONAL PHONETIC ALPHABET* | SIMPLIFIED PHONICS** |
|------|----------------------------------|----------------------|
| **Verdun** | vɚ ˈdʌn<br>və ˈdʌn ◊ | vər duhn<br>və duhn ◊ |
| **Vernon** | ˈvɚ nən<br>ˈvɜ nən ◊ | vər nuhn<br>və nuhn ◊ |
| **Wallon** | wə ˈlɔn | wuh lawn |
| **Walloon** | wɑ ˈlun<br>wə ˈlun<br>wɒ ˈlun ◊ | wah loon<br>wuh loon<br>wo loon ◊ |
| **Warwick** | ˈwɑ rɪk<br>ˈwɔ rɪk<br>ˈwɔr wɪk<br>ˈwɒ rɪk ◊ | wah rik<br>waw rik<br>wawr wik<br>wo rik ◊ |
| **Washford** | ˈwɑʃ fɚd<br>ˈwɒʃ fəd ◊ | wahsh fərd<br>wosh fəd ◊ |
| **Waterford** | ˈwɑ tɚ fɚd<br>ˈwɔ tɚ fɚd<br>ˈwɔ tə fəd ◊ | wah tər fərd<br>waw tər fərd<br>waw tə fəd ◊ |
| **Westminster** | ˈwɛst mɪn stɚ<br>ˈwɛst mɪn stə ◊ | west min stər<br>west min stə ◊ |
| **William** | ˈwɪl jəm | wil yuhm |
| **Winchester** | ˈwɪn tʃɛ stɚ<br>ˈwɪn tʃɪ stə ◊ | win che stər<br>win chi stə ◊ |
| **Windsor** | ˈwɪn zɚ<br>ˈwɪn zə ◊ | win zər<br>win zə ◊ |
| **Wingfield** | ˈwɪŋ fild | wing feeld |
| **Woodvile/<br>  Woodville** | ˈwʊd vɪl | wood vil |
| **York** | ˈjɔrk<br>ˈjɔk ◊ | yawrk<br>yawk ◊ |

| NAME | INTERNATIONAL PHONETIC ALPHABET* | SIMPLIFIED PHONICS** |
|---|---|---|
| **Absyrtus** | əb 'sɝ təs<br>əb 'sɜ təs ◊ | uhb sər tuhs<br>uhb sə tuhs ◊ |
| **Achilles** | ə 'kɪ liz | uh ki leez |
| **Adam** | 'æ dəm | a duhm |
| **Aeacida** | i 'æ sɪ də | ee a si duh |
| **Aeacides** | i 'æ sɪ diz | ee a si deez |
| **Aeneas** | ɪ 'ni əs<br>i 'ni əs | i nee uhs<br>ee nee uhs |
| **Ajax** | 'eɪ dʒæks | ei jaks |
| **[Saint] Alban**<br>-folio **Albon,**<br>**Albone** | [seɪnt] 'ɔl bən<br>[sɪnt] 'ɔl bən ◊ | [seint] awl buhn<br>[sint] awl buhn ◊ |
| **Albion** | 'æl biən | al bee uhn |
| **Alençon** | æ lən 'soʊn<br>ə 'lɛn sən<br>'æ lən sɒn ◊<br>ə 'len sɒn ◊ | a luhn son<br>uh len suhn<br>a luhn son ◊<br>uh len son ◊ |
| **Alexander** | æ lɪg 'zæn dɚ<br>æ lɪg 'zɑn də ◊ | a lig zan dər<br>a lig zahn də ◊ |
| **Althaea/Althea** | æl 'θiə | al *the*e uh |

*International Phonetic Alphabet Pronunciation Key: (General American) i-see, happy, Juliet; ɪ-sit; eɪ-say; ɛ-set; æ-sat; ɑ-father; ʌ-sun; ə-about; ɔ-saw; oʊ-so; o-hero; ʊ-shook; u-soon; aɪ-sigh; ɔɪ-soy; aʊ-south; ju-cube; ɚ-supper; ɛr-fair; ɝ-bird; k-cut, kite; g-go; dʒ-joy; j-yes; ŋ-sing; ʃ-shoe; tʃ-chop; ð-that; θ-thin; ʒ-measure; (Additional symbols for British RP) e-set; ɛə-fair; ə-supper; ɜ-bird; ɒ-stop; əʊ-so, hero; o-(followed by l) pole.

**Simplified Phonics Pronunciation Key: (General American) ee-see, happy; i-sit; ei-say; e-set; a-sat; ah-father; uh-sun, about; aw-saw; o-so; oo-shook; oo-soon; ai-sigh; oy-soy; ow-south; yoo-cube; ər-bird, supper; k-cut, kite; g-go; j-joy; ng-sing; kw-quick; sh-shoe; ch-chop; th-that; *th*-thin; zh-measure; (Additional symbols for British RP) ə-bird; ə-supper; ǫ-stop; ... indicates pronunciation variance too subtle for Simplified Phonics transcription see International Phonetic Alphabet transcription.

◊ British RP pronunciation-see Introduction.

| NAME | INTERNATIONAL PHONETIC ALPHABET* | SIMPLIFIED PHONICS** |
|------|----------------------------------|----------------------|
| **Anchises** | æn 'kaɪ siz | an kai seez |
| | æŋ 'kaɪ siz | ang kai seez |
| **Anjou** | ɑn 'ʤu | ahn joo |
| | ɑn 'ʒu | ahn zhoo |
| **Anne** | 'æn | an |
| **Ascanius** | ə 'skeɪ niəs | uh skei nee uhs |
| **Ascapart** | 'æs kə pɑrt | as kuh pahrt |
| | 'æs kə pɑt ◊ | as kūh paht ◊ |
| **Ashford** | 'æʃ fɚd | ash fərd |
| | 'æʃ fəd ◊ | ash fəd ◊ |
| **Asmath** | 'æz məθ | az muh*th* |
| **Bargulus** | 'bɑr gju ləs | bahr gyoo luhs |
| | 'bɑ gju ləs ◊ | bah gyoo luhs ◊ |
| **Basimecu** | bə zɪ mə 'kju | buh zi muh kyoo |
| | bæ zɪ mə 'kju | ba zi muh kyoo |
| | beɪ zɪ mə 'kju | bei zi muh kyoo |
| **Beaufort** | 'boʊ fɚt | bo fərt |
| | 'bəʊ fət ◊ | bo fət ◊ |
| **Bedford** | 'bɛd fɚd | bed fərd |
| | 'bed fəd ◊ | bed fəd ◊ |
| **Bedlam** | 'bɛd ləm | bed luhm |
| | 'bed ləm ◊ | ... ◊ |
| **Berwick** -folio | 'bɛ rɪk | be rik |
|    **Barwick** | 'be rɪk ◊ | be rik ◊ |
| **Besonian/** | bə 'zoʊ niən | buh zo nee uhn |
|    **Bezonian** | bɪ 'zəʊ niən ◊ | bi zo nee uhn ◊ |

| NAME | INTERNATIONAL PHONETIC ALPHABET* | SIMPLIFIED PHONICS** |
|------|-----------------------------------|----------------------|
| Best | 'bɛst<br>'best ◊ | best<br>… ◊ |
| Bevis | 'bi vɪs<br>'bɛ vɪs<br>'be vɪs ◊ | bee vis<br>be vis<br>… ◊ |
| Bolingbroke | 'bɑ lɪŋ brʊk<br>'hoʊ lɪŋ brʊk<br>'bʊ lɪŋ brʊk ◊<br>'bɒ lɪŋ brʊk ◊ | bah ling brook<br>bo ling brook<br>boo ling brook ◊<br>bo ling brook ◊ |
| Bona | 'boʊ nə<br>'bəʊ nə ◊ | bo nuh<br>… ◊ |
| Bristol | 'brɪ stəl | bri stuhl |
| Britaigne/<br>  Bretagne | 'brɪ tən<br>brə 'tæŋ | bri tuhn<br>bruh tang |
| Britain | 'brɪ tən | bri tuhn |
| Buckingham | 'bʌ kɪŋ hæm<br>'bʌ kɪŋ əm | buh king ham<br>buh king uhm |
| Bury St Edmunds | 'bɛ ri seɪnt<br>  'ɛdməndz<br>'be ri sɪnt<br>  'ɛdməndz ◊ | be ree seint<br>  ed muhndz<br>be ree sint<br>  ed muhndz ◊ |
| Butcher | 'bʊ tʃɚ<br>'bʊ tʃə ◊ | boo chər<br>boo chə ◊ |
| Cade | 'keɪd | keid |
| Caesar | 'si zɚ<br>'si zə ◊ | see zər<br>see zə ◊ |
| Calaber | 'kæ lə bɚ<br>'kæ lə bə ◊ | ka luh bər<br>ka luh bə ◊ |

| NAME | INTERNATIONAL PHONETIC ALPHABET* | SIMPLIFIED PHONICS** |
|------|----------------------------------|----------------------|
| **Calydon** | 'kæ lə dɑn<br>'kæ lɪ dən<br>'kæ lə dɒn ◊<br>'kæ lɪ dən ◊ | ka luh dahn<br>ka luh duhn<br>ka luh don ◊<br>ka li duhn ◊ |
| **Cambridge** | 'keɪm brɪʤ | keim brij |
| **Canon/Cannon** | 'kæ nən | ka nuhn |
| **Ceres** | 'sɪ riz<br>'sɪə riz ◊ | si reez<br>siə reez |
| **Charles** | 'ʧɑrlz<br>'ʧɑlz ◊ | chahrlz<br>chahlz ◊ |
| **Chatham** -folio<br>  **Chartham** | 'ʧæ təm | cha tuhm |
| **Cheapside** | 'ʧip saɪd | cheep said |
| **Christ** | 'kraɪst | kraist |
| **Christendom** | 'krɪ sən dəm | kri suhn duhm |
| **Christian** | 'krɪs ʧən | kris chuhn |
| **Clarence** | 'klæ rəns | kla ruhns |
| **Clifford** | 'klɪ fɚd<br>'klɪ fəd ◊ | kli fərd<br>kli fəd ◊ |
| **Cobham** | 'kɑ bəm<br>'kɒ bəm ◊ | kah buhm<br>ko buhm ◊ |
| **Cromer** | 'kroʊ mɚ<br>'krəʊ mə ◊ | kro mər<br>kro mə ◊ |
| **Cumberland** | 'kʌm bɚ lənd<br>'kʌm bə lənd ◊ | kuhm bər luhnd<br>kuhm bə luhnd ◊ |
| **Cyprus** | 'saɪ prəs | sai pruhs |

| NAME | INTERNATIONAL PHONETIC ALPHABET* | SIMPLIFIED PHONICS** |
|------|----------------------------------|----------------------|
| **Dartford** | 'dɑrt fɚd<br>'dɑt fəd ◊ | dahrt fərd<br>daht fəd ◊ |
| **Dauphin** -folio<br>   **Dolphin**<br>   (see below) | 'dɔ fin<br>do 'fæn<br>   [gen Am var] | daw fin<br>do fan<br>   [gen Am var] |
| **Davy** | 'deɪ vi | dei vee |
| **Dick** | 'dɪk | dik |
| **Dido** | 'daɪ do<br>'daɪ dəʊ ◊ | dai do<br>... ◊ |
| **Dolphin/**<br>   **Dauphin**<br>   (see above) | 'dɑl fɪn<br>'dɒl fɪn ◊ | dahl fin<br>dol fin ◊ |
| **Downs** | 'daʊnz | downz |
| **Edmund** | 'ɛd mənd<br>'ed mənd ◊ | ed muhnd<br>... ◊ |
| **[Bury St] Edmunds** | 'ɛd məndz | ed muhndz |
| **Edward** | 'ɛd wɚd<br>'ed wəd ◊ | ed wərd<br>ed wəd ◊ |
| **Eleanor** | 'ɛ lɪ nɚ<br>'e lɪ nə ◊ | e li nər<br>e li nə ◊ |
| **Elysium** -folio<br>   **Elizium** | ɪ 'lɪ ziəm<br>ɪ 'lɪ ʒiəm | i li zee uhm<br>i li zhee uhm |
| **Emanuell** | ɪ 'mæ nju əl<br>ɪ 'mæ njʊ əl ◊ | i ma nyoo uhl<br>i ma nyoo uhl ◊ |
| **England** | 'ɪŋ glənd | ing gluhnd |
| **English** | 'ɪŋ glɪʃ | ing glish |

| NAME | INTERNATIONAL PHONETIC ALPHABET* | SIMPLIFIED PHONICS** |
|------|----------------------------------|----------------------|
| **Fish** | 'fɪʃ | fish |
| **Fleet** | 'flit | fleet |
| **French** | 'frɛntʃ<br>'frɛntʃ ◊ | french<br>… ◊ |
| **Gaultier** | 'goʊ tjɚ<br>'gəʊ tjə ◊ | go tyər<br>go tyə ◊ |
| **Gaunt** | 'gɔnt | gawnt |
| **[Saint] George** | [seɪnt] 'ʤɔrʤ<br>[sɪnt] 'ʤɔʤ ◊ | [seint] jawrj<br>[sint] jawj ◊ |
| **Glendower** | 'glɛn daʊ ɚ<br>glɛn 'daʊ ɚ<br>'glen daʊ ə ◊<br>glen 'daʊ ə ◊ | glen dow ər<br>glen dow ər<br>glen dow ə ◊<br>glen dow ə ◊ |
| **Gloucester** | 'glɑ stɚ<br>'glɔ stɚ<br>'glɒ stə ◊ | glah stər<br>glaw stər<br>glo stə ◊ |
| **Goffe/Gough** | 'gɔf<br>'gɒf ◊ | gawf<br>gof ◊ |
| **Goodman** | 'gʊd mən | good muhn |
| **Hart** | 'hɑrt<br>'hɑt ◊ | hahrt<br>haht ◊ |
| **Hatfield** | 'hæt fild | hat feeld |
| **Henry** | 'hɛn ri<br>'hen ri ◊ | hen ree<br>… ◊ |
| **Holland** | 'hɑ lənd<br>'hɒ lənd ◊ | hah luhnd<br>ho luhnd ◊ |

| NAME | INTERNATIONAL PHONETIC ALPHABET* | SIMPLIFIED PHONICS** |
|---|---|---|
| Horner | 'hɔr nɚ<br>'hɔ nə ◊ | hawr nər<br>haw nə ◊ |
| Hume | 'hjum | hyoom |
| Humphrey | 'hʌm fri<br>'hʌmp fri | huhm free<br>huhmp free |
| Iden | 'aɪ dən | ai duhn |
| Illyrian | ɪ 'lɪ riən | i li ree uhn |
| Ireland | 'aɪ ɚ lənd<br>'aɪ ə lənd ◊ | ai ər luhnd<br>ai ə luhnd ◊ |
| Iris | 'aɪ rɪs | ai ris |
| Irish | 'aɪ rɪʃ | ai rish |
| Isle of Man | 'aɪl əv 'mæn | ail uhv man |
| Jack | 'ʤæk | jak |
| James | 'ʤeɪmz | jeimz |
| Jerusalem | ʤə 'ru sə ləm | juh roo suh luhm |
| Jesu | 'ʤi zu<br>'ʤi su<br>'ʤi zju ◊ | jee zoo<br>jee soo<br>jee zyoo ◊ |
| Jesus | 'ʤi zəs | jee zuhs |
| Joan -folio Ioane | 'ʤoʊn<br>'ʤəʊn ◊ | jon<br>... ◊ |
| John | 'ʤɑn<br>'ʤɒn ◊ | jahn<br>jon ◊ |

| NAME | INTERNATIONAL PHONETIC ALPHABET[a] | SIMPLIFIED PHONICS** |
|------|-------------------------------------|----------------------|
| **Jourdain** -folio **Jordan, Jordane** | dʒʊr ˈdeɪn<br>dʒʊə ˈdeɪn ◊ | joor dein<br>jooə dein ◊ |
| **Jove** | ˈdʒoʊv<br>ˈdʒəʊv ◊ | jov<br>… ◊ |
| **Julius** | ˈdʒu liəs<br>ˈdʒul jəs | joo lee uhs<br>jool yuhs |
| **Kenelworth/ Kenilworth** -folio **Killingworth** | ˈkɛ nəl wɚθ<br>ˈke nɪl wəθ ◊ | ke nuhl wᵉrth<br>ke nil wᵉth ◊ |
| **Kent** | ˈkɛnt<br>ˈkent ◊ | kent<br>… ◊ |
| **Kentish** | ˈkɛn tɪʃ<br>ˈken tɪʃ ◊ | ken tish<br>… ◊ |
| **Lacies** | ˈleɪ siz | lei siz |
| **Lancaster** | ˈlæŋ kæ stɚ<br>ˈlæŋ kə stɚ<br>ˈlæŋ kə stə ◊ | lang ka stər<br>lang kuh stər<br>lang kuh stə ◊ |
| **Langley** | ˈlæŋ li | lang lee |
| **Latin** | ˈlæ tən<br>ˈlæ tɪn | la tuhn<br>la tin |
| **Lent** | ˈlɛnt<br>ˈlent ◊ | lent<br>… ◊ |
| **Lionel** | ˈlaɪ ə nəl | lai uh nuhl |
| **London** | ˈlʌn dən | luhn duhn |
| **[Saint] Magnus** | [seɪnt] ˈmæg nəs<br>[sɪnt] ˈmæg nəs ◊ | [seint] mag nuhs<br>[sint] mag nuhs ◊ |

| NAME | INTERNATIONAL PHONETIC ALPHABET* | SIMPLIFIED PHONICS** |
|---|---|---|
| **Maine** | 'meɪn | mein |
| **March** | 'martʃ<br>'matʃ ◊ | mahrch<br>mahch ◊ |
| **Margeret** | 'mar grɪt<br>'mar gə rɪt<br>'ma grɪt ◊<br>'ma gə rɪt ◊ | mahr grit<br>mahr guh rit<br>mah grit ◊<br>mah guh rit ◊ |
| **Margery** | 'mar dʒə ri<br>'ma dʒə ri ◊ | mahr juh ree<br>mah juh ree ◊ |
| **Matthew** | 'mæ θju | ma *th*yoo |
| **May** | 'meɪ | mei |
| **Medea** | mɪ 'di ə | mi dee uh |
| **Meg** | 'mɛg<br>'meg ◊ | meg<br>... ◊ |
| **Meleager** | mɛ li 'eɪ dʒɚ<br>me li 'eɪ dʒə ◊ | me lee ei jər<br>me lee ei jə ◊ |
| **Melford** | 'mɛl fɚd<br>'mel fəd ◊ | mel fərd<br>mel fəd ◊ |
| **Mortimer** | 'mɔr tə mɚ<br>'mɔ tɪ mə ◊ | mawr tuh mər<br>maw ti mə ◊ |
| **Naples** | 'neɪ pəlz | nei puhlz |
| **Neapolitan** | niə 'pa li tən<br>niə 'pɒ li tən ◊ | nee uh pah li tuhn<br>nee uh p*o* li tuhn ◊ |
| **Nell** | 'nɛl<br>'nel ◊ | nel<br>... ◊ |
| **Nevil** | 'nɛ vəl<br>'ne vɪl ◊ | ne vuhl<br>ne vil ◊ |

| NAME | INTERNATIONAL PHONETIC ALPHABET* | SIMPLIFIED PHONICS** |
|------|----------------------------------|----------------------|
| Nicholas | 'nɪ kə ləs | ni kuh luhs |
| Norman | 'nɔr mən | nawr muhn |
| | 'nɔ mən ◊ | naw muhn ◊ |
| Normandy | 'nɔr mən di | nawr muhn dee |
| | 'nɔ mən di ◊ | naw muhn dee ◊ |
| Orleans | 'ɔr liənz | awr lee uhnz |
| | ɔr 'li ənz | … |
| | 'ɔ liənz ◊ | aw lee uhnz ◊ |
| | ɔ 'li ənz ◊ | … ◊ |
| Owen | 'oʊ ɪn | o in |
| | 'oʊ ən | o uhn |
| | 'əʊ ɪn ◊ | … ◊ |
| Paris | 'pæ rɪs | pa ris |
| Peter | 'pi tɚ | pee tər |
| | 'pi tə ◊ | pee tə ◊ |
| Picardy | 'pɪ kɚ di | pi kər dee |
| | 'pɪ kə di ◊ | pi kə dee ◊ |
| Philippe | 'fɪ lɪp | fi lip |
| | fɪ 'lip | fi leep |
| Plantagenet | plæn 'tæ ʤə nɪt | plan ta juh nit |
| | plæn 'tæ ʤɪ nɪt | plan ta ji nit |
| [de la] Pole/ Poole | 'poʊl | pol |
| | 'pol ◊ | … ◊ |
| Pomfret | 'pʌm frɪt | puhm frit |
| | 'pɑm frɪt [gen Am var] | pahm frit [gen Am var] |
| | 'pɒm frɪt [Brit RP var] | pom frit [Brit RP var] |

| NAME | INTERNATIONAL PHONETIC ALPHABET* | SIMPLIFIED PHONICS** |
|------|----------------------------------|----------------------|
| **Pompey** | 'pɑm pi<br>'pɒm pi ◊ | pahm pee<br>pom pee ◊ |
| **Reignier** | 'reɪn jei<br>reɪn 'jei | rein yei<br>rein yei |
| **Rheims** -folio<br> **Rheimes** | 'rimz | reemz |
| **Richard** | 'rɪ tʃɚd<br>'rɪ tʃəd ◊ | ri chərd<br>ri chəd ◊ |
| **Robin** | 'rɑ bɪn<br>'rɒ bɪn ◊ | rah bin<br>ro bin ◊ |
| **Roger** | 'rɑ ʤɚ<br>'rɒ ʤə ◊ | rah jər<br>ro jə ◊ |
| **Roman** | 'roʊ mən<br>'rəʊ mən ◊ | ro muhn<br>... ◊ |
| **Romanos** | ro 'mɑ nos<br>rə 'mɑ nos<br>rəʊ 'mɑ nəʊs ◊ | ro mah nos<br>ruh mah nos<br>... ◊ |
| **Rome** | 'roʊm<br>'rəʊm ◊ | rom<br>... ◊ |
| **Salisbury** | 'sɔlz bɛ ri<br>'sælz bɛ ri<br>'sɔlz bə ri ◊ | sawlz be ree<br>salz be ree<br>sawlz buh ree ◊ |
| **Saunder** | 'sɔn dɚ<br>'sɔn də ◊ | sawn dər<br>sawn də ◊ |
| **Savoy** | sə 'vɔɪ | suh voy |
| **Say** | 'seɪ | sei |
| **Sicil** | 'sɪ sɪl | si sil |

| NAME | INTERNATIONAL PHONETIC ALPHABET* | SIMPLIFIED PHONICS** |
|---|---|---|
| **Sicilia** | sɪ 'sɪ liə <br> sɪ 'sɪl jə | si si lee uh <br> si sil yuh |
| **Simon** | 'saɪ mən | sai muhn |
| **Simpcox** | 'sɪmp kɑks <br> 'sɪmp kɒks ◊ <br> 'sɪm kɒks ◊ | simp kahks <br> simp koks ◊ <br> sim koks ◊ |
| **Smith** | 'smɪθ | smi*th* |
| **Smithfield** | 'smɪθ fild | smi*th* feeld |
| **Somerset** | 'sʌ mɚ sɛt <br> 'sʌ mə sɪt ◊ <br> 'sʌ mə set ◊ | suh mər set <br> suh mə sit ◊ <br> suh mə set ◊ |
| **Southwark** | 'sʌ ðɚk <br> 'sʌ ðək ◊ | suh thərk <br> suh thək ◊ |
| **Southwell** | 'saʊθ wəl <br> 'sʌ ðəl ◊ | sow*th* wuhl <br> suh thuhl ◊ |
| **Stafford** | 'stæ fɚd <br> 'stæ fəd ◊ | sta fərd <br> sta fəd ◊ |
| **Stanley** | 'stæn li | stan lee |
| **Suffolk** | 'sʌ fək | suh fuhk |
| **Sylla** | 'sɪ lə | si luh |
| **Telamonius** | tɛ lə 'moʊ niəs <br> te lə 'məʊ niəs ◊ | te luh mo nee uhs <br> … ◊ |
| **Thames** | 'tɛmz <br> 'temz ◊ | temz <br> … ◊ |
| **Thomas** | 'tɑ məs <br> 'tɒ məs ◊ | tah muhs <br> t*o* muhs ◊ |

| NAME | INTERNATIONAL PHONETIC ALPHABET* | SIMPLIFIED PHONICS** |
|---|---|---|
| **Thump** | ˈθʌmp | *th*uhmp |
| **Tom** | ˈtɑm<br>ˈtɒm ◊ | tahm<br>tom ◊ |
| **Tours** | ˈtuɚ<br>ˈtʊə ◊ | tooər<br>tooə ◊ |
| **Troy** | ˈtrɔɪ<br>ˈtʃrɔɪ | troy<br>chroy |
| **Tully** | ˈtʌ li | tuh lee |
| **Vaux** | ˈvɔks<br>ˈvɔz | vawks<br>vawz |
| **Wales** | ˈweɪlz | weilz |
| **Walter (Water)** | ˈwɔ tɚ<br>ˈwɔl tɚ<br>ˈwɔ tə ◊<br>ˈwɔl tə ◊ | waw tər<br>wawl tər<br>waw tə ◊<br>wawl tə ◊ |
| **Warwick** | ˈwɔ rɪk<br>ˈwɔr wɪk<br>ˈwɑ rɪk<br>ˈwɒ rɪk ◊ | waw rik<br>wawr wik<br>wah rik<br>wo rik ◊ |
| **Warwickshire** | ˈwɔ rɪk ʃɚ<br>ˈwɒ rɪk ʃə ◊ | war rik shər<br>wo rik shə ◊ |
| **Westminster** | ˈwɛst mɪn stɚ<br>ˈwest mɪn stə ◊ | west min stər<br>west min stə ◊ |
| **Whitmore** | ˈwɪt mɔr<br>ˈwɪt mɔ ◊ | wit mawr<br>wit maw ◊ |
| **Will** | ˈwɪl | wil |
| **William** | ˈwɪl jəm | wil yuhm |

| NAME | INTERNATIONAL PHONETIC ALPHABET* | SIMPLIFIED PHONICS** |
|------|----------------------------------|----------------------|
| **Winchester** | 'wɪn tʃɛ stɚ<br>'wɪn tʃɪ stə ◊ | win che stər<br>win chi stə ◊ |
| **Windsor** | 'wɪn zɚ<br>'wɪn zə ◊ | win zər<br>win zə ◊ |
| **Wingham** | 'wɪŋ əm | wing uhm |
| **Woodstock** | 'wʊd stɑk<br>'wʊd stɒk ◊ | wood stahk<br>wood stok ◊ |
| **York** | 'jɔrk<br>'jɔk ◊ | yawrk<br>yawk ◊ |

| NAME | INTERNATIONAL PHONETIC ALPHABET* | SIMPLIFIED PHONICS** |
|---|---|---|
| **Aesop** | 'i sɑp<br>'i sɒp ◊ | ee sahp<br>ee s*o*p ◊ |
| **Agamemnon** | æ gə 'mɛm nɑn<br>æ gə 'mem nɒn ◊<br>æ gə 'mɛm nən<br>æ gə 'mɛm nən ◊ | a guh mem nahn<br>a guh mem n*o*n ◊<br>a guh mem nuhn<br>… ◊ |
| **[Saint] Alban**<br>-folio **Albon,**<br>**Albone** | [seɪnt] 'ɔl bən<br>[sɪnt] 'ɒl bən ◊ | [seint] awl buhn<br>[sint] *o*l buhn ◊ |
| **Albion** | 'æl biən | al bee uhn |
| **Amazon** | 'æ mə zɑn<br>'æ mə zɒn ◊ | a muh zahn<br>a muh z*o*n ◊ |
| **Amazonian** | æ m ə 'zoʊ niən<br>æ m ə 'zəʊ niən ◊ | a muh zo nee uhn<br>… ◊ |
| **Atlas** | 'æt ləs | at luhs |
| **Aubrey** | 'ɔ bri | aw bree |
| **Barnet** | 'bɑr nɪt<br>'bɑ nɪt ◊ | bahr nit<br>bah nit ◊ |
| **Belgia** | 'bɛl ʤə<br>'bel ʤiə ◊ | bel juh<br>bel jee uh ◊ |
| **Berwick** -folio<br>**Barwick** | 'bɛ rɪk<br>'be rɪk ◊ | be rik<br>… ◊ |

| NAME | INTERNATIONAL PHONETIC ALPHABET* | SIMPLIFIED PHONICS** |
|---|---|---|
| Bess | 'bɛs<br>'bes ◊ | bes<br>... ◊ |
| Bona | 'boʊ nə<br>'bəʊ nə ◊ | bo nuh<br>... ◊ |
| Bonville | 'bɑn vɪl<br>'bɒn vɪl ◊ | bahn vil<br>bon vil ◊ |
| Bourbon -folio<br>  Burbon | 'bɝ bən<br>'bʊə bən ◊ | bər buhn<br>booə buhn ◊ |
| Britany/Brittany | 'brɪ tə ni | bri tuh nee |
| Buckingham | 'bʌ kɪŋ hæm<br>'bʌ kɪŋ əm ◊ | buh king ham<br>buh king uhm ◊ |
| Burgundy | 'bɝ gən di<br>'bɜ gən di ◊ | bər guhn dee<br>bə guhn dee ◊ |
| Caesar | 'si zɚ<br>'si zə ◊ | see zər<br>see zə ◊ |
| Calais | 'kæ leɪ<br>kə 'leɪ<br>    [gen Am var] | ka lei<br>kuh lei<br>    [gen Am var] |
| Christendom | 'krɪ sən dəm | kri suhn duhm |
| Clarence | 'klæ rəns | kla ruhns |
| Clifford | 'klɪ fɚd<br>'klɪ fəd ◊ | kli fərd<br>kli fəd ◊ |
| Cobham | 'kɑ bəm<br>'kɒ bəm ◊ | kah buhm<br>ko buhm ◊ |
| Coventry | 'kʌ vən tri<br>'kʌ vən tʃri<br>'kɒ vən tri ◊ | kuh vuhn tree<br>kuh vuhn chree<br>ko vuhn tree ◊ |

142

| NAME | INTERNATIONAL PHONETIC ALPHABET* | SIMPLIFIED PHONICS** |
|---|---|---|
| **Crete** | 'krit | kreet |
| **[Mortimer's] Cross** | 'krɔs<br>'krɑs<br>'krɒs ◊ | kraws<br>krahs<br>kros ◊ |
| **Daedalus** | 'dɛ də ləs<br>'di də ləs ◊ | de duhl uhs<br>dee duh luhs ◊ |
| **Daintree/ Daintry** | 'dein tri<br>'deɪn tʃri | dein tree<br>dein chree |
| **Dauphin** -folio<br>**Dolphin**<br>(see below) | 'dɔ fɪn<br>do 'fæn<br>    [gen Am var] | daw fin<br>do fan<br>    [gen Am var] |
| **Dian** | 'daɪ ən<br>'daɪ æn | dai uhn<br>dai an |
| **Dick** | 'dɪk | dik |
| **Dicky** | 'dɪ ki | di kee |
| **Diomede** | 'daɪ ə mid | dai uh meed |
| **Dolphin/ Dauphin**<br>(see above) | 'dɑl fɪn<br>'dɒl fɪn ◊ | dahl fin<br>dol fin ◊ |
| **Dunsmore** | 'dʌnz mɔr<br>'dʌnz mɔ ◊ | duhnz mawr<br>duhnz maw ◊ |
| **Edmund** | 'ɛd mənd<br>'ed mənd ◊ | ed muhnd<br>... ◊ |
| **Edward** | 'ɛd wɚd<br>'ed wəd ◊ | ed wərd<br>ed wəd ◊ |
| **Elizabeth** | ɪ 'lɪ zə bəθ | i li zuh buh*th* |

| NAME | INTERNATIONAL PHONETIC ALPHABET* | SIMPLIFIED PHONICS** |
|---|---|---|
| **Elysium** -folio<br>  **Elizium** | ɪ 'lɪ ziəm<br>ɪ 'lɪ ʒiəm | i li zee uhm<br>i li zhee uhm |
| **England** | 'ɪŋ glənd | ing gluhnd |
| **English** | 'ɪŋ glɪʃ | ing glish |
| **Essex** | 'ɛ sɪks<br>'e sɪks ◊ | e siks<br>... ◊ |
| **Europe** | 'jʊ rəp<br>'jʊə rəp ◊ | y*oo* ruhp<br>y*oo*ə ruhp ◊ |
| **Exeter** | 'ɛk sɪ tɚ<br>'ek sɪ tə ◊ | ek si tər<br>ek si tə ◊ |
| **Faulconbridge/<br>  Falconbridge** | 'fɔ kən brɪʤ<br>'fɔl kən brɪʤ<br>'fæl kən brɪʤ<br>  [gen Am var] | faw kuhn brij<br>fawl kuhn brij<br>fal kuhn brij<br>  [gen Am var] |
| **Flanders** | 'flæn dɚz<br>'flɑn dəz ◊ | flan dərz<br>flahn dəz ◊ |
| **French** | 'frɛnʧ<br>'frɛnʃ ◊ | french<br>... ◊ |
| **Gabriel** (folio only) | 'geɪ briəl | gei bree uhl |
| **Gallia** | 'gæ liə | ga lee uh |
| **Gaunt** | 'gɔnt | gawnt |
| **[Saint] George** | [seɪnt] 'ʤɔrʤ<br>[sɪnt] 'ʤɔʤ ◊ | [seint] jawrj<br>[sint] jawj ◊ |
| **German** | 'ʤɚ mən<br>'ʤɜ mən ◊ | jər muhn<br>jə muhn ◊ |

144

| NAME | INTERNATIONAL PHONETIC ALPHABET* | SIMPLIFIED PHONICS** |
|---|---|---|
| Gloucester | 'glɑ stɚ<br>'glɔ stɚ<br>'glɒ stə ◊ | glah stər<br>glaw stər<br>glo stə ◊ |
| Greece | 'gris | grees |
| Greek | 'grik | greek |
| Grey | 'greɪ | grei |
| Hammes/Hames | 'hæmz<br>'heɪmz | hamz<br>heimz |
| Hastings | 'heɪ stɪŋz | hei stingz |
| Hector | 'hɛk tɚ<br>'hek tə ◊ | hek tər<br>hek tə ◊ |
| Helen | 'hɛ lɪn<br>'hɛ lən<br>'he lən ◊ | he lin<br>he luhn<br>... ◊ |
| Henry | 'hɛn ri<br>'hen ri ◊ | hen ree<br>... ◊ |
| Hercules | 'hɝ kjə liz<br>'hɝ kju liz<br>'hɜ kjʊ liz ◊ | hər kyuh leez<br>hər kyoo leez<br>hə kyoo leez ◊ |
| Holland | 'hɑ lənd<br>'hɒ lənd ◊ | hah luhnd<br>ho luhnd ◊ |
| Hugh | 'hju | hyoo |
| Humfrey<br>(folio only) | 'hʌm fri<br>'hʌmp fri | huhm free<br>huhmp free |
| Hungerford | 'hʌŋ gɚ fɚd<br>'hʌŋ gə fəd ◊ | huhng gər fərd<br>huhng gə fəd ◊ |

| NAME | INTERNATIONAL PHONETIC ALPHABET* | SIMPLIFIED PHONICS** |
|------|-----------------------------------|----------------------|
| **Hyrcania** | hɝ ˈkeɪ niə<br>hɜ ˈkeɪ niə ◊ | hər kei nee uh<br>hə kei nee uh ◊ |
| **Icarus** | ˈɪ kə rəs<br>ˈaɪ kə rəs<br>  [Brit RP var] | i kuh ruhs<br>ai kuh ruhs<br>  [Brit RP var] |
| **Indian** | ˈɪn diən | in dee uhn |
| **Ireland** | ˈaɪ ɚ lənd<br>ˈaɪ ə lənd ◊ | ai ər luhnd<br>ai ə luhnd ◊ |
| **Jephthah** | ˈʤɛf θə<br>ˈʤɛp θə<br>ˈʤef θə ◊ | jef *th*uh<br>jep *th*uh<br>… ◊ |
| **Jerusalem** | ʤə ˈru sə ləm | juh roo suh luhm |
| **Jesus** | ˈʤi zəs | jee zuhs |
| **John** | ˈʤɑn<br>ˈʤɒn ◊ | jahn<br>jon ◊ |
| **Jove** | ˈʤoʊv<br>ˈʤəʊv ◊ | jov<br>… ◊ |
| **Judas** | ˈʤu dəs | joo duhs |
| **Kent** | ˈkɛnt<br>ˈkent ◊ | kent<br>… ◊ |
| **Kentish** | ˈkɛn tɪʃ<br>ˈken tɪʃ ◊ | ken tish<br>… ◊ |
| **Lancaster** | ˈlæŋ kæ stɚ<br>ˈlæŋ kə stɚ<br>ˈlæŋ kə stə ◊ | lang ka stər<br>lang kuh stər<br>lang kuh stə ◊ |
| **Leistershire** | ˈlɛ stɚʃɚ<br>ˈle stə ʃə ◊ | le stər shər<br>le stə shə ◊ |

146

| NAME | INTERNATIONAL PHONETIC ALPHABET* | SIMPLIFIED PHONICS** |
|------|----------------------------------|----------------------|
| **Lewis** | 'lu ɪs | loo is |
| **Lynn** | 'lɪn | lin |
| **Machiavel** | 'mæ kjə vɛl<br>mæ kiə 'vɛl<br>mæ kiə 'vel ◊ | ma kyuh vel<br>ma kee uh vel<br>... ◊ |
| **March** | 'mɑrtʃ<br>'mɑtʃ ◊ | mahrch<br>mahch ◊ |
| **Margaret** | 'mɑr gə rɪt<br>'mɑ gə rɪt ◊ | mahr guh rit<br>mah guh rit ◊ |
| **Menalaus** | mɛ nə 'leɪ əs<br>me nə 'leɪ əs ◊ | me nuh lei uhs<br>... ◊ |
| **Middleham [Castle]** | 'mɪ də ləm<br>['kæ səl]<br>'mɪ də ləm<br>['kɑ səl] ◊ | mi duh luhm<br>[ka suhl]<br>mi duh luhm<br>[kah suhl] ◊ |
| **Minos** | 'maɪ nəs<br>'maɪ nɑs<br>'maɪ nɒs ◊ | mai nuhs<br>mai nahs<br>mai nos ◊ |
| **Montague** -folio<br>**Mountague,**<br>**Mountacute** | 'man tə gju<br>'mɒn tə gju ◊ | mahn tuh gyoo<br>mon tuh gyoo ◊ |
| **Montgomery** | mənt 'gʌm ri<br>mənt 'gʌ mə ri | muhnt guhm ree<br>muhnt guh muh ree |
| **Mortimer** | 'mɔr tə mɚ<br>'mɔ tɪ mə ◊ | mawr tuh mər<br>maw ti mə ◊ |
| **Naples** | 'neɪ pəlz | nei puhlz |
| **Ned** | 'nɛd<br>'ned ◊ | ned<br>... ◊ |

| NAME | INTERNATIONAL PHONETIC ALPHABET* | SIMPLIFIED PHONICS** |
|------|----------------------------------|----------------------|
| Nero | 'ni ro<br>'nɪə rəʊ ◊ | nee ro<br>ni ro ◊ |
| Nestor | 'nɛs tɚ<br>'nes tə ◊ | nes tər<br>nes tə ◊ |
| Norfolk | 'nɔr fək<br>'nɔ fək ◊ | nawr fuhk<br>naw fuhk ◊ |
| Northampton | nɔrθ 'hæmp tən<br>nɔ 'θæm tən ◊ | nawr*th* hamp tuhn<br>naw *th*am tuhn ◊ |
| Northumberland | nɔr 'θʌm bɚ lənd<br>nɔ 'θʌm bə lənd ◊ | nawr *th*uhm bər luhnd<br>naw *th*uhm bə luhnd ◊ |
| Olympian | ə 'lɪm piən | uh lim pee uhn |
| Oxford | 'aks fɚd<br>'ɒks fəd ◊ | ahks fərd<br>*o*ks fəd ◊ |
| Oxfordshire | 'aks fɚd ʃɚ<br>'ɒks fəd ʃə ◊ | ahks fərd shər<br>*o*ks fəd shə ◊ |
| Pembroke | 'pɛm broʊk<br>'pɛm brʊk<br>'pem brʊk ◊ | pem brok<br>pem br*oo*k<br>… ◊ |
| Phaeton/<br>  Phaethon | 'feɪ ə tən<br>'feɪ ə θan<br>'feɪ ə θɒn ◊ | fei uh tuhn<br>fei uh *th*ahn<br>fei uh *th*on ◊ |
| Phoebus | 'fi bəs | fee buhs |
| Phoenix | 'fi nɪks | fee niks |
| Plantagenet | plæn 'tæ ʤə nɪt<br>plæn 'tæ ʤɪ nɪt | plan ta juh nit<br>plan ta ji nit |
| Priam | 'praɪ əm | prai uhm |

| NAME | INTERNATIONAL PHONETIC ALPHABET* | SIMPLIFIED PHONICS** |
|------|----------------------------------|----------------------|
| **Proteus** | 'proʊ tiəs<br>'prəʊ tiəs ◊ | pro tee uhs<br>… ◊ |
| **Ravenspurgh** | 'reɪ vənz pɚg<br>'reɪnz pɚ<br>'reɪ vənz pəg ◊<br>'reɪnz pə ◊ | rei vuhnz pərg<br>reinz pər<br>rei vuhnz pəg ◊<br>reinz pə ◊ |
| **Reignier** | 'reɪn jei<br>reɪn 'jei | rein yei<br>rein yei |
| **Rhesus** | 'ri səs | ree suhs |
| **Richard** | 'rɪ tʃɚd<br>'rɪ tʃəd ◊ | ri chərd<br>ri chəd ◊ |
| **Richmond** | 'rɪtʃ mənd | rich muhnd |
| **Rivers** | 'rɪ vɚz<br>'rɪ vəz ◊ | ri vərz<br>ri vəz ◊ |
| **Roger** | 'rɑ dʒɚ<br>'rɒ dʒə ◊ | rah jər<br>ro jə ◊ |
| **Roscius** | 'rɑ ʃiəs<br>'rɒ ʃiəs ◊ | rah shee uhs<br>ro shee uhs ◊ |
| **Rutland** | 'rʌt lənd | ruht luhnd |
| **Sandal [Castle]** | 'sæn dəl ['kæ səl]<br>'sæn dəl ['kɑ səl] ◊ | san duhl [ka suhl]<br>san duhl [kah suhl] ◊ |
| **Saxton** | 'sæks tən | saks tuhn |
| **Scales** | 'skeɪlz | skeilz |
| **Scotland** | 'skɑt lənd<br>'skɒt lənd ◊ | skaht luhnd<br>skot luhnd ◊ |
| **Sicil** | 'sɪ sɪl | si sil |

| NAME | INTERNATIONAL PHONETIC ALPHABET* | SIMPLIFIED PHONICS** |
|---|---|---|
| **Sinon** | 'saɪ nən | sai nuhn |
| **Somerset** | 'sʌ mɚ sɛt<br>'sʌ mə sɪt ◊<br>'sʌ mə set ◊ | suh mər set<br>suh mə sit ◊<br>suh mə set ◊ |
| **Somerville** | 'sʌ mɚ vɪl<br>'sʌ mə vɪl ◊ | suh mər vil<br>suh mə vil ◊ |
| **Southam** | 'saʊ ðəm | sow thuhm |
| **Spain** | 'speɪn | spein |
| **Stafford** | 'stæ fɚd<br>'stæ fəd ◊ | sta fərd<br>sta fəd ◊ |
| **Stanley** | 'stæn li | stan lee |
| **Suffolk** | 'sʌ fək | suh fuhk |
| **Tewksbury** | 'tuks bɛ ri<br>'tjuks bə ri ◊ | tooks be ree<br>tyooks buh ree ◊ |
| **Thracian** | 'θreɪ ʃən | *th*rei shuhn |
| **Towton** | 'taʊ tən | tow tuhn |
| **Troy** | 'trɔɪ<br>'ʧrɔɪ | troy<br>chroy |
| **Ulysses** | ju 'lɪ siz | yoo li seez |
| **Vere** | 'vir<br>'vɪr<br>'vɪə ◊ | veer<br>vir<br>viə ◊ |
| **Wakefield** | 'weɪk fild | weik feeld |

| NAME | INTERNATIONAL PHONETIC ALPHABET* | SIMPLIFIED PHONICS** |
|------|----------------------------------|----------------------|
| **Warwick** | ˈwɔ rɪk<br>ˈwɔr wɪk<br>ˈwɑ rɪk<br>ˈwɒ rɪk ◊ | waw rik<br>wawr wik<br>wah rik<br>wo rik ◊ |
| **Warwickshire** | ˈwɔ rɪk ʃɚ<br>ˈwɒ rɪk ʃə ◊ | war rik shər<br>wo rik shiə ◊ |
| **Welsh** | ˈwɛlʃ<br>ˈwelʃ ◊ | welsh<br>… ◊ |
| **Westmoreland** | ˈwɛst mɚ lənd<br>ˈwest mə lənd ◊ | west mər luhnd<br>west mə luhnd ◊ |
| **Will** | ˈwɪl | wil |
| **William** | ˈwɪl jəm | wil yuhm |
| **Wiltshire** | ˈwɪlt ʃɚ<br>ˈwɪlt ʃə ◊ | wilt shər<br>wilt shə ◊ |
| **York** | ˈjɔrk<br>ˈjɔk ◊ | yawrk<br>yawk ◊ |

| NAME | INTERNATIONAL PHONETIC ALPHABET* | SIMPLIFIED PHONICS** |
|---|---|---|
| **Abergavenny** | æ bɚ ˈgɛ ni | a bər ge nee |
| -folio | æ bɚ gə vɛ ni | a bər guh ve nee |
| **Aburgany,** | æ bə ˈge ni ◊ | a bə ge nee ◊ |
| **Aburgavenny** | æ bə gə ˈve ni ◊ | a bə guh ve nee ◊ |
| **Alençon** | æ lən ˈsoʊn | a luhn son |
| | ə ˈlɛn sən | uh len suhn |
| | ˈæ lən sɒn ◊ | a luhn sɒn ◊ |
| | ə ˈlen sɒn ◊ | uh len sɒn ◊ |
| **Amphthill/ Ampthill** | ˈæmt hɪl | amt hil |
| **Andren** | ˈæn drən | an dren |
| | ˈæn dʒrən | an jruhn |
| **Anne** | ˈæn | an |
| **Arde** | ˈɑrd | ahrd |
| | ˈɑd ◊ | ahd ◊ |
| **Arthur** | ˈɑr θɚ | ahr *thər* |
| | ˈɑ θə ◊ | ah *thə* ◊ |
| **[Saint] Asaph** | [seint] ˈæ səf | [seint] a suhf |
| | [sɪnt] ˈæ səf ◊ | [sint] a suhf ◊ |
| **Asher** | ˈæ ʃɚ | a shər |
| | ˈæ ʃə ◊ | a shə ◊ |
| **Banister** | ˈbæ nɪ stɚ | ba ni stər |
| | ˈbæ nɪ stə ◊ | ba ni stə ◊ |

*International Phonetic Alphabet Pronunciation Key: (General American) i-s<u>ee</u>, happy, Jul<u>ie</u>t; ɪ-s<u>i</u>t; eɪ-s<u>ay</u>; ɛ-s<u>e</u>t; æ-s<u>a</u>t; ɑ-f<u>a</u>ther; ʌ-s<u>u</u>n; ə-<u>a</u>bout; ɔ-s<u>aw</u>; oʊ-s<u>o</u>; o-h<u>e</u>ro; ʊ-sh<u>oo</u>k; u-s<u>oo</u>n; aɪ-s<u>igh</u>; ɔɪ-s<u>oy</u>; aʊ-s<u>ou</u>th; ju-c<u>u</u>be; ɚ-s<u>upp</u>er; ɛr-f<u>air</u>; ɝ-b<u>ir</u>d; k-<u>c</u>ut, <u>k</u>ite; g-<u>g</u>o; dʒ-<u>j</u>oy; j-<u>y</u>es; ŋ-si<u>ng</u>; ʃ-<u>sh</u>oe; tʃ-<u>ch</u>op; ð-<u>th</u>at; θ-<u>th</u>in; ʒ-mea<u>s</u>ure; (Additional symbols for British RP) e-s<u>e</u>t; ɛə-f<u>air</u>; ə-s<u>upp</u>er; ɜ-b<u>ir</u>d; ɒ-st<u>o</u>p; əʊ-s<u>o</u>, hero; o-(followed by l) p<u>o</u>le.

**Simplified Phonics Pronunciation Key: (General American) ee-s<u>ee</u>, happy; i-s<u>i</u>t; ei-s<u>ay</u>; e-s<u>e</u>t; a-s<u>a</u>t; ah-f<u>a</u>ther; uh-s<u>u</u>n, <u>a</u>bout; aw-s<u>aw</u>; o-s<u>o</u>; oo-sh<u>oo</u>k; oo-s<u>oo</u>n; ai-s<u>igh</u>; oy-s<u>oy</u>; ow-s<u>ou</u>th; yoo-c<u>u</u>be; ər-b<u>ir</u>d, supper; k-<u>c</u>ut, <u>k</u>ite; g-<u>g</u>o; j-<u>j</u>oy; ng-si<u>ng</u>; kw-<u>qu</u>ick; sh-<u>sh</u>oe; ch-<u>ch</u>op; th-<u>th</u>at; *th*-<u>th</u>in; zh-mea<u>s</u>ure; (Additional symbols for British RP) ə-b<u>ir</u>d; ə-s<u>upp</u>er; o-st<u>o</u>p; ... indicates pronunciation variance too subtle for Simplified Phonics transcription see International Phonetic Alphabet transcription.

◊ British RP pronunciation-see Introduction.

| NAME | INTERNATIONAL PHONETIC ALPHABET* | SIMPLIFIED PHONICS** |
|---|---|---|
| **Bayonne** -folio **Bayon** | baɪ ˈɑn<br>baɪ ˈoʊn<br>beɪ ˈoʊn<br>baɪ ˈɒn ◊ | bai ahn<br>bai on<br>bei on<br>bai *o*n ◊ |
| **Bevis** | ˈbi vɪs<br>ˈbɛ vɪs<br>ˈbe vɪs ◊ | bee vis<br>be vis<br>... ◊ |
| **Blackfriars** | ˈblæk fraɪ ɚz<br>ˈblæk fraɪ əz ◊ | blak frai ərz<br>blak frai əz ◊ |
| **Blomer/Bulmer** (see below) | ˈbloʊ mɚ<br>ˈbləʊ mə ◊ | blo mər<br>blo mə ◊ |
| **Bohun** | ˈbun<br>ˈboʊ ən<br>    [gen Am var]<br>ˈbəʊ ən<br>    [Brit RP var] | boon<br>bo uhn<br>    [gen Am var]<br>...<br>    [Brit RP var] |
| **Bourdeaux/ Bordeaux** | ˈbɔr do<br>bɔr ˈdo<br>ˈbɔ dəʊ ◊<br>bɔr ˈdəʊ ◊ | bawr do<br>...<br>baw do ◊<br>... ◊ |
| **Brandon** | ˈbræn dən | bran duhn |
| **Britain** | ˈbrɪ tən | bri tuhn |
| **Buckingham** | ˈbʌ kɪŋ hæm<br>ˈbʌ kɪŋ əm ◊ | buh king ham<br>buh king uhm ◊ |
| **Bullen** | ˈbʊ lɪn | b*oo* lin |
| **Bulmer/Blomer** (see above) | ˈbʊl mɚ<br>ˈbʊl mə ◊ | b*oo*l mər<br>b*oo*l mə ◊ |
| **Butts** | ˈbʌts | buhts |

| NAME | INTERNATIONAL PHONETIC ALPHABET* | SIMPLIFIED PHONICS** |
|------|------|------|
| **Campeius** -folio<br>**Campian** | kæm ˈpi əs<br>kæm ˈpeɪ əs | kam pee uhs<br>kam pei uhs |
| **Capucius** -folio<br>**Capuchius** | kə ˈpju ʧəs | kuh pyoo chuhs |
| **Carnarvonshire** | kə˞ ˈnɑr vən ʃə˞<br>kə ˈnɑ vən ʃə ◊ | kər nahr vuhn shər<br>kə nah vuhn shə ◊ |
| **[de] Cassado**<br>-folio<br>**de Casalis** | deɪ kə ˈsɑ do<br>deɪ kə ˈsɑ dəʊ ◊ | dei kuh sah do<br>… ◊ |
| **[de la] Car/Court**<br>(see balow) | dɛ lə ˈkɑr<br>de lə ˈkɑ ◊ | de luh kahr<br>de luh kah ◊ |
| **[de la] Court**<br>(see above) | dɛ lə ˈkɔrt<br>de lə ˈkɔt ◊ | de luh kawrt<br>de luh kawt ◊ |
| **Charles** | ˈʧɑrlz<br>ˈʧɑlz ◊ | chahrlz<br>chahlz |
| **Chartreaux** | ˈʃɑr trə<br>ˈʃɑ trə ◊ | shahr truh<br>shah truh ◊ |
| **Christendom** | ˈkrɪ sən dəm | kri suhn duhm |
| **Christian** | ˈkrɪs ʧən | kris chuhn |
| **Cinque-ports** | ˈsɪŋk pɔrts<br>ˈsɪŋk pɔts ◊ | singk pawrts<br>singk pawts ◊ |
| **Clotharius** | klo ˈtɛ riəs<br>kləʊ ˈte riəs ◊ | klo te ree uhs<br>… ◊ |
| **Colbrand** | ˈkoʊl brænd<br>ˈkol brænd ◊ | kol brand<br>… ◊ |
| **Cranmer** | ˈkræn mə˞<br>ˈkræn mə ◊ | kran mər<br>kran mə ◊ |

154

| NAME | INTERNATIONAL PHONETIC ALPHABET* | SIMPLIFIED PHONICS** |
|------|------|------|
| Cromwell | 'krɑm wɛl | krahm wel |
| | 'krɑm wəl | krahm wuhl |
| | 'krɒm wel ◊ | krom wel ◊ |
| | 'krɒm wəl ◊ | krom wuhl ◊ |
| Denny | 'dɛ ni | de nee |
| | 'de ni ◊ | … ◊ |
| Dorset | 'dɔr sɪt | dawr sit |
| | 'dɔ sɪt ◊ | daw sit ◊ |
| Dunstable | 'dʌn stə bəl | duhn stuh buhl |
| Edward | 'ɛd wɚd | ed wərd |
| | 'ed wəd ◊ | ed wəd ◊ |
| Egypt | 'i ʤɪpt | ee jipt |
| Elizabeth | ɪ 'lɪ zə bəθ | i li zuh buh*th* |
| Ely | 'i li | ee lee |
| England | 'ɪŋ glənd | ing gluhnd |
| English | 'ɪŋ glɪʃ | ing glish |
| Farrara | fə 'rɑ rə | fuh rah ruh |
| Ferdinand | 'fɚ dɪ nænd | fər di nand |
| | 'fɜ dɪ nənd ◊ | fə di nand ◊ |
| Ferrara/Farrara | fə 'rɑ rə | fuh rah ruh |
| Flanders | 'flæn dɚz | flan dərz |
| | 'flan dəz ◊ | flahn dəz ◊ |
| French | 'frɛntʃ | french |
| | 'frɛntʃ ◊ | … ◊ |
| Gardiner | 'gɑrd nər | gahrd nər |
| | 'gɑd nə ◊ | gahd nə ◊ |

| NAME | INTERNATIONAL PHONETIC ALPHABET* | SIMPLIFIED PHONICS** |
|------|-------------------|----------------|
| **Germany** | 'ʤɝ mə ni<br>'ʤɜ mə ni ◊ | jər muh nee<br>jə muh nee ◊ |
| **Gilbert** | 'gɪl bɚt<br>'gɪl bət ◊ | gil bərt<br>gil bət ◊ |
| **Greenwich** | 'grɛ nɪʧ<br>'gre nɪʧ ◊ | gre nich<br>... ◊ |
| **Griffith** | 'grɪ fɪθ | gri fi*th* |
| **Guilford** | 'gɪl fɚd<br>'gɪl fəd ◊ | gil fərd<br>gil fəd ◊ |
| **Guy** | 'gaɪ | gai |
| **Guynes** | 'gin | geen |
| **Henry** | 'hɛn ri<br>'hen ri ◊ | hen ree<br>... ◊ |
| **Henton** -folio<br>  **Hopkins** | 'hɛn tən<br>'hen tən ◊ | hen tuhn<br>... ◊ |
| **Hereford** | 'hɛ rɪ fɚd<br>'he rɪ fəd ◊ | he ri fərd<br>he ri fəd ◊ |
| **India** | 'ɪn diə | in dee uh |
| **Indian** | 'ɪn diən | in dee uhn |
| **Ipswich** | 'ɪps wɪʧ | ips wich |
| **Ireland** | 'aɪ ɚ lənd<br>'aɪ ə lənd ◊ | ai ər luhnd<br>ai ə luhnd ◊ |
| **John** | 'ʤan<br>'ʤɒn ◊ | jahn<br>jon ◊ |
| **July** | 'ʤu laɪ<br>ʤə 'laɪ | joo lai<br>juh lai |

156

| NAME | INTERNATIONAL PHONETIC ALPHABET* | SIMPLIFIED PHONICS** |
|---|---|---|
| Kate | 'keɪt | keit |
| Katherine | 'kæθ rɪn<br>'kæ θə rɪn | ka*th* rin<br>ka *th*uh rin |
| Kildare | kɪl 'dɛɚ<br>kɪl 'dɛə ◊ | kil deər<br>kil deə ◊ |
| Kimbolton -folio<br>Kymmalton | 'kɪm bəl tən<br>kɪm 'bol tən | kim buhl tuhn<br>kim bol tuhn |
| Latin | 'læ tən<br>'læ tɪn | la tuhn<br>la tin |
| Lawrence -folio<br>Laurence | 'lɔ rəns<br>'lɒ rəns ◊ | law ruhns<br>l*o* ruhns ◊ |
| Leister | 'lɛ stɚ<br>'le stə ◊ | le stər<br>le stə ◊ |
| Limbo | 'lɪm bo<br>'lɪm bəʊ ◊ | lim bo<br>… ◊ |
| Limehouse | 'laɪm haʊs | laim hows |
| Lincoln | 'lɪŋ kən | ling kuhn |
| London | 'lʌn dən | luhn duhn |
| Louvre | 'luv<br>'luvrə | loov<br>loovruh |
| Lovell | 'lʌ vəl | luh vuhl |
| Lucifer | 'lu sɪ fɚ<br>'lu sɪ fə ◊ | loo si fər<br>loo si fə ◊ |
| Lutheran | 'lu θə rən<br>'lu θə rɪn | loo *th*uh ruhn<br>loo *th*uh rin |

| NAME | INTERNATIONAL PHONETIC ALPHABET* | SIMPLIFIED PHONICS** |
|------|------|------|
| Marshalsea | 'mɑr ʃəl si<br>'mɑ ʃəl si ◊ | mahr shul see<br>mah shul see ◊ |
| Mary | 'mɛ ri<br>'mɛə ri ◊ | me ree<br>… ◊ |
| May-day | 'meɪ deɪ | mei dei |
| Michael | 'maɪ kəl | mai kuhl |
| Moorfields | 'mʊr fildz<br>'mʊə fildz ◊ | moor feeldz<br>mooə feeldz ◊ |
| Mountacute/<br>  Montacute | 'man tə kjut<br>'mɒn tə kjut ◊ | mahn tuh kyoot<br>mon tuh kyoot ◊ |
| Nicholas | 'nɪ kləs<br>'nɪ kə ləs | ni kluhs<br>ni kuh luhs |
| Norfolk | 'nɔr fək<br>'nɔ fək ◊ | nawr fuhk<br>naw fuhk ◊ |
| Northampton | nɔrθ 'hæmp tən<br>nɔ 'θæm tən ◊ | nawrth hamp tuhn<br>naw tham tuhn ◊ |
| Northumberland | nɔr 'θʌm bɚ lənd<br><br>nɔ 'θʌm bə lənd ◊ | nawr thuhm bər<br>  luhnd<br>naw thuhm bə<br>  luhnd ◊ |
| Orleans -folio<br>  Orleance | 'ɔr liənz<br>ɔr 'liənz<br>'ɔ li ənz ◊<br>ɔ 'liənz ◊ | awr lee uhnz<br>…<br>aw lee uhnz ◊<br>… ◊ |
| Orpheus | 'ɔr fiəs<br>'ɔr fjus<br>'ɔ fjus ◊ | awr fee uhs<br>awr fyoos<br>aw fyoos ◊ |
| Oxford | 'ɑks fɚd<br>'ɒks fəd ◊ | ahks fərd<br>oks fəd ◊ |

158

| NAME | INTERNATIONAL PHONETIC ALPHABET* | SIMPLIFIED PHONICS** |
|------|----------------------------------|----------------------|
| Pace | ˈpeɪs | peis |
| Paris/ Parish Garden | ˈpæ rɪs ˈgɑr dən<br>ˈpæ rɪʃ ˈgɑr dən<br>ˈpæ rɪs ˈgɑ dən ◊<br>ˈpæ rɪʃ ˈgɑ dən ◊ | pa ris gahr duhn<br>pa rish gahr duhn<br>pa ris gah duhn ◊<br>pa rish gah duhn ◊ |
| Patience | ˈpeɪ ʃəns | pei shuhns |
| [Saint] Paul | [seɪnt] ˈpɔl<br>[sɪnt] ˈpɔl ◊ | [seint] pawl<br>[sint] pawl ◊ |
| Peck | ˈpɛk<br>ˈpek ◊ | pek<br>... ◊ |
| Pembroke | ˈpɛm broʊk<br>ˈpɛm brʊk<br>ˈpem brʊk ◊ | pem brok<br>pem brook<br>... ◊ |
| Pepin | ˈpɛ pɪn<br>ˈpɪ pɪn<br>ˈpe pɪn ◊ | pe pin<br>pi pin<br>... ◊ |
| Phoenix | ˈfi nɪks | fee niks |
| Poultney | ˈpoʊlt ni<br>ˈpolt ni ◊ | polt nee<br>... ◊ |
| Powle's/Paul['s] (see above) | ˈpɔlz | pawlz |
| Richard | ˈrɪ tʃɚd<br>ˈrɪ tʃəd ◊ | ri chərd<br>ri chəd ◊ |
| Rochester | ˈrɑ tʃɛ stɚ<br>ˈrɒ tʃɪ stə ◊ | rah che stər<br>ro chi stə ◊ |
| Rochford | ˈrɑtʃ fɚd<br>ˈrɒtʃ fəd ◊ | rahch fərd<br>roch fəd ◊ |

| NAME | INTERNATIONAL PHONETIC ALPHABET* | SIMPLIFIED PHONICS** |
|------|----------------------------------|----------------------|
| **Rome** | 'roʊm<br>'rəʊm ◊ | rom<br>... ◊ |
| **Rose** | 'roʊz<br>'rəʊz ◊ | roz<br>... ◊ |
| **Saba** | seɪ bə | sei buh |
| **Salisbury** | 'sɔlz bɛ ri<br>'sælz bɛ ri<br>'sɔlz bə ri ◊ | sawlz be ree<br>salz be ree<br>sawlz buh ree ◊ |
| **Sampson** | 'sæmp sən | samp suhn |
| **Sands** -folio<br>  **Sandys** | 'sændz | sandz |
| **Sheba** -folio **Saba** | 'ʃi bə | shee buh |
| **Spain** | 'speɪn | spein |
| **Spaniard** | 'spæn jɚd<br>'spæn jəd ◊ | span yərd<br>span yəd ◊ |
| **Stafford** | 'stæ fɚd<br>'stæ fəd ◊ | sta fərd<br>sta fəd ◊ |
| **Stokesly** | 'stoʊks li<br>'stəʊks li ◊ | stoks lee<br>... ◊ |
| **Suffolk** | 'sʌ fək | suh fuhk |
| **Surrey** | 'sɝi<br>'sʌ ri | səree<br>suh ree |
| **Thomas** | 'tɑ məs<br>'tɒ məs ◊ | tah muhs<br>to muhs ◊ |
| **Toledo** | tə 'leɪ do<br>tə 'li do<br>tɒ 'leɪ dəʊ ◊ | tuh lei do<br>tuh lee do<br>to lei do ◊ |

| NAME | INTERNATIONAL PHONETIC ALPHABET* | SIMPLIFIED PHONICS** |
|---|---|---|
| **Tower** | 'taʊ ɚ<br>'taʊ ə ◊ | tow ər<br>tow ə ◊ |
| **Vaux** | 'vɔks<br>'vɔz ◊ | vawks<br>vawz ◊ |
| **Walter**<br>(folio only) | 'wɔl tɚ<br>'wɔl tə ◊ | wawl tər<br>wawl tə ◊ |
| **Washes** | 'wɑ ʃɪz<br>'wɒ ʃɪz ◊ | wah shiz<br>wo shiz ◊ |
| **Whitehall** | 'waɪt hɔl | wait hawl |
| **William** | 'wɪl jəm | wil yuhm |
| **Winchester** | 'wɪn ʧɛ stɚ<br>'wɪn ʧɪ stə ◊ | win che stər<br>win chi stə ◊ |
| **Wolsey** | 'wʊl zi | wool zee |
| **York** | 'jɔrk<br>'jɔk ◊ | yawrk<br>yawk ◊ |

| NAME | INTERNATIONAL PHONETIC ALPHABET* | SIMPLIFIED PHONICS** |
|------|----------------------------------|----------------------|
| **Aemilius** | ɪ 'mi liəs | i mee lee uhs |
| | ɪ 'mil jəs | i meel yuhs |
| **Aeneas** | ɪ 'ni əs | i nee uhs |
| | i 'ni əs | ee nee uhs |
| **Anchises** | æn 'kaɪ siz | an kai seez |
| | æŋ 'kaɪ siz | ang kai seez |
| **Anthony** | 'æn θə ni | an *th*uh nee |
| **Antonio** | æn 'toʊ nio | an to nee o |
| | æn 'təʊ niəʊ ◊ | ... ◊ |
| **Antonius** | æn 'toʊ niəs | an to nee uhs |
| | æn təʊ niəs ◊ | an ton ee uhs ◊ |
| **Antony** | 'æn tə ni | an tuh nee |
| **Artemidorus** | ɑr tə mɪ 'dɔ rəs | ahr tuh mi daw ruhs |
| | ɑ tə mɪ 'dɔ rəs ◊ | ah tuh mi daw ruhs ◊ |
| **Ate** | 'eɪ ti | ei tee |
| | 'ɑ ti | ah tee |
| **Brute** | 'bru teɪ | broo tei |
| | 'bru ti | broo tee |
| **Brutus** | 'bru təs | broo tuhs |

| NAME | INTERNATIONAL PHONETIC ALPHABET* | SIMPLIFIED PHONICS** |
|---|---|---|
| Caesar | 'si zɚ<br>'si zə ◊ | see zər<br>see zə ◊ |
| Caius | 'kai əs<br>'keɪ əs | kai suhs<br>kei suhs |
| Calpurnia -folio<br>  Calphurnia | kæl 'pɚ ni ə<br>kæl 'pɜ niə ◊ | kal pər nee uh<br>kal pə nee uh ◊ |
| Capitol | 'kæ pɪ təl | ka pi tuhl |
| Casca | 'kæ skə | ka skuh |
| Cassius | 'kæ ʃəs<br>'kæ siəs | ka shuhs<br>ka see uhs |
| Cato | 'keɪ to<br>'keɪ təʊ ◊ | kei to<br>… ◊ |
| Cicero | 'sɪ sə ro<br>'sɪ sə rəʊ ◊ | si suh ro<br>… ◊ |
| Cimber | 'sɪm bɚ<br>'sɪm bə ◊ | sim bər<br>sim bə ◊ |
| Cinna | 'sɪ nə | si nuh |
| Claudio | 'klɔ dio<br>'klɔ diəʊ ◊ | klaw dee o<br>… ◊ |
| Claudius | 'klɔ diəs | klaw dee uhs |
| Clitus | 'klaɪ təs | klai tuhs |
| Cnidos | 'naɪ dəs | nai duhs |
| Colossus | kə 'lɑ səs<br>kə 'lɒ səs ◊ | kuh lah suhs<br>kuh lo suhs ◊ |
| Dardanius | dɑr 'deɪ niəs<br>dɑ 'deɪ niəs ◊ | dahr dei nee uhs<br>dah dei nee uhs ◊ |

| NAME | INTERNATIONAL PHONETIC ALPHABET* | SIMPLIFIED PHONICS** |
|------|----------------------------------|----------------------|
| **Decius** | ˈdi ʃəs | dee shuhs |
| **Epicurus** | ˌɛ pɪ ˈkjʊ rəs<br>ˌe pɪ ˈkjʊə rəs ◊ | e pi ky*oo* ruhs<br>e pi ky*ooə* ruhs ◊ |
| **Erebus** | ˈɛ rə bəs<br>ˈe rɪ bəs ◊ | e ruh buhs<br>e ri buhs ◊ |
| **Flavia** | ˈfleɪ viə | flei vee uh |
| **Flavio** | ˈfleɪ vio<br>ˈfleɪ viəʊ ◊ | flei vee o<br>… ◊ |
| **Flavius** | ˈfleɪ viəs | flei vee uhs |
| **Greek** | ˈgrik | greek |
| **Hybla** | ˈhaɪ blə | hai bluh |
| **Italy** | ˈɪ tə li | i tuh lee |
| **Julius** | ˈdʒu liəs<br>ˈdʒul jəs | joo lee uhs<br>jool yuhs |
| **Labeo** | ˈleɪ bio<br>ˈleɪ biəʊ ◊ | lei bee o<br>… ◊ |
| **Lena** | ˈli nə | lee nuh |
| **Lepidus** | ˈlɛ pɪ dəs<br>ˈle pɪ dəs ◊ | le pi duhs<br>… ◊ |
| **Ligarius** | lɪ ˈgɛ riəs<br>lɪ ˈgɛə riəs | li ge ree uhs<br>… |
| **Lucilius** | lu ˈsɪ liəs | loo si lee uhs |
| **Lucius** | ˈlu ʃəs | loo shuhs |

| NAME | INTERNATIONAL PHONETIC ALPHABET* | SIMPLIFIED PHONICS** |
|------|----------------------------------|----------------------|
| **Lupercal** | 'lu pɚ kæl<br>'lu pɚ kəl<br>'lu pə kæl ◊ | loo pər kal<br>loo pər kuhl<br>loo pə kal |
| **March** | 'mɑrtʃ<br>'mɑtʃ ◊ | mahrch<br>mahch ◊ |
| **Marcus** | 'mɑr kəs<br>'mɑ kəs ◊ | mahr kuhs<br>mah kuhs ◊ |
| **Mark** | 'mɑrk<br>'mɑk ◊ | mahrk<br>mahk ◊ |
| **Marullus/<br>Marellus**<br>(folio only) | mə 'rʌ ləs | muh ruh luhs |
| **Messala** | mə 'seɪ lə<br>mə 'sɑ lə | muh sei luh<br>muh sah luh |
| **Metellus** | mɪ 'tɛ ləs<br>mɪ 'te ləs ◊ | mi te luhs<br>… ◊ |
| **Nervii** | 'nɝ vi aɪ<br>'nɜ vi aɪ ◊ | nər vee ai<br>nə vee ai ◊ |
| **Octavius** | ɑk 'teɪ viəs<br>ɒk 'teɪ viəs ◊ | ahk tei vee uhs<br>*o*k tei vee uhs ◊ |
| **Olympus** | o 'lɪm pəs<br>ə 'lɪm pəs | o lim puhs<br>uh lim puhs |
| **Parthia** | 'pɑr θiə<br>'pɑ θiə ◊ | pahr *th*ee uh<br>pah *th*ee uh ◊ |
| **Pella** | 'pɛ lə<br>'pe lə ◊ | pe luh<br>… ◊ |
| **Phillipi** | fɪ 'lɪ paɪ<br>'fɪ lɪ paɪ | fi li pai<br>fi li pai |

| NAME | INTERNATIONAL PHONETIC ALPHABET* | SIMPLIFIED PHONICS** |
|------|------|------|
| Pindarus | ˈpɪn də rəs | pin duh ruhs |
| Pluto | ˈplu to<br>ˈplu təʊ ◊ | ploo to<br>… ◊ |
| Plutus | ˈplu təs | ploo tuhs |
| Pompey | ˈpɑm pi<br>ˈpɒm pi ◊ | pahm pee<br>pom pee ◊ |
| Popilius | po ˈpɪl jəs<br>po ˈpɪ liəs<br>pəʊ ˈpɪ liəs ◊ | po pil yuhs<br>po pi lee uhs<br>… ◊ |
| Portia | ˈpɔr ʃə<br>ˈpɔ ʃə ◊ | pawr shuh<br>paw shuh ◊ |
| Publius | ˈpʌ bliəs | puh blee uhs |
| Roman | ˈroʊ mən<br>ˈrəʊ mən ◊ | ro muhn<br>… ◊ |
| Rome | ˈroʊm<br>ˈrəʊm ◊ | rom<br>… ◊ |
| Sardian | ˈsɑr diən<br>ˈsɑ diən ◊ | sahr dee uhn<br>sah dee uhn ◊ |
| Sardis | ˈsɑr dɪs<br>ˈsɑ dɪs ◊ | sahr dis<br>sah dis ◊ |
| Spain | ˈspeɪn | spein |
| Statilius | stə ˈtɪ liəs<br>stə ˈtɪl jəs<br>stæ ˈtɪ liəs | stuh ti lee uhs<br>stuh til yuhs<br>sta ti lee uhs |
| Strato | ˈstreɪ to<br>ˈstreɪ təʊ ◊ | strei to<br>… ◊ |

| NAME | INTERNATIONAL PHONETIC ALPHABET* | SIMPLIFIED PHONICS** |
|---|---|---|
| **Tarquin** | 'tɑr kwɪn<br>'tɑ kwɪn ◊ | tahr kwin<br>tah kwin ◊ |
| **Tarsus/Tharsus** | 'tɑr səs<br>'tɑ səs ◊ | tahr suhs<br>tah suhs ◊ |
| **Thassos/Thasos** | 'θeɪ sɑs<br>'θeɪ sɒs ◊ | *the*i sahs<br>*the*i sos ◊ |
| **Tiber** | 'taɪ bɚ<br>'taɪ bə ◊ | tai bər<br>tai bə ◊ |
| **Titinius** | tɪ 'tɪ niəs<br>taɪ 'tɪ niəs | ti ti nee uhs<br>tai ti nee uhs |
| **Trebonius** | ʧrɪ 'boʊ niəs<br>trɪ 'boʊ niəs<br>trɪ 'bəʊ niəs ◊ | chri bo nee uhs<br>tri bo nee uhs<br>... ◊ |
| **Troy** | 'trɔɪ<br>'ʧrɔɪ | troy<br>chroy |
| **Varo/Varro** -folio<br>    **Varrus** | 'væ ro<br>'væ rəʊ ◊ | va ro<br>... ◊ |
| **Volumnius** | və 'lʌm niəs | vuh luhm nee uhs |

| NAME | INTERNATIONAL PHONETIC ALPHABET* | SIMPLIFIED PHONICS** |
|------|----------------------------------|----------------------|
| **Alcides** | æl ˈsaɪ diz | al sai deez |
| **Alps** | ˈælps | alps |
| **Amazon** | ˈæ mə zɑn | a muh zahn |
|  | ˈæ mə zɒn ◊ | a muh zon ◊ |
| **Angiers** | ˈæn dʒɪrz | an jirz |
|  | ˈæn dʒɪəz ◊ | an jiəz ◊ |
| **Anjou** | ɑn ˈdʒu | ahn joo |
|  | ɑn ˈʒu | ahn zhoo |
|  | ˈæn dʒu | an joo |
| **Apennines** | ˈæ pə naɪnz | a puh nainz |
| **April** | ˈeɪ prəl | ei pruhl |
| **Arthur** | ˈɑr θɚ | ahr *th*ər |
|  | ˈɑ θə ◊ | ah *th*ə ◊ |
| **Ate** | ˈeɪ ti | ei tee |
|  | ˈɑ ti | ah tee |
| **Austria** | ˈɔ striə | aw stree uh |
|  | ˈɔs tʃriə | aws chree uh |
| **Basilisco** | bæ sə ˈlɪ sko | ba suh li sko |
|  | bæ zə lɪ skəʊ ◊ | ba zuh li sko ◊ |
| **Bastard** | ˈbæs tɚd | bas tərd |
|  | ˈbɑs təd ◊ | bahs təd ◊ |

*International Phonetic Alphabet Pronunciation Key: (General American) i-s<u>ee</u>, happ<u>y</u>, J<u>u</u>liet; ɪ-s<u>i</u>t; eɪ-s<u>ay</u>; ɛ-s<u>e</u>t; æ-s<u>a</u>t; ɑ-f<u>a</u>ther; ʌ-s<u>u</u>n; ə-<u>a</u>bout; ɔ-s<u>aw</u>; oʊ-s<u>o</u>; o-her<u>o</u>; ʊ-sh<u>oo</u>k; u-s<u>oo</u>n; aɪ-s<u>igh</u>; ɔɪ-s<u>oy</u>; aʊ-s<u>outh</u>; ju-c<u>u</u>be; ɚ-s<u>upp</u>er; ɛr-f<u>air</u>; ɝ-b<u>ir</u>d; k-<u>c</u>ut, <u>k</u>ite; g-<u>g</u>o; dʒ-<u>j</u>oy; j-<u>y</u>es; ŋ-si<u>ng</u>; ʃ-<u>sh</u>oe; tʃ-<u>ch</u>op; ð-<u>th</u>at; θ-<u>th</u>in; ʒ-mea<u>s</u>ure; (Additional symbols for British RP) e-s<u>e</u>t; ɛə-f<u>air</u>; ə-s<u>upp</u>er; ɜ-b<u>ir</u>d; ɒ-st<u>o</u>p; əʊ-s<u>o</u>, her<u>o</u>; o-(followed by l) p<u>o</u>le.

**Simplified Phonics Pronunciation Key: (General American) ee-s<u>ee</u>, happ<u>y</u>; i-s<u>i</u>t; ei-s<u>ay</u>; e-s<u>e</u>t; a-s<u>a</u>t; ah-f<u>a</u>ther; uh-s<u>u</u>n, <u>a</u>bout; aw-s<u>aw</u>; o-s<u>o</u>; oo-sh<u>oo</u>k; oo-s<u>oo</u>n; ai-s<u>igh</u>; oy-s<u>oy</u>; ow-s<u>outh</u>; yoo-c<u>u</u>be; ər-b<u>ir</u>d, s<u>upp</u>er; k-<u>c</u>ut, <u>k</u>ite; g-<u>g</u>o; j-<u>j</u>oy; ng-si<u>ng</u>; kw-<u>qu</u>ick; sh-<u>sh</u>oe; ch-<u>ch</u>op; th-<u>th</u>at; *th*-<u>th</u>in; zh-mea<u>s</u>ure; (Additional symbols for British RP) ə-b<u>ir</u>d; ə-s<u>upp</u>er; <u>o</u>-stop; ... indicates pronunciation variance too subtle for Simplified Phonics transcription see International Phonetic Alphabet transcription.

◊ British RP pronunciation-see Introduction.

| NAME | INTERNATIONAL PHONETIC ALPHABET* | SIMPLIFIED PHONICS** |
|------|----------------------------------|----------------------|
| **Bigot** | ˈbɪ gət | bi guht |
| **Blanch** | ˈblæntʃ<br>ˈblɑntʃ ◊ | blanch<br>blahnch ◊ |
| **Brabbler** | ˈbræ blɚ<br>ˈbræ blə ◊ | bra blər<br>bra blə ◊ |
| **Bretagne** | ˈbrɪ tən<br>brə ˈtæŋ | bri tuhn<br>bruh tang |
| **[de] Burgh** | [də] ˈbɝg<br>[də] ˈbɜg ◊ | [duh] bərg<br>[duh] bəg ◊ |
| **Bury** | ˈbɛ ri<br>ˈbe ri ◊ | be ree<br>… ◊ |
| **Bury St Edmunds** | ˈbɛ ri seɪnt<br> ˈɛd məndz<br>ˈbe ri sɪnt<br> ˈed məndz ◊ | be ree seint<br> ed muhndz<br>be ree sint<br> ed muhndz ◊ |
| **Cain** | ˈkeɪn | kein |
| **Calais** | ˈkæ leɪ<br>kə ˈleɪ<br> [gen Am var] | ka lei<br>kuh lei<br> [gen Am var] |
| **Canturbury** | ˈkæn tɚ bɛ ri<br>ˈkæn tə bə ri ◊ | kan tər be ree<br>kan tə buh ree ◊ |
| **Chatillon**-folio<br>**Chatillion,**<br>**Chattylion** | ʃə ˈtɪl jən<br>ʃə ˈtɪ lən | shuh til yuhn<br>shuh ti luhn |
| **Christendom** | ˈkrɪ sən dəm | kri suhn duhm |
| **Christian** | ˈkrɪs tʃən | kris chuhn |
| **Coeur de Lion** | kɚ də ˈli an<br>kɜ də ˈli ɒn ◊ | kər duh lee ahn<br>kə duh lee on ◊ |

169

| NAME | INTERNATIONAL PHONETIC ALPHABET* | SIMPLIFIED PHONICS** |
|---|---|---|
| **Colbrand** | 'koʊl brænd<br>'kol brænd ◊ | kol brand<br>… ◊ |
| **Constance** | 'kɑn stəns<br>'kɒn stəns ◊ | kahn stuhns<br>kon stuhns ◊ |
| **Dauphin/<br> Dolphin**<br>(see below) | 'dɔ fin<br>do 'fæn<br>    [gen Am var] | daw fin<br>do fan<br>    [gen Am var] |
| **Dolphin/<br> Dauphin**<br>(see above) | 'dɑl fin<br>'dɒl fin ◊ | dahl fin<br>dol fin ◊ |
| **Dover [Castle]** | 'doʊ vɚ [kæ səl]<br>'dəʊ və [kɑ səl] ◊ | do vər [ka suhl]<br>do və [kah suhl] ◊ |
| **[Saint]<br> Edmundsbury** | [seɪnt] 'ɛd<br>    məndz bɛ ri<br>[sɪnt] 'ɛd<br>    məndz bə ri ◊ | [seint] ed muhndz<br>    be ree<br>[sint] ed muhndz<br>    buh ree ◊ |
| **Elinor** | 'ɛ lɪ nɚ<br>'e lɪ nə ◊ | e li nər<br>e li nə ◊ |
| **England** | 'ɪŋ glənd | ing gluhnd |
| **English** | 'ɪŋ glɪʃ | ing glish |
| **Essex** | 'ɛ sɪks<br>'e sɪks ◊ | e siks<br>… ◊ |
| **Faulconbridge/<br> Falconbridge** | 'fɔ kən brɪdʒ<br>'fɔl kən brɪdʒ<br>'fæl kən brɪdʒ<br>    [gen Am var] | faw kuhn brij<br>fawl kuhn brij<br>fal kuhn brij<br>    [gen Am var] |
| **France** | 'fræns<br>'frɑns ◊ | frans<br>frahns ◊ |

| NAME | INTERNATIONAL PHONETIC ALPHABET* | SIMPLIFIED PHONICS** |
|------|----------------------------------|----------------------|
| French | 'frɛntʃ<br>'frentʃ ◊ | french<br>... ◊ |
| Friday | 'fraɪ deɪ<br>'fraɪ di ◊ | frai dei<br>frai dee ◊ |
| Geffrey/Geoffrey | 'dʒɛ fri<br>'dʒe fri ◊ | je free<br>... ◊ |
| [Saint] George | [seɪnt] 'dʒɔrdʒ<br>[sɪnt] 'dʒɔdʒ ◊ | [seint] jawrj<br>[sint] jawj ◊ |
| Germany | 'dʒɚ mə ni<br>'dʒɜ mə ni ◊ | jər muh nee<br>jə muh nee ◊ |
| Goodwin Sands | 'gʊd wɪn 'sændz | good win sandz |
| Gurney | 'gɚ ni<br>'gɜ ni ◊ | gər nee<br>gə nee ◊ |
| Henry | 'hɛn ri<br>'hen ri ◊ | hen ree<br>... ◊ |
| Hubert | 'hju bɚt<br>'hju bət ◊ | hyoo bərt<br>hyoo bət ◊ |
| Innocent | 'ɪ nə sənt | i nuh suhnt |
| Ireland | 'aɪ ɚ lənd<br>'aɪ ə lənd ◊ | ai ər luhnd<br>aiə luhnd ◊ |
| Italian | ɪ 'tæl jən | i tal yuhn |
| James | 'dʒeɪmz | jeimz |
| Jerusalem | dʒə 'ru sə ləm | juh roo suh luhm |
| Joan | 'dʒoʊn<br>'dʒəʊn ◊ | jon<br>... ◊ |

| NAME | INTERNATIONAL PHONETIC ALPHABET* | SIMPLIFIED PHONICS** |
|---|---|---|
| John | 'ʤɑn<br>'ʤɒn ◊ | jahn<br>jon ◊ |
| Kent | 'kɛnt<br>'kent ◊ | kent<br>... ◊ |
| Langton | 'læŋ tən | lang tuhn |
| Lewis | 'lu ɪs | loo is |
| Lincoln Washes | 'lɪŋ kən 'wɑ ʃɪz<br>'lɪŋ kən 'wɒ ʃɪz ◊ | ling kuhn wah shiz<br>ling kuhn wo shiz ◊ |
| London | 'lʌn dən | luhn duhn |
| Lucifer | 'lu sɪ fɚ<br>'lu sɪ fə ◊ | loo si fər<br>loo si fə ◊ |
| Lymoges | lɪ 'moʊʒ<br>lɪ 'məʊʒ ◊ | li mozh<br>... ◊ |
| Maine | 'meɪn | mein |
| [Saint] Mary | [seɪnt] mɛ ri<br>[sɪnt] mɛə ri ◊ | [seint] me ree<br>[sint] meə ree ◊ |
| Melun | mə 'lʌn<br>mə 'lun | muh luhn<br>muh loon |
| Mercury | 'mɝ kjə ri<br>'mɜ kjʊ ri ◊ | mər kyuh ree<br>mə kyoo ree ◊ |
| Milan | mɪ 'lɑn<br>mɪ 'læn<br>'mɪ lən | mi lahn<br>mi lan<br>mi luhn |
| Neptune | 'nɛp tun<br>'nep tjun ◊ | nep toon<br>nep tyoon ◊ |
| Nero | 'ni ro<br>'nɪə rəʊ ◊ | nee ro<br>niə ro ◊ |

| NAME | INTERNATIONAL PHONETIC ALPHABET* | SIMPLIFIED PHONICS** |
|------|-----------------------------------|----------------------|
| Nob | 'nɑb<br>'nɒb ◊ | nahb<br>nob ◊ |
| Norfolk | 'nɔr fək<br>'nɔ fək ◊ | nawr fuhk<br>naw fuhk ◊ |
| Northampton-<br>shire | nɔrθ 'hæmp tən ʃɚ<br><br>nɔ 'θæm tən ʃə ◊ | nawrth hamp<br>  tuhn shər<br>nawr tham<br>  tuhn shə ◊ |
| Palestine | 'pæ lə staɪn<br>'pæ lɪ staɪn | pa luh stain<br>pa li stain |
| Pandulph | 'pæn dəlf | pan duhlf |
| Pembroke | 'pɛm broʊk<br>'pɛm brʊk<br>'pem brʊk ◊ | pem brok<br>pem brook<br>… ◊ |
| Peter | 'pi tɚ<br>'pi tə ◊ | pee tər<br>pee tə ◊ |
| Phillip | 'fɪ lɪp | fi lip |
| Pigmy | 'pɪg mi | pig mee |
| Plantagenet | plæn 'tæ ʤə nɪt<br>plæn 'tæ ʤɪ nɪt | plan ta juh nit<br>plan ta ji nit |
| Po | 'poʊ<br>'pəʊ ◊ | po<br>… ◊ |
| Poictiers | pwɑ ti 'eɪ<br>pɔɪ 'tiɚz [Ang.<br>  gen Am var]<br>pɔɪ 'tiəz [Ang.<br>  Brit RP var] | pwah tee ei<br>poy tee ərz [Ang.<br>  gen Am var]<br>poy tee əz [Ang.<br>  Brit RP var] |

| NAME | INTERNATIONAL PHONETIC ALPHABET* | SIMPLIFIED PHONICS** |
|---|---|---|
| Pomfret | ˈpʌm frɪt<br>ˈpɑm frɪt<br>　[gen Am var]<br>ˈpɒm frɪt<br>　[Brit RP var] | puhm frit<br>pahm frit<br>　[gen Am var]<br>pom frit<br>　[Brit RP var] |
| Pyrenean | pɪ rə ˈni ən | pi ruh nee uhn |
| Richard | ˈrɪ tʃɚd<br>ˈrɪ tʃəd ◊ | ri chərd<br>ri chəd ◊ |
| Richmond | ˈrɪtʃ mənd | rich muhnd |
| Robert | ˈrɑ bɚt<br>ˈrɒ bət ◊ | rah bərt<br>ro bət ◊ |
| Rome | ˈroʊm<br>ˈrəʊm ◊ | rom<br>… ◊ |
| Salisbury | ˈsɔlz bɛ ri<br>ˈsælz bɛ ri<br>ˈsɔlz bə ri ◊ | sawlz be ree<br>salz be ree<br>sawlz buh ree ◊ |
| Sands | ˈsændz | sandz |
| Spain | ˈspeɪn | spein |
| Stephen | ˈsti vən | stee vuhn |
| Swinstead | ˈswɪn stɛd<br>ˈswɪn sted ◊ | swin sted<br>… ◊ |
| Touraine -folio<br>　Torayne | tʊ ˈreɪn<br>ˈtu reɪn | too rein<br>too rein |
| Volquessen | vɑl ˈkɛ sən<br>vɒl ˈke sən ◊ | vahl ke suhn<br>vol ke suhn ◊ |
| Worcester | ˈwʊ stɚ<br>ˈwʊ stə ◊ | woo stər<br>woo stə ◊ |

| NAME | INTERNATIONAL PHONETIC ALPHABET* | SIMPLIFIED PHONICS** |
|---|---|---|
| **Ajax** | 'eɪ ʤæks | ei jaks |
| **Albany** | 'ɔl bə ni | awl buh nee |
| **Albion** | 'æl biən | al bee uhn |
| **Apollo** | ə 'pɑ lo<br>ə 'pɒ ləʊ ◊ | uh pah lo<br>uh p*o* lo ◊ |
| **Athenian** | ə 'θi niən | uh *th*ee nee uhn |
| **Bedlam** | 'bɛd ləm<br>'bed ləm ◊ | bed luhm<br>... ◊ |
| **Bessy** | 'bɛ si<br>'be si ◊ | be see<br>... ◊ |
| **Blanch** | 'blænʧ<br>'blɑnʧ ◊ | blanch<br>blahnch ◊ |
| **Britain** | 'brɪ tən | bri tuhn |
| **British** | 'brɪ tɪʃ | bri tish |
| **Burgundy** | 'bɝ gən di<br>'bɜ gən di ◊ | bər guhn dee<br>bə guhn dee ◊ |
| **Caius** | 'kai əs<br>'keɪ əs | kai uhs<br>kei uhs |
| **Camelot** | 'kæ mə lɑt<br>'kæ mə lɒt ◊ | ka muh laht<br>ka muh l*o*t ◊ |

*International Phonetic Alphabet Pronunciation Key: (General American) i-s<u>ee</u>, happ<u>y</u>, Jul<u>i</u>et; ɪ-s<u>i</u>t; eɪ-s<u>ay</u>; ɛ-s<u>e</u>t; æ-s<u>a</u>t; ɑ-f<u>a</u>ther; ʌ-s<u>u</u>n; ə-<u>a</u>bout; ɔ-s<u>aw</u>; oʊ-s<u>o</u>; o-her<u>o</u>; ʊ-sh<u>oo</u>k; u-s<u>oo</u>n; aɪ-s<u>igh</u>; ɔɪ-s<u>oy</u>; aʊ-s<u>outh</u>; ju-c<u>u</u>be; ə-s<u>upper</u>; ɛr-f<u>air</u>; ɝ-b<u>ir</u>d; k-<u>c</u>ut, <u>k</u>ite; g-<u>g</u>o; ʤ-<u>j</u>oy; j-<u>y</u>es; ŋ-si<u>ng</u>; ʃ-<u>sh</u>oe; ʧ-<u>ch</u>op; ð-<u>th</u>at; θ-<u>th</u>in; ʒ-mea<u>s</u>ure; (Additional symbols for British RP) e-s<u>e</u>t; ɛə-f<u>air</u>; ə-s<u>upper</u>; ɜ-b<u>ir</u>d; ɒ-st<u>o</u>p; əʊ-s<u>o</u>, her<u>o</u>; o-(followed by l) p<u>o</u>le.

**Simplified Phonics Pronunciation Key: (General American) ee-s<u>ee</u>, happ<u>y</u>; i-s<u>i</u>t; ei-s<u>ay</u>; e-s<u>e</u>t; a-s<u>a</u>t; ah-f<u>a</u>ther; uh-s<u>u</u>n, <u>a</u>bout; aw-s<u>aw</u>; o-s<u>o</u>; *o*-sh<u>oo</u>k; oo-s<u>oo</u>n; ai-s<u>igh</u>; oy-s<u>oy</u>; ow-s<u>outh</u>; yoo-c<u>u</u>be; ər-b<u>ir</u>d, s<u>upper</u>; k-<u>c</u>ut, <u>k</u>ite; g-<u>g</u>o; j-<u>j</u>oy; ng-si<u>ng</u>; kw-<u>qu</u>ick; sh-<u>sh</u>oe; ch-<u>ch</u>op; th-<u>th</u>at; *th*-<u>th</u>in; zh-mea<u>s</u>ure; (Additional symbols for British RP) ə-b<u>ir</u>d; ə-s<u>upper</u>; *o*-st<u>o</u>p; ... indicates pronunciation variance too subtle for Simplified Phonics transcription see International Phonetic Alphabet transcription.

◊ British RP pronunciation-see Introduction.

| NAME | INTERNATIONAL PHONETIC ALPHABET* | SIMPLIFIED PHONICS** |
|---|---|---|
| **Centaur** | 'sɛn tɔr<br>'sen tɔ ◊ | sen tawr<br>sen taw ◊ |
| **Cordelia** | kɔr 'di liə<br>kɔr 'dil jə<br>kɔ 'di liə ◊ | kawr dee lee uh<br>kawr deel yuh<br>kaw dee lee uh ◊ |
| **Cornwall** | 'kɔrn wɔl<br>'kɔrn wɑl<br>'kɔn wɔl ◊<br>'kɔn wəl ◊ | kawrn wawl<br>kawrn wahl<br>kawn wawl ◊<br>kawn wuhl ◊ |
| **Cupid** | 'kju pɪd | kyoo pid |
| **Curan** | 'kʌ rən | kuh ruhn |
| **Dauphin/<br>Dolphin**<br>(see below) | 'dɔ fɪn<br>do 'fæn<br>[gen Am var] | daw fin<br>do fan<br>[gen Am var] |
| **Dolphin/<br>Dauphin**<br>(see below) | 'dɑl fɪn<br>'dɒl fɪn ◊ | dahl fin<br>dol fin ◊ |
| **Dover** | 'doʊ vɚ<br>'dəʊ və ◊ | do vər<br>do və ◊ |
| **Edgar** | 'ɛd gɚ<br>'ed gə ◊ | ed gər<br>ed gə ◊ |
| **Edmund** | 'ɛd mʌnd<br>'ed mʌnd ◊ | ed muhnd<br>... ◊ |
| **[de la] Far** | [dɛ lə] 'fɑr<br>[de lə] 'fɑ ◊ | [de luh] fahr<br>[de luh] fah ◊ |
| **Flibbertigibbet** | 'flɪ bɚ ti 'ʤɪ bɪt<br>'flɪ bə ti 'ʤɪ bɪt ◊ | fli bər tee ji bit<br>fli bə tee ji bit ◊ |
| **Fool** | 'ful | fool |

| NAME | INTERNATIONAL PHONETIC ALPHABET* | SIMPLIFIED PHONICS** |
|------|-----------------------------------|----------------------|
| France | 'fræns<br>'frɑns ◊ | frans<br>frahns ◊ |
| Frateretto | fræ tə 'rɛ to<br>fræ tə 're təʊ ◊ | fra tuh re to<br>… ◊ |
| Germany | 'dʒɝ mə ni<br>'dʒɜ mə ni ◊ | jər muh nee<br>jə muh nee ◊ |
| Gloucester | 'glɑ stɚ<br>'glɔ stɚ<br>'glɒ stə ◊ | glah stər<br>glaw stər<br>glo stə ◊ |
| Goneril | 'gɑ nə rəl<br>'gɑ nə rɪl<br>'gɒ nə rɪl ◊ | gah nuh ruhl<br>gah nuh ril<br>go nuh ril ◊ |
| Hecate | 'hɛ kɪt<br>'he kɪt ◊ | he kit<br>… ◊ |
| Hobbididence | hɑ bɪ 'dɪ dəns<br>hɒ bɪ 'dɪ dəns ◊ | hah bi di duhns<br>ho bi di duhns ◊ |
| Hopdance | 'hap dæns<br>'hɒp dɑns ◊ | hahp dans<br>hop dahns ◊ |
| Jove | 'dʒoʊv<br>'dʒəʊv ◊ | jov<br>… ◊ |
| Jug | 'dʒʌg | juhg |
| Juno | 'dʒu no<br>'dʒu nəʊ ◊ | joo no<br>… ◊ |
| Jupiter | 'dʒu pɪ tɚ<br>'dʒu pɪ tə ◊ | joo pi tər<br>joo pi tə ◊ |
| Kent | 'kɛnt<br>'kɛnt ◊ | kent<br>… ◊ |

| NAME | INTERNATIONAL PHONETIC ALPHABET* | SIMPLIFIED PHONICS** |
|------|-----------------------------------|----------------------|
| **Lear** | 'lir | leer |
| | 'lɪɚ | liər |
| | lɪə ◊ | liə ◊ |
| **Lipsbury** | 'lɪps bɛ ri | lips be ree |
| | 'lɪps bə ri ◊ | lips buh ree ◊ |
| **Mahu** | 'mɑ hu | mah hoo |
| **Merlin** | 'mɝ lɪn | mər lin |
| | 'mɜ lɪn ◊ | mə lin ◊ |
| **Modo** | 'moʊ do | mo do |
| | 'məʊ dəʊ ◊ | ... ◊ |
| **Nero** | 'ni ro | nee ro |
| | 'nɪə rəʊ ◊ | ni ro ◊ |
| **o'Bedlam** | ə 'bɛd ləm | uh bed luhm |
| | o 'bɛd ləm | o bed luhm |
| | ə 'bed ləm ◊ | ... ◊ |
| | o 'bed ləm ◊ | ... ◊ |
| **Obidicut** | o 'bɪ dɪ kət | o bi di kuht |
| **Oswald** | 'ɑz wɔld | ahz wawld |
| | 'ɒz wəld ◊ | *o*z wuhld ◊ |
| **Phoebus** | 'fi bəs | fee buhs |
| **Pigmy** | 'pɪg mi | pig mee |
| **Pillicock** | 'pɪ li kɑk | pi lee kahk |
| | 'pɪ li kɒk ◊ | pi lee k*o*k ◊ |
| **Regan** | 'ri gən | ree guhn |
| **Rowland** | 'roʊ lənd | ro luhnd |
| | 'ro lənd ◊ | ... ◊ |

179

# A Lover's Complaint

| NAME | INTERNATIONAL PHONETIC ALPHABET* | SIMPLIFIED PHONICS** |
|------|----------------------------------|----------------------|
| **Adonis** | ə 'dɑ nɪs | uh dah nis |
| | ə 'doʊ nɪs | uh do nis |
| | ə 'dəʊ nɪs ◊ | ... ◊ |
| **May** | 'meɪ | mei |

*International Phonetic Alphabet Pronunciation Key: (General American) i-see, happy, Juliet; ɪ-sit; eɪ-say; ɛ-set; æ-sat; ɑ-father; ʌ-sun; ə-about; ɔ-saw; oʊ-so; o-hero; ʊ-shook; u-soon; aɪ-sigh; ɔɪ-soy; aʊ-south; ju-cube; ɚ-supper; ɛr-fair; ɝ-bird; k-cut, kite; g-go; ʤ-joy; j-yes; ŋ-sing; ʃ-shoe; tʃ-chop; ð-that; θ-thin; ʒ-measure; (Additional symbols for British RP) e-set; ɛə-fair; ə-supper; ɜ-bird; ɒ-stop; əʊ-so, hero; o-(followed by l) pole.

**Simplified Phonics Pronunciation Key: (General American) ee-see, happy, i-sit; ei-say; e-set; a-sat; ah-father; uh-sun, about; aw-saw; o-so; oo-shook; oo-soon; ai-sigh; oy-soy; ow-south; yoo-cube; ər-bird, supper; k-cut, kite; g-go; j-joy; ng-sing; kw-quick; sh-shoe; ch-chop; th-that; th-thin; zh-measure; (Additional symbols for British RP) ə-bird; ə-supper; o-stop; ... indicates pronunciation variance too subtle for Simplified Phonics transcription see International Phonetic Alphabet transcription.

◊ British RP pronunciation-see Introduction.

| NAME | INTERNATIONAL PHONETIC ALPHABET* | SIMPLIFIED PHONICS** |
|------|----------------------------------|----------------------|
| **Abraham** | 'eɪ brə hæm | ei bruh ham |
| **Academe** -folio | 'æ kə dim | a kuh deem |
|    **Achademe** | æ kə 'dim | ... |
| **Achilles** | ə 'kɪ liz | uh ki leez |
| **Adam** | 'æd əm | a duhm |
| **Adriamadio** | eɪ dʒriə 'mɑ dio | ei jree uh mah dee o |
| | eɪ driə 'mɑ dio | ei dree uh mah dee o |
| | eɪ driə mɑ diəʊ ◊ | ... ◊ |
| **Adriana** | eɪ dʒri 'æ nə | ei jree a nuh |
| | eɪ dri 'æ nə | ei dree a nuh |
| | eɪ dʒri 'ɑ nə | ei jree ah nuh |
| | eɪ dri 'ɑ nə | ei dree ah nuh |
| **Adriano** | eɪ dʒri 'ɑ no | ei jree ah no |
| | eɪ dri 'ɑ no | ei dree ah no |
| | eɪ dri 'ɑ nəʊ ◊ | ... ◊ |
| **Ajax** | 'eɪ dʒæks | ei jaks |
| **Alençon** | æ lən 'soʊn | a luhn son |
| | ə 'lɛn sən | uh len suhn |
| | 'æ lən sɒn ◊ | a luhn son ◊ |
| | ə 'len sɒn ◊ | uh len son ◊ |
| **Alexander** | æ lɪg 'zæn dɚ | a lig zan dər |
| | æ lɪg 'zɑn də ◊ | a lig zahn də ◊ |

---

*International Phonetic Alphabet Pronunciation Key: (General American) i-s<u>ee</u>, happ<u>y</u>, Jul<u>i</u>et; ɪ-s<u>i</u>t; eɪ-s<u>ay</u>; ɛ-s<u>e</u>t; æ-s<u>a</u>t; ɑ-f<u>a</u>ther; ʌ-s<u>u</u>n; ə-<u>a</u>bout; ɔ-s<u>aw</u>; oʊ-s<u>o</u>; o-h<u>e</u>ro; u-s<u>oon</u>; aɪ-s<u>igh</u>; ɔɪ-s<u>oy</u>; aʊ-s<u>outh</u>; ju-c<u>u</u>be; ɚ-s<u>upper</u>; ɜr-f<u>air</u>; ɝ-b<u>ir</u>d; k-<u>c</u>ut, <u>k</u>ite; g-<u>g</u>o; dʒ-<u>j</u>oy; j-<u>y</u>es; ŋ-si<u>ng</u>; ʃ-<u>sh</u>oe; tʃ-<u>ch</u>op; ð-<u>th</u>at; θ-<u>th</u>in; ʒ-mea<u>s</u>ure; (Additional symbols for British RP) e-s<u>e</u>t; ɛə-f<u>air</u>; ə-s<u>upper</u>; ɜ-b<u>ir</u>d; ɒ-st<u>o</u>p; əʊ-s<u>o</u>, h<u>e</u>ro; o-(followed by l) p<u>o</u>le.

**Simplified Phonics Pronunciation Key: (General American) ee-s<u>ee</u>, happ<u>y</u>; i-s<u>i</u>t; ei-s<u>ay</u>; e-s<u>e</u>t; a-s<u>a</u>t; ah-f<u>a</u>ther; uh-s<u>u</u>n, <u>a</u>bout; aw-s<u>aw</u>; o-s<u>o</u>; oo-sh<u>oo</u>k; oo-s<u>oon</u>; ai-s<u>igh</u>; oy-s<u>oy</u>; ow-s<u>outh</u>; yoo-c<u>u</u>be; ər-b<u>ir</u>d, s<u>upper</u>; k-<u>c</u>ut, <u>k</u>ite; g-<u>g</u>o; j-<u>j</u>oy; ng-si<u>ng</u>; kw-<u>qu</u>ick; sh-<u>sh</u>oe; ch-<u>ch</u>op; th-<u>th</u>at; *th*-<u>th</u>in; zh-mea<u>s</u>ure; (Additional symbols for British RP) ə-b<u>ir</u>d; ə-s<u>upper</u>; <u>o</u>-st<u>o</u>p; ... indicates pronunciation variance too subtle for Simplified Phonics transcription see International Phonetic Alphabet transcription.

◊ British RP pronunciation-see Introduction.

| NAME | INTERNATIONAL PHONETIC ALPHABET* | SIMPLIFIED PHONICS** |
|---|---|---|
| **Alisander** | æ lı 'sæn dɚ<br>æ lı 'sɑn də ◊ | a li san dər<br>a li sahn də ◊ |
| **Anthony** | 'æn θə ni | an *th*uh nee |
| **Antony** | 'æn tə ni | an tuh nee |
| **Apollo** | ə 'pɑ lo<br>ə 'pɒ ləʊ ◊ | uh pah lo<br>uh p*o* lo ◊ |
| **Argus** | 'ɑr gəs<br>'ɑ gəs ◊ | ahr guhs<br>ah guhs ◊ |
| **[de] Armado** | [deɪ] ɑr 'mɑ do<br>[deɪ] ɑ 'mɑ dəʊ ◊ | [dei] ahr mah do<br>[dei] ah mah do ◊ |
| **Armatho** | ɑr 'mɑ ðo<br>ɑ 'mɑ ðəʊ ◊ | ahr mah tho<br>ah mah tho ◊ |
| **Arme** | 'ɑrm<br>'ɑm ◊ | ahrm<br>ahm ◊ |
| **Ate** | 'eɪ ti<br>'ɑ ti | ei tee<br>ah tee |
| **Bacchus** | 'bæ kəs<br>'bɑ kəs | ba kuhs<br>bah kuhs |
| **Berowne/Biron**<br>-folio **also,**<br>**Beroune** | bɪ 'run | bi roon |
| **Boyet** | bɔɪ 'ɛt<br>bɔɪ 'et ◊ | boy et<br>… ◊ |
| **Brabant** | brə 'bænt<br>'brɑ bənt | bruh bant<br>brah buhnt |
| **Britain** | 'brɪ tən | bri tuhn |

182

| NAME | INTERNATIONAL PHONETIC ALPHABET* | SIMPLIFIED PHONICS** |
|---|---|---|
| Caesar | 'si zɚ<br>'si zə ◊ | see zər<br>see zə ◊ |
| Cain | 'keɪn | kein |
| Cerberus | 'sɝ bə rəs<br>'sɜ bə rəs ◊ | sər buh ruhs<br>sə buh ruhs ◊ |
| Charles | 'tʃɑrlz<br>'tʃɑlz ◊ | chahrlz<br>chahlz ◊ |
| Christmas | 'krɪs məs | kris muhs |
| Cophetua | kə 'fɛ tʃu ə<br>kəʊ 'fe tju ə ◊ | kuh fe choo uh<br>ko fe tyoo uh ◊ |
| Costard | 'kɑ stɚd<br>'kɒ stəd ◊ | kah stərd<br>ko stəd ◊ |
| [Saint] Cupid | [seɪnt] 'kju pɪd<br>[sɪnt] 'kju pɪd ◊ | [seint] kyoo pid<br>[sint] kyoo pid ◊ |
| Dennis | 'dɛ nɪs<br>'de nɪs ◊ | de nis<br>... ◊ |
| Dick | 'dɪk | dik |
| Dictynna/<br>Dyctynna folio<br>Dictisima,<br>Dictima | dɪk 'tɪ nə | dik ti nuh |
| Dull | 'dʌl | duhl |
| Dumain | du 'meɪn<br>dju 'meɪn ◊ | doo mein<br>dyoo mein ◊ |
| Dutch | 'dʌtʃ | duhch |
| Ethiop | 'i θiɑp<br>'i θiɒp ◊ | ee *thee* ahp<br>ee *thee* op ◊ |

| NAME | INTERNATIONAL PHONETIC ALPHABET* | SIMPLIFIED PHONICS** |
|------|----------------------------------|----------------------|
| Ethiope | 'i θiop<br>'i θiəʊp ◊ | ee thee op<br>… ◊ |
| Eve | 'iv | eev |
| Faulconbridge/<br>  Falconbridge | 'fɔ kən brɪdʒ<br>'fɔl kən brɪdʒ<br>'fæl kən brɪdʒ<br>  [gen Am var] | faw kuhn brij<br>fawl kuhn brij<br>fal kuhn brij<br>  [gen Am var] |
| Fauste | 'faʊ steɪ<br>'fɔ sti | fow stei<br>faws tee |
| Ferdinand | 'fɝ dɪ nænd<br>'fɜ dɪ nənd ◊ | fər di nand<br>fə di nand ◊ |
| France | 'fræns<br>'frɑns ◊ | frans<br>frahns ◊ |
| Frances | 'fræn sɪs<br>'frɑn sɪs ◊ | fran sis<br>frahn sis ◊ |
| French | 'frɛntʃ<br>'frɛntʃ ◊ | french<br>… ◊ |
| George | 'dʒɔrdʒ<br>'dʒɔdʒ ◊ | jawrj<br>jawj ◊ |
| German | 'dʒɝ mən<br>'dʒɜ mən ◊ | jər muhn<br>jə muhn ◊ |
| Guinever/<br>  Guinover | 'gwɪ nə vɪr<br>'gwɪ nə vɪə ◊<br>'gɪ nə və ◊ | gwi nuh vir<br>gwi nuh viə ◊<br>gi nuh və ◊ |
| Hannibal | 'hæ nə bəl<br>'hæ nɪ bəl | ha nuh buhl<br>ha ni buhl |
| Hector | 'hɛk tɚ<br>'hek tə ◊ | hek tər<br>hek tə ◊ |

| NAME | INTERNATIONAL PHONETIC ALPHABET* | SIMPLIFIED PHONICS** |
|---|---|---|
| Hercules | 'hɝ kjə liz<br>'hɝ kju liz<br>'hɜ kjʊ liz ◊ | hər kyuh leez<br>hər kyoo leez<br>hə ky*oo* leez ◊ |
| Hesperides | hɛs 'pɛ rə diz<br>hɛs 'pɛ rɪ diz<br>hes 'pe rɪ diz ◊ | hes pe ruh deez<br>hes pe ri deez<br>... ◊ |
| Hiems | haɪ əmz | hai uhmz |
| Holofernes | 'hɑ lo fɝ niz<br>'hɒ ləʊ fə niz ◊ | hah lo fər neez<br>ho lo fə neez ◊ |
| Horace | 'hɔ rəs<br>'hɑ rəs<br>'hɒ rəs ◊ | haw ruhs<br>hah ruhs<br>ho ruhs ◊ |
| Ilion | 'ɪ liən<br>'aɪ liən | i lee uhn<br>ai lee uhn |
| Ind/Inde | 'ɪnd<br>'aɪnd | ind<br>aind |
| Iscariot | ɪs 'kæ riət | is ka ree uht |
| Jack -folio Iacke | 'ʤæk | jak |
| Jaquenetta | ʤæ kwə 'nɛ tə<br>ʤæ kə 'nɛ tə<br>ʤæ kə 'ne tə ◊ | ja kwuh ne tuh<br>ja kuh ne tuh<br>... ◊ |
| Jaques/Jacques | 'ʤeɪ kwiz | jei kweez |
| Jew | 'ʤu | joo |
| Joan -folio Ioane | 'ʤoʊn<br>'ʤəʊn ◊ | jon<br>... ◊ |
| Joshua | 'ʤɑ ʃuə<br>'ʤɒ ʃuə ◊<br>'ʤɒ ʃwə ◊ | jah shoo uh<br>jo sh*oo* uh ◊<br>jo shwuh ◊ |

185

| NAME | INTERNATIONAL PHONETIC ALPHABET* | SIMPLIFIED PHONICS** |
|---|---|---|
| Jove | 'dʒoʊv<br>'dʒəʊv ◊ | jov<br>… ◊ |
| Judas | 'dʒu dəs | joo duhs |
| Jude | 'dʒud | jood |
| Juno | 'dʒu noʊ<br>'dʒu nəʊ ◊ | joo no<br>… ◊ |
| Kate | 'keɪt | keit |
| Katherine | 'kæ θrɪn<br>'kæ θə rɪn | ka *th*rin<br>ka *th*uh rin |
| Latin | 'læ tən<br>'læ tɪn | la tuhn<br>la tin |
| Longaville | 'lɔ ŋə vɪl<br>'lɔŋ vaɪl<br>'lɒ ŋə vɪl ◊<br>'lɒŋ vaɪl ◊ | law nguh vil<br>lawng vail<br>l*o* nguh vil ◊<br>l*o*ng vail ◊ |
| Luna | 'lu nə | loo nuh |
| Maccabaeus -folio<br>  Machabeus | mæ kə 'bi əs<br>'mæ kə biz | ma kuh bee uhs<br>ma kuh beez |
| Mantuan | 'mæn tʃu ən<br>'mæn tju ən ◊ | man choo uhn<br>man ty*oo* uhn ◊ |
| Marcade/<br>  Mercade | 'mɑr kə di<br>'mɑ kə di ◊ | mahr kuh dee<br>mah kuh dee ◊ |
| Maria | mə 'ri ə<br>mə 'raɪ ə | muh ree uh<br>muh rai uh |
| Marian | 'mɛ riən<br>'mæ riən<br>'mɛə riən ◊ | me ree uhn<br>ma ree uhn<br>meə ree uhn ◊ |

| NAME | INTERNATIONAL PHONETIC ALPHABET* | SIMPLIFIED PHONICS** |
|---|---|---|
| **Mars** | 'mɑrz | mahrz |
| | 'mɑz ◊ | mahz ◊ |
| **Mediterranean** | mɛ dɪ tə 'reɪ niən | me di tuh rei nee uhn |
| | me dɪ tə 'reɪ niən ◊ | ... ◊ |
| **Mediterraneum** -can also be pronounced as **Mediterranean** -see above | mɛ dɪ tə 'reɪ niəm | me di tuh rei nee uhm |
| | mɛ dɪ tə reɪ niəm ◊ | ... ◊ |
| **Mercade/ Marcade** | 'mɑr kə di | mahr kuh dee |
| | 'mɑ kə di ◊ | mah kuh dee ◊ |
| **Mercury** | 'mɝ kjə ri | mər kyuh ree |
| | 'mɜ kjʊ ri ◊ | mə ky*oo* ree ◊ |
| **Monarcho** | mɑ 'nɑr ko | mah nahr ko |
| | mə 'nɑr ko | muh nahr ko |
| | mɒ 'nɑ kəʊ ◊ | m*o* nah ko ◊ |
| | mə 'nɑ kəʊ ◊ | muh nah ko ◊ |
| **Moor** | 'mur | moor |
| | 'mʊɝ | m*oo*ər |
| | 'mʊə ◊ | m*oo*ə ◊ |
| **Moth** | 'mɔθ | maw*th* |
| | 'mɒθ ◊ | m*oth* ◊ |
| **Muscovite** | 'mʌs kə vaɪt | muhs kuh vait |
| **Muscovy** | 'mʌs kə vi | muhs kuh vee |
| **[Ovidus] Naso** | 'neɪ zo | nei zo |
| | 'nɑ so | nah so |
| | 'neɪ zəʊ ◊ | ... ◊ |
| | 'nɑ səʊ ◊ | ... ◊ |
| **Nathaniel** | nə 'θæn jəl | nuh *th*an yuhl |

| NAME | INTERNATIONAL PHONETIC ALPHABET* | SIMPLIFIED PHONICS** |
|------|------|------|
| **Navarre** | nə 'vɑr | nuh vahr |
|  | nə 'vɑ ◊ | nuh vah ◊ |
| **Nemean** | 'ni miən | nee mee uhn |
|  | nɪ 'mi ən | nuh mee uhn |
| **Nestor** | 'nɛs tɚ | nes tər |
|  | 'ne stə ◊ | nes tə ◊ |
| **Normandy** | 'nɔr mən di | nawr muhn dee |
|  | 'nɔ mən di ◊ | naw muhn dee ◊ |
| **Ovidius [Naso]** | o 'vɪ diəs | o vi dee uhs |
|  | əʊ 'vɪ diəs ◊ | … ◊ |
| **Penelophon** -folio | pə 'nɛ lə fɑn | puh ne luh fahn |
|   **Zenelophon** | pə 'ne lə fɒn ◊ | puh ne luh fon ◊ |
| **Pepin** -folio | 'pɛ pɪn | pe pin |
|   also **Pippin** | 'pɪ pɪn | pi pin |
|  | 'pe pɪn ◊ | … ◊ |
| **Perigort** | 'pɛ rɪ gɔrt | pe ri gawrt |
|  | 'pe rɪ gɔt ◊ | pe ri gawt ◊ |
| **Phoebe** | 'fi bi | fee bee |
| **Pompey** | 'pɑm pi | pahm pee |
|  | 'pɒm pi ◊ | pom pee ◊ |
| **Pompion** | 'pɑm piən | pahm pee uhn |
|  | 'pɒm piən ◊ | pom pee uhn ◊ |
| **Priscian** | 'prɪ ʃiən | pri shee uhn |
| **Promethian** | prə 'mi θiən | pruh mee *th*ee uhn |
|  | pro 'mi θiən | pro mee *th*ee uhn |
|  | prəʊ 'mi θiən ◊ | … ◊ |
| **Roman** | 'roʊ mən | ro muhn |
|  | 'rəʊ mən ◊ | … ◊ |

188

| NAME | INTERNATIONAL PHONETIC ALPHABET* | SIMPLIFIED PHONICS** |
|------|----------------------------------|----------------------|
| **Rome** | 'roʊm<br>'rəʊm ◊ | rom<br>… ◊ |
| **Rosaline** | 'rɑ zə laɪn<br>'rɒ zə laɪn ◊ | rah zuh lain<br>ro zuh lain ◊ |
| **Russian** | 'rʌ ʃən | ruh shuhn |
| **Sampson** | 'sæmp sən | samp suhn |
| **Saturday** | 'sæ tɚ deɪ<br>'sæ tə di ◊ | sa tər dei<br>sa tə dee ◊ |
| **Soloman** | 'sɑ lə mən<br>'sɒ lə mən ◊ | sah luh muhn<br>so luh muhn ◊ |
| **Spain** | 'speɪn | spein |
| **Spaniard** | 'spæn jɚd<br>'spæn jəd ◊ | span yərd<br>span yəd ◊ |
| **Sphinx** | 'sfɪŋks | sfingks |
| **Timon** | 'taɪ mən | tai muhn |
| **Tom** | 'tɑm<br>'tɒm ◊ | tahm<br>tom ◊ |
| **Trojan/Troyan** | 'tʃroʊ ʤən<br>'troʊ ʤən<br>'trəʊ ʤən ◊ | chro juhn<br>tro juhn<br>… ◊ |
| **Troy** | 'trɔɪ<br>'tʃrɔɪ | troy<br>chroy |
| **Venetia** | və 'ni ʃiə<br>vɛ 'ni ʃiə<br>ve 'ni ʃiə ◊ | vuh nee shyuh<br>ve nee shyuh<br>… ◊ |
| **Venice** | 'vɛ nɪs<br>'ve nɪs ◊ | ve nis<br>… ◊ |

| NAME | INTERNATIONAL PHONETIC ALPHABET* | SIMPLIFIED PHONICS** |
|------|----------------------------------|----------------------|
| **Ver** | ˈvɝ | vər |
| | ˈvɜ ◊ | və ◊ |
| **Winter** | ˈwɪn tɚ | win tər |
| | ˈwɪn tə ◊ | win tə ◊ |
| **Zenelephon** | zə ˈnɛ lə fɑn | zuh ne luh fahn |
| | zə ˈne lə fɒn ◊ | zuh ne luh fon ◊ |

| NAME | INTERNATIONAL PHONETIC ALPHABET* | SIMPLIFIED PHONICS** |
|---|---|---|
| **Acheron** | 'æ kə rɑn<br>'æ kə rən<br>'æ kə rɒn ◊ | a kuh rahn<br>a kuh ruhn<br>a kuh ron ◊ |
| **Aleppo** | ə 'lɛ po<br>ə 'le pəʊ ◊ | uh le po<br>... ◊ |
| **Angus** | 'æŋ gəs | ang guhs |
| **Anthony** | 'æn θə ni | an *th*uh nee |
| **Antony** | 'æn tə ni | an tuh nee |
| **Arabia** | ə 'reɪ biə | uh rei bee uh |
| **Banquo** | 'bæŋ kwo<br>'bæŋ kwəʊ ◊ | bang kwo<br>... ◊ |
| **Beelzabub** | bi 'ɛl zɪ bəb<br>bi 'el zɪ bəb ◊ | bee el zi buhb<br>... ◊ |
| **Bellona** | bə 'loʊ nə<br>bə 'ləʊ nə ◊ | buh lo nuh<br>... ◊ |
| **Birnam** | 'bɝ nəm<br>'bɜ nəm ◊ | bər nuhm<br>bə nuhm ◊ |
| **Caesar** | 'si zɚ<br>'si zə ◊ | see zər<br>see zə ◊ |
| **Caithness** -folio<br>  **Cathnes** | 'keɪθ nɛs<br>'keɪθ nes ◊ | kei*th* nes<br>... ◊ |

*International Phonetic Alphabet Pronunciation Key: (General American) i-s<u>ee</u>, happ<u>y</u>, Jul<u>ie</u>t; ɪ-s<u>i</u>t; eɪ-s<u>ay</u>; ɛ-s<u>e</u>t; æ-s<u>a</u>t; ɑ-f<u>a</u>ther; ʌ-s<u>u</u>n; ə-<u>a</u>bout; ɔ-s<u>a</u>w; oʊ-s<u>o</u>; o-h<u>e</u>ro; ʊ-sh<u>oo</u>k; u-s<u>oo</u>n; aɪ-s<u>igh</u>; ɔɪ-s<u>oy</u>; aʊ-s<u>ou</u>th; ju-c<u>u</u>be; ɚ-s<u>upp</u>er; ɛr-f<u>air</u>; ɝ-b<u>ir</u>d; k-<u>c</u>ut, <u>k</u>ite; g-<u>g</u>o; ʤ-<u>j</u>oy; j-<u>y</u>es; ŋ-si<u>ng</u>; ʃ-<u>sh</u>oe; ʧ-<u>ch</u>op; ð-<u>th</u>at; θ-<u>th</u>in; ʒ-mea<u>s</u>ure; (Additional symbols for British RP) e-s<u>e</u>t; ɛə-f<u>air</u>; ə-s<u>upp</u>er; ɜ-b<u>ir</u>d; ɒ-s<u>to</u>p; əʊ-s<u>o</u>, h<u>e</u>ro; o-(followed by l) p<u>o</u>le.

**Simplified Phonics Pronunciation Key: (General American) ee-s<u>ee</u>, happ<u>y</u>; i-s<u>i</u>t; ei-s<u>ay</u>; e-s<u>e</u>t; a-s<u>a</u>t; ah-f<u>a</u>ther; uh-s<u>u</u>n, <u>a</u>bout; aw-s<u>aw</u>; o-s<u>o</u>; oo-sh<u>oo</u>k; oo-s<u>oo</u>n; ai-s<u>igh</u>; oy-s<u>oy</u>; ow-s<u>ou</u>th; yoo-c<u>u</u>be; ər-b<u>ir</u>d, s<u>upp</u>er; k-<u>c</u>ut, <u>k</u>ite; g-<u>g</u>o; j-<u>j</u>oy; ng-si<u>ng</u>; kw-<u>qu</u>ick; sh-<u>sh</u>oe; ch-<u>ch</u>op; th-<u>th</u>at; *th*-<u>th</u>in; zh-mea<u>s</u>ure; (Additional symbols for British RP) ə-b<u>ir</u>d; ə-s<u>upp</u>er; <u>o</u>-stop; ... indicates pronunciation variance too subtle for Simplified Phonics transcription see International Phonetic Alphabet transcription.

◊ British RP pronunciation-see Introduction.

| NAME | INTERNATIONAL PHONETIC ALPHABET* | SIMPLIFIED PHONICS** |
|------|----------------------------------|----------------------|
| Cawdor | 'kɔ dɚ<br>'kɔ də ◊ | kaw dər<br>kaw də ◊ |
| Christendom | 'krɪ sən dəm | kri suhn duhm |
| [Saint]<br>  Colme's Inch | [seɪnt] 'kal mɪz<br>[sɪnt] 'kɒl mɪz ◊ | [seint] kahl miz<br>[sint] kol miz ◊ |
| Colme-kill/<br>  Colmes-kill | 'koʊm kɪl<br>'kəʊm kɪl ◊ | kom kil<br>… ◊ |
| Cumberland | 'kʌm bɚ lənd<br>'kʌm bə lənd ◊ | kuhm bər luhnd<br>kuhm bə luhnd ◊ |
| Donalbain -folio e<br>  Donalbain | 'dɑ nəl beɪn<br>'dɒ nəl beɪn ◊ | dah nuhl bein<br>do nuhl bein ◊ |
| Duff | 'dʌf | duhf |
| Duncan | 'dʌŋ kən | duhng kuhn |
| Dunsinane | 'dʌn sɪ neɪn<br>dʌn 'sɪ neɪn<br>dʌn sɪ 'neɪn | duhn si nein<br>…<br>… |
| Edward | 'ɛd wɚd<br>'ed wəd ◊ | ed wərd<br>ed wəd ◊ |
| England | 'ɪŋ glənd | ing gluhnd |
| English | 'ɪŋ glɪʃ | ing glish |
| Fife | 'faɪf | faif |
| Fleance | 'fli əns<br>'fli ɑns | flee uhns<br>flee ahns |
| Forres/Fores<br>  -folio Soris | 'fɔ rɪs<br>'fɑ rɪs<br>'fɒ rɪs ◊ | faw ris<br>fah ris<br>fo ris ◊ |

| NAME | INTERNATIONAL PHONETIC ALPHABET* | SIMPLIFIED PHONICS** |
|------|------|------|
| French | 'frɛntʃ<br>'frɛntʃ ◊ | french<br>... ◊ |
| Glamis | 'glamz<br>'glɑ mɪs | glahmz<br>glah mis |
| Golgatha | 'gɑl gə θə<br>'gɒl gə θə ◊ | gahl guh *th*uh<br>gol guh *th*uh ◊ |
| Gorgan | 'gɔr gən<br>'gɔ gən ◊ | gawr guhn<br>gaw guhn ◊ |
| Harpier/Harper/<br>Harpy | 'hɑr piɚ<br>'hɑ piə ◊ | hahr pee ər<br>hah pee ə ◊ |
| Hecate | 'hɛ kɪt<br>'he kɪt ◊ | he kit<br>... ◊ |
| Hyrcan | 'hɝ kən<br>'hɜ kən ◊ | hər kuhn<br>hə kuhn ◊ |
| Inverness | ɪn vɚ 'nɛs<br>ɪn və 'nes ◊ | in vər nes<br>in və nes ◊ |
| Ireland | 'aɪ ɚ lənd<br>'aɪ ə lənd ◊ | ai ər luhnd<br>ai ə luhnd ◊ |
| Jew | 'ʤu | joo |
| Lennox | 'lɛ nəks<br>'le nəks ◊ | le nuhks<br>... ◊ |
| Macbeth | mæk 'bɛθ<br>mək 'bɛθ<br>mæk 'beθ ◊<br>mək 'beθ ◊ | mak be*th*<br>muhk be*th*<br>... ◊<br>... ◊ |
| MacDonwald | mək 'dɑ nəld<br>mæk 'dɑ nəld<br>mək 'dɒ nəld ◊<br>mæk 'dɒ nəld ◊ | muhk dah nuhld<br>mak dah nuhld<br>muhk do nuhld ◊<br>mak do nuhld ◊ |

| NAME | INTERNATIONAL PHONETIC ALPHABET* | SIMPLIFIED PHONICS** |
|---|---|---|
| Macduff | mæk ˈdʌf<br>mək ˈdʌf | mak duhf<br>muhk duhf |
| Malcom | ˈmæl kəm | mal kuhm |
| Mark | ˈmɑrk<br>ˈmɑk ◊ | mahrk<br>mahk ◊ |
| Menteith | mɛn ˈtiθ<br>men ˈtiθ | men tee*th*<br>… ◊ |
| Neptune | ˈnɛp tun<br>ˈnep tjun ◊ | nep toon<br>nep tyoon ◊ |
| Northumberland | nɔr ˈθʌm bɚ lənd<br><br>nɔ ˈθʌm bə lənd ◊ | nawr *th*uhm bər luhnd<br>naw *th*uhm bə luhnd ◊ |
| Norway | ˈnɔr weɪ<br>ˈnɔ weɪ ◊ | nawr wei<br>naw wei ◊ |
| Norweyan | nɔr ˈweɪ ən<br>nɔ ˈweɪ ən ◊ | nawr wei uhn<br>naw wei uhn ◊ |
| Roman | ˈroʊ mən<br>ˈrəʊ mən ◊ | ro muhn<br>… ◊ |
| Ross/Rosse | ˈrɔs<br>ˈrɒs ◊ | raws<br>r*o*s ◊ |
| Scotland | ˈskɑt lənd<br>ˈskɒt lənd ◊ | skaht luhnd<br>sk*o*t luhnd ◊ |
| Seyton | ˈsi tən | see tuhn |
| Sinel | ˈsaɪ nəl | sai nuhl |
| Siward | ˈsu ɚd<br>ˈsu əd ◊<br>ˈsi wəd ◊ | soo ərd<br>soo əd ◊<br>see wəd ◊ |

194

| NAME | INTERNATIONAL PHONETIC ALPHABET* | SIMPLIFIED PHONICS** |
|------|----------------------------------|----------------------|
| **Sweno** | 'swi no<br>'swi nəʊ ◊ | swee no<br>… ◊ |
| **Tarquin** | 'tɑr kwɪn<br>'tɑ kwɪn ◊ | tahr kwin<br>tah kwin ◊ |
| **Tartar** | 'tɑr tɚ<br>'tɑ tə ◊ | tahr tər˙<br>tah tə ◊ |
| **Tiger** | 'taɪ gɚ<br>'taɪ gə ◊ | tai gər<br>tai gə ◊ |
| **Tuesday** | 'tuz deɪ<br>'tjuz di ◊ | tooz dei<br>tyooz dee ◊ |
| **Turk** | tɝk<br>tɝk ◊ | tərk<br>tək ◊ |

# Measure For Measure

| NAME | INTERNATIONAL PHONETIC ALPHABET* | SIMPLIFIED PHONICS** |
|---|---|---|
| **Abhorson** | əb ˈhɔr sən<br>əb ˈhɔ sən ◊ | uh bawr suhn<br>uh baw suhn ◊ |
| **Angelo** | ˈæn ʤə lo<br>ˈæn ʤə ləʊ ◊ | an juh lo<br>… ◊ |
| **Balthasar/<br>  Balthazar** | bæl θə ˈzɑr<br>ˈbæl θə zɑr<br>bæl θə ˈzɑ ◊ | bal *th*uh zahr<br>…<br>bal *th*uh zah ◊ |
| **Barnadine** | ˈbɑr nə din<br>ˈbɑ nə din ◊ | bahr nuh deen<br>bah nuh deen ◊ |
| **Bohemia** | bo ˈhi miə<br>bəʊ ˈhi miə ◊ | bo hee mee uh<br>… ◊ |
| **Bohemian** | boʊ ˈhi miən<br>bəʊ ˈhi miən ◊ | bo hee mee uhn<br>… ◊ |
| **Bridget** | ˈbrɪ ʤɪt | bri jit |
| **Bunch of Grapes** | ˈbʌntʃ əv ˈgreɪps | buhnch uhv greips |
| **Caesar** | ˈsi zɚ<br>ˈsi zə ◊ | see zər<br>see zə ◊ |
| **Caper** | ˈkeɪ pɚ<br>ˈkeɪ pə ◊ | kei pər<br>kei pə ◊ |
| **Christian** | ˈkrɪs tʃən | kris chuhn |
| **[Saint] Clare** | [seɪnt] ˈklɛr<br>[sɪnt] ˈklɛə ◊ | [seint] kler<br>[sint] kleə ◊ |

| NAME | INTERNATIONAL PHONETIC ALPHABET* | SIMPLIFIED PHONICS** |
|---|---|---|
| Claudio | 'klɔ dio<br>'klɔ diəʊ ◊ | klaw dee o<br>... ◊ |
| Copper-spur | 'kɑ pɚ 'spɚ<br>'kɒ pə 'spɜ ◊ | kah pər spər<br>ko pə spə ◊ |
| Crassus | 'kræ səs | kra suhs |
| Deep-vow | 'dip 'vaʊ | deep vow |
| Dizy -folio Dizie | 'dɪ zi | di zee |
| Drop-heir | 'drɑp ɛr<br>'drɒp ɛə ◊ | drahp er<br>drop eə ◊ |
| Edward | 'ɛd wɚd<br>'ed wəd ◊ | ed wərd<br>ed wəd ◊ |
| Elbow | 'ɛl bo<br>'el bəʊ ◊ | el bo<br>... ◊ |
| English | 'ɪŋ glɪʃ | ing glish |
| Escalus | 'ɛs kə ləs<br>'es kə ləs ◊ | es kuh luhs<br>... ◊ |
| Flavius | 'fleɪ viəs | flei vee uhs |
| Forthright/<br>  Forthlight | 'fɔr θraɪt<br>'fɔ θraɪt ◊ | fawr thrait<br>faw thrait ◊ |
| Francisca | fræn 'sɪs kə | fran sis kuh |
| Frederick | 'frɛd rɪk<br>'frɛ də rɪk<br>'fred rɪk ◊<br>'fre də rɪk ◊ | fred rik<br>fre duh rik<br>... ◊<br>... ◊ |
| French | 'frɛntʃ<br>'frentʃ ◊ | french<br>... ◊ |

| NAME | INTERNATIONAL PHONETIC ALPHABET* | SIMPLIFIED PHONICS** |
|------|----------------------------------|----------------------|
| Friday | 'frai dei<br>'frai di ◊ | frai dei<br>frai dee ◊ |
| Froth | 'frɔθ<br>'frɑθ<br>'frɒθ ◊ | fraw*th*<br>frah*th*<br>fr*oth* ◊ |
| Halfcan | 'hæf kæn<br>'hɑf kæn ◊ | haf kan<br>hahf kan ◊ |
| Hallowmas | 'hæ lo mæs<br>'hæ ləʊ mæs ◊ | ha lo mas<br>... ◊ |
| Hannibal | 'hæ nə bəl<br>'hæ nɪ bəl | ha nuh buhl<br>ha ni buhl |
| [All] Holland | 'hɑ lənd<br>'hɒ lənd ◊ | hah luhnd<br>h*o* luhnd ◊ |
| Hungary | 'hʌŋ gə ri | huhng guh ree |
| Isabel | 'ɪ zə bɛl<br>'ɪ zə bel ◊ | i zuh bel<br>... ◊ |
| Isabella | ɪ zə 'bɛ lə<br>ɪ zə 'be lə ◊ | i zuh be luh<br>... ◊ |
| Jacob | 'ʤeɪ kəb | jei kuhb |
| Jewry | 'ʤu ri | joo ree |
| Jove | 'ʤoʊv<br>'ʤəʊv ◊ | jov<br>... ◊ |
| Juliet | 'ʤu liɛt<br>  [gen Am var]<br>'ʤu liet<br>  [Brit RP var]<br>'ʤu liət | joo lee et<br>  [gen Am var]<br>...<br>  [Brit RP var]<br>... |

| NAME | INTERNATIONAL PHONETIC ALPHABET* | SIMPLIFIED PHONICS** |
|------|------|------|
| **Julietta** | ʤu li 'ɛ tə<br>ʤu li 'e tə ◊ | joo lee e tuh<br>... ◊ |
| **Kate** | 'keɪt | keit |
| **Keepdown** | 'kip daʊn | keep down |
| **Lodowick** | 'loʊ də wɪk<br>'lɒ də wɪk ◊ | lo duh wik<br>lo duh wik ◊ |
| **Lucio** | 'lu ʧio<br>'lu ʧiəʊ ◊<br>'lu ʃio<br>'lu ʃiəʊ ◊<br>'lu sio<br>'lu siəʊ ◊ | loo chee o<br>... ◊<br>loo shee o<br>... ◊<br>loo see o<br>... ◊ |
| **[Saint] Luke** | [seɪnt] luk<br>[sɪnt] luk ◊ | [seint] look<br>[sint] look |
| **Mariana** | mæ ri 'æ nə<br>mɛ ri 'æ nə<br>mɛə ri 'ɑ nə ◊ | ma ree a nuh<br>me ree a nuh<br>me ree ah nuh ◊ |
| **Mitigation** | mɪ tə 'geɪ ʃən<br>mɪ tɪ 'geɪ ʃən | mi tuh gei shuhn<br>mi ti gei shuhn |
| **Overdone** | 'oʊ vɚ dən<br>'əʊ və dən ◊ | o vər duhn<br>o və duhn ◊ |
| **Peter** | 'pi tɚ<br>'pi tə ◊ | pee tər<br>pee tə ◊ |
| **Philip** | 'fɪ lɪp | fi lip |
| **Poland** | 'poʊ lənd<br>'po lənd ◊ | po luhnd<br>... ◊ |
| **Pompey** | 'pɑm pi<br>'pɒm pi ◊ | pahm pee<br>pom pee ◊ |

| NAME | INTERNATIONAL PHONETIC ALPHABET* | SIMPLIFIED PHONICS** |
|---|---|---|
| **Pots** | 'pɑts<br>'pɒts ◊ | pahts<br>pots ◊ |
| **Pudding** | 'pʊ dɪŋ | poo ding |
| **Pygmalion** | pɪg 'meɪ liən<br>pɪg meɪl jən | pig mei lee uhn<br>pig meil yuhn |
| **Ragozine** | 'ræ gə zin<br>'ræ gə zɪn | ra guh zeen<br>ra guh zin |
| **Rash** | 'ræʃ | rash |
| **Rome** | 'roʊm<br>'rəʊm ◊ | rom<br>… ◊ |
| **Rowland** | 'roʊ lənd<br>'ro lənd ◊ | ro luhnd<br>… ◊ |
| **Russia** | 'rʌ ʃə | ruh shuh |
| **Shoetie/Shoetye**<br>-folio **Shootie** | 'ʃu taɪ | shoo tai |
| **Starve-lackey** | 'stɑrv læ ki<br>'stɑv læ ki ◊ | stahrv la kee<br>stahv la kee ◊ |
| **Tapster** | 'tæp stɚ<br>'tæp stə ◊ | tap stər<br>tap stə ◊ |
| **Thomas** | 'tɑ məs<br>'tɒ məs ◊ | tah muhs<br>to muhs ◊ |
| **Three-pile** | 'θri paɪl | *th*ree pail |
| **Trot** | 'trɑt<br>'tʃrɑt<br>'trɒt ◊ | traht<br>chraht<br>trot ◊ |
| **Tuesday** | 'tuz deɪ<br>'tjuz di ◊ | tooz dei<br>tyooz dee ◊ |

| NAME | INTERNATIONAL PHONETIC ALPHABET* | SIMPLIFIED PHONICS** |
|------|-----------------------------------|----------------------|
| **Valencius** | və 'lɛn ʃəs | vuh len shuhs |
| **Valentinus** | væ lɛn 'taɪ nəs | va luhn tai nuhs |
| **Varrius** | 'væ riəs | va ree uhs |
| **Vienna** | vi 'ɛ nə | vee e nuh |
|  | vi 'e nə ◊ | vee e nuh ◊ |
| **Vincentio** | vɪn 'sɛn tio | vin sen tee o |
|  | vɪn 'sɛn tʃo | vin sen cho |
|  | vɪn 'sɛn ʃio | vin sen shee o |
|  | vɪn 'sen ʃiəʊ ◊ | ... ◊ |

| NAME | INTERNATIONAL PHONETIC ALPHABET* | SIMPLIFIED PHONICS** |
|------|----------------------------------|----------------------|
| **Abram** | 'ei brəm | ei bruhm |
| **Aeson** | 'i sən | ee suhn |
| **Alcides** | æl 'saɪ diz | al sai deez |
| **Andrew** | 'æn dru | an droo |
| | 'æn ʤru | an jroo |
| **Antonio** | æn 'toʊ nio | an to nee o |
| | æn 'təʊ niəʊ ◊ | ... ◊ |
| **April** | 'eɪ prəl | ei pruhl |
| **Arabia** | ə 'reɪ biə | uh rei bee uh |
| **Aragon/Arragon** | 'æ rə gɑn | a ruh gahn |
| | 'æ rə gən ◊ | a ruh guhn ◊ |
| **Argus** | 'ɑr gəs | ahr guhs |
| | 'ɑ gəs ◊ | ah guhs ◊ |
| **Balthasar/** | bæl θə 'zɑr | bal *th*uh zahr |
| **Balthazar** | 'bæl θə zɑr | bal *th*uh zahr |
| | bæl θə 'zɑ ◊ | bal *th*uh zah |
| **Barabas/** | 'bæ rə bəs | ba ruh buhs |
| **Barabbas** | bə 'ræ bəs | buh ra buhs |
| **Barbary** -folio | 'bɑr bə ri | bahr buh ree |
| **Barbarie** | 'bɑ bə ri ◊ | bah buh ree ◊ |

---

*International Phonetic Alphabet Pronunciation Key: (General American) i-s<u>ee</u>, happ<u>y</u>, Jul<u>i</u>et; ɪ-s<u>i</u>t; eɪ-s<u>ay</u>; ɛ-s<u>e</u>t; æ-s<u>a</u>t; ɑ-f<u>a</u>ther; ʌ-s<u>u</u>n; ə-<u>a</u>bout; ɔ-s<u>aw</u>; oʊ-s<u>o</u>; o-h<u>e</u>ro; ʊ-sh<u>oo</u>k; u-s<u>oo</u>n; aɪ-s<u>igh</u>; ɔɪ-s<u>oy</u>; aʊ-s<u>ou</u>th; ju-c<u>u</u>be; ə-supp<u>er</u>; ɛr-f<u>air</u>; ɝ-b<u>ir</u>d; k-<u>c</u>ut, <u>k</u>ite; g-go; ʤ-joy; j-<u>y</u>es; ŋ-si<u>ng</u>; ʃ-<u>sh</u>oe; ʧ-<u>ch</u>op; ð-<u>th</u>at; θ-<u>th</u>in; ʒ-mea<u>s</u>ure; (Additional symbols for British RP) e-s<u>e</u>t; ɛə-f<u>air</u>; ə-supp<u>er</u>; ɜ-b<u>ir</u>d; ɒ-st<u>o</u>p; əʊ-s<u>o</u>, h<u>e</u>ro; o-(followed by l) p<u>o</u>le.

**Simplified Phonics Pronunciation Key: (General American) ee-s<u>ee</u>, happ<u>y</u>; i-s<u>i</u>t; ei-s<u>ay</u>; e-s<u>e</u>t; a-s<u>a</u>t; ah-f<u>a</u>ther; uh-s<u>u</u>n, <u>a</u>bout; aw-s<u>aw</u>; o-s<u>o</u>; oo-sh<u>oo</u>k; oo-s<u>oo</u>n; ow-s<u>ou</u>th; yoo-c<u>u</u>be; ər-b<u>ir</u>d, supp<u>er</u>; k-<u>c</u>ut, <u>k</u>ite; g-go; j-joy; ng-si<u>ng</u>; kw-<u>qu</u>ick; sh-<u>sh</u>oe; ch-<u>ch</u>op; th-<u>th</u>at; *th*-<u>th</u>in; zh-mea<u>s</u>ure; (Additional symbols for British RP) ə-b<u>ir</u>d; ə-supp<u>er</u>; <u>o</u>-st<u>o</u>p; ... indicates pronunciation variance too subtle for Simplified Phonics transcription see International Phonetic Alphabet transcription.

◊ British RP pronunciation-see Introduction.

| NAME | INTERNATIONAL PHONETIC ALPHABET* | SIMPLIFIED PHONICS** |
|------|----------------------------------|----------------------|
| **Bassanio** | bə 'sɑ nio<br>bə 'sɑ nɪəʊ ◊ | buh sah nee o<br>… ◊ |
| **Bellario** -folio<br>   **Belario** | bə 'lɑ rio<br>bə 'lɑ rɪəʊ ◊ | buh lah ree o<br>… ◊ |
| **Belmont** | 'bɛl mɑnt<br>'bel mɒnt ◊ | bel mahnt<br>bel mont ◊ |
| **[le] Bon** | lə 'bɑn<br>lə 'bɒn ◊ | luh bahn<br>luh bon ◊ |
| **Caper** | 'keɪ pɚ<br>'keɪ pə ◊ | kei pər<br>kei pə ◊ |
| **Carthage** | 'kɑr θɪʤ<br>'kɑ θɪʤ ◊ | kahr *th*ij<br>kah *th*ij ◊ |
| **Cato** | 'keɪ toʊ<br>'keɪ təʊ ◊ | kei to<br>… ◊ |
| **Charybdis** | kə 'rɪb dɪs | kuh rib dis |
| **Christian** | 'krɪs ʧən | kris chuhn |
| **Colchos** | 'kɑl kɪs<br>'kɒl kɪs ◊ | kahl kis<br>kol kis ◊ |
| **Cressid** | 'krɛ sɪd<br>'kre sɪd ◊ | kre sid<br>… ◊ |
| **Cupid** | 'kju pɪd | kyoo pid |
| **Daniel** | 'dæn jəl | dan yuhl |
| **Dardanian** | dɑr 'deɪ nɪən<br>dɑ 'deɪ nɪən ◊ | dahr dei nee uhn<br>dah dei nee uhn ◊ |
| **Diana** | daɪ 'æ nə | dai a nuh |

| NAME | INTERNATIONAL PHONETIC ALPHABET* | SIMPLIFIED PHONICS** |
|------|-----------------------------------|----------------------|
| **Dido** | 'daɪ do<br>'daɪ dəʊ ◊ | dai do<br>… ◊ |
| **Dobbin** | 'dɑ bɪn<br>'dɒ bɪn ◊ | dah bin<br>do bin ◊ |
| **Endymion** | ɛn 'dɪ miən<br>en 'dɪ miən ◊ | en di mee uhn<br>en di mee uhn ◊ |
| **England** | 'ɪŋ glənd | ing gluhnd |
| **English** | 'ɪŋ glɪʃ | ing glish |
| **Erebus** | 'ɛ rə bəs<br>'e rɪ bəs ◊ | e ruh buhs<br>e ri buhs ◊ |
| **Faulconbridge/<br>Falconbridge** | 'fɔ kən brɪʤ<br>'fɔl kən brɪʤ<br>'fæl kən brɪʤ<br>    [gen Am var] | faw kuhn brij<br>fawl kuhn brij<br>fal kuhn brij<br>    [gen Am var] |
| **France** | 'fræns<br>'frɑns ◊ | frans<br>frahns ◊ |
| **Frankfort** | 'fræŋk fɚt<br>'fræŋk fət ◊ | frangk fərt<br>frangk fət ◊ |
| **French** | 'frɛnʧ<br>'frɛnʧ ◊ | french<br>… ◊ |
| **Friday** | 'fraɪ deɪ<br>'fraɪ di ◊ | frai dei<br>frai dee ◊ |
| **Genoa** -folio also<br>    **Genowa** | 'ʤɛ noə<br>'ʤe nəʊə ◊ | je no uh<br>… ◊ |
| **German** | 'ʤɝ mən<br>'ʤɜ mən ◊ | jər muhn<br>jə muhn ◊ |
| **Germany** | 'ʤɝ mə ni<br>'ʤɜ mə ni ◊ | jər muh nee<br>jə muh nee ◊ |

| NAME | INTERNATIONAL PHONETIC ALPHABET* | SIMPLIFIED PHONICS** |
|---|---|---|
| Gobbo | 'ɡɑ bo<br>'ɡɒ bəʊ ◊ | gah bo<br>go bo ◊ |
| Goodwin | 'ɡʊd wɪn | good win |
| Goodwin Sands | 'ɡʊd wɪn 'sændz | good win sandz |
| Gratiano | ɡræ ʃi 'ɑ no<br>ɡræ ʃi 'ɑ nəʊ ◊<br>ɡrɑt zi 'ɑ no<br>   [gen Am var] | gra shee ah no<br>… ◊<br>graht zee ah no<br>   [gen Am var] |
| Hagar | 'heɪ ɡɑr<br>'heɪ ɡɑ ◊ | hei gahr<br>he gah ◊ |
| Hebrew | 'hi bru | hee broo |
| Hercules | 'hɝ kjə liz<br>'hɝ kju liz<br>'hɜ kjʊ liz ◊ | hər kyuh leez<br>hər kyoo leez<br>hə kyoo leez ◊ |
| Hyrcanian | hɝ 'keɪ niən<br>hɜ 'keɪ niən ◊ | hər kei nee uhn<br>hə kei nee uhn ◊ |
| India | 'ɪn diə | in dee uh |
| Indian | 'ɪn diən | in dee uhn |
| Italian | ɪ 'tæl jən | i tal yuhn |
| Italy | 'ɪ tə li | i tuh lee |
| Jack | 'dʒæk | jak |
| Jacob | 'dʒeɪ kəb | jei kuhb |
| Janus | 'dʒeɪ nəs | jei nuhs |
| Jessica | 'dʒɛ sɪ kə<br>'dʒe sɪ kə ◊ | je si kuh<br>… ◊ |

| NAME | INTERNATIONAL PHONETIC ALPHABET* | SIMPLIFIED PHONICS** |
|------|----------------------------------|----------------------|
| Jew | ˈʤu | joo |
| Jewish | ˈʤu ɪʃ | joo ish |
| Latin | ˈlæ tən <br> ˈlæ tɪn | la tuhn <br> la tin |
| Launcelot | ˈlɔn sə lət <br> ˈlɑn sə lət | lawn suh laht <br> lahn suh laht |
| le Bon | lə ˈbɑn <br> lə ˈbɒn ◊ | luh bahn <br> luh bon ◊ |
| Leah | ˈliə | leeuh |
| Leonardo | li ə ˈnɑr do <br> liə ˈnɑ dəʊ ◊ | leeuh nahr do <br> leeuh nah do ◊ |
| Lichas | ˈlaɪ kəs | lai kuhs |
| Lisbon | ˈlɪz bən | liz buhn |
| Lorenzo | lə ˈrɛn zo <br> lə ˈren zəʊ ◊ <br> lo ˈrɛn zo <br> lɒ ˈren zəʊ ◊ | luh ren zo <br> … ◊ <br> lo ren zo <br> lo ren zo ◊ |
| Margery | ˈmɑr ʤə ri <br> ˈmɑ ʤə ri ◊ | mahr juh ree <br> mah juh ree ◊ |
| Mars | ˈmɑrz <br> ˈmɑz ◊ | mahrz <br> mahz ◊ |
| Medea | mɪ ˈdiə | mi dee uh |
| Mexico | ˈmɛk sɪ ko <br> ˈmek sɪ kəʊ ◊ | mek si ko <br> … ◊ |
| Midas | ˈmaɪ dəs | mai duhs |
| Montferrat | mɑnt fə ˈræt <br> mɒnt fə ˈræt ◊ | mahnt fuh rat <br> mont fuh rat ◊ |

206

| NAME | INTERNATIONAL PHONETIC ALPHABET* | SIMPLIFIED PHONICS** |
|------|-----------------------------------|----------------------|
| **Moor** | 'mur | moor |
| | 'mʊr | moor |
| | 'mʊə ◊ | mooə ◊ |
| **Morocco** -folio | mə 'rɑ ko | muh rah ko |
| **Moroco,** | mə 'rɒ kəʊ ◊ | muh ro ko ◊ |
| **Morocho,** | | |
| **Morrocho** | | |
| **Nazarite** | 'næ zə raɪt | na zuh rait |
| **Neapolitan** | niə 'pɑ lə tən | nee uh pah luh tuhn |
| | niə 'pɒ lɪ tən ◊ | nee uh po luh tuhn ◊ |
| **Nerissa** -folio | nɪə 'rɪ sə | nuh ri suh |
| **Nerrissa,** | nɪ 'rɪ sə | ni ri suh |
| **Nerrysa** | | |
| **Nestor** | 'nɛs tɚ | nes tər |
| | 'nes tə ◊ | nes tə ◊ |
| **Oracle** | 'ɔ rə kəl | aw ruh kuhl |
| | 'ɑ rə kəl | ah ruh kuhl |
| | 'ɒ rə kəl ◊ | o ruh kuhl ◊ |
| **Orpheus** | 'ɔr fiəs | awr fee uhs |
| | 'ɔr fjus | awr fyoos |
| | 'ɔ fjus ◊ | aw fyoos ◊ |
| **Padua** | 'pæ ʤu ə | pa joo uh |
| | 'pæ dju ə ◊ | pa dyoo uh ◊ |
| **Palatine** | 'pæ lə taɪn | pa luh tain |
| **Phoebus** | 'fi bəs | fee buhs |
| **Portia** | 'pɔr ʃə | pawr shuh |
| | 'pɔ ʃə ◊ | paw shuh ◊ |

| NAME | INTERNATIONAL PHONETIC ALPHABET* | SIMPLIFIED PHONICS** |
|---|---|---|
| **Pythagorus** | pə ˈθæ gə rəs<br>paɪ ˈθæ gə res ◊ | puh *tha* guh ruhs<br>pai *tha* guh ruhs ◊ |
| **Rhenish** | ˈrɛ nɪʃ<br>ˈre nɪʃ ◊ | re nish<br>… ◊ |
| **Rialto** | ri ˈæl to<br>rɪ ˈæl təʊ ◊ | ree al to<br>… ◊ |
| **Roman** | ˈroʊ mən<br>ˈrəʊ mən ◊ | ro muhn<br>… ◊ |
| **Rome** | ˈroʊm<br>ˈrəʊm ◊ | rom<br>… ◊ |
| **Salanio/Solanio** | sə ˈlɑ nio<br>sə ˈlɑ nɪəʊ ◊ | suh lah nee o<br>… ◊ |
| **Salarino** | sæ lə ˈri no<br>sæ lə ˈri nəʊ ◊ | sa luh ree no<br>… ◊ |
| **Salerio** | sə ˈlɛ ri o<br>sə ˈlɪə rɪəʊ ◊ | suh le ree o<br>… ◊ |
| **Saxony** | ˈsæk sə ni | sak suh nee |
| **Scylla** | ˈsɪ lə | si luh |
| **Shylock** | ˈʃaɪ lɑk<br>ˈʃaɪ lɒk ◊ | shai lahk<br>shai l*o*k ◊ |
| **Sibylla** | sɪ ˈbɪ lə | si bi luh |
| **Solanio/Salanio** | sə ˈlɑ nio<br>sə ˈlɑ nɪəʊ ◊ | suh lah nee o<br>… ◊ |
| **Solyman** | ˈsɑ lə mən<br>ˈsɒ lə mən ◊ | sah luh muhn<br>s*o* luh muhn ◊ |
| **Sophy** | ˈsoʊ fi<br>ˈsəʊ fi ◊ | so fee<br>… ◊ |

| NAME | INTERNATIONAL PHONETIC ALPHABET* | SIMPLIFIED PHONICS** |
|------|----------------------------------|----------------------|
| **Stephano** | stə 'fa no<br>ste 'fa nəʊ ◊ | stuh fah no<br>ste fah no ◊ |
| **Tartar** | 'tɑr tɚ<br>'ta tə ◊ | tahr tər<br>tah tə ◊ |
| **Thisbe** | 'θɪz bi | *th*iz bee |
| **Tripoli/Tripoly/ Tripolis** | 'trɪ pə li<br>'ʧrɪ pə li | tri puh lee<br>chri puh lee |
| **Troilus** | 'ʧrɔɪ ləs<br>'trɔɪ ləs<br>'trəʊɪ ləs ◊ | chroy luhs<br>troy luhs<br>... ◊ |
| **Trojan** | 'ʧroʊ ʤən<br>'troʊ ʤən<br>'trəʊ ʤən ◊ | chro juhn<br>tro juhn<br>... ◊ |
| **Troy** | 'trɔɪ<br>'ʧrɔɪ | troy<br>chroy |
| **Tubal** | 'tu bəl<br>'tju bəl ◊ | too buhl<br>tyoo buhl ◊ |
| **Turk** | 'tɚk<br>'tɜk ◊ | tərk<br>tək ◊ |
| **Varrius** | 'væ riəs | va ree uhs |
| **Venetian** | və 'ni ʃən<br>vɪ 'ni ʃən | vuh nee shuhn<br>vi nee shuhn |
| **Venice** | 'vɛ nɪs<br>'ve nɪs ◊ | ve nis<br>... ◊ |
| **Venus** | 'vi nəs | vee nuhs |
| **Wednesday** | 'wɛnz deɪ<br>'wenz di ◊ | wenz dei<br>wenz dee ◊ |

# The Merry Wives of Windsor

| NAME | INTERNATIONAL PHONETIC ALPHABET* | SIMPLIFIED PHONICS** |
|------|----------------------------------|----------------------|
| **Abraham** | 'eɪ brə hæm | ei bruh ham |
| **Actaeon** | æk 'ti ən | ak tee uhn |
| **Aesculapius** | ɛs kjə 'leɪ piəs | es kyuh lei pee uhs |
| | is kju 'leɪ piəs | ees kyoo lei pee uhs |
| **Aetna/Etna** | 'ɛt nə | et nuh |
| | 'et nə ◊ | ... ◊ |
| **Alice** | 'æ lɪs | a lis |
| **All Hallowmas** | ɔl 'hæ lo mæs | awl ha lo mas |
| | ɔl 'hæ ləʊ mæs ◊ | ... ◊ |
| **Amaimon/ Amamon** | ə 'meɪ mɑn | uh mei mahn |
| | ə 'meɪ mən | uh mei muhn |
| | ə 'meɪ mɒn ◊ | uh mei mon ◊ |
| **Anne** | 'æn | an |
| **Ape** | 'eɪp | eip |
| **April** | 'eɪ prəl | ei pruhl |
| **Babylon** | 'bæ bɪ lən | ba bi luhn |
| | 'bæ bə lɑn [gen Am var] | ba buh lahn [gen Am var] |
| **Banbury** | 'bæn bɛ ri | ban be ree |
| | 'bæn bə ri ◊ | ban buh ree ◊ |

---

*International Phonetic Alphabet Pronunciation Key: (General American) i-s<u>ee</u>, happ<u>y</u>, Jul<u>ie</u>t; ɪ-s<u>i</u>t; eɪ-s<u>ay</u>; ɛ-s<u>e</u>t; æ-s<u>a</u>t; ɑ-f<u>a</u>ther; ʌ-s<u>u</u>n; ə-<u>a</u>bout; ɔ-s<u>aw</u>; oʊ-s<u>o</u>; o-h<u>e</u>ro; ʊ-sh<u>oo</u>k; u-s<u>oo</u>n; aɪ-s<u>igh</u>; ɔɪ-s<u>oy</u>; aʊ-s<u>ou</u>th; ju-c<u>u</u>be; ɚ-s<u>upp</u>er; ɛr-f<u>air</u>; ɝ-b<u>ir</u>d; k-<u>c</u>ut, <u>k</u>ite; g-<u>g</u>o; ʤ-<u>j</u>oy; j-<u>y</u>es; ŋ-si<u>ng</u>; ʃ-<u>sh</u>oe; ʧ-<u>ch</u>op; ð-<u>th</u>at; θ-<u>th</u>in; ʒ-mea<u>s</u>ure; (Additional symbols for British RP) e-s<u>e</u>t; ɛə-f<u>air</u>; ə-s<u>upp</u>er; ɜ-b<u>ir</u>d; ɒ-st<u>o</u>p; əʊ-s<u>o</u>, h<u>e</u>ro; o-(followed by l) p<u>o</u>le.

**Simplified Phonics Pronunciation Key: (General American) ee-s<u>ee</u>, happ<u>y</u>; i-s<u>i</u>t; ei-s<u>ay</u>; e-s<u>e</u>t; a-s<u>a</u>t; ah-f<u>a</u>ther; uh-s<u>u</u>n, <u>a</u>bout; aw-s<u>aw</u>; o-s<u>o</u>; oo-sh<u>oo</u>k; oo-s<u>oo</u>n; ow-s<u>ou</u>th; yoo-c<u>u</u>be; ar-b<u>ir</u>d, s<u>upp</u>er; k-<u>c</u>ut, <u>k</u>ite; g-<u>g</u>o; j-<u>j</u>oy; ng-si<u>ng</u>; kw-<u>qu</u>ick; sh-<u>sh</u>oe; ch-<u>ch</u>op; th-<u>th</u>at; th-<u>th</u>in; zh-mea<u>s</u>ure; (Additional symbols for British RP) ə-b<u>ir</u>d; ə-s<u>upp</u>er; <u>o</u>-st<u>o</u>p; ... indicates pronunciation variance too subtle for Simplified Phonics transcription see International Phonetic Alphabet transcription.

◊ British RP pronunciation-see Introduction.

| NAME | INTERNATIONAL PHONETIC ALPHABET* | SIMPLIFIED PHONICS** |
|------|----------------------------------|----------------------|
| **Barbason** | 'bɑr bə sən<br>'bɑ bə sən ◊ | bahr buh suhn<br>bah buh suhn ◊ |
| **Bardolph** | 'bɑr dɑlf<br>'bɑ dɒlf ◊ | bahr dahlf<br>bah dolf ◊ |
| **Bead/Bede** | 'bid | beed |
| **Bohemian** | boʊ 'hi miən<br>bəʊ 'hi miən ◊ | bo hee mee uhn<br>… ◊ |
| **Brentford** -folio<br>**Brainford,<br>Braineford** | 'brɛnt fɚd<br>'brent fəd ◊ | brent fərd<br>brent fəd ◊ |
| **Bridget** | 'brɪ dʒɪt | bri jit |
| **Brook** | 'brʊk | brook |
| **Bucklersbury** | 'bʌk lɚz bɛ ri<br>'bʌk ləz bə ri ◊ | buh klərz be ree<br>buh kləz buh ree ◊ |
| **Caesar** | 'si zɚ<br>'si zə ◊ | see zər<br>see zə ◊ |
| **Caius** | 'kiz | keez |
| **Castalion/<br>Castilian** | kæ 'steɪ liən<br>kæ 'steɪl jən | ka stei lee uhn<br>ka steil yuhn |
| **Cataian** | kə 'teɪ ən | kuh tei uhn |
| **Christian** | 'krɪs tʃən | kris chuhn |
| **Colebrook** | 'koʊl brʊk<br>'kol brʊk ◊ | kol brook<br>kol brook ◊ |
| **Cotsall/Cotsale** | 'kɑt səl<br>'kɒt səl ◊ | kaht suhl<br>kot suhl ◊ |

211

| NAME | INTERNATIONAL PHONETIC ALPHABET* | SIMPLIFIED PHONICS** |
|------|-----------------------------------|----------------------|
| **Counter-gate** | 'kaʊn tɚ geɪt <br> 'kaʊn tə geɪt ◊ | kown tər geit <br> kown tə geit ◊ |
| **Cricket** | 'krɪ kɪt | kri kit |
| **Cupid** | 'kju pɪd | kyoo pid |
| **Datchet** | 'dæ tʃɪt | da chit |
| **Dutch** | 'dʌtʃ | duhch |
| **Edward** | 'ɛd wɚd <br> 'ed wəd ◊ | ed wərd <br> ed wəd ◊ |
| **England** | 'ɪŋ glənd | ing gluhnd |
| **English** | 'ɪŋ glɪʃ | ing glish |
| **Ephesian** | ɪ 'fi ʒən <br> ɪ 'fi ʒiən | i fee zhuhn <br> i fee zhee uhn |
| **Epicurian** | ɛ pɪ 'kju riən <br> ɛ pɪ kju 'ri ən <br> e pɪ kju 'riən ◊ | e pi kyoo ree uhn <br> ... <br> ... ◊ |
| **Ethiopian** | i θi 'oʊ piən <br> i θi 'əʊ piən ◊ | ee _thee_ o pee uhn <br> ... ◊ |
| **Etna/Aetna** | 'ɛt nə <br> 'et nə ◊ | et nuh <br> ... ◊ |
| **Eton** | 'i tən | ee tuhn |
| **Europa** | jʊ 'roʊ pə <br> jʊə 'rəʊ pə ◊ | _yoo_ ro puh <br> ... ◊ |
| **Evans** | 'ɛ vənz <br> 'e vənz ◊ | e vuhnz <br> ... ◊ |
| **Eve** | 'iv | eev |

| NAME | INTERNATIONAL PHONETIC ALPHABET* | SIMPLIFIED PHONICS** |
|------|----------------------------------|----------------------|
| **Falstaff** | 'fɔl stæf<br>'fɔl staf ◊ | fawl staf<br>fawl stahf ◊ |
| **Faustus** | 'faʊ stəs | fow stuhs |
| **Fenton** | 'fɛn tən<br>'fen tən ◊ | fen tuhn<br>... ◊ |
| **Fleming** | 'flɛ mɪŋ<br>'fle mɪŋ ◊ | fle ming<br>... ◊ |
| **Flemish** | 'flɛ mɪʃ<br>'fle mɪʃ ◊ | fle mish<br>... ◊ |
| **Ford** | 'fɔrd<br>'fɔd ◊ | fawrd<br>fawd ◊ |
| **France** | 'fræns<br>'frɑns ◊ | frans<br>frahns ◊ |
| **Francisco** | fræn 'sɪs ko<br>fræn 'sɪs kəʊ ◊ | fran sis ko<br>... ◊ |
| **Frank** | 'fræŋk | frangk |
| **French** | 'frɛntʃ<br>'frentʃ ◊ | french<br>... ◊ |
| **Frogmore** | 'frɑg mɔr<br>'frɒg mɔ ◊ | frahg mawr<br>frog maw ◊ |
| **Galen** | 'geɪ lən | gei luhn |
| **Gallia** | 'gæ liə | ga lee uh |
| **Garter [Inn]** | 'gɑr tɚ<br>'gɑ tə ◊ | gahr tər<br>gah tə ◊ |
| **Gaul** -folio **Gaule** | 'gɔl | gawl |

213

| NAME | INTERNATIONAL PHONETIC ALPHABET* | SIMPLIFIED PHONICS** |
|---|---|---|
| George | 'ʤɔrʤ<br>'ʤɔʤ ◊ | jawrj<br>jawj ◊ |
| German | 'ʤɝ mən<br>'ʤɜ mən ◊ | jər muhn<br>jə muhn ◊ |
| Germany | 'ʤɝ mə ni<br>'ʤɜ mə ni ◊ | jər muh nee<br>jə muh nee ◊ |
| Gloucester | 'glɑ stɚ<br>'glɔ stɚ<br>'glɒ stə ◊ | glah stər<br>glaw stər<br>glo stə ◊ |
| Gloucestershire | 'glɑ stɚ ʃɚ<br>'glɔ stɚ ʃɚ<br>'glɒ stə ʃə ◊ | glah stər shər<br>glaw stər shər<br>glo stə shə ◊ |
| Goliath | gə 'laɪ əθ | guh lai uh*th* |
| Greece | 'gris | grees |
| Guiana | gi 'æ nə<br>gi 'ɑ nə | gee a nuh<br>gee ah nuh |
| [All] Hallowmas | ɔl 'hæ lo mæs<br>ɔl 'hæ ləʊ mæs ◊ | awl ha lo mas<br>… ◊ |
| [Pickt] Hatch | 'pɪkt hæʧ | pikt hach |
| Hector | 'hɛk tɚ<br>'hek tə ◊ | hek tər<br>hek tə ◊ |
| Hecuba | 'hɛ kju bə<br>'he kjʊ bə ◊ | he kyoo buh<br>he ky*oo* buh ◊ |
| Hercules | 'hɝ kjə liz<br>'hɝ kju liz<br>'hɜ kjʊ liz ◊ | hər kyuh leez<br>hər kyoo leez<br>hə ky*oo* leez ◊ |
| Herne | 'hɝn<br>'hɜn ◊ | hərn<br>hən ◊ |

| NAME | INTERNATIONAL PHONETIC ALPHABET* | SIMPLIFIED PHONICS** |
|------|----------------------------------|----------------------|
| **Herod** | 'hɛ rəd<br>'he rəd ◊ | he ruhd<br>… ◊ |
| **Hibocrates** | hɪ 'ba krə tiz | hi bah kruh teez |
| **Hippocrates** | hɪ 'pa krə tiz<br>hɪ 'pɒ krə tiz ◊ | hi pah kruh teez<br>hi po kruh teez ◊ |
| **Hobgoblin** | 'hab ga blɪn<br>'hɒb gɒ blɪn ◊ | hahb gah blin<br>hob go blin ◊ |
| **Hugh** | 'hju | hyoo |
| **Hungarian/<br>    Gongarian** | hʌŋ 'gɛ riən<br>hʌŋ 'ge riən ◊ | huhng ge ree uhn<br>… ◊ |
| **Indies** | 'ɪn diz | in deez |
| **Irish** | 'aɪ rɪʃ | ai rish |
| **Jack** | 'ʤæk | jak |
| **Jamany/Jarmany** | 'ʤar mə ni<br>'ʤa mə ni ◊ | jahr muh nee<br>jah muh nee ◊ |
| **Jarteer/Jarterre** | 'ʒar tɛr<br>'ʒa teə ◊ | zhahr ter<br>zhah teə ◊ |
| **Jenny** | 'ʤɛ ni<br>'ʤe ni ◊ | je nee<br>je nee ◊ |
| **Job** | 'ʤoʊb<br>'ʤəʊb ◊ | job<br>… ◊ |
| **John** | 'ʤan<br>'ʤɒn ◊ | jahn<br>jon ◊ |
| **Jove** | 'ʤoʊv<br>'ʤəʊv ◊ | jov<br>… ◊ |

| NAME | INTERNATIONAL PHONETIC ALPHABET* | SIMPLIFIED PHONICS** |
|---|---|---|
| **Jupiter** | 'ʤu pɪ tɚ<br>'ʤu pɪ tə ◊ | joo pi tər<br>joo pi tə ◊ |
| **Keisar/Keiser** | 'kaɪ zɚ<br>'kaɪ zə ◊ | kai zər<br>kai zə ◊ |
| **Latin** | 'læ tən<br>'læ tɪn | la tuhn<br>la tin |
| **Leda** | 'li də | lee duh |
| **Lucifer** | 'lu sɪ fɚ<br>'lu sɪ fə ◊ | loo si fər<br>loo si fə ◊ |
| **Machiavel** | 'mæ kjə vɛl<br>mæ kiə 'vɛl<br>mæ kiə 'vel ◊ | ma kyuh vel<br>ma kee uh vel<br>... ◊ |
| **Maidenhead** | 'meɪ dən hɛd<br>'meɪ dən hed ◊ | mei duhn hed<br>... ◊ |
| **Mars** | 'mɑrz<br>'mɑz ◊ | mahrz<br>mahz ◊ |
| **May** | 'meɪ | mei |
| **Meg** | 'mɛg<br>'meg ◊ | meg<br>... ◊ |
| **Mephistopholus** | mɛ fɪ 'stɑ fə ləs<br>me fɪ 'stɒ fə ləs ◊ | me fi stah fuh luhs<br>me fi sto fuh luhs ◊ |
| **Michaelmas** | 'mɪ kəl məs | mi kuhl muhs |
| **[Yead] Miller** | 'jɛd 'mɪ lɚ<br>'jed 'mɪ lə ◊ | yed mi lər<br>yed mi lə ◊ |
| **Mock/<br>  Muck-water** | 'mɑk wɔ tɚ<br>'mɒk wɔ tə ◊ | mahk waw tər<br>mok waw tə ◊ |
| **Nan** | 'næn | nan |

| NAME | INTERNATIONAL PHONETIC ALPHABET* | SIMPLIFIED PHONICS** |
|------|----------------------------------|----------------------|
| Nym | 'nɪm | nim |
| Pabylon | 'pæ bə lən | pa buh luhn |
| Page | 'peɪʤ | peij |
| Pandarus | 'pæn də rəs | pan duh ruhs |
| Pede/Pead | 'pid | peed |
| Pelion | 'pɛ liən<br>'pe liən ◊ | pe lee uhn<br>... ◊ |
| Peter | 'pi tɚ<br>'pi tə ◊ | pee tər<br>pee tə ◊ |
| Pheezar/Phaesar<br>folio **Pheazar** | 'fi zɚ<br>'fi zə ◊ | fee zər<br>fee zə ◊ |
| Phrygian | 'frɪ ʤiən | fri jee uhn |
| Pickt Hatch | 'pɪkt hæʧ | pikt hach |
| Pistol | 'pɪ stəl | pi stuhl |
| Poins/Poines | 'pɔɪnz | poynz |
| Prat | 'præt | prat |
| Quickly | 'kwɪk li | kwik lee |
| Reading | 'rɛ dɪŋ<br>'re dɪŋ ◊ | re ding<br>... ◊ |
| Readins | 'rɛ dɪnz<br>'re dɪnz ◊ | re dinz<br>... ◊ |
| Ringwood | 'rɪŋ wʊd | ring wood |
| Robert | 'rɑ bɚt<br>'rɒ bət ◊ | rah bərt<br>ro bət ◊ |

217

| NAME | INTERNATIONAL PHONETIC ALPHABET* | SIMPLIFIED PHONICS** |
|------|----------------------------------|----------------------|
| **Robin** | 'rɑ bɪn <br> 'rɒ bɪn ◊ | rah bin <br> ro bin ◊ |
| **Rugby** | 'rʌg bi | ruhg bee |
| **Sackerson** | 'sæ kɚ sən <br> 'sæ kə sən ◊ | sa kər suhn <br> sa kə suhn ◊ |
| **Satan** | 'seɪ tən | sei tuhn |
| **Scarlet** | 'skɑr lɪt <br> 'skɑ lɪt ◊ | skahr lit <br> skah lit ◊ |
| **Shallow** | 'ʃæ lo <br> 'ʃæ ləʊ ◊ | sha lo <br> … ◊ |
| **Shortcake** | 'ʃɔrt keɪk <br> 'ʃɔt keɪk ◊ | shawrt keik <br> shawt keik ◊ |
| **Simple** | 'sɪm pəl | sim puhl |
| **Slender** | 'slɛn dɚ <br> 'slɛn də ◊ | slen dər <br> slen də ◊ |
| **Star-chamber** | 'stɑr 'ʧeɪm bɚ <br> 'stɑ 'ʧeɪm bə ◊ | stahr cheim bər <br> stah cheim bə ◊ |
| **Tartar** | 'tɑr tɚ <br> 'tɑ tə ◊ | tahr tər <br> tah tə ◊ |
| **Thames** | 'tɛmz <br> 'tɛmz ◊ | temz <br> … ◊ |
| **Thomas** | 'tɑ məs <br> 'tɒ məs ◊ | tah muhs <br> to muhs ◊ |
| **Troy** | 'trɔɪ <br> 'ʧrɔɪ | troy <br> chroy |
| **Turk** | 'tɝk <br> 'tɜk ◊ | tərk <br> tək ◊ |

| NAME | INTERNATIONAL PHONETIC ALPHABET* | SIMPLIFIED PHONICS** |
|------|----------------------------------|----------------------|
| **Venetian** | və 'ni ʃən<br>vɪ 'ni ʃən | vuh nee shuhn<br>vi nee shuhn |
| **Welsh** | 'wɛlʃ<br>'wɛlʃ ◊ | welsh<br>... ◊ |
| **William** | 'wɪl jəm | wil yuhm |
| **Windsor** | 'wɪn zɚ<br>'wɪn zə ◊ | win zər<br>win zə ◊ |
| **Yead Miller** | 'jɛd 'mɪ lɚ<br>'jed 'mɪ lə ◊ | yed mi lər<br>yed mi lə ◊ |

# A Midsummer Night's Dream

| NAME | INTERNATIONAL PHONETIC ALPHABET* | SIMPLIFIED PHONICS** |
|------|-------------------------------|---------------------|
| **Acheron** | 'æ kə ɑɑn<br>'æ kə rən<br>'æ kə rɒn ◊ | a kuh rahn<br>a kuh ruh<br>a kuh ron ◊ |
| **Aegle** | 'i gli | ee glee |
| **Amazon** | 'æ mə zɑn<br>'æ mə zɒn ◊ | a muh zahn<br>a muh zon ◊ |
| **Antiopa**<br>-folio **Atiopa** | æn 'taɪ ə pə | an tai uh puh |
| **Apollo** | ə 'pɑ lo<br>ə 'pɒ ləʊ ◊ | uh pah lo<br>uh po lo ◊ |
| **Ariadne** | æ ri 'æd ni | a ree ad nee |
| **Athenian** | ə 'θi niən | uh *thee* nee uhn |
| **Athens** | 'æ θɪnz<br>'æ θənz | a *th*inz<br>a *th*uhnz |
| **Aurora** | ə 'rɔ rə<br>ɔ 'rɔ rə | uh raw ruh<br>aw raw ruh |
| **Bacchanal** | bæ kə 'næl<br>'bæ kə næl<br>bɑ kə 'næl<br>[gen Am var] | ba kuh nal<br>ba kuh nal<br>bah kuh nal<br>[gen Am var] |
| **Bergomask** | 'bɝ gə mæsk<br>'bɜ gə mɑsk ◊ | bər guh mask<br>bə guh mahsk ◊ |

*International Phonetic Alphabet Pronunciation Key: (General American) i-s<u>ee</u>, happ<u>y</u>, Jul<u>i</u>et;
ɪ-s<u>i</u>t; eɪ-s<u>ay</u>; ɛ-s<u>e</u>t; æ-s<u>a</u>t; ɑ-f<u>a</u>ther; ʌ-s<u>u</u>n; ə-<u>a</u>bout; ɔ-s<u>aw</u>; oʊ-s<u>o</u>; o-h<u>e</u>ro; ʊ-sh<u>oo</u>k; u-s<u>oo</u>n;
aɪ-s<u>igh</u>; ɔɪ-s<u>oy</u>; aʊ-s<u>ou</u>th; ju-c<u>u</u>be; ɚ-s<u>u</u>pper; ɛr-f<u>air</u>; ɝ-b<u>ir</u>d; k-<u>c</u>ut, <u>k</u>ite; g-<u>g</u>o; dʒ-<u>j</u>oy; j-<u>y</u>es;
ŋ-si<u>ng</u>; ʃ-<u>sh</u>oe; tʃ-<u>ch</u>op; ð-<u>th</u>at; θ-<u>th</u>in; ʒ-mea<u>s</u>ure; (Additional symbols for British RP) e-s<u>e</u>t;
ɛə-f<u>air</u>; ə-s<u>u</u>pper; ɜ-b<u>ir</u>d; ɒ-st<u>o</u>p; əʊ-s<u>o</u>, h<u>e</u>ro; o-(followed by l) p<u>o</u>le.

**Simplified Phonics Pronunciation Key: (General American) ee-s<u>ee</u>, happ<u>y</u>; i-s<u>i</u>t; ei-s<u>ay</u>;
e-s<u>e</u>t; a-s<u>a</u>t; ah-f<u>a</u>ther; uh-s<u>u</u>n, ab<u>ou</u>t; aw-s<u>aw</u>; o-s<u>o</u>; oo-sh<u>oo</u>k; oo-s<u>oo</u>n; ai-s<u>igh</u>; oy-s<u>oy</u>;
ow-s<u>ou</u>th; yoo-c<u>u</u>be; ər-b<u>ir</u>d, s<u>u</u>pper; k-<u>c</u>ut, <u>k</u>ite; g-<u>g</u>o; j-<u>j</u>oy; ng-si<u>ng</u>; kw-<u>qu</u>ick; sh-<u>sh</u>oe;
ch-<u>ch</u>op; th-<u>th</u>at; th-<u>th</u>in; zh-mea<u>s</u>ure; (Additional symbols for British RP) ə-b<u>ir</u>d; ə-s<u>u</u>pper;
<u>o</u>-stop; ... indicates pronunciation variance too subtle for Simplified Phonics transcription
see International Phonetic Alphabet transcription.

◊ British RP pronunciation-see Introduction.

| NAME | INTERNATIONAL PHONETIC ALPHABET* | SIMPLIFIED PHONICS** |
|---|---|---|
| Bottom | 'bɑ təm<br>'bɒ təm ◊ | bah tuhm<br>bo tuhm ◊ |
| Cadmus | 'kæd məs | kad muhs |
| Carthage | 'kɑr θɪʤ<br>'kɑ θɪʤ ◊ | kahr *th*ij<br>kah *th*ij ◊ |
| Cobweb | 'kɑb wɛb<br>'kɒb web ◊ | kahb web<br>k*o*b web ◊ |
| Corin | 'kɔ rɪn<br>'kɑ rɪn<br>'kɒ rɪn ◊ | kaw rin<br>kah rin<br>k*o* rin ◊ |
| Crete | 'krit | kreet |
| Cupid | 'kju pɪd | kyoo pid |
| Daphne | 'dæf ni | daf nee |
| Demetrius | dɪ 'mi triəs<br>dɪ 'mi ʧriəs | di mee tree uhs<br>di mee chree uhs |
| Dian | 'daɪ ən<br>'daɪ æn | dai uhn<br>dai an |
| Diana | daɪ 'æ nə | dai a nuh |
| Egeus | i 'ʤi əs | ee jee uhs |
| Egypt | 'i ʤɪpt | ee jipt |
| Ercles | 'ɝ kliz<br>'ɜ kliz ◊ | ər kleez<br>ə kleez ◊ |
| Ethiop | 'i θiɑp<br>'i θiɒp ◊ | ee *th*ee ahp<br>ee *th*i *o*p ◊ |
| Ethiope | 'i θiop<br>'i θiəʊp ◊ | ee *th*ee op<br>… ◊ |

221

| NAME | INTERNATIONAL PHONETIC ALPHABET* | SIMPLIFIED PHONICS** |
|---|---|---|
| **Flute** | 'flut | floot |
| **Francis** | 'fræn sɪs<br>'frɑn sɪs ◊ | fran sis<br>frahn sis ◊ |
| **French** | 'frɛntʃ<br>'frɛntʃ ◊ | french<br>… ◊ |
| **Goodfellow** | 'gʊd fɛ lo<br>'gʊd fe ləʊ ◊ | good fe lo<br>… ◊ |
| **Hecate** | 'hɛ kɪt<br>'he kɪt ◊ | he kit<br>… ◊ |
| **Helen** | 'hɛ lən<br>'hɛ lɪn<br>'he lɪn ◊ | he luhn<br>he lin<br>… ◊ |
| **Helena** | 'hɛ lɪ nə<br>'he lɪ nə ◊ | he li nuh<br>… ◊ |
| **Hercules** | 'hɝ kjə liz<br>'hɝ kju liz<br>'hɜ kjʊ liz ◊ | hər kyuh leez<br>hər kyoo leez<br>hə kyoo leez ◊ |
| **Hermia** | 'hɝ miə<br>'hɜ miə ◊ | hər mee uh<br>hə mee uh ◊ |
| **Hero** | 'hi ro<br>'hɪə rəʊ ◊ | hee ro<br>hi ro ◊ |
| **Hiems**<br>  -folio **Hyem's** | 'haɪ əmz | hai uhmz |
| **Hippolyta** | hɪ 'pa lɪ tə<br>hɪ 'pɒ lɪ tə ◊ | hi pah li tuh<br>hi po li tuh ◊ |
| **Hobgobblin** | 'hab ga blɪn<br>'hɒb gɒ blɪn ◊ | hahb gah blin<br>hob go blin ◊ |
| **India** | 'ɪn diə | in dee uh |

222

| NAME | INTERNATIONAL PHONETIC ALPHABET* | SIMPLIFIED PHONICS** |
|------|----------------------------------|----------------------|
| **Indian** | 'ɪn diən | in dee uhn |
| **Jack** | 'dʒæk | jak |
| **Jew** | 'dʒu | joo |
| **Jill** | 'dʒɪl | jil |
| **Jove** | 'dʒoʊv 'dʒəʊv ◊ | jov ... ◊ |
| **Limander** | li 'mæn dɚ li 'mæn də ◊ | lee man dər lee man də ◊ |
| **Lion** | 'laɪ ən | lai uhn |
| **Lysander** | laɪ 'sæn dɚ laɪ 'sæn də ◊ | lai san dər lai san də ◊ |
| **May** | 'meɪ | mei |
| **Moth** | 'mɔθ 'mɒθ ◊ | maw*th* m*oth* ◊ |
| **Mustardseed** | 'mʌ stɚd sid 'mʌ stəd sid ◊ | muh stərd seed muh stəd seed ◊ |
| **Nedar** | 'ni dɚ 'ni də ◊ | nee dər nee də ◊ |
| **Neptune** | 'nɛp tun 'nep tjun ◊ | nep toon nep tyoon ◊ |
| **Nick/Nicke** | 'nɪk | nik |
| **Ninny** | 'nɪ ni | ni nee |
| **Ninus** | 'nai nəs | nai nuhs |

| NAME | INTERNATIONAL PHONETIC ALPHABET* | SIMPLIFIED PHONICS** |
|------|----------------------------------|----------------------|
| Oberon | 'oʊ bə rɑn | o buh rahn |
| | 'oʊ bə rən | o buh ruhn |
| | 'əʊ bə rɒn ◊ | o buh ron ◊ |
| | 'əʊ bə rən ◊ | ... ◊ |
| Peascod/ Peasecod | 'piz kɑd | peez kahd |
| | 'piz kɒd ◊ | peez kod ◊ |
| Peaseblossom | 'piz blɑ səm | peez blah suhm |
| | 'piz blɒ səm ◊ | peez blo suhm |
| Peregenia/ Perigounia -folio **Perginia** | pɛ rɪ 'dʒi niə | pe ri jee nee uh |
| | pe rɪ 'dʒi niə ◊ | ... ◊ |
| Peter | 'pi tɚ | pee tər |
| | 'pi tə ◊ | pee tə ◊ |
| Phibbus | 'fi bəs | fee buhs |
| | 'fɪ bəs ◊ | fi buhs ◊ |
| Phillida | 'fɪ lɪ də | fi li duh |
| Philomel | 'fɪ lə mɛl | fi luh mel |
| | 'fɪ lo mel ◊ | fi lo mel ◊ |
| Philomela | fɪ lə 'mi lə | fi luh mee luh |
| | fɪ lo 'mi lə | fi lo mee luh |
| Philostrate | 'fɪ lə streit | fi luh streit |
| Phoebe | 'fi bi | fee bee |
| Phoebus | 'fi bəs | fee buhs |
| Procrus | 'proʊ krəs | pro kruhs |
| | 'prɑ krəs | prah kruhs |
| | 'prəʊ krəs ◊ | ... ◊ |
| | 'prɒ krəs ◊ | pro kruhs ◊ |
| Puck | 'pʌk | puhk |

| NAME | INTERNATIONAL PHONETIC ALPHABET* | SIMPLIFIED PHONICS** |
|---|---|---|
| **Pyramus** | 'pɪ rə məs | pi ruh muhs |
| **Quince** | 'kwɪns | kwins |
| **Robin** | 'rɑ bɪn<br>'rɒ bɪn ◊ | rah bin<br>ro bin ◊ |
| **Shafalus** | 'ʃæ fə ləs | sha fuh luhs |
| **Snout** -folio<br> **Snowt** | 'snaʊt | snowt |
| **Snug** | 'snʌg | snuhg |
| **Sparta** | 'spɑr tə<br>'spɑ tə ◊ | spahr tuh<br>spah tuh ◊ |
| **Squash** | 'skwɑʃ<br>'skwɒʃ ◊ | skwahsh<br>skwosh ◊ |
| **Starvling** | 'stɑrv lɪŋ<br>'stɑv lɪŋ ◊ | stahrv ling<br>stahv ling ◊ |
| **Tartar** | 'tɑr tɚ<br>'tɑ tə ◊ | tahr tər<br>tah tə ◊ |
| **Taurus** | 'tɔ rəs<br>'tɑ rəs<br>[gen Am var] | taw ruhs<br>tah ruhs<br>[gen Am var] |
| **Thebes** | 'θibz | *th*eebz |
| **Theseus** | 'θi siəs | *th*ee see uhs |
| **Thessalian** | θə 'seɪ liən<br>θə 'seɪl jən | *th*uh sei lee uhn<br>*th*uh seil yuhn |
| **Thessaly** | 'θɛ sə li<br>'θe sə li ◊ | *th*e suh lee<br>... ◊ |
| **Thisbe/Thisby** | 'θɪz bi | *th*iz bee |

| NAME | INTERNATIONAL PHONETIC ALPHABET* | SIMPLIFIED PHONICS** |
|---|---|---|
| **Thisne** | 'θɪz ni | *th*iz nee |
| **Thracian** | 'θreɪ ʃən | *th*rei shuhn |
| **Titania** -folio<br>  **Tytania** | tɪ 'teɪ niə<br>tɪ 'tɑ niə<br>taɪ 'teɪ niə<br>taɪ 'tɑ niə | ti tei nee uh<br>ti tah nee uh<br>tai tei nee uh<br>tai tah nee uh |
| **Tom** | 'tɑm<br>'tɒm ◊ | tahm<br>tom ◊ |
| **Trojan** | 'ʧroʊ ʤən<br>'troʊ ʤən<br>'trəʊ ʤən ◊ | chro juhn<br>tro juhn<br>... ◊ |
| **[Saint] Valentine** | [seɪnt] 'væ lən taɪn<br>[sɪnt] 'væ lən taɪn ◊ | [seint] va luhn tain<br>[sint] va luhn tain ◊ |
| **Venus** | 'vi nəs | vee nuhs |
| **Wall** | 'wɔl | wawl |

| NAME | INTERNATIONAL PHONETIC ALPHABET* | SIMPLIFIED PHONICS** |
|------|----------------------------------|----------------------|
| **Adam** | 'æ dəm | a duhm |
| **Anthony** | 'æn θə ni | an *th*uh nee |
| **Antonio** | æn 'toʊ nio<br>æn 'təʊ niəʊ ◊ | an to nee o<br>... ◊ |
| **Antony** | 'æn tə ni | an tuh nee |
| **Aragon/Arragon** | 'æ rə gɑn<br>'æ rə gən<br>'æ rə gɒn ◊ | a ruh gahn<br>a ruh guhn<br>a ruh gon ◊ |
| **Asia** | 'eɪ ʒə<br>'eɪ ʃə ◊ | ei zhuh<br>ei shuh ◊ |
| **Ate** | 'eɪ ti<br>'ɑ ti | ei tee<br>ah tee |
| **Balthasar** -folio<br>**Iacke Wilson** | bæl θə 'zɑr<br>'bæl θə zɑr<br>bæl θə 'zɑ ◊ | bal *th*uh zahr<br>...<br>bal *th*uh zah ◊ |
| **Beatrice** | 'biə trɪs<br>'biə tʃrɪs | bee uh tris<br>bee uh chris |
| **Bel** | 'bɛl<br>'beɪl<br>'bel ◊ | bel<br>beil<br>bel ... ◊ |
| **Benedick** -folio<br>also **Benedicke,**<br>**Benedict** | 'bɛ nə dɪk<br>'be nɪ dɪk ◊ | be nuh dik<br>... ◊ |

*International Phonetic Alphabet Pronunciation Key: (General American) i-s<u>ee</u>, happ<u>y</u>, Jul<u>ie</u>t; ɪ-s<u>i</u>t; eɪ-s<u>ay</u>; ɛ-s<u>e</u>t; æ-s<u>a</u>t; ɑ-f<u>a</u>ther; ʌ-s<u>u</u>n; ə-<u>a</u>bout; ɔ-s<u>aw</u>; oʊ-s<u>o</u>; o-h<u>e</u>ro; ʊ-sh<u>oo</u>k; u-s<u>oo</u>n; aɪ-s<u>igh</u>; ɔɪ-s<u>oy</u>; aʊ-s<u>ou</u>th; ju-c<u>u</u>be; ɚ-s<u>uppe</u>r; ɛr-f<u>air</u>; ɝ-b<u>ir</u>d; k-<u>c</u>ut, <u>k</u>ite; g-<u>g</u>o; ʤ-<u>j</u>oy; j-<u>y</u>es; ŋ-si<u>ng</u>; ʃ-<u>sh</u>oe; ʧ-<u>ch</u>op; ð-<u>th</u>at; θ-<u>th</u>in; ʒ-mea<u>s</u>ure; (Additional symbols for British RP) e-s<u>e</u>t; ɛə-f<u>air</u>; ə-s<u>uppe</u>r; ɜ-b<u>ir</u>d; ɒ-st<u>o</u>p; əʊ-s<u>o</u>, h<u>e</u>ro; o-(followed by l) p<u>o</u>le.

**Simplified Phonics Pronunciation Key: (General American) ee-s<u>ee</u>, happ<u>y</u>; i-s<u>i</u>t; ei-s<u>ay</u>; e-s<u>e</u>t; a-s<u>a</u>t; ah-f<u>a</u>ther; uh-s<u>u</u>n, <u>a</u>bout; aw-s<u>aw</u>; o-s<u>o</u>; oo-sh<u>oo</u>k; oo-s<u>oo</u>n; ai-s<u>igh</u>; oy-s<u>oy</u>; ow-s<u>ou</u>th; yoo-c<u>u</u>be; ər-b<u>ir</u>d, s<u>uppe</u>r; k-<u>c</u>ut, <u>k</u>ite; g-<u>g</u>o; j-<u>j</u>oy; ng-si<u>ng</u>; kw-<u>qu</u>ick; sh-<u>sh</u>oe; ch-<u>ch</u>op; th-<u>th</u>at; *th*-<u>th</u>in; zh-mea<u>s</u>ure; (Additional symbols for British RP) ɚ-b<u>ir</u>d; ə-s<u>uppe</u>r; <u>o</u>-st<u>o</u>p; ... indicates pronunciation variance too subtle for Simplified Phonics transcription see International Phonetic Alphabet transcription.

◊ British RP pronunciation-see Introduction.

| NAME | INTERNATIONAL PHONETIC ALPHABET* | SIMPLIFIED PHONICS** |
|---|---|---|
| **Benedictus** | bɛ nɪ 'dɪk təs<br>be nɪ 'dɪk təs ◊ | be ni dik tuhs<br>… ◊ |
| **Borachio** | bə 'ra ʧio<br>bo 'ra ʧio<br>bəʊ 'ra ʧiəʊ ◊ | buh rah chee o<br>bo rah chee o<br>… ◊ |
| **Cham** | 'kæm | kam |
| **Christian** | 'krɪs ʧən | kris chuhn |
| **Claudio** | 'klɔ dio<br>'klɔ diəʊ ◊ | klaw dee o<br>… ◊ |
| **Comfect** | 'kʌm fɪt<br>'kɑm fɪt<br>  [gen Am var]<br>'kɒm fɪt<br>  [Brit RP var] | kuhm fit<br>kahm fit<br>  [gen Am var]<br>kom fit<br>  [Brit RP var] |
| **Conrade** | 'kɑn ræd<br>'kɒn ræd ◊ | kahn rad<br>kon rad ◊ |
| **Cupid** | 'kju pɪd | kyoo pid |
| **December** | di 'sɛm bɚ<br>dɪ 'sem bə ◊ | dee sem bər<br>di sem bə ◊ |
| **Deformed** | dɪ 'fɔrmd<br>dɪ 'fɔmd ◊ | di fawrmd<br>di fawmd ◊ |
| **Dian** | 'daɪ ən<br>'daɪ æn | dai uhn<br>dai an |
| **Diana** | daɪ 'æ nə | dai a nuh |
| **Disdain** | dɪs 'deɪn | dis dein |
| **Dogberry** | 'dɔg bɛ ri<br>'dɒg bə ri ◊ | dawg be ree<br>dog buh ree ◊ |

| NAME | INTERNATIONAL PHONETIC ALPHABET* | SIMPLIFIED PHONICS** |
|------|------|------|
| **Dutch** | 'dʌtʃ | duhch |
| **Ethiop** | 'i θiɑp | ee *thee* ahp |
| | 'i θiɒp ◊ | ee *thee* op ◊ |
| **Ethiope** | 'i θiop | ee *thee* op |
| | 'i θiəʊp ◊ | ... ◊ |
| **Europa** | jʊ 'roʊ pə | y*oo* ro puh |
| | jʊə 'rəʊ pə ◊ | ... ◊ |
| **February** | 'fɛ bru ɛ ri | fe br*oo* e ree |
| | 'fe brʊ ɛə ri ◊ | fe br*oo* e ree ◊ |
| **Florentine** | 'flɔ rən tin | flaw ruhn teen |
| | 'flɑ rən tin | flah ruhn teen |
| | 'flɒ rən taɪn ◊ | fl*o* ruhn tain ◊ |
| **Francis** | 'fræn sɪs | fran sis |
| | 'frɑn sɪs ◊ | frahn sis ◊ |
| **French** | 'frɛntʃ | french |
| | 'frentʃ ◊ | ... ◊ |
| **George** | 'dʒɔrdʒ | jawrj |
| | 'dʒɔdʒ ◊ | jawj ◊ |
| **German** | 'dʒɝ mən | jər muhn |
| | 'dʒɜ mən ◊ | jə muhn ◊ |
| **Hector** | 'hɛk tɚ | hek tər |
| | 'hek tə ◊ | hek tə ◊ |
| **Hercules** | 'hɝ kjə liz | hər ky*oo* leez |
| | 'hɝ kju liz | hər kyuh leez |
| | 'hɜ kjʊ liz ◊ | hə ky*oo* leez ◊ |
| **Hero** | 'hi ro | hee ro |
| | 'hɪə rəʊ ◊ | hiə ro ◊ |
| **Hugh** | 'hju | hjoo |

| NAME | INTERNATIONAL PHONETIC ALPHABET* | SIMPLIFIED PHONICS** |
|---|---|---|
| **Hymen** | 'haɪ mən<br>'haɪ men ◊ | hai muhn<br>hai men ◊ |
| **Italy** | 'ɪ tə li | i tuh lee |
| **Jack** | 'dʒæk | jak |
| **January** | 'dʒæn ju ɛ ri<br>'dʒæn jʊ ə ri ◊ | jan yoo e ree<br>jan yoo uh ree ◊ |
| **Jew** | 'dʒu | joo |
| **John** | 'dʒɑn<br>'dʒɒn ◊ | jahn<br>jon ◊ |
| **Jove** | 'dʒoʊv<br>'dʒəʊv ◊ | jov<br>… ◊ |
| **July** | dʒə 'laɪ | juh lai |
| **Lackbeard** | 'læk bɪrd<br>'læk bɪəd ◊ | lak bird<br>lak biəd ◊ |
| **Leander** | li 'æn dɚ<br>li 'æn də ◊ | lee an dər<br>lee an də ◊ |
| **Leonato** | liə 'nɑ to<br>liə 'nɑ təʊ ◊ | lee uh nah to<br>… ◊ |
| **Margeret** | 'mɑr grɪt<br>'mɑr gə rɪt<br>'mɑ grɪt ◊<br>'mɑ gə rɪt ◊ | mahr grit<br>mahr guh rit<br>mah grit ◊<br>mah guh rit ◊ |
| **May** | 'meɪ | mei |
| **Meg** | 'mɛg<br>'meg ◊ | meg<br>… ◊ |

| NAME | INTERNATIONAL PHONETIC ALPHABET* | SIMPLIFIED PHONICS** |
|---|---|---|
| **Messina** | mə 'si nə<br>mɛ 'si nə<br>me 'si nə ◊ | muh see nuh<br>me see nuh<br>... ◊ |
| **Milan** -folio<br>**Millaine** | mɪ 'læn<br>mɪ 'lɑn<br>'mɪ lən | mi lan<br>mi lahn<br>mi luhn |
| **Monday** | 'mʌn deɪ<br>'mʌn di ◊ | muhn dei<br>muhn dee ◊ |
| **Montanto/<br>Mountanto** | mɑn 'tɑn to<br>mɒn 'tæn təʊ ◊<br>mɒn 'tɑn təʊ ◊ | mahn tahn to<br>mon tan to ◊<br>mon tahn to ◊ |
| **Oatcake/Otecake** | 'oʊt 'keɪk<br>'əʊt 'keɪk ◊ | ot keik<br>... ◊ |
| **Padua** | 'pæ ʤu ə<br>'pæ dju ə ◊ | pa joo uh<br>pa dyoo uh ◊ |
| **Pedro** | 'pɛɪ dro<br>'peɪ ʤro<br>'pe drəʊ ◊<br>'pi drəʊ ◊ | pɛi dro<br>pei jro<br>pe dro ◊<br>pee dro ◊ |
| **[Saint] Peter** | [seɪnt] 'pi tɚ<br>[sɪnt] 'pi tə ◊ | [seint] pee tər<br>[sint] pee tə ◊ |
| **Pharoah** | 'fɛ ro<br>'fɛə rəʊ ◊ | fe ro<br>... ◊ |
| **Philemon** | fə 'li mən<br>fɪ 'li mɒn ◊ | fuh lee muhn<br>fi lee mon ◊ |
| **Phoebus** | 'fi bəs | fee buhs |
| **Pigmy** | 'pɪg mi | pig mee |
| **Prester John** | 'prɛ stɚ 'ʤɑn<br>'pre stə 'ʤɒn ◊ | pre stər jahn<br>pre stə jon ◊ |

| NAME | INTERNATIONAL PHONETIC ALPHABET* | SIMPLIFIED PHONICS** |
|------|----------------------------------|----------------------|
| **Saturn** | 'sæ tɚn<br>'sæ tən ◊ | sa tərn<br>sa tən ◊ |
| **Sea-Cole/Seacole** | 'si kol<br>'si ko | see kol<br>see ko |
| **Spaniard** | 'spæn jɚd<br>'spæn jəd ◊ | span yərd<br>span yəd ◊ |
| **Sunday** | 'sʌn deɪ<br>'sʌn di | suhn dei<br>suhn dee |
| **Troilus** | 'ʧrɔɪ ləs<br>'trɔɪ ləs<br>'trəʊɪ ləs ◊ | chroy luhs<br>troy luhs<br>… ◊ |
| **Tuesday** | 'tuz deɪ<br>'tjuz di ◊ | tooz dei<br>tyooz dee ◊ |
| **Turk** | 'tɝk<br>'tɜk ◊ | tərk<br>tək ◊ |
| **Ursula** | 'ɝ sə lə<br>'ɝs lə<br>'ɜ sə lə ◊<br>'ɜs lə ◊ | ər suh luh<br>ərs luh<br>ə suh luh ◊<br>əs luh ◊ |
| **Venice** | 'vɛ nɪs<br>'ve nɪs ◊ | ve nis<br>… ◊ |
| **Venus** | 'vi nəs | vee nuhs |
| **Verges** | 'vɝ ʤɪs<br>'vɝ ʤəs<br>'vɜ ʤɪs ◊<br>'vɜ ʤəs ◊ | vər jis<br>vər juhs<br>və jis ◊<br>və juhs ◊ |
| **Vulcan** | 'vʌl kən | vuhl kuhn |
| **Wilson**<br>(folio only) | 'wɪl sən | wil suhn |

| NAME | INTERNATIONAL PHONETIC ALPHABET* | SIMPLIFIED PHONICS** |
|---|---|---|
| **Aemilia/Emilia** | ɪ 'mi liə<br>ɪ 'mil jə | i mee lee uh<br>i meel yuh |
| **Aleppo** | ə 'lɛ po<br>ə 'le pəʊ ◊ | uh le po<br>… ◊ |
| **Almain** | 'æl meɪn | al mein |
| **Angelo** | 'æn ʤə lo<br>'æn ʤɪ ləʊ ◊ | an juh lo<br>an ji lo ◊ |
| **Anthropophagai** | æn θrə 'pɑ fə ʤaɪ<br><br>æn θrə 'pɒ fə ʤaɪ ◊ | an *th*ruh pah fuh jai<br>an *th*ruh po fuh jai ◊ |
| **Arabian** | ə 'reɪ biən | uh rei bee uhn |
| **Barbara/Barbary** (see below) | 'bɑr bə rə<br>'bɑ bə rə ◊ | bahr buh ruh<br>bah buh ruh ◊ |
| **Barbary** -folio **Barbarie** can also be pronounced as **Barbara** -see above | 'bɑr bə ri<br>'bɑ bə ri ◊ | bahr buh ree<br>bah buh ree ◊ |
| **Bianca** | bi 'æŋ kə<br>bi 'ɑŋ kə ◊ | bee ang kuh<br>bee ahng kuh ◊ |
| **Brabantio** | brə 'ban tio<br>brə 'bæn tio<br>brə 'bæn tiəʊ ◊<br>brə 'bæn ʃəʊ ◊ | bruh bahn tee o<br>bruh ban tee o<br>… ◊<br>bruh ban sho ◊ |

*International Phonetic Alphabet Pronunciation Key: (General American) i-s<u>ee</u>, happ<u>y</u>, J<u>u</u>liet; ɪ-s<u>i</u>t; eɪ-s<u>ay</u>; ɛ-s<u>e</u>t; æ-s<u>a</u>t; ɑ-f<u>a</u>ther; ʌ-s<u>u</u>n; ə-<u>a</u>bout; ɔ-s<u>aw</u>; oʊ-s<u>o</u>; o-h<u>e</u>ro; ʊ-sh<u>oo</u>k; u-s<u>oo</u>n; aɪ-s<u>igh</u>; ɔɪ-s<u>oy</u>; aʊ-s<u>ou</u>th; ju-c<u>u</u>be; ə-s<u>u</u>pper; ɛr-f<u>air</u>; ɜ-b<u>ir</u>d; k-<u>c</u>ut, <u>k</u>ite; g-<u>g</u>o; ʤ-<u>j</u>oy; j-<u>y</u>es; ŋ-si<u>ng</u>; ʃ-<u>sh</u>oe; ʧ-<u>ch</u>op; ð-<u>th</u>at; θ-<u>th</u>in; ʒ-mea<u>s</u>ure; (Additional symbols for British RP) e-s<u>e</u>t; ɛə-f<u>air</u>; ə-s<u>u</u>pper; ɜ-b<u>ir</u>d; ɒ-st<u>o</u>p; əʊ-s<u>o</u>, h<u>e</u>ro; o-(followed by l) p<u>o</u>le.

**Simplified Phonics Pronunciation Key: (General American) ee-s<u>ee</u>, happ<u>y</u>; i-s<u>i</u>t; ei-s<u>ay</u>; e-s<u>e</u>t; a-s<u>a</u>t; ah-f<u>a</u>ther; uh-s<u>u</u>n, <u>a</u>bout; aw-s<u>aw</u>; o-s<u>o</u>; oo-sh<u>oo</u>k; oo-s<u>oo</u>n; ai-s<u>igh</u>; oy-s<u>oy</u>; ow-s<u>ou</u>th; yoo-c<u>u</u>be; ər-b<u>ir</u>d, supp<u>er</u>; k-<u>c</u>ut, <u>k</u>ite; g-<u>g</u>o; j-<u>j</u>oy; ng-si<u>ng</u>; kw-<u>qu</u>ick; sh-<u>sh</u>oe; ch-<u>ch</u>op; th-<u>th</u>at; *th*-<u>th</u>in; zh-mea<u>s</u>ure; (Additional symbols for British RP) ə-b<u>ir</u>d; ə-s<u>u</u>pper; <u>o</u>-stop; … indicates pronunciation variance too subtle for Simplified Phonics transcription see International Phonetic Alphabet transcription.

◊ British RP pronunciation-see Introduction.

| NAME | INTERNATIONAL PHONETIC ALPHABET* | SIMPLIFIED PHONICS** |
|------|----------------------------------|----------------------|
| **Cassio** | 'kæ sio<br>'kæ siəʊ ◊ | ka see o<br>... ◊ |
| **Christian** | 'krɪs tʃən | kris chuhn |
| **Cupid** | 'kju pɪd | kyoo pid |
| **Cyprus** | 'saɪ prəs | sai pruhs |
| **Dane** | 'deɪn | dein |
| **Desdemon** | dɛz də 'moʊn<br>'dɛz də mon<br>dez dɪ 'məʊn ◊<br>'dez dɪ məʊn ◊ | dez duh mon<br>...<br>dez di mon ◊<br>... ◊ |
| **Desdemona** | dɛz də 'moʊ nə<br>dez dɪ 'məʊ nə ◊ | dez duh mo nuh<br>dez di mo nuh ◊ |
| **Dian** | 'daɪ ən<br>'daɪ æn | dai uhn<br>dai an |
| **Egyptian** | i 'dʒɪp ʃən | ee jip shuhn |
| **Emilia/Aemilia** | ɪ 'mi liə<br>ɪ 'mil jə | i mee lee uh<br>i meel yuh |
| **England** | 'ɪŋ glənd | ing gluhnd |
| **English** | 'ɪŋ glɪʃ | ing glish |
| **Florence** | 'flɔ rɪns | flaw rins |
| **Florentine** | 'flɔ rən tin<br>'flɑ rən tin<br>'flɒ rən taɪn ◊ | flaw ruhn teen<br>flah ruhn teen<br>flo ruhn tain ◊ |
| **German** | 'dʒɝ mən<br>'dʒɜ mən ◊ | jər muhn<br>jə muhn ◊ |

| NAME | INTERNATIONAL PHONETIC ALPHABET* | SIMPLIFIED PHONICS** |
|------|----------------------------------|----------------------|
| **Gratiano** | græ ʃi 'ɑ no<br>greɪ ʃi 'ɑ nəʊ ◊<br>grɑt zi 'ɑ no<br>[gen Am var] | gra shee ah no<br>grei shee ah no ◊<br>graht zee ah no<br>[gen Am var] |
| **Hallowmas** | 'hæ lo mæs<br>'hæ ləʊ mæs ◊ | ha lo mas<br>... ◊ |
| **Hellespont** | 'hɛ ləs pɑnt<br>'he lɪs pɒnt ◊ | he luhs pahnt<br>he lis pont ◊ |
| **Holland** | 'hɑ lənd<br>'hɒ lənd ◊ | hah luhnd<br>ho luhnd ◊ |
| **Hydra** | 'haɪ drə<br>'haɪ dʒrə | hai druh<br>hai jruh |
| **Iago** | i 'ɑ go<br>'jɑ go<br>i 'ɑ gəʊ ◊<br>'jɑ gəʊ ◊ | ee ah go<br>yah go<br>... ◊<br>... ◊ |
| **Indian/Judean**<br>-folio **Iudean** | 'ɪn diən | in dee uhn |
| **Isabel** | 'ɪ zə bɛl<br>'ɪ zə bel ◊ | i zuh bel<br>... ◊ |
| **Janus** | 'dʒeɪ nəs | jei nuhs |
| **Jove** | 'dʒoʊv<br>'dʒəʊv ◊ | jov<br>... ◊ |
| **Lodovico** | loʊ də 'vi ko<br>ləʊ də 'vi kəʊ ◊ | lo duh vee ko<br>... ◊ |
| **Luccicos/**<br>**Lucchese** | lu 'tʃi kəs | loo chee kuhs |
| **Marcus** | 'mɑr kəs<br>'mɑ kəs ◊ | mahr kuhs<br>mah kuhs ◊ |

| NAME | INTERNATIONAL PHONETIC ALPHABET* | SIMPLIFIED PHONICS** |
|------|-----------------------------------|----------------------|
| **Mauretania** | mɔ rə 'teɪ nɪə | maw ruh tei nee uh |
|  | mɑ rə 'teɪ nɪə | mah ruh tei nee uh |
|  | mɒ rə 'teɪ nɪə ◊ | mo ruh tei nee uh ◊ |
| **Michael** | 'maɪ kəl | mai kuhl |
| **Montano** | mɑn 'tæ no | mahn ta no |
|  | mɒn 'tæ nəʊ ◊ | mon ta no ◊ |
|  | mɒn 'tɑ nəʊ ◊ | mon tah no ◊ |
| **Moor** | 'mur | moor |
|  | 'mʊr | moor |
|  | 'mʊə ◊ | mooə ◊ |
| **Naples** | 'neɪ pəlz | nei puhlz |
| **Othello** | o 'θɛ lo | o *the* lo |
|  | ə 'θɛ lo | uh *the* lo |
|  | əʊ 'θe ləʊ ◊ | … ◊ |
|  | ɒ 'θe ləʊ ◊ | *o the* lo ◊ |
|  | ə 'θe ləʊ ◊ | … ◊ |
| **Ottoman** | 'ɑ tə mən | ah tuh muhn |
|  | 'ɒ tə mən ◊ | *o* tuh muhn ◊ |
| **Ottomites** | 'ɑ tə maɪts | ah tuh maits |
|  | 'ɒ tə maɪts ◊ | *o* tuh maits ◊ |
| **Palestine** | 'pæ lə staɪn | pa luh stain |
|  | 'pæ lɪ staɪn | pa li stain |
| **[Saint] Peter** | [seɪnt] 'pi tɚ | [seint] pee tər |
|  | [sɪnt] 'pi tə ◊ | [sint] pee tə ◊ |
| **Pontic/Ponticke** | 'pɑn tɪk | pahn tik |
|  | 'pɒn tɪk ◊ | p*o*n tik ◊ |

236

| NAME | INTERNATIONAL PHONETIC ALPHABET* | SIMPLIFIED PHONICS** |
|------|----------------------------------|----------------------|
| Promethean | prə 'mi θiən<br>pro 'mi θiən<br>prəʊ 'mi θiən ◊ | pruh mee *thee* uhn<br>pro mee *thee* uhn<br>… ◊ |
| Propontic/<br>  Propontick | pro 'pɑn tɪk<br>prəʊ 'pɒn tɪk ◊ | pro pahn tik<br>pro pon tik ◊ |
| Rhodes | 'roʊdz<br>'rəʊdz ◊ | rodz<br>… ◊ |
| Roderigo -folio<br>  Rodorigo | rɑ də 'ri go<br>rɒ də 'ri gəʊ ◊ | rah duh ree go<br>ro duh ree go ◊ |
| Roman | 'roʊ mən<br>'rəʊ mən ◊ | ro muhn<br>… ◊ |
| Sagittary | 'sæ ʤɪ tɛ ri<br>'sæ ʤɪ tɛə ri ◊ | sa ji te ree<br>… ◊ |
| Spain | 'speɪn | spein |
| Stephen | 'sti vən | stee vuhn |
| Tuesday | 'tuz deɪ<br>'tjuz di ◊ | tooz dei<br>tyooz dee ◊ |
| Turk | 'tɝk<br>'tɜk ◊ | tərk<br>tək ◊ |
| Venetian | və 'ni ʃən | vuh nee shuhn |
| Venice | 'vɛ nɪs<br>'ve nɪs ◊ | ve nis<br>… ◊ |
| Veronesa/<br>  Veronessa/<br>  Veronese -folio<br>  Verennessa | vɛ rə 'nɛ sə<br>ve rə 'ne sə ◊ | ve ruh ne suh<br>… ◊ |
| Wednesday | 'wɛnz deɪ<br>'wenz di ◊ | wenz dei<br>wenz dee ◊ |

## The Passionate Pilgrum

| NAME | INTERNATIONAL PHONETIC ALPHABET* | SIMPLIFIED PHONICS** |
|------|----------------------------------|----------------------|
| **Adon** | 'æ dɑn | a dahn |
| | 'æ don | a don |
| | 'æ dəʊn ◊ | ... ◊ |
| **Adonis** | ə 'dɑ nɪs | uh dah nis |
| | ə 'doʊ nɪs | uh do nis |
| | ə 'dəʊ nɪs ◊ | ... ◊ |
| **Corydon** | 'kɔ rɪ dən | kaw ri duhn |
| **Cytherea** | sɪ θə 'riə | si *th*uh ree uh |
| **Dowland** | 'daʊ lənd | dow luhnd |
| **English** | 'ɪŋ glɪʃ | ing glish |
| **Ethiop** | 'i θiap | ee *th*ee ahp |
| | 'i θiɒp ◊ | ee *th*ee op ◊ |
| **Ethiope** | 'i θiop | ee *th*ee op |
| | 'i θiəʊp ◊ | ... ◊ |
| **Juno** | 'ʤu no | joo no |
| | 'ʤu nəʊ ◊ | ... ◊ |
| **Mars** | 'mɑrz | mahrz |
| | 'mɑz ◊ | mahz ◊ |
| **May** | 'meɪ | mei |
| **Pandion** | 'pæn diən | pan dee uhn |
| **Philomela** | fɪ lə 'mi lə | fi luh mee luh |

*International Phonetic Alphabet Pronunciation Key: (General American) i-s<u>ee</u>, happ<u>y</u>, Jul<u>ie</u>t; ɪ-s<u>i</u>t; eɪ-s<u>ay</u>; ɛ-s<u>e</u>t; æ-s<u>a</u>t; ɑ-f<u>a</u>ther; ʌ-s<u>u</u>n; ə-<u>a</u>bout; ɔ-s<u>aw</u>; oʊ-s<u>o</u>; o-her<u>o</u>; ʊ-sh<u>oo</u>k; u-s<u>oo</u>n; aɪ-s<u>igh</u>; ɔɪ-s<u>oy</u>; aʊ-s<u>ou</u>th; ju-c<u>u</u>be; ə-s<u>upper</u>; ɛr-f<u>air</u>; ɝ-b<u>ir</u>d; k-<u>c</u>ut, <u>k</u>ite; g-<u>g</u>o; ʤ-<u>j</u>oy; j-<u>y</u>es; ŋ-si<u>ng</u>; ʃ-<u>sh</u>oe; ʧ-<u>ch</u>op; ð-<u>th</u>at; θ-<u>th</u>in; ʒ-mea<u>s</u>ure; (Additional symbols for British RP) e-s<u>e</u>t; ɛə-f<u>air</u>; ə-s<u>upper</u>; ɜ-b<u>ir</u>d; ɒ-s<u>to</u>p; əʊ-s<u>o</u>, her<u>o</u>; o-(followed by l) p<u>o</u>le.

**Simplified Phonics Pronunciation Key: (General American) ee-s<u>ee</u>, happ<u>y</u>; i-s<u>i</u>t; ei-s<u>ay</u>; e-s<u>e</u>t; ah-f<u>a</u>ther; uh-s<u>u</u>n, <u>a</u>bout; aw-s<u>aw</u>; o-s<u>o</u>; oo-sh<u>oo</u>k; oo-s<u>oo</u>n; ow-s<u>ou</u>th; yoo-c<u>u</u>be; ər-b<u>ir</u>d, s<u>upper</u>; k-<u>c</u>ut, <u>k</u>ite; g-<u>g</u>o; j-<u>j</u>oy; ng-si<u>ng</u>; kw-<u>qu</u>ick; sh-<u>sh</u>oe; ch-<u>ch</u>op; th-<u>th</u>at; *th*-<u>th</u>in; zh-mea<u>s</u>ure; (Additional symbols for British RP) ə-b<u>ir</u>d; ə-s<u>upper</u>; <u>o</u>-st<u>o</u>p; ... indicates pronunciation variance too subtle for Simplified Phonics transcription see International Phonetic Alphabet transcription.

◊ British RP pronunciation-see Introduction.

| NAME | INTERNATIONAL PHONETIC ALPHABET* | SIMPLIFIED PHONICS** |
|------|----------------------------------|----------------------|
| **Phoebus** | 'fi bəs | fee buhs |
| **Spencer** | 'spɛn sɚ<br>'spɛn sə ◊ | spen sər<br>spen sə ◊ |
| **Venus** | 'vi nəs | vee nuhs |

| NAME | INTERNATIONAL PHONETIC ALPHABET* | SIMPLIFIED PHONICS** |
|------|----------------------------------|----------------------|
| **Aesculapius** | ɛs kjə 'leɪ piəs | es kyuh lei pee uhs |
| | is kju 'leɪ piəs | ees kyoo lei pee uhs |
| **Antioch** | 'æn ti ɑk | an tee ahk |
| | 'æn tɪ ɒk ◊ | an tee *o*k ◊ |
| **Antiochus** | æn 'taɪ ə kəs | an tai uh kuhs |
| **Apollo** | ə 'pɑ lo | uh pah lo |
| | ə 'pɒ ləʊ ◊ | uh p*o* lo ◊ |
| **Bawd** | 'bɔd | bawd |
| **Boult** | 'boʊlt | bolt |
| | 'bolt ◊ | ... ◊ |
| **Cerimon** | 'sɛ rɪ mɑn | se ri mahn |
| | 'se rɪ mɒn ◊ | se ri m*o*n ◊ |
| **Cleon** | 'kli ɑn | klee ahn |
| | 'kli ɒn ◊ | klee *o*n ◊ |
| **Cupid** | 'kju pɪd | kyoo pid |
| **Cynthia** | 'sɪn θiə | sin *th*ee uh |
| **Dian** | 'daɪ ən | dai uhn |
| | 'daɪ æn | dai an |
| **Diana** | daɪ 'æ nə | dai a nuh |

| NAME | INTERNATIONAL PHONETIC ALPHABET* | SIMPLIFIED PHONICS** |
|---|---|---|
| **Dionyza** | dai ə 'naɪ zə | dai uh nai zuh |
| **Egyptian** | i 'dʒɪp ʃən | ee jip shuhn |
| **Ephesus/Ephess** | 'ɛ fɪ səs<br>'e fɪ səs ◊ | e fi suhs<br>… ◊ |
| **Escanes** | 'ɛs kə niz<br>'es kə niz ◊ | es kuh neez<br>… ◊ |
| **Ethiop** | 'i θiɑp<br>'i θiɒp ◊ | ee *thee* ahp<br>ee *thee* op ◊ |
| **Ethiope** | 'i θiop<br>'i θiəʊp ◊ | ee *thee* op<br>… ◊ |
| **Gower** | 'gaʊ ɚ<br>'gaʊ ə ◊ | gow ər<br>gow ə ◊ |
| **Greece** | 'gris | grees |
| **Helicane** | hɛ lɪ 'keɪn<br>'hɛ lɪ keɪn<br>he lɪ 'keɪn ◊<br>'hɛ lɪ keɪn ◊ | he li kein<br>he li kein<br>… ◊<br>… ◊ |
| **Helicanus** | hɛ lɪ 'keɪ nəs<br>he lɪ 'keɪ nəs ◊ | he li kei nuhs<br>… ◊ |
| **Hesperedes** | hɛ 'spɛ rə diz<br>he 'spe rɪ diz ◊ | he spe ruh deez<br>he spe ri deez ◊ |
| **Hymen** | 'haɪ mən | hai muhn |
| **Jove** | 'dʒoʊv<br>'dʒəʊv ◊ | jov<br>… ◊ |
| **Juno** | 'dʒu no<br>'dʒu nəʊ ◊ | joo no<br>… ◊ |
| **Leonine** | 'li ə naɪn | lee uh nain |

241

| NAME | INTERNATIONAL PHONETIC ALPHABET* | SIMPLIFIED PHONICS** |
|---|---|---|
| Lucina | lu 'si nə<br>lu 'ʧi nə<br>lu 'saɪ nə | loo see nuh<br>loo chee nuh<br>loo sai nuh |
| Lychorida | laɪ 'kɔ rɪ də<br>laɪ 'kɑ rɪ də<br>laɪ 'kɒ rɪ də ◊ | lai kaw ri duh<br>lai kah ri duh<br>lai ko ri duh ◊ |
| Lysimachus | laɪ 'sɪ mə kəs | lai si muh kuhs |
| Macedon | 'mæ sɪ dɑn<br>'mæ sɪ dən ◊ | ma si dahn<br>ma si duhn ◊ |
| Marina | mə 'ri nə | muh ree nuh |
| Mitylene/<br>  Mytelene | mɪ tə 'li ni<br>'mɪ tə lɪn<br>mɪ tɪ 'lɪ ni | mi tuh lee nee<br>mi tuh lin<br>mi ti li nee |
| Neptune | 'nɛp tun<br>'nep tjun ◊ | nep toon<br>nep tyoon ◊ |
| Nestor | 'nɛs tɚ<br>'nes tə ◊ | nes tər<br>nes tə ◊ |
| Nicander | naɪ 'kæn dɚ<br>naɪ 'kæn də ◊ | nai kan dər<br>nai kan də ◊ |
| Pandar | 'pæn dɚ<br>'pæn də ◊ | pan dər<br>pan də ◊ |
| Paphos | 'peɪ fɑs<br>'peɪ fɒs ◊ | pei fahs<br>pei fos ◊ |
| Patch Breech | 'pæʧ 'briʧ | pach breech |
| Pentapolis | pɛn 'tæ pə lɪs<br>pen 'tæ pə lɪs ◊ | pen ta puh lis<br>… ◊ |
| Pericles | 'pɛ rə kliz<br>'pe rɪ kliz ◊ | pe ruh kleez<br>pe ri kleez ◊ |

| NAME | INTERNATIONAL PHONETIC ALPHABET* | SIMPLIFIED PHONICS** |
|---|---|---|
| **Philemon** | fə 'li mən<br>fɪ 'li mɒn ◊ | fuh lee muhn<br>fi lee mon ◊ |
| **Philoten** | 'faɪ lo tɛn<br>'faɪ ləʊ ten ◊ | fai lo ten<br>... ◊ |
| **Pilch** | 'pɪltʃ | pilch |
| **Priapus** | praɪ 'eɪ pəs | prai ei puhs |
| **Simonides** | saɪ 'ma nə diz<br>saɪ 'mɒ nə diz ◊ | sai mah nuh deez<br>sai mo nuh deez ◊ |
| **Smooth** | 'smuð | smooth |
| **Spaniard** | 'spæn jɚd<br>'spæn jəd ◊ | span yərd<br>span yəd ◊ |
| **Spanish** | 'spæ nɪʃ | spa nish |
| **Sparta** | 'spɑr tə<br>'spɑ tə ◊ | spahr tuh<br>spah tuh ◊ |
| **Syria** | 'sɪ riə<br>'sɪə riə ◊ | si ree uh<br>siə ree uh ... ◊ |
| **Tarsus/Tharsus** | 'tɑr səs<br>'tɑ səs ◊ | tahr suhs<br>tah suhs ◊ |
| **Tellus** | 'tɛ ləs<br>'te ləs ◊ | te luhs<br>... ◊ |
| **Thaisa** | θeɪ 'ɪ sə | *th*ei i suh |
| **Thaliard** | 'θæl jɚd<br>'θæl jəd ◊ | *th*al yərd<br>*th*al yəd ◊ |
| **Tib** | 'tɪb | tib |

243

| NAME | INTERNATIONAL PHONETIC ALPHABET* | SIMPLIFIED PHONICS** |
|------|----------------------------------|----------------------|
| **Transilvanian/ Transylvanian** | træn sɪl 'veɪ niən<br>træn sɪl 'veɪn jən<br>tʃræn sɪl 'veɪn jən | tran sil vei nee uhn<br>tran sil vein yuhn<br>chran sil vein yuhn |
| **Trojan** | 'tʃroʊ ʤən<br>'troʊ ʤən<br>'trəʊ ʤən ◊ | chro juhn<br>tro juhn<br>... ◊ |
| **Tyre** | 'taɪr<br>'taɪə ◊ | tair<br>tai ə ◊ |
| **Tyrian** | 'tɪ riən<br>'tɪə riən ◊ | ti ree uhn<br>tiə ree uhn ... ◊ |
| **Tyrus** | 'taɪ rəs<br>'taɪ ə rəs ◊ | tai ruhs<br>tai ə ruhs ◊ |
| **Valdes** | 'væl dɪs | val dis |
| **Veroles/Verollus** | və 'rɑ ləs<br>və 'rɒ ləs ◊ | vuh rah luhs<br>vuh ro luhs ◊ |

# The Phoenix and the Turtle

| NAME | INTERNATIONAL PHONETIC ALPHABET* | SIMPLIFIED PHONICS** |
|------|----------------------------------|----------------------|
| **Arabian** | ə 'reɪ biən | uh rei bee uhn |
| **Phoenix** | 'fi nɪks | fee niks |

*International Phonetic Alphabet Pronunciation Key: (General American) i-s<u>ee</u>, happ<u>y</u>, Jul<u>i</u>et; ɪ-s<u>i</u>t; eɪ-s<u>ay</u>; ɛ-s<u>e</u>t; æ-s<u>a</u>t; ɑ-f<u>a</u>ther; ʌ-s<u>u</u>n; ə-<u>a</u>bout; ɔ-s<u>aw</u>; oʊ-s<u>o</u>; o-her<u>o</u>; ʊ-sh<u>oo</u>k; u-s<u>oo</u>n; aɪ-s<u>igh</u>; ɔɪ-s<u>oy</u>; aʊ-s<u>ou</u>th; ju-c<u>u</u>be; ɚ-supp<u>er</u>; ɛr-f<u>air</u>; ɝ-b<u>ir</u>d; k-<u>c</u>ut, <u>k</u>ite; g-<u>g</u>o; dʒ-<u>j</u>oy; j-<u>y</u>es; ŋ-si<u>ng</u>; ʃ-<u>sh</u>oe; tʃ-<u>ch</u>op; ð-<u>th</u>at; θ-<u>th</u>in; ʒ-mea<u>s</u>ure; (Additional symbols for British RP) e-s<u>e</u>t; ɛə-f<u>air</u>; ə-supp<u>er</u>; ɜ-b<u>ir</u>d; ɒ-st<u>o</u>p; əʊ-s<u>o</u>, her<u>o</u>; o-(followed by l) p<u>o</u>le.

**Simplified Phonics Pronunciation Key: (General American) ee-s<u>ee</u>, happ<u>y</u>; i-s<u>i</u>t; ei-s<u>ay</u>; e-s<u>e</u>t; a-s<u>a</u>t; ah-f<u>a</u>ther; uh-s<u>u</u>n, <u>a</u>bout; aw-s<u>aw</u>; o-s<u>o</u>; oo-sh<u>oo</u>k; oo-s<u>oo</u>n; ai-s<u>igh</u>; oy-s<u>oy</u>; ow-s<u>ou</u>th; yoo-c<u>u</u>be; ər-b<u>ir</u>d, supp<u>er</u>; k-<u>c</u>ut, <u>k</u>ite; g-<u>g</u>o; j-<u>j</u>oy; ng-si<u>ng</u>; kw-<u>qu</u>ick; sh-<u>sh</u>oe; ch-<u>ch</u>op; th-<u>th</u>at; th-<u>th</u>in; zh-mea<u>s</u>ure; (Additional symbols for British RP) ə-b<u>ir</u>d; ə-supp<u>er</u>; o-st<u>o</u>p; … indicates pronunciation variance too subtle for Simplified Phonics transcription see International Phonetic Alphabet transcription.

◊ British RP pronunciation-see Introduction.

# The Rape of Lucrece

| NAME | INTERNATIONAL PHONETIC ALPHABET* | SIMPLIFIED PHONICS** |
|------|------|------|
| **Achilles** | ə ˈkɪ liz | uh ki leez |
| **Aetna/Etna** | ˈɛt nə <br> ˈet nə ◊ | et nuh <br> … ◊ |
| **Ajax** | ˈeɪ ʤæks | ei jaks |
| **April** | ˈeɪ prəl | ei pruhl |
| **Ardea** | ˈɑr diə <br> ˈɑ diə ◊ | ahr dee uh <br> ah dee uh ◊ |
| **Brutus** | ˈbru təs | broo tuhs |
| **Capitol** | ˈkæ pɪ təl | ca pi tuhl |
| **Collatine** | ˈkɑ lə taɪn <br> ˈkɒ lə taɪn ◊ | kah luh tain <br> ko luh tain ◊ |
| **Collatinus** | kɑ lə ˈtaɪ nəs <br> kɒ lə ˈtaɪ nəs ◊ | kah luh tai nuhs <br> ko luh tai nuhs ◊ |
| **Collatium** | kə ˈleɪ ʃəm <br> kɒ ˈleɪ ʃəm ◊ | kuh lei shuhm <br> ko lei shuhm ◊ |
| **Dardan** | ˈdɑr dən <br> ˈdɑ dən ◊ | dahr duhn <br> dah duhn ◊ |
| **Etna/Aetna** | ˈɛt nə <br> ˈet nə ◊ | et nuh <br> … ◊ |
| **Greece** | ˈgris | grees |

*International Phonetic Alphabet Pronunciation Key: (General American) i-s_ee_, happy, Jul_ie_t; ɪ-s_i_t; eɪ-s_ay_; ɛ-s_e_t; æ-s_a_t; ɑ-f_a_ther; ʌ-s_u_n; ə-_a_bout; ɔ-s_aw_; oʊ-s_o_; o-h_e_ro; ʊ-sh_oo_k; u-s_oo_n; aɪ-s_igh_; ɔɪ-s_oy_; aʊ-s_ou_th; ju-c_u_be; ɚ-s_upp_er; ɛr-f_air_; ɝ-b_ir_d; k-_c_ut, _k_ite; g-_g_o; ʤ-_j_oy; j-_y_es; ŋ-si_ng_; ʃ-_sh_oe; ʧ-_ch_op; ð-_th_at; θ-_th_in; ʒ-mea_s_ure; (Additional symbols for British RP) e-s_e_t; ɛə-f_air_; ə-s_upp_er; ɜ-b_ir_d; ɒ-s_to_p; əʊ-s_o_, h_e_ro; o-(followed by l) p_o_le.

**Simplified Phonics Pronunciation Key: (General American) ee-s_ee_, happy; i-s_i_t; ei-s_ay_; e-s_e_t; a-s_a_t; ah-f_a_ther; uh-s_u_n, _a_bout; aw-s_aw_; o-s_o_; oo-sh_oo_k; oo-s_oo_n; ai-s_igh_; oy-s_oy_; ow-s_ou_th; yoo-c_u_be; ər-b_ir_d; supper; k-_c_ut, _k_ite; g-_g_o; j-_j_oy; ng-si_ng_; kw-_qu_ick; sh-_sh_oe; ch-_ch_op; th-_th_at; _th_-_th_in; zh-mea_s_ure; (Additional symbols for British RP) ə-b_ir_d; ə-s_upp_er; _o_-s_to_p; … indicates pronunciation variance too subtle for Simplified Phonics transcription see International Phonetic Alphabet transcription.

◊ British RP pronunciation-see Introduction.

| NAME | INTERNATIONAL PHONETIC ALPHABET* | SIMPLIFIED PHONICS** |
|------|----------------------------------|----------------------|
| **Greek** | 'grik | greek |
| **Hector** | 'hɛk tɚ<br>'hek tə ◊ | hek tər<br>hek tə ◊ |
| **Hecuba** | 'hɛ kju bə<br>'he kjʊ bə ◊ | he kyoo buh<br>he ky*oo* buh ◊ |
| **Henry** | 'hɛn ri<br>'hen ri ◊ | hen ree<br>… ◊ |
| **Ilion** | 'ɪ liən<br>'aɪ liən ◊ | i lee uhn<br>ai lee uhn ◊ |
| **Italy** | 'ɪ tə li | i tuh lee |
| **Jove** | 'dʒoʊv<br>'dʒəʊv ◊ | jov<br>… ◊ |
| **Junius** | 'dʒu niəs | joo nee uhs |
| **Lucrece** | 'lu kris<br>lu 'kris | loo krees<br>… |
| **Lucretia** | lu 'kri ʃə | loo kree shuh |
| **Lucretius** | lu 'kri ʃəs | loo kree shuhs |
| **Narcissus** | nɑr 'sɪ səs<br>nɑ 'sɪ səs ◊ | nahr si suhs<br>nah si suhs ◊ |
| **Nestor** | 'nɛs tɚ<br>'nes tə ◊ | nes tər<br>nes tə ◊ |
| **Orpheus** | 'ɔr fiəs<br>'ɔr fjus<br>'ɔ fjus ◊ | awr fee uhs<br>awr fyoos<br>aw fyoos ◊ |
| **Paris** | 'pæ rɪs | pa ris |

| NAME | INTERNATIONAL PHONETIC ALPHABET* | SIMPLIFIED PHONICS** |
|---|---|---|
| **Philomel** | 'fɪ lə mɛl<br>'fɪ ləʊ mel ◊ | fi luh mel<br>fi lo mel ◊ |
| **Phrygian** | 'frɪ ʤən | fri juhn |
| **Pluto** | 'plu to<br>'plu təʊ ◊ | ploo to<br>… ◊ |
| **Priam** | 'praɪ əm | prai uhm |
| **Publius** | 'pʌ bliəs | puh blee uhs |
| **Pyrrhus** | 'pɪ rəs<br>'pɪə rəs ◊ | pi ruhs<br>piə ruhs … ◊ |
| **Roman** | 'roʊ mən<br>'rəʊ mən ◊ | ro muhn<br>… ◊ |
| **Rome** | 'roʊm<br>'rəʊm ◊ | rom<br>… ◊ |
| **Sextus** | 'sɛks təs<br>'seks təs ◊ | seks tuhs<br>… ◊ |
| **Simois** | 'sɪ mə wɪs<br>'sɪ məʊ ɪs ◊ | si muh wis<br>si mo is ◊ |
| **Sinon** | 'saɪ nən | sai nuhn |
| **Southampton** | saʊθ 'hæmp tən<br>saʊ θæmp tən | sow*th* hamp tuhn<br>sow *th*amp tuhn |
| **Tantalus** | 'tæn tə luhs | tan tuh luhs |
| **Tarquin** | 'tɑr kwɪn<br>'tɑ kwɪn ◊ | tahr kwin<br>tah kwin ◊ |
| **Tarquinius** | tɑr 'kwɪ niəs<br>tɑ 'kwɪ niəs ◊ | tahr kwi nee uhs<br>tah kwi nee uhs ◊ |
| **Tereus** | 'ti rus | tee roos |

| NAME | INTERNATIONAL PHONETIC ALPHABET* | SIMPLIFIED PHONICS** |
|------|--------------------------------|----------------------|
| **Troilus** | 'tʃrɔɪ ləs<br>'trɔɪ ləs<br>'trəʊɪ ləs ◊ | chroy luhs<br>troy luhs<br>... ◊ |
| **Trojan** | 'tʃroʊ dʒən<br>'troʊ dʒən<br>'trəʊ dʒən ◊ | chro juhn<br>tro juhn<br>... ◊ |
| **Troy** | 'trɔɪ<br>'tʃrɔɪ | troy<br>chroy |
| **Tullius** | 'tʌ liəs | tuh lee uhs |
| **Ulysses** | ju 'lɪ siz | yoo li seez |
| **Venus** | 'vi nəs | vee nuhs |

# Richard the Second

| NAME | INTERNATIONAL PHONETIC ALPHABET* | SIMPLIFIED PHONICS** |
|------|----------------------------------|----------------------|
| **Abel** | 'eɪ bəl | ei buhl |
| **Abraham** | 'eɪ brə hæm | ei bruh ham |
| **Adam** | 'æ dəm | a duhm |
| **Alps** | 'ælps | alps |
| **Arundel** | 'æ rən dəl<br>ə 'rʌn dəl<br>[gen Am var] | a ruhn duhl<br>uh ruhn duhl<br>[gen Am var] |
| **Aumerle** | ɔ 'mɝl<br>ɔ 'məl ◊ | aw mərl<br>aw məl ◊ |
| **Bagot** | 'bæ gət | ba guht |
| **Barbary** | 'bɑr bə ri<br>'bɑ bə ri ◊ | bahr buh ree<br>bah buh ree ◊ |
| **Barkloughly [Castle]** | bɑrk 'loʊ li [kæ səl]<br>bak 'ləʊ li [kɑ səl] ◊ | bahrk lo lee<br>bahk lo lee ◊ |
| **Beaumond/ Beaumont** | 'boʊ mɑnd<br>'boʊ mənd<br>'bəʊ mənd ◊ | bo mahnd<br>bo muhnd<br>… ◊ |
| **Bennet** | 'bɛ nɪt<br>'be nɪt ◊ | be nit<br>… ◊ |

*International Phonetic Alphabet Pronunciation Key: (General American) i-s<u>ee</u>, happ<u>y</u>, Jul<u>ie</u>t; ɪ-s<u>i</u>t; eɪ-s<u>ay</u>; ɛ-s<u>e</u>t; æ-s<u>a</u>t; ɑ-f<u>a</u>ther; ʌ-s<u>u</u>n; ə-<u>a</u>bout; ɔ-s<u>aw</u>; oʊ-s<u>o</u>; o-h<u>e</u>ro; ʊ-sh<u>oo</u>k; u-s<u>oo</u>n; aɪ-s<u>igh</u>; ɔɪ-s<u>oy</u>; aʊ-s<u>outh</u>; ju-c<u>u</u>be; ɚ-s<u>upper</u>; ɛr-f<u>air</u>; ɝ-b<u>ir</u>d; k-<u>c</u>ut, <u>k</u>ite; g-<u>g</u>o; ʤ-<u>j</u>oy; j-<u>y</u>es; ŋ-si<u>ng</u>; ʃ-<u>sh</u>oe; ʧ-<u>ch</u>op; ð-<u>th</u>at; θ-<u>th</u>in; ʒ-mea<u>s</u>ure; (Additional symbols for British RP) e-s<u>e</u>t; ɛə-f<u>air</u>; ə-s<u>upper</u>; ɜ-b<u>ir</u>d; ɒ-st<u>o</u>p; əʊ-s<u>o</u>, h<u>e</u>ro; o-(followed by l) p<u>o</u>le.

**Simplified Phonics Pronunciation Key: (General American) ee-s<u>ee</u>, happ<u>y</u>; i-s<u>i</u>t; ei-s<u>ay</u>; e-s<u>e</u>t; a-s<u>a</u>t; ah-f<u>a</u>ther; uh-s<u>u</u>n, <u>a</u>bout; aw-s<u>aw</u>; o-s<u>o</u>; oo-sh<u>oo</u>k; oo-s<u>oo</u>n; ai-s<u>igh</u>; oy-s<u>oy</u>; ow-s<u>outh</u>; yoo-c<u>u</u>be; ər-b<u>ir</u>d, s<u>upper</u>; k-<u>c</u>ut, <u>k</u>ite; g-<u>g</u>o; j-<u>j</u>oy; ng-si<u>ng</u>; kw-<u>qu</u>ick; sh-<u>sh</u>oe; ch-<u>ch</u>op; th-<u>th</u>at; th-<u>th</u>in; zh-mea<u>s</u>ure; (Additional symbols for British RP) ə-b<u>ir</u>d; ə-s<u>upper</u>; o-st<u>o</u>p; … indicates pronunciation variance too subtle for Simplified Phonics transcription see International Phonetic Alphabet transcription.

◊ British RP pronunciation-see Introduction.

| NAME | INTERNATIONAL PHONETIC ALPHABET* | SIMPLIFIED PHONICS** |
|------|-----------------------------------|----------------------|
| **Berkeley/Berkley** | 'bɑrk li | bahrk lee |
| folio **Barkely,** | 'bɝˑk li | bərk lee |
| **Barkley,** | [gen Am var] | |
| **Berkley** | 'bɑk li ◊ | bahk lee ◊ |
| **[Port le] Blanc** | 'blɑŋk | blahngk |
| | 'blɒŋk ◊ | blongk ◊ |
| **Blunt/Blount** | 'blʌnt | bluhnt |
| **Bolingbroke** | 'ba lɪŋ brʊk | bah ling brook |
| -folio | 'boʊ lɪŋ brʊk | bo ling brook |
| **Bullingbrooke,** | 'bʊ lɪŋ brʊk ◊ | boo ling brook ◊ |
| **Bollingbrooke,** | 'bɒ lɪŋ brʊk ◊ | bo ling brook ◊ |
| **Bullinbroke** | | |
| **Bourdeaux/** | 'bɔr doʊ | bawr do |
| **Bordeaux** | bɔr 'doʊ | ... |
| | 'bɔ dəʊ ◊ | baw do ◊ |
| | bɔ 'dəʊ ◊ | ... ◊ |
| **Bristol [Castle]** | 'brɪ stəl [kæ səl] | bri stuhl [ka suhl] |
| -folio **Bristow** | 'brɪ stəl [kɑ səl] ◊ | bri stuhl [kah suhl] ◊ |
| **Britaigne/** | 'brɪ tən | bri tuhn |
| **Bretagne** | brə 'tæŋ | bruh tang |
| **Britany/Brittany** | 'brɪ tə ni | bri tuh nee |
| **Brocas** | 'brɑ kəs | brah kuhs |
| -folio **Broccas** | 'broʊ kəs | bro kuhs |
| | 'brɒ kəs ◊ | bro kuhs ◊ |
| | 'brəʊ kəs ◊ | ... ◊ |
| **Bushy** | 'bʊ ʃi | boo shee |
| **Caesar** | 'si zɚ | see zər |
| | 'si zə ◊ | see zə ◊ |
| **Cain** | 'keɪn | kein |

| NAME | INTERNATIONAL PHONETIC ALPHABET* | SIMPLIFIED PHONICS** |
|------|----------------------------------|----------------------|
| **Canterbury** | 'kæn tɚ bɛ ri<br>'kæn tə bə rɪ ◊ | kan tər be ree<br>kan tə buh ree ◊ |
| **Carlisle** -folio<br>   **Carlile** | kɑr 'laɪl<br>'kɑr laɪl<br>kɑ 'laɪl ◊ | kahr lail<br>…<br>kah lail ◊ |
| **Caucasus** | 'kɔ kə səs<br>'kɑ kə səs | kaw kuh suhs<br>kah kuh suhs |
| **Christ** | 'kraɪst | kraist |
| **Christian** | 'krɪs tʃən | kris chuhn |
| **Cicester/**<br>   **Cirenster** | 'sɪ sɪ tɚ<br>'sɪ sɪ tə ◊ | si si tər<br>si si tə ◊ |
| **Cobham** | 'kɑ bəm<br>'kɒ bəm ◊ | kah buhm<br>ko buhm ◊ |
| **Cotswold** | 'kats wəld<br>'kɒts wold ◊ | kahts wuhld<br>kots wold ◊ |
| **Coventry** | 'kʌ vən tri<br>'kʌ vən tʃri<br>'kɒ vən tri ◊ | kuh vuhn tree<br>kuh vuhn chree<br>ko vuhn tree ◊ |
| **December** | di 'sɛm bɚ<br>dɪ 'sɛm bə ◊ | dee sem bər<br>di sem bə ◊ |
| **Derby** | 'dɑr bi<br>'dɝ bi<br>'dɑ bi ◊ | dahr bee<br>dər bee<br>dah bee ◊ |
| **Eden** | 'i dən | ee duhn |
| **Edmund** | 'ɛd mʌnd<br>'ed mʌnd ◊ | ed muhnd<br>… ◊ |
| **Edward** | 'ɛd wɚd<br>'ed wəd ◊ | ed wərd<br>ed wəd ◊ |

| NAME | INTERNATIONAL PHONETIC ALPHABET* | SIMPLIFIED PHONICS** |
|---|---|---|
| **Ely** | 'i li | ee lee |
| **England** | 'ɪŋ glənd | ing gluhnd |
| **English** | 'ɪŋ glɪʃ | ing glish |
| **Erpingham** | 'ɝ pɪŋ hæm<br>'ɝ pɪŋ əm ◊ | ər ping ham<br>ə ping uhm ◊ |
| **Eve** | 'iv | eev |
| **Exeter** | 'ɛk sɪ tɚ<br>'ek sɪ tə ◊ | ek si tər<br>ek si tə ◊ |
| **Exton** | 'ɛks tən<br>'eks tən ◊ | eks tuhn<br>... ◊ |
| **Fitzwater** | fits 'wɔ tɚ<br>'fɪts wɔ tɚ<br>fɪts 'wɔ tə ◊ | fits waw tər<br>...<br>fits waw tə ◊ |
| **Flint [Castle]** | 'flɪnt [kæ səl]<br>'flɪnt [kɑ səl] ◊ | flint [ka suhl]<br>flint [kah suhl] ◊ |
| **Francis** | 'fræn sɪs<br>'frɑn sɪs ◊ | fran sis<br>frahn sis ◊ |
| **French** | 'frɛntʃ<br>'frɛntʃ ◊ | french<br>... ◊ |
| **Gaunt** | 'gɔnt | gawnt |
| **Glendower** -folio<br>    **Glendoure** | 'glɛn daʊ ɚ<br>glɛn 'daʊ ɚ<br>'glen daʊ ə ◊<br>glen 'daʊ ə ◊ | glen dow ər<br>...<br>glen dow ə ◊<br>... ◊ |
| **Gloucester** | 'glɑ stɚ<br>'glɔ stɚ<br>'glɒ stə ◊ | glah stər<br>glaw stər<br>glo stə ◊ |

| NAME | INTERNATIONAL PHONETIC ALPHABET* | SIMPLIFIED PHONICS** |
|---|---|---|
| Gloucestershire | 'glɑ stɚ ʃɚ<br>'glɔ stɚ ʃɚ<br>'glɒ stə ʃə ◊ | glah stər shər<br>glaw stər shər<br>glo stə shə ◊ |
| Golgatha | 'gɑl gə θə<br>'gɒl gə θə ◊ | gahl guh *th*uh<br>g*o*l guh *th*uh ◊ |
| Green | 'grin | green |
| Hallowmas | 'hæ lo mæs<br>'hæ ləʊ mæs ◊ | ha lo mas<br>... ◊ |
| Harry | 'hæ ri | ha ree |
| Henry | 'hɛn ri<br>'hen ri ◊ | hen ree<br>... ◊ |
| Hereford | 'hɛ rɪ fɚd<br>'hɝ fɚd<br>'he rɪ fəd ◊<br>'hɜ fəd ◊ | he ri fərd<br>hər fərd<br>he ri fəd ◊<br>hə fəd |
| Hotspur | 'hɑt spɚ<br>'hɒt spə ◊ | haht spər<br>h*o*t spə ◊ |
| Ireland | 'aɪ ɚ lənd<br>'aɪ ə lənd ◊ | ai ər luhnd<br>ai ə luhnd ◊ |
| Irish | 'aɪ rɪʃ | ai rish |
| Italy | 'ɪ tə li | i tuh lee |
| Jack -folio **Iacke** | 'ʤæk | jak |
| Jesu | 'ʤi zu<br>'ʤi su<br>'ʤi zju ◊ | jee zoo<br>jee soo<br>jee zyoo ◊ |
| Jew | 'ʤu | joo |
| Jewry | 'ʤu ri | joo ree |

| NAME | INTERNATIONAL PHONETIC ALPHABET* | SIMPLIFIED PHONICS** |
|---|---|---|
| John | 'ʤan<br>'ʤɒn ◊ | jahn<br>jon ◊ |
| John a Gaunt | 'ʤan ə gɔnt<br>'ʤɒn ə gɔnt ◊ | jahn uh gawnt<br>jon uh gawnt ◊ |
| Judas | 'ʤu dəs | joo duhs |
| Julius | 'ʤu liəs<br>'ʤul jəs | joo lee uh<br>jool yuhs |
| Kent | 'kɛnt<br>'kent ◊ | kent<br>... ◊ |
| [Saint] Lambert | [seɪnt] 'læm bət<br>[sɪnt] 'læm bət ◊ | [seint] lam bərt<br>[sint] lam bət ◊ |
| Lancaster | 'læŋ kæ stɚ<br>'læŋ kə stɚ<br>'læŋ kə stə ◊ | lang ka stər<br>lang kuh stər<br>lang kuh stə ◊ |
| Langley | 'læŋ li | lang lee |
| London | 'lʌn dən | luhn duhn |
| Mary | 'mɛ ri<br>'mɛə ri ◊ | me ree<br>... ◊ |
| Mars | 'mɑrz<br>'mɑz ◊ | mahrz<br>mahz ◊ |
| May | 'meɪ | mei |
| Mowbray | 'moʊ bri<br>'məʊ bri ◊<br>'məʊ breɪ ◊ | mo bree<br>... ◊<br>mo brei ◊ |
| Neptune | 'nɛp tun<br>'nɛp tjun ◊ | nep toon<br>nep tyoon ◊ |

| NAME | INTERNATIONAL PHONETIC ALPHABET* | SIMPLIFIED PHONICS** |
|------|----------------------------------|----------------------|
| **Norberry** | 'nɔr bɛ ri<br>'nɔ bə ri ◊ | nawr be ree<br>naw buh ree ◊ |
| **Norfolk** | 'nɔr fək<br>'nɔ fək ◊ | nawr fuhk<br>naw fuhk ◊ |
| **Northumberland** | nɔr 'θʌm bɚ lənd<br><br>nɔ 'θʌm bə lənd ◊ | nawr *th*uhm bər luhnd<br>naw *th*uhm bə luhnd ◊ |
| **Oxford** | 'ɑks fɚd<br>'ɒks fəd ◊ | ahks fərd<br>*o*ks fəd ◊ |
| **[Saint] Paul** | [seɪnt] 'pɔl<br>[sɪnt] 'pɔl ◊ | [seint] pawl<br>[sint] pawl ◊ |
| **Percy** | 'pɝ si<br>'pɜ si ◊ | pər see<br>pə see ◊ |
| **Phaeton/ Phaethon** | 'feɪ ə tən<br>'feɪ ə θɑn<br>[gen Am var]<br>'feɪ ə θɒn ◊<br>[Brit RP var] | fei uh tuhn<br>fei uh *th*ahn<br>[gen Am var]<br>fei uh *th*o*n<br>[Brit RP var] ◊ |
| **Pierce** | 'pirs<br>'pɪrs<br>'pɪəs ◊ | peers<br>pirs<br>piəs ◊ |
| **Pilate** | 'paɪ lət | pai luht |
| **Plashy** | 'plæ ʃi | pla shee |
| **Pomfret** | 'pʌm frɪt<br>'pɑm frɪt<br>[gen Am var]<br>'pɒm frɪt<br>[Brit RP var] ◊ | puhm frit<br>pahm frit<br>[gen Am var]<br>p*o*m frit<br>[Brit RP var] ◊ |

| NAME | INTERNATIONAL PHONETIC ALPHABET* | SIMPLIFIED PHONICS** |
|---|---|---|
| **Port le Blanc** | 'pɔrt lə 'blaŋk<br>'pɔt lə 'blɒŋk ◊ | pawrt luh blahngk<br>pawt luh blongk ◊ |
| **Quoint** | 'kwɔɪnt | kwoynt |
| **Rainold/Reignold**<br>folio **Rainald** | 're nəld<br>'re nəld ◊ | re nuhld<br>... ◊ |
| **Ramston** | 'ræm stən | ram stuhn |
| **Ravenspurgh** | 'reɪ vənz pɚg<br>'reɪnz pɚ<br>'reɪ vənz pəg ◊<br>'reɪnz pə ◊ | rei vuhnz pərg<br>reinz pər<br>rei vuhnz pəg ◊<br>reinz pə ◊ |
| **Richard** | 'rɪ ʧɚd<br>'rɪ ʧəd ◊ | ri chərd<br>ri chəd ◊ |
| **Robert** | 'rɑ bɚt<br>'rɒ bət ◊ | rah bərt<br>ro bət ◊ |
| **Ross/Rosse** | 'rɔs<br>'rɒs ◊ | raws<br>ros ◊ |
| **Rutland** | 'rʌt lənd | ruht luhnd |
| **Salisbury** | 'sɔlz bɛ ri<br>'sælz bɛ ri<br>'sɔlz bə ri ◊ | sawlz be ree<br>salz be ree<br>sawlz buh ree ◊ |
| **Saracen** | 'sæ rə sən | sa ruh suhn |
| **Scroop** | 'skrup | skroop |
| **Seely** | 'si li | see lee |
| **Seymour** | 'si mɔr<br>'si mɔ ◊ | see mawr<br>see maw ◊ |
| **Spencer** | 'spɛn sɚ<br>'spen sə ◊ | spen sər<br>spen sə ◊ |
| **Stephen** | 'sti vən | stee vuhn |

257

| NAME | INTERNATIONAL PHONETIC ALPHABET* | SIMPLIFIED PHONICS** |
|------|-----------------------------------|----------------------|
| **Surrey** | 'sɜ·i | səree |
| | 'sʌ ri | suh ree |
| **Thomas** | 'tɑ məs | tah muhs |
| | 'tɒ məs ◊ | to muhs ◊ |
| **Troy** | 'trɔɪ | troy |
| | 'tʃrɔɪ | chroy |
| **Turk** | 'tɝk | tərk |
| | 'tɜk ◊ | tək ◊ |
| **Venice** | 'vɛ nɪs | ve nis |
| | 've nɪs ◊ | … ◊ |
| **Wales** | 'weɪlz | weilz |
| **Waterton** | 'wɔ tɚ tən | waw tər tuhn |
| | 'wɔ tə tən ◊ | waw tə tuhn ◊ |
| **Wednesday** | 'wɛnz deɪ | wenz dei |
| | 'wenz di ◊ | wenz dee ◊ |
| **Welsh** | 'wɛlʃ | welsh |
| | 'welʃ ◊ | … ◊ |
| **Westminster** | 'wɛst mɪn stɚ | west min stər |
| | 'west mɪn stə ◊ | west min stə ◊ |
| **Willoughby** | 'wɪ lə bi | wi luh bee |
| **Wiltshire** | 'wɪlt ʃɚ | wilt shər |
| | 'wɪlt ʃə ◊ | wilt shə ◊ |
| **Woodstock** | 'wʊd stak | wood stahk |
| | 'wʊd stɒk ◊ | wood stok ◊ |
| **Worcester** | 'wʊ stɚ | woo stər |
| | 'wʊ stə ◊ | woo stə ◊ |
| **York** | 'jɔrk | yawrk |
| | 'jɔk ◊ | yawk ◊ |

| NAME | INTERNATIONAL PHONETIC ALPHABET* | SIMPLIFIED PHONICS** |
|---|---|---|
| **Abraham** | 'eɪ brə hæm | ei bruh ham |
| **[Saint] Alban** -folio **Albon, Albone** | [seɪnt] 'ɔl bən<br>[sɪnt] 'ɔl bən ◊ | [seint] awl buhn<br>[sint] awl buhn ◊ |
| **All Souls' Day** | ɔl 'soʊlz deɪ<br>ɔl 'solz deɪ ◊ | awl solz dei<br>… ◊ |
| **Anne** | 'æn | an |
| **Anthony** | 'æn θə ni | an *th*uh nee |
| **Antony** | 'æn tə ni | an tuh nee |
| **Baynard's [Castle]** | 'beɪ nɚdz ['kæ səl]<br>'beɪ nədz ['ka səl] ◊ | bei nərdz [ka suhl]<br>bei nədz [kah suhl] ◊ |
| **Berkeley/Berkley** folio **Barkely, Barkley, Berkley** | 'bɑrk li<br>'bɝk li<br>'bɑk li ◊ | bahrk lee<br>bərk lee<br>bahk lee ◊ |
| **Blunt/Blount** | 'blʌnt | bluhnt |
| **Bona** | 'boʊ nə<br>'bəʊ nə ◊ | bo nuh<br>… ◊ |
| **Bosworth Field** | 'bɑz wɚθ fild<br>'bɒz wəθ fild ◊ | bahz wərth<br>boz wəth ◊ |

*International Phonetic Alphabet Pronunciation Key: (General American) i-s<u>ee</u>, happ<u>y</u>, Jul<u>i</u>et; ɪ-s<u>i</u>t; eɪ-s<u>ay</u>; ɛ-s<u>e</u>t; æ-s<u>a</u>t; ɑ-f<u>a</u>ther; ʌ-s<u>u</u>n; ə-<u>a</u>bout; ɔ-s<u>aw</u>; oʊ-s<u>o</u>; o-h<u>e</u>ro; ʊ-sh<u>oo</u>k; u-s<u>oo</u>n; aɪ-s<u>igh</u>; ɔɪ-s<u>oy</u>; aʊ-s<u>ou</u>th; ju-c<u>u</u>be; ɚ-s<u>u</u>pp<u>er</u>; er-f<u>air</u>; ɝ-b<u>ir</u>d; k-<u>c</u>ut, <u>k</u>ite; g-<u>g</u>o; ʤ-<u>j</u>oy; j-<u>y</u>es; ŋ-si<u>ng</u>; ʃ-<u>sh</u>oe; ʧ-<u>ch</u>op; ð-<u>th</u>at; θ-<u>th</u>in; ʒ-mea<u>s</u>ure; (Additional symbols for British RP) e-s<u>e</u>t; ɛə-f<u>air</u>; ə-s<u>u</u>pp<u>er</u>; ɜ-b<u>ir</u>d; ɒ-st<u>o</u>p; əʊ-s<u>o</u>, h<u>e</u>ro; o-(followed by l) p<u>o</u>le.

**Simplified Phonics Pronunciation Key: (General American) ee-s<u>ee</u>, happ<u>y</u>; i-s<u>i</u>t; ei-s<u>ay</u>; e-s<u>e</u>t; a-s<u>a</u>t; ah-f<u>a</u>ther; uh-s<u>u</u>n, <u>a</u>bout; aw-s<u>aw</u>; o-s<u>o</u>; oo-sh<u>oo</u>k; oo-s<u>oo</u>n; ai-s<u>igh</u>; oy-s<u>oy</u>; ow-s<u>ou</u>th; yoo-c<u>u</u>be; ər-b<u>ir</u>d; supper; k-<u>c</u>ut, <u>k</u>ite; g-<u>g</u>o; j-<u>j</u>oy; ng-si<u>ng</u>; kw-<u>qu</u>ick; sh-<u>sh</u>oe; ch-<u>ch</u>op; th-<u>th</u>at; *th*-<u>th</u>in; zh-mea<u>s</u>ure; (Additional symbols for British RP) ə-b<u>ir</u>d; ə-s<u>u</u>pp<u>er</u>; <u>o</u>-st<u>o</u>p; … indicates pronunciation variance too subtle for Simplified Phonics transcription see International Phonetic Alphabet transcription.

◊ British RP pronunciation-see Introduction.

| NAME | INTERNATIONAL PHONETIC ALPHABET* | SIMPLIFIED PHONICS** |
|------|----------------------------------|----------------------|
| **Bourchier** | 'baʊ ʧɚ<br>bu 'ʃeɪ<br>'baʊ ʧə ◊ | bow chər<br>boo shei<br>bow chə ◊ |
| **Brakenbury** | 'bræ kən bɛ ri<br>'bræ kən bə ri ◊ | bra kuhn be ree<br>bra kuhn buh ree ◊ |
| **Brandon** | 'bræn dən | bran duhn |
| **Brecknock** | 'brɛk nək<br>'brɛk nɑk<br>'brek nək ◊ | brek nuhk<br>brek nahk<br>… ◊ |
| **Bretagne** | 'brɪ tən<br>brə 'tæŋ | bri tuhn<br>bruh tang |
| **Breton** | 'brɛ tən<br>'bre tən ◊ | bre tuhn<br>… ◊ |
| **Britany** | 'brɪ tə ni | bri tuh nee |
| **Buckingham** | 'bʌ kɪŋ hæm<br>'bʌ kɪŋ əm | buh king ham<br>buh king uhm |
| **Burgundy** | 'bɝ gən di<br>'bɜ gən di ◊ | bər guhn dee<br>bə guhn dee ◊ |
| **Caesar** | 'si zɚ<br>'si zə ◊ | see zər<br>see zə ◊ |
| **Calais** | 'kæ leɪ<br>kə 'leɪ<br>   [gen Am var] | ka lei<br>kuh lei<br>   [gen Am var] |
| **Catesby** | 'keɪts bi | keits bee |
| **Charon** | 'kɛ rən<br>'kɛə rən ◊ | ke ruhn<br>keə ruhn ◊ |
| **Chertsey** | 'ʧɝt si<br>'ʧɜt si ◊ | chərt see<br>chət see ◊ |

| NAME | INTERNATIONAL PHONETIC ALPHABET* | SIMPLIFIED PHONICS** |
|---|---|---|
| **Christendom** | ˈkrɪ sən dəm | kri suhn duhm |
| **Christian** | ˈkrɪs tʃən | kris chuhn |
| **Christopher** | ˈkrɪ stə fɚ | kri stuh fər |
| | ˈkrɪ stə fə ◊ | kri stuh fə ◊ |
| **Clarence** | ˈklæ rəns | kla ruhns |
| **Clifford** | ˈklɪ fɚd | kli fərd |
| | ˈklɪ fəd ◊ | kli fəd ◊ |
| **Courtney** | ˈkɔrt ni | kawrt nee |
| | ˈkɔt ni ◊ | kawt nee ◊ |
| **Crosby Place** | ˈkrɔz bi | krawz bee |
| -folio **Crosbie** | ˈkrɑz bi | krahz bee |
| **House** | ˈkrɒz bi ◊ | kroz bee ◊ |
| | ˈkrɒs bi ◊ | kros bee ◊ |
| **Derby** | ˈdɑr bi | dahr bee |
| | ˈdɝ bi | dər bee |
| | ˈdɑ bi ◊ | dah bee ◊ |
| **Devonshire** | ˈdɛ vən ʃɚ | de vuhn shər |
| | ˈde vən ʃə ◊ | de vuhn shə ◊ |
| **Dickon** | ˈdɪ kən | di kuhn |
| **Dighton** | ˈdaɪ tən | dai tuhn |
| **Dorset** | ˈdɔr sɪt | dawr sit |
| | ˈdɔ sɪt ◊ | daw sit ◊ |
| **Dorsetshire** | ˈdɔr sɪt ʃɚ | dawr sit shər |
| | ˈdɔ sɪt ʃə ◊ | daw sit shə ◊ |
| **Edward** | ˈɛd wɚd | ed wərd |
| | ˈed wəd ◊ | ed wəd ◊ |
| **Elizabeth** | ɪ ˈlɪ zə bəθ | i li zuh buh*th* |

261

| NAME | INTERNATIONAL PHONETIC ALPHABET* | SIMPLIFIED PHONICS** |
|---|---|---|
| Ely | 'i li | ee lee |
| England | 'ɪŋ glənd | ing gluhnd |
| English | 'ɪŋ glɪʃ | ing glish |
| Exeter | 'ɛk sɪ tɚ<br>'ek sɪ tə ◊ | ek si tər<br>ek si tə ◊ |
| Ferrers | 'fɛ rɚz<br>'fe rəz ◊ | fe rərz<br>fe rəz ◊ |
| Forrest | 'fɔ rɪst<br>'fɑ rɪst<br>'fɒ rɪst ◊ | faw rist<br>fah rist<br>fo rist ◊ |
| George | 'dʒɔr dʒ<br>'dʒɔ dʒ ◊ | jawrj<br>jawj ◊ |
| Gilbert | 'gɪl bɚt<br>'gɪl bət ◊ | gil bərt<br>gil bət ◊ |
| Gloucester | 'glɑ stɚ<br>'glɔ stɚ<br>'glɒ stə ◊ | glah stər<br>glaw stər<br>glo stə ◊ |
| Grey | 'greɪ | grei |
| Guilford/<br>   Guildford | 'gɪl fɚd<br>'gɪl fəd ◊ | gil fərd<br>gil fəd ◊ |
| Guildhall | 'gɪld hɔl | gild hawl |
| Ha'rford West | 'hɑr fɚd 'wɛst<br>'heɪ vɚ fɚd 'wɛst<br>'hɑ fəd 'wɛst ◊<br>'heɪ və fəd 'wɛst ◊ | hahr fərd west<br>hei vər fərd west<br>hah fəd west ◊<br>hei və fəd west ◊ |
| Hastings | 'heɪ stɪŋz | hei stingz |

| NAME | INTERNATIONAL PHONETIC ALPHABET* | SIMPLIFIED PHONICS** |
|------|----------------------------------|----------------------|
| **Henry** | 'hɛn ri<br>'hen ri ◊ | hen ree<br>... ◊ |
| **Herbert** | 'hɝ bə·t<br>'hɜ bət ◊ | hər bərt<br>hə bət ◊ |
| **Hereford** | 'hɛ rɪ fə·d<br>'he rɪ fəd ◊ | he ri fərd<br>he ri fəd ◊ |
| **Holborn** | 'hoʊ bə·n<br>'hoʊl bə·n<br>'ho bən ◊ | ho bərn<br>hol bərn<br>ho bən ◊ |
| **Hour** -folio<br>  **Hower** | 'aʊ ə·<br>'aʊ ə ◊ | au ər<br>au ə ◊ |
| **Humphrey** -folio<br>  **Humfrey** | 'hʌm fri<br>'hʌmp fri | huhm free<br>huhmp free |
| **Ireland** | 'aɪ ə· lənd<br>'aɪ ə lənd ◊ | ai ər luhnd<br>ai ə luhnd ◊ |
| **Jack** -folio **Iacke** | 'dʒæk | jak |
| **James** | 'dʒeɪmz | jeimz |
| **Jesu** | 'dʒi zu<br>'dʒi su<br>'dʒi zju ◊ | jee zoo<br>jee soo<br>jee zyoo ◊ |
| **John** | 'dʒɑn<br>'dʒɒn ◊ | jahn<br>jon ◊ |
| **Jove** | 'dʒoʊv<br>'dʒəʊv ◊ | jov<br>... ◊ |
| **Julius** | 'dʒu liəs<br>'dʒul jəs | joo lee uhs<br>jool yuhs |
| **Kent** | 'kɛnt<br>'kent ◊ | kent<br>... ◊ |

| NAME | INTERNATIONAL PHONETIC ALPHABET* | SIMPLIFIED PHONICS** |
|---|---|---|
| Leicester | 'lɛ stɚ | le stər |
| | 'le stə ◊ | le stə ◊ |
| Lethe | 'li θi | lee *thee* |
| London | 'lʌn dən | luhn duhn |
| Lucy | 'lu si | loo see |
| Ludlow | 'lʌd lo | luhd lo |
| | 'lʌd ləʊ ◊ | … ◊ |
| Margeret | 'mɑr grɪt | mahr grit |
| | 'mɑr gə rɪt | mahr guh rit |
| | 'mɑ grɪt ◊ | mah grit ◊ |
| | 'mɑ gə rɪt ◊ | mah guh rit ◊ |
| May | 'meɪ | mei |
| Mercury | 'mɝk jə ri | mər kyuh ree |
| | 'mɜk jʊ ri ◊ | mə ky*oo* ree ◊ |
| Milford | 'mɪl fɚd | mil fərd |
| | 'mɪl fəd ◊ | mil fəd ◊ |
| Morton | 'mɔr tən | mawr tuhn |
| | 'mɔ tən ◊ | maw tuhn ◊ |
| Ned | 'nɛd | ned |
| | 'ned ◊ | … ◊ |
| Norfolk | 'nɔr fək | nawr fuhk |
| | 'nɔ fək ◊ | naw fuhk ◊ |
| Northampton | nɔrθ 'hæmp tən | nawr*th* hamp tuhn |
| | nɔ 'θæm tən ◊ | naw *th*am tuhn ◊ |
| Northumberland | nɔr 'θʌm bɚ lənd | nawr *th*uhm bər luhnd |
| | nɔ 'θʌm bə lənd ◊ | naw *th*uhm bə luhnd ◊ |

264

| NAME | INTERNATIONAL PHONETIC ALPHABET* | SIMPLIFIED PHONICS** |
|---|---|---|
| Oxford | 'ɑks fɚd<br>'ɒks fəd ◊ | ahks fərd<br>oks fəd ◊ |
| Paris | 'pæ rɪs | pa ris |
| [Saint] Paul | [seɪnt] 'pɔl<br>[sɪnt] 'pɔl ◊ | [seint] pawl<br>[sint] pawl ◊ |
| Pembroke | 'pɛm brok<br>'pɛm brʊk<br>'pem brʊk ◊ | pem brok<br>pem brook<br>… ◊ |
| Penker | 'pɛŋ kɚ<br>'peŋ kə ◊ | peng kər<br>peng kə ◊ |
| Pilate | 'paɪ lət | pai luht |
| Plantagenet | plæn 'tæ ʤə nɪt<br>plæn 'tæ ʤɪ nɪt | plan ta juh nit<br>plan ta ji nit |
| Pomfret [Castle] | 'pʌm frɪt<br>'pɑm frɪt [kæ səl]<br>[gen Am var]<br>'pɒm frɪt [kɑ səl]<br>[Brit RP var] | puhm frit<br>pahm frit [ka suhl]<br>[gen Am var]<br>pom frit [kah suhl]<br>[Brit RP var] |
| Ratcliff | 'ræt klɪf | rat klif |
| Rice ap Thomas | 'raɪs æp 'tɑ məs<br>'raɪs æp 'tɒ məs ◊ | rais ap tah muhs<br>rais ap to muhs ◊ |
| Richard | 'rɪ ʧɚd<br>'rɪ ʧəd ◊ | ri chərd<br>ri chəd ◊ |
| Richmond | 'rɪʧ mənd | rich muhnd |
| Rivers | 'rɪ vɚz<br>'rɪ vəz ◊ | ri vərz<br>ri vəz ◊ |
| Robert | 'rɑ bɚt<br>'rɒ bət ◊ | rah bərt<br>ro bət ◊ |

265

| NAME | INTERNATIONAL PHONETIC ALPHABET* | SIMPLIFIED PHONICS** |
|---|---|---|
| **Rotherham** | 'rɑ ðə rəm<br>'rɒ ðə rəm ◊ | rah thə ruhm<br>ro thə ruhm ◊ |
| **Rougemont** | 'ruʒ mɑnt<br>'ruʒ mɒnt ◊ | roozh mahnt<br>roozh mont ◊ |
| **Rutland** | 'rʌt lənd | ruht luhnd |
| **Salisbury** | 'sɔlz bɛ ri<br>'sælz bɛ ri<br>'sɔlz bə ri ◊ | sawlz be ree<br>salz be ree<br>sawlz buh ree ◊ |
| **Scales** | 'skeɪlz | skeilz |
| **Scotland** | 'skɑt lənd<br>'skɒt lənd ◊ | skaht luhnd<br>skot luhnd ◊ |
| **Shaw** | 'ʃɔ | shaw |
| **Shore** | 'ʃɔr<br>'ʃɔ ◊ | shawr<br>shaw ◊ |
| **Stanley** | 'stæn li | stan lee |
| **Stony-Stratford** | 'stoʊ ni 'stræt fɚd<br>'stəʊ ni 'stræt fəd ◊ | sto nee strat fərd<br>sto nee strat fəd ◊ |
| **Stratford** | 'stræt fɚd<br>'stræt fəd ◊ | strat fərd<br>strat fəd ◊ |
| **Surrey** | 'sɝi<br>'sʌ ri | səree<br>suh ree |
| **Talbot** | 'tɔl bət<br>'tæl bət | tawl buht<br>tal buht |
| **Tamworth** | 'tæm wɚθ<br>'tæm wəθ ◊ | tam wər*th*<br>tam wə*th* ◊ |
| **Tewksbury** | 'tuks bɛ ri<br>'tjuks bə ri ◊ | tooks be ree<br>tyooks buh ree ◊ |

| NAME | INTERNATIONAL PHONETIC ALPHABET* | SIMPLIFIED PHONICS** |
|------|----------------------------------|----------------------|
| **Thomas** | 'tɑ məs<br>'tɒ məs ◊ | tah muhs<br>to muhs ◊ |
| **Tower** | 'taʊ ɚ<br>'taʊ ə ◊ | tow ər<br>tow ə ◊ |
| **Tressel** | 'tʃrɛ səl<br>'trɛ səl<br>'tre səl ◊ | chre suhl<br>tre suhl<br>... ◊ |
| **Turk** | 'tɝk<br>'tɜk ◊ | tərk<br>tək ◊ |
| **Tyrrel** | 'tɪ rəl<br>'tɪə rəl ◊ | ti ruhl<br>tiə ruhl ... ◊ |
| **Urswick** | 'ɝz wɪk<br>'ɝ zɪk<br>'ɜz wɪk ◊<br>'ɜ zɪk ◊ | ərz wik<br>ər zik<br>əz wik ◊<br>ə zik ◊ |
| **Vaughan** | 'vɔn<br>'vɑn<br>   [gen Am var] | vawn<br>vahn<br>   [gen Am var] |
| **Wales** | 'weɪlz | weilz |
| **Walter** | 'wɔl tɚ<br>'wɔl tə ◊ | wawl tər<br>wawl tə ◊ |
| **Warwick** | 'wɔ rɪk<br>'wɔr wɪk<br>'wɑ rɪk<br>'wɒ rɪk ◊ | waw rik<br>wawr wik<br>wah rik<br>wo rik ◊ |
| **Welsh** | 'wɛlʃ<br>'welʃ ◊ | welsh<br>... ◊ |
| **Westminster** | 'wɛst mɪn stɚ<br>'west mɪn stə ◊ | west min stər<br>west min stə ◊ |

| NAME | INTERNATIONAL PHONETIC ALPHABET* | SIMPLIFIED PHONICS** |
|------|----------------------------------|---------------------|
| **White-friars** | 'waɪt fraɪ ɚz<br>'waɪt fraɪ əz ◊ | wait frai ərz<br>wait frai əz ◊ |
| **William** | 'wɪl jəm | wil yuhm |
| **Wiltshire** | 'wɪlt ʃɚ<br>'wɪlt ʃə ◊ | wilt shər<br>wilt shə ◊ |
| **Woodvile/<br>Woodville** | 'wʊd vɪl | wood vil |
| **York** | 'jɔrk<br>'jɔk ◊ | yawrk<br>yawk ◊ |
| **Yorkshire** | 'jɔrk ʃɚ<br>'jɔk ʃə ◊ | yawrk shər<br>yawk shə ◊ |

| NAME | INTERNATIONAL PHONETIC ALPHABET* | SIMPLIFIED PHONICS** |
|---|---|---|
| **Abraham** | 'eɪ brə hæm | ei bruh ham |
| **Abram** | 'eɪ brəm | ei bruhm |
| **Adam** | 'æ dəm | a duhm |
| **Angelica** | æn 'dʒɛ lɪ kə<br>æn 'dʒe lɪ kə ◊ | an je li kuh<br>... ◊ |
| **Anselme** | 'æn sɛlm<br>'æn selm ◊ | an selm<br>... ◊ |
| **Anthony** | 'æn θə ni | an *th*uh nee |
| **Antony** | 'æn tə ni | an tuh nee |
| **April** | 'eɪ prəl | ei pruhl |
| **Aurora** | ə 'rɔ rə<br>ɔ 'rɔ rə | uh raw ruh<br>aw raw ruh |
| **Balthasar/ Balthazar** | bæl θə 'zɑr<br>'bæl θə zɑr<br>bæl θə 'zɑ ◊ | bal *th*uh zahr<br>...<br>bal *th*uh zah ◊ |
| **Benvolio** | bɛn 'voʊ lio<br>ben 'vo liəʊ ◊ | ben vo lee o<br>... ◊ |
| **Capel** | 'kæ pəl | ka puhl |
| **Capulet** | 'kæ pju lɪt<br>'kæ pju lət | ka pyoo lit<br>ka pyoo luht |

| NAME | INTERNATIONAL PHONETIC ALPHABET* | SIMPLIFIED PHONICS** |
|------|----------------------------------|---------------------|
| **Catling** | ˈkæt lɪŋ | kat ling |
| **Cleopatra** | kliə ˈpæ trə<br>kliə ˈpæ tʃrə<br>kliə ˈpɑ trə<br>    [Brit RP var] | klee uh pa truh<br>klee uh pa chruh<br>klee uh pah truh<br>    [Brit RP var] |
| **Cophetua** | kə ˈfɛ tʃu ə<br>kəʊ ˈfe tju ə ◊ | kuh fe choo uh<br>ko fe tyoo uh ◊ |
| **Cupid** | ˈkju pɪd | kyoo pid |
| **Cynthia** | ˈsɪn θiə | sin *th*ee uh |
| **Dian** | ˈdaɪ ən<br>ˈdaɪ æn | dai uhn<br>dai an |
| **Dido** | ˈdaɪ do<br>ˈdaɪ dəʊ ◊ | dai do<br>… ◊ |
| **Easter** | ˈi stɚ<br>ˈi stə ◊ | ee star<br>ee stə ◊ |
| **Echo** -folio **Eccho** | ˈɛ ko<br>ˈe kəʊ ◊ | e ko<br>… ◊ |
| **Escalus** -folio<br>    **Eskales** | ˈɛs kə ləs<br>ˈes kə ləs ◊ | es kuh luhs<br>… ◊ |
| **Ethiop** | ˈi θiɑp<br>ˈi θiɒp ◊ | ee *th*ee ahp<br>ee *th*ee op ◊ |
| **Ethiope** | ˈi θiop<br>ˈi θiəʊp ◊ | ee *th*ee op<br>… ◊ |
| **[Saint] Francis** | [seɪnt] ˈfræn sɪs<br>[sɪnt] ˈfrɑn sɪs ◊ | [seint]fran sis<br>[sint] frahn sis ◊ |
| **Free-Town** | ˈfri taʊn | free town |

270

| NAME | INTERNATIONAL PHONETIC ALPHABET* | SIMPLIFIED PHONICS** |
|------|----------------------------------|----------------------|
| **French** | 'frɛntʃ <br> 'frɛntʃ ◊ | french <br> ... ◊ |
| **Gregory** | 'grɛ gə ri <br> 'gre gə ri ◊ | gre guh ree <br> ... ◊ |
| **Grindstone** | 'graɪnd ston <br> 'graɪnd stəʊn ◊ | graind ston <br> ... ◊ |
| **Helen** | 'hɛ lən <br> 'hɛ lɪn <br> 'he lɪn ◊ | he luhn <br> he lin <br> ... ◊ |
| **Helena** | 'hɛ lɪ nə <br> 'he lɪ nə ◊ | he li nuh <br> ... ◊ |
| **Hero** | 'hi ro <br> 'hɪə rəʊ ◊ | hee ro <br> ... ◊ |
| **Hora** (folio only) | 'hɔ rə | haw ruh |
| **Hugh** | 'hju | hyoo |
| **Italy** | 'ɪ tə li | i tuh lee |
| **Jack** | 'dʒæk | jak |
| **James** | 'dʒeɪmz | jeimz |
| **Jesu** | 'dʒi zu <br> 'dʒi su <br> 'dʒi zju ◊ | jee zoo <br> jee soo <br> jee zyoo ◊ |
| **John** | 'dʒɑn <br> 'dʒɒn ◊ | jahn <br> jon ◊ |
| **Jove** | 'dʒoʊv <br> 'dʒəʊv ◊ | jov <br> ... ◊ |
| **Jule** | 'dʒul | jool |

| NAME | INTERNATIONAL PHONETIC ALPHABET* | SIMPLIFIED PHONICS** |
|------|----------------------------------|----------------------|
| **Juliet** | 'dʒu liɛt [gen Am var] | joo lee et |
|  | 'dʒu liet [Brit RP var] | ... |
|  | 'dʒu liət | ... |
| **Laura** | 'lɔ rə | law ruh |
| **Lawrence** -folio | 'lɔ rəns | law ruhns |
|    **Laurence** | 'lɒ rəns ◊ | lo ruhns ◊ |
| **Lent** | 'lɛnt | lent |
|  | 'lent ◊ | ... ◊ |
| **Livia** | 'lɪ viə | li vee uh |
| **Lucentio** | lu 'sɛn tio | loo sen tee o |
|  | lu 'sɛn tʃio | loo sen chee o |
|  | lu 'sen tʃiəʊ ◊ | ... ◊ |
| **Lucio** | 'lu tʃio | loo chee o |
|  | 'lu tʃiəʊ ◊ | ... ◊ |
|  | 'lu ʃio | loo shee o |
|  | 'lu ʃiəʊ ◊ | ... ◊ |
|  | 'lu sio | loo see o |
|  | 'lu si əʊ ◊ | ... ◊ |
| **Mab** | 'mæb | mab |
| **Mantua** | 'mæn tʃuə | man choo uh |
|  | 'mæn tjʊə ◊ | man ty*oo* uh ◊ |
| **Maria** | mə 'ri ə | muh ree uh |
|  | mə 'raɪ ə | muh rai uh |
| **Martino** | mɑr 'ti no | mahr tee no |
|  | mɑ 'ti nəʊ ◊ | mah tee no ◊ |
| **Mercutio** | mɝ 'kju ʃi o | mər kyoo shee o |
|  | mɜ 'kju ʃi əʊ ◊ | mə kyoo shee o ◊ |

| NAME | INTERNATIONAL PHONETIC ALPHABET* | SIMPLIFIED PHONICS** |
|------|----------------------------------|----------------------|
| **Monday** | 'mʌn deɪ<br>'mʌn di ◊ | muhn dei<br>muhn dee ◊ |
| **Montague** -folio<br>**Mountague** | 'mɑn tə gju<br>'mɒn tə gju ◊ | mahn tuh gyoo<br>mon tuh gyoo ◊ |
| **Nell** | 'nɛl<br>'nel ◊ | nel<br>... ◊ |
| **Paris** | 'pæ rɪs | pa ris |
| **Pentecost** | 'pɛn tə kɔst<br>'pɛn tə kɑst<br>'pen tə kɔst ◊ | pen tuh kawst<br>pen tuh kahst<br>...◊ |
| **[Saint] Peter** | [seɪnt] 'pi tɚ<br>[sɪnt] 'pi tə ◊ | [seint] pee tər<br>[sint] pee tə ◊ |
| **Petrarch** | 'pɛ trɑrk<br>'pɛ tʃrɑrk<br>'pe trɑk ◊ | pe trahrk<br>pe chrahrk<br>pe trahk ◊ |
| **Petruchio** -folio<br>**Petrucio** | pə 'tru kio<br>pə 'tru tʃio<br>pə 'tru tʃiəʊ ◊ | puh troo kee o<br>puh troo chee o<br>... ◊ |
| **Phaeton/**<br>**Phaethon** | 'feɪ ə tən<br>'feɪ ə θɑn<br>　[gen Am var]<br>'feɪ ə θɒn<br>　[Brit RP var] | fei uh tuhn<br>fei uh *th*ahn<br>　[gen Am var]<br>fei uh *th*on<br>　[Brit RP var] |
| **Phoebus** | 'fi bəs | fee buhs |
| **Placentio** | plə 'sɛn tio<br>plə sɛn ʃo<br>plə 'sen ʃəʊ ◊ | pluh sen tee o<br>pluh sen sho<br>... ◊ |
| **Potpan** | 'pɑt pæn<br>'pɒt pæn ◊ | paht pan<br>pot pan ◊ |

| NAME | INTERNATIONAL PHONETIC ALPHABET* | SIMPLIFIED PHONICS** |
|---|---|---|
| Rebeck/Rebicke | 'ri bɛk<br>'ri bek ◊ | ree bek<br>... ◊ |
| Romeo | 'roʊ mio<br>'rəʊ miəʊ ◊ | ro mee o<br>... ◊ |
| Rosaline | 'rɑ zə laɪn<br>'rɒ zə laɪn ◊ | rah zuh lain<br>ro zuh lain ◊ |
| Sampson/<br>Samson | 'sæmp sən | samp suhn |
| Simon | 'saɪ mən | sai muhn |
| Soundpost | 'saʊnd post<br>'saʊnd pəʊst ◊ | sownd post<br>... ◊ |
| Spanish | 'spæ nɪʃ | spa nish |
| Susan | 'su zən | soo zuhn |
| Tartar | 'tɑr tɚ<br>'tɑ tə ◊ | tahr tər<br>tah tə ◊ |
| Thisbe | 'θɪz bi | *th*iz bee |
| Thursday | 'θɝz deɪ<br>'θɜz di ◊ | *th*ərz dei<br>*th*əz dee ◊ |
| Tiberio | taɪ 'bɪ rio<br>taɪ 'bɪ riəʊ ◊ | tai bi ree o<br>... ◊ |
| Titan | 'taɪ tən | tai tuhn |
| Tybalt -folio<br>Tibalt | 'tɪ bəlt | ti buhlt |
| [Saint] Valentine | [seɪnt] 'væ lən taɪn<br>[sɪnt] 'væ lən taɪn ◊ | [seint] va luhn tain<br>[sint] va luhn tain ◊ |

| NAME | INTERNATIONAL PHONETIC ALPHABET* | SIMPLIFIED PHONICS** |
|---|---|---|
| **Valentio** | və 'lɛn tio | vuh len tee o |
| | və 'lɛn ʃo | vuh len sho |
| | və 'len ʃəʊ ◊ | ... ◊ |
| | væ 'len ʃəʊ ◊ | va len sho ◊ |
| **Venus** | 'vi nəs | vee nuhs |
| **Verona** | və 'roʊ nə | vuh ro nuh |
| | və 'rəʊ nə ◊ | ... ◊ |
| **Vitruvio** | vɪ 'ʧru vio | vi chroo vee o |
| | vɪ 'tru vio | vi troo vee o |
| | vɪ 'tru viəʊ ◊ | ... ◊ |
| **Wednesday** | 'wɛnz deɪ | wenz dei |
| | 'wenz di ◊ | wenz dee ◊ |

# The Sonnets

| NAME | INTERNATIONAL PHONETIC ALPHABET* | SIMPLIFIED PHONICS** |
|------|----------------------------------|----------------------|
| **Adonis** | ə 'dɑ nɪs | uh dah nis |
|  | ə 'doʊ nɪs | uh do nis |
|  | ə 'dəʊ nɪs ◊ | ... ◊ |
| **Cupid** | 'kju pɪd | kyoo pid |
| **December** | di 'sɛm bɚ | dee sem bər |
|  | dɪ 'sɛm bə ◊ | dee sem bə ◊ |
| **Dian** | 'daɪ ən | dai uhn |
|  | 'daɪ æn | dai an |
| **Eve** | 'iv | eev |
| **Grecian** | 'gri ʃən | gree shuhn |
| **Helen** | 'hɛ lən | he luhn |
|  | 'hɛ lɪn | he lin |
|  | 'he lɪn ◊ | ... ◊ |
| **Jack** | 'ʤæk | jak |
| **June** | 'ʤun | joon |
| **Mars** | 'mɑrz | mahrz |
|  | 'mɑz ◊ | mahz ◊ |
| **May** | 'meɪ | mei |
| **Philomel** | 'fɪ lə mɛl | fi luh mel |
|  | 'fɪ lo mel ◊ | fi lo mel ◊ |
| **Phoenix** | 'fi nɪks | fee niks |

*International Phonetic Alphabet Pronunciation Key: (General American) i-s<u>ee</u>, happ<u>y</u>, J<u>u</u>li<u>e</u>t; ɪ-s<u>i</u>t; eɪ-s<u>ay</u>; ɛ-s<u>e</u>t; æ-s<u>a</u>t; ɑ-f<u>a</u>ther; ʌ-s<u>u</u>n; ə-<u>a</u>bout; ɔ-s<u>aw</u>; oʊ-s<u>o</u>; o-her<u>o</u>; ʊ-sh<u>oo</u>k; u-s<u>oo</u>n; aɪ-s<u>igh</u>; ɔɪ-s<u>oy</u>; aʊ-s<u>ou</u>th; ju-c<u>u</u>be; ɚ-supp<u>er</u>; ɛr-f<u>air</u>; ɝ-b<u>ir</u>d; k-<u>c</u>ut, <u>k</u>ite; g-<u>g</u>o; ʤ-<u>j</u>oy; j-<u>y</u>es; ŋ-si<u>ng</u>; ʃ-<u>sh</u>oe; ʧ-<u>ch</u>op; ð-<u>th</u>at; θ-<u>th</u>in; ʒ-mea<u>s</u>ure; (Additional symbols for British RP) e-s<u>e</u>t; ɛə-f<u>air</u>; ə-supp<u>er</u>; ɜ-b<u>ir</u>d; ɒ-st<u>o</u>p; aʊ-s<u>o</u>, her<u>o</u>; o-(followed by l) p<u>o</u>le.

**Simplified Phonics Pronunciation Key: (General American) ee-s<u>ee</u>, happ<u>y</u>; i-s<u>i</u>t; ei-s<u>ay</u>; e-s<u>e</u>t; a-s<u>a</u>t; ah-f<u>a</u>ther; uh-s<u>u</u>n, ab<u>ou</u>t; aw-s<u>aw</u>; o-s<u>o</u>; oo-sh<u>oo</u>k; oo-s<u>oo</u>n; ai-s<u>igh</u>; oy-s<u>oy</u>; ow-s<u>ou</u>th; yoo-c<u>u</u>be; ər-b<u>ir</u>d, supp<u>er</u>; k-<u>c</u>ut, <u>k</u>ite; g-<u>g</u>o; j-<u>j</u>oy; ng-si<u>ng</u>; kw-<u>qu</u>ick; sh-<u>sh</u>oe; ch-<u>ch</u>op; th-<u>th</u>at; th-<u>th</u>in; zh-mea<u>s</u>ure; (Additional symbols for British RP) ə-b<u>ir</u>d; ə-supp<u>er</u>; <u>o</u>-stop; ... indicates pronunciation variance too subtle for Simplified Phonics transcription see International Phonetic Alphabet transcription.

◊ British RP pronunciation-see Introduction.

| NAME | INTERNATIONAL PHONETIC ALPHABET* | SIMPLIFIED PHONICS** |
|------|----------------------------------|----------------------|
| **Saturn** | ˈsæ tɚn<br>ˈsæ tən ◊ | sa tərn<br>sa tən ◊ |

# The Taming of the Shrew

| NAME | INTERNATIONAL PHONETIC ALPHABET* | SIMPLIFIED PHONICS** |
|---|---|---|
| **Adam** | 'æ dəm | a duhm |
| **Adonis** | ə 'dɑ nɪs | uh dah nis |
| | ə 'doʊ nɪs | uh do nis |
| | ə 'dəʊ nɪs ◊ | … ◊ |
| **Adriatic** | eɪ dri 'æ tɪk | ei dree a tik |
| | eɪ dʒri 'æ tɪk | ei jree a tik |
| **Aeacides** | i 'æ sɪ diz | ee a si deez |
| **Agenor** | ə 'dʒi nɔr | uh jee nawr |
| | ə 'dʒi nɔ ◊ | uh jee naw ◊ |
| **Ajax** | 'eɪ dʒæks | ei jaks |
| **Al'ce** | 'æls | als |
| | 'æ lɪs | a lis |
| **Alcides** | æl 'saɪ diz | al sai deez |
| **Anna** | 'æ nə | a nuh |
| **[Saint] Anne** | [seint] 'æn | [seint] an |
| | [sɪnt] 'æn ◊ | [sint] an ◊ |
| **Antonio** | æn 'toʊ nio | an to nee o |
| | æn 'təʊ niəʊ ◊ | … ◊ |
| **Apollo** | ə 'pɑ lo | uh pah lo |
| | ə 'pɒ ləʊ ◊ | uh po lo ◊ |

---

*International Phonetic Alphabet Pronunciation Key: (General American) i-s<u>ee</u>, happ<u>y</u>, J<u>u</u>li<u>e</u>t; ɪ-s<u>i</u>t; eɪ-s<u>ay</u>; ɛ-s<u>e</u>t; æ-s<u>a</u>t; ɑ-f<u>a</u>ther; ʌ-s<u>u</u>n; ə-<u>a</u>bout; ɔ-s<u>aw</u>; oʊ-s<u>o</u>; o-h<u>e</u>ro; ʊ-sh<u>oo</u>k; u-s<u>oo</u>n; aɪ-s<u>igh</u>; ɔɪ-s<u>oy</u>; aʊ-s<u>ou</u>th; ju-c<u>u</u>be; ə-supp<u>er</u>; ɛr-f<u>air</u>; ɚ-b<u>ir</u>d; k-<u>c</u>ut, <u>k</u>ite; g-<u>g</u>o; dʒ-<u>j</u>oy; j-<u>y</u>es; ŋ-si<u>ng</u>; ʃ-<u>sh</u>oe; tʃ-<u>ch</u>op; ð-<u>th</u>at; θ-<u>th</u>in; ʒ-mea<u>s</u>ure; (Additional symbols for British RP) e-s<u>e</u>t; ɛə-f<u>air</u>; ə-supp<u>er</u>; ɜ-b<u>ir</u>d; ɒ-st<u>o</u>p; əʊ-s<u>o</u>, h<u>e</u>ro; o-(followed by l) p<u>o</u>le.

**Simplified Phonics Pronunciation Key: (General American) ee-s<u>ee</u>, happ<u>y</u>; i-s<u>i</u>t; ei-s<u>ay</u>; e-s<u>e</u>t; a-s<u>a</u>t; ah-f<u>a</u>ther; uh-s<u>u</u>n, <u>a</u>bout; aw-s<u>aw</u>; o-s<u>o</u>; oo-sh<u>oo</u>k; oo-s<u>oo</u>n; ai-s<u>igh</u>; oy-s<u>oy</u>; ow-s<u>ou</u>th; yoo-c<u>u</u>be; ər-b<u>ir</u>d, supp<u>er</u>; k-<u>c</u>ut, <u>k</u>ite; g-<u>g</u>o; j-<u>j</u>oy; ng-si<u>ng</u>; kw-<u>qu</u>ick; sh-<u>sh</u>oe; ch-<u>ch</u>op; th-<u>th</u>at; <i>th</i>-<u>th</u>in; zh-mea<u>s</u>ure; (Additional symbols for British RP) ə-b<u>ir</u>d; ə-supp<u>er</u>; <u>o</u>-st<u>o</u>p; … indicates pronunciation variance too subtle for Simplified Phonics transcription see International Phonetic Alphabet transcription.

◊ British RP pronunciation-see Introduction.

| NAME | INTERNATIONAL PHONETIC ALPHABET* | SIMPLIFIED PHONICS** |
|------|----------------------------------|----------------------|
| Aristotle | 'æ rə stɑ təl<br>'æ rə stɒ təl ◊ | a ruh stah tuhl<br>a ruh sto tuhl ◊ |
| Baptista | bæp 'tɪstə<br>bæp 'tistə | bap tis tuh<br>bap tees tuh |
| Bartholomew/<br>Bartolmew | bɑr 'θɑ lə mju<br><br>'bɑr təl mju<br>ba 'θɒ lə mju ◊<br>'bɑ təl mju ◊ | bahr thah luh<br>myoo<br>bahr tuhl myoo<br>bahr tho luh myoo ◊<br>bah tuhl myoo ◊ |
| Belman | 'bɛl mən<br>'bel mən ◊ | bel muhn<br>... ◊ |
| Bentivolii | bɛn tɪ 'voʊ li aɪ<br>ben tɪ vəʊ li aɪ ◊ | ben ti vo lee ai<br>... ◊ |
| Bergamo | 'bɝ gə mo<br>'bɜ gə məʊ ◊ | bər guh mo<br>bə guh mo ◊ |
| Bianca | bi 'æŋ kə<br>bi 'aŋ kə | bee ang kuh<br>bee ahng kuh |
| Biondello | bi ən 'dɛ lo<br>bi ən 'de ləʊ ◊ | bee uhn de lo<br>... ◊ |
| Burton | 'bɝ tən<br>'bɜ tən ◊ | bər tuhn<br>bə tuhn ◊ |
| Cambio | 'kæm bio<br>'kæm biəʊ ◊ | kam bee o<br>... ◊ |
| Carthage | 'kɑr θɪdʒ<br>'kɑ θɪdʒ ◊ | kahr thij<br>kah thij ◊ |
| Christendom | 'krɪ sən dəm | kri suhn duhm |
| Christian | 'krɪs tʃən | kris chuhn |
| Christmas | 'krɪs məs | kris muhs |

279

| NAME | INTERNATIONAL PHONETIC ALPHABET* | SIMPLIFIED PHONICS** |
|---|---|---|
| **Christopher** | ˈkrɪ stə fɚ <br> ˈkrɪ stə fə ◊ | kri stuh fər <br> kri stuh fə ◊ |
| **Christophero** | krɪ ˈsta fə ro <br> krɪ ˈstɒ fə rəʊ ◊ | kri stah fuh ro <br> kri sto fuh ro ◊ |
| **Cicely** | ˈsɪ sə li <br> ˈsɪs li | si suh lee <br> sis lee |
| **Clowder** | ˈklaʊ dɚ <br> ˈklaʊ də ◊ | klow dər <br> klow də ◊ |
| **Cock** | ˈkɑk <br> ˈkɒk ◊ | kahk <br> kok ◊ |
| **Cretan** | ˈkri tən | kree tuhn |
| **Cytherea** | sɪ θə ˈriə | si thuh ree uh |
| **Daphne** | ˈdæf ni | daf nee |
| **Dian** | ˈdaɪ ən <br> ˈdaɪ æn | dai uhn <br> dai an |
| **Echo** -folio **Eccho** | ˈɛ koʊ <br> ˈe kəʊ ◊ | e ko <br> … ◊ |
| **Europa** | jʊ ˈroʊ pə <br> jʊə ˈrəʊ pə ◊ | yoo ro puh <br> … ◊ |
| **Ferdinand** | ˈfɚ dɪ nænd <br> ˈfɜ dɪ nənd ◊ | fər di nand <br> fə di nand ◊ |
| **Florence** | ˈflɔ rɪns | flaw rins |
| **Florentine** | ˈflɔ rən tin <br> ˈflɑ rən tin <br> ˈflɒ rən taɪn ◊ | flaw ruhn teen <br> flah ruhn teen <br> flo ruhn tain ◊ |

| NAME | INTERNATIONAL PHONETIC ALPHABET* | SIMPLIFIED PHONICS** |
|------|----------------------------------|----------------------|
| **Florentius** | flɔ 'rɛn ʃəs | flaw ren shuhs |
| | flɑ 'rɛn ʃəs | flah ren shuhs |
| | flɒ 'ren ʃəs ◊ | fl*o* ren shuhs ◊ |
| **Gabriel** -folio **Gabrel** | 'geɪ briəl | gei bree uhl |
| **Genoa** -folio also **Genowa** | 'ʤɛ noʊə | je no uh |
| | 'ʤe nəʊə ◊ | ... ◊ |
| **George** | 'ʤɔrʤ | jawrj |
| | 'ʤɔʤ ◊ | jawj ◊ |
| **Greece** | 'gris | grees |
| **Greek** | 'grik | greek |
| **Gregory** | 'grɛ gə ri | gre guh ree |
| | 'gre gə ri ◊ | ... ◊ |
| **Gremio** | 'gri mio | gree mee o |
| | 'gri miəʊ ◊ | ... ◊ |
| | 'gre miəʊ ◊ | gre mee o ◊ |
| **Grissel** | 'grɪ səl | gri suhl |
| **Grumio** | 'gru mio | groo mee o |
| | 'gru miəʊ ◊ | ... ◊ |
| **Hacket** | 'hæ kɪt | ha kit |
| **Henry** | 'hɛn ri | hen ree |
| | 'hen ri ◊ | ... ◊ |
| **Hercules** | 'hɝ kjə liz | hər kyuh leez |
| | 'hɝ kju liz | hər kyoo leez |
| | 'hɝ kjʊ liz ◊ | hə ky*oo* leez ◊ |
| **Hortensio** -folio **Hortentio** | hɔr 'tɛn sio | hawr ten see o |
| | hɔ 'ten siəʊ ◊ | haw ten see o ◊ |
| | hɔ 'ten ʃəʊ ◊ | haw ten sho ◊ |

| NAME | INTERNATIONAL PHONETIC ALPHABET* | SIMPLIFIED PHONICS** |
|------|----------------------------------|----------------------|
| Io | 'aɪ o<br>'aɪ əʊ ◊ | ai o<br>... ◊ |
| Italian | ɪ 'tæl jən | i tal yuhn |
| Italy | 'ɪ tə li | i tuh lee |
| Jack | 'dʒæk | jak |
| [Saint] Jamy | [seɪnt] 'dʒeɪ mi<br>[sɪnt] 'dʒeɪ mi ◊ | [seint] jei mee<br>[sint] jei mee ◊ |
| Jeronimy | dʒə 'rɑ nɪ mi<br>dʒə 'rɒ nɪ mi ◊ | juh rah ni mee<br>juh ro ni mee ◊ |
| Jill | 'dʒɪl | jil |
| Joan | 'dʒoʊn<br>'dʒəʊn ◊ | jon<br>... ◊ |
| John | 'dʒɑn<br>'dʒɒn ◊ | jahn<br>jon ◊ |
| Joseph | 'dʒoʊ zəf<br>'dʒoʊ səf<br>'dʒəʊ zɪf ◊ | jo zuhf<br>jo suhf<br>jo zif ◊ |
| Jove | 'dʒoʊv<br>'dʒəʊv ◊ | jov<br>... ◊ |
| Kate | 'keɪt | keit |
| Katherina | kæ θə 'ri nə<br>kæ tə 'ri nə | ka *th*uh ree nuh<br>ka tuh ree nuh |
| Katherine | 'kæ θrɪn<br>'kæ θə rɪn | ka *th*rin<br>ka *th*uh rin |
| Latin | 'læ tən<br>'læ tɪn | la tuhn<br>la tin |

| NAME | INTERNATIONAL PHONETIC ALPHABET* | SIMPLIFIED PHONICS** |
|---|---|---|
| **Leda** | 'li də | lee duh |
| **Licio** | 'lı ʧio | li chee o |
|  | 'lı ʃio | li shee o |
|  | 'lı ʧiəʊ ◊ | ... ◊ |
|  | 'lı ʃiəʊ ◊ | ... ◊ |
| **Lombardy** -folio **Lumbardie** | 'lɑm bɚ di | lahm bər dee |
|  | 'lʌm bɚ di | luhm bər dee |
|  | 'lɒm bə di ◊ | lom bə dee ◊ |
|  | 'lʌm bə di ◊ | luhm bə dee ◊ |
| **Long-Lane** | 'lɔŋ 'leın | lawng lein |
|  | 'lɒŋ 'leın ◊ | long lein ◊ |
| **Lucentio** | lu 'sɛn tio | loo sen tee o |
|  | lu 'sɛn ʃio | loo sen shee o |
|  | lu 'sen ʃiəʊ ◊ | lu sen shee o ◊ |
| **Lucrece** | 'lu kris | loo krees |
|  | lu 'kris | ... |
| **[Saint] Luke** | [seınt] 'luk | [seint] look |
|  | [sınt] 'luk ◊ | [sint] look ◊ |
| **Mantua** | 'mæn ʧuə | man choo uh |
|  | 'mæn tjuə ◊ | man tyoo uh ◊ |
| **Marian** | 'mɛ riən | me ree uhn |
|  | 'mɛə riən ◊ | meə ree uhn ◊ |
| **Marseilles** | mɑr 'seı | mahr sei |
|  | mɑ 'seı ◊ | mah sei ◊ |
| **Merriman** | 'mɛ rı mən | me ri muhn |
|  | 'me rı mən ◊ | ... ◊ |
| **Minerva** | mə 'nɝ və | muh nər vuh |
|  | mı 'nɜ və ◊ | mi nə vuh ◊ |
| **Minola** | 'mı nə lə | mi nuh luh |

| NAME | INTERNATIONAL PHONETIC ALPHABET* | SIMPLIFIED PHONICS** |
|---|---|---|
| Naps | 'næps | naps |
| Nathaniel | nə 'θæn jəl | nuh *th*an yuhl |
| Neapolitan | niə 'pɑ lə tən | nee uh pah luh tuhn |
| | niə 'pɒ lɪ tən ◊ | nee uh p*o* li tuhn ◊ |
| Nicholas | 'nɪ kə ləs | ni kuh luhs |
| Nicke | 'nɪk | nik |
| Ovid | 'ɑ vɪd | ah vid |
| | 'ɒ vɪd ◊ | *o* vid ◊ |
| Padua | 'pæ ʤuə | pa joo uh |
| | 'pæ djuə ◊ | pa dyoo uh ◊ |
| Paris | 'pæ rɪs | pa ris |
| Pedascule | pɪ 'dæ skjʊ li | pi da sky*oo* lee |
| Pegasus | 'pɛ gə səs | pe guh suhs |
| | 'pe gə səs ◊ | … ◊ |
| Peter | 'pi tɚ | pee tər |
| | 'pi tə ◊ | pee tə ◊ |
| Petruchio | pə 'tru kio | puh troo kee o |
| | pə 'tru tʃio | puh troo chee o |
| | pə 'tru tʃiəʊ ◊ | … ◊ |
| Philip | 'fɪ lɪp | fi lip |
| Pimpernell | 'pɪm pɚ nɛl | pim pər nel |
| | 'pɪm pə nel ◊ | pim pə nel ◊ |
| Pisa | 'pi zə | pee zuh |
| Priami | 'praɪ ə maɪ | prai uh mai |

284

| NAME | INTERNATIONAL PHONETIC ALPHABET* | SIMPLIFIED PHONICS** |
|------|----------------------------------|----------------------|
| **Ralph** | 'rælf<br>'reɪf<br>  [Brit RP var] | ralf<br>reif<br>  [Brit RP var] |
| **Rheims** -folio<br>  **Rheimes** | 'rimz | reemz |
| **Richard** | 'rɪ tʃɚd<br>'rɪ tʃəd ◊ | ri chərd<br>ri chəd ◊ |
| **Roman** | 'roʊ mən<br>'rəʊ mən ◊ | ro muhn<br>... ◊ |
| **Rome** | 'roʊm<br>'rəʊm ◊ | rom<br>... ◊ |
| **Semiramus** | sə 'mɪrə mɪs | suh mi ruh mis |
| **Sibyl/Sybil** | 'sɪ bəl<br>'sɪ bɪl | si buhl<br>si bil |
| **Sibylla** | sɪ 'bɪ lə | si bi luh |
| **Sigeia** | sɪ 'dʒiə | si jee uh |
| **Silver** | 'sɪl vɚ<br>'sɪl və ◊ | sil vər<br>sil və ◊ |
| **Simois** | 'sɪ mə wɪs<br>'sɪ məʊ ɪs ◊ | si muh wis<br>si mo is ◊ |
| **Sincklo**<br>  (folio only) | 'sɪŋ klo<br>'sɪŋ kləʊ ◊ | sing klo<br>... ◊ |
| **Sly** | 'slaɪ | slai |
| **Socrates** | 'su krə tiz<br>'sɒ krə tiz ◊ | sah kruh teez<br>so kruh teez ◊ |
| **Soto** | 'soʊ to<br>'səʊ təʊ ◊ | so to<br>... ◊ |

| NAME | INTERNATIONAL PHONETIC ALPHABET* | SIMPLIFIED PHONICS** |
|---|---|---|
| **Stephen** | 'sti vən | stee vuhn |
| **Sugarsop** | 'ʃʊ gɚ sap | sh*oo* gər sahp |
| | 'ʃʊ gə sɒp ◊ | sh*oo* gə s*o*p ◊ |
| **Sunday** | 'sʌn deɪ | suhn dei |
| | 'sʌn di ◊ | suhn dee ◊ |
| **Tranio** -folio o | 'tʃreɪ nio | chrei nee o |
| **Taino, Tayn** | 'treɪ nio | trei nee o |
| | 'treɪ niəʊ ◊ | … ◊ |
| | 'tʃrɑ nio | chrah nee o |
| | 'trɑ nio | trah nee o |
| | 'trɑ niəʊ ◊ | … ◊ |
| **Tripoli** -folio | 'trɪ pə li | tri puh lee |
| **Tripolie** | 'tʃrɪ pə li | chri puh lee |
| **Troilus** | 'tʃrɔɪ ləs | chroy luhs |
| | 'trɔɪ ləs | troy luhs |
| | 'trəʊɪ ləs ◊ | troi luhs ◊ |
| **Turf/Turph** | 'tɚf | tərf |
| | 'tɜf ◊ | təf ◊ |
| **Turkey** | 'tɚ ki | tər kee |
| | 'tɜ ki ◊ | tə kee ◊ |
| **Tyrian** | 'tɪ riən | ti ree uhn |
| | 'tɪə riən ◊ | tiə ree uhn … ◊ |
| **Venice** | 'vɛ nɪs | ve nis |
| | 've nɪs ◊ | … ◊ |
| **Verona** | və 'roʊ nə | vuh ro nuh |
| | və rəʊ nə ◊ | … ◊ |
| **Vincentio** | vɪn 'sɛn tio | vin sen tee o |
| | vɪn 'sɛn tʃo | vin sen cho |
| | vɪn 'sɛn ʃio | vin sen shee o |
| | vɪn 'sen ʃiəʊ ◊ | … ◊ |

| NAME | INTERNATIONAL PHONETIC ALPHABET* | SIMPLIFIED PHONICS** |
|------|----------------------------------|----------------------|
| **Walter** | 'wɔl tɚ <br> 'wɔl tə ◊ | wawl tər <br> wawl tə ◊ |
| **Wincot/ <br> Wincote/ <br> Wilnecote** | 'wɪŋ kət | wing kuht |
| **Xantippe/ <br> Xanthippe** | zæn 'θɪ pi <br> zæn 'tɪ pi | zan *th*i pee <br> zan ti pee |

| NAME | INTERNATIONAL PHONETIC ALPHABET* | SIMPLIFIED PHONICS** |
|------|----------------------------------|----------------------|
| **Adrian** | 'eɪ driən<br>'eɪ dʒriən | ei dree uhn<br>ei jree uhn |
| **Aeneas** | ɪ 'niəs<br>i 'niəs | i nee uhs<br>ee nee uhs |
| **Afric** | 'æ frɪk | a frik |
| **African** | 'æ frɪ kən | a fri kuhn |
| **Alonso** | ə 'lɑn zo<br>ə 'lɒn zəʊ ◊ | uh lahn zo<br>uh lon zo ◊ |
| **Antonio** | æn 'toʊ nio<br>æn 'təʊ niəʊ ◊ | an to nee o<br>… ◊ |
| **April** | 'eɪ prəl | ei pruhl |
| **Arabia** | ə 'reɪ biə | uh rei bee uh |
| **Argier** | ɑr 'dʒɪr<br>ɑ 'dʒɪə ◊ | ahr jir<br>ah jiə ◊ |
| **Ariel** | 'ɛ ri əl<br>'æ ri əl<br>ɛə ri əl ◊ | e ree uhl<br>a ree uhl<br>… ◊ |
| **August** | 'ɔ gəst | aw guhst |
| **Bermoothes** | bɚ 'mu ðəz<br>bə 'mu ðəz ◊ | bər moo thuhz<br>bə moo thuhz ◊ |

*International Phonetic Alphabet Pronunciation Key: (General American) i-s<u>ee</u>, happ<u>y</u>, J<u>u</u>liet; ɪ-s<u>i</u>t; eɪ-s<u>ay</u>; ɛ-s<u>e</u>t; æ-s<u>a</u>t; ɑ-f<u>a</u>ther; ʌ-s<u>u</u>n; ə-<u>a</u>bout; ɔ-s<u>aw</u>; oʊ-s<u>o</u>; o-h<u>e</u>ro; ʊ-sh<u>oo</u>k; u-s<u>oo</u>n; aɪ-s<u>igh</u>; ɔɪ-s<u>oy</u>; aʊ-s<u>ou</u>th; ju-c<u>u</u>be; ɚ-s<u>u</u>pper; ɛr-f<u>air</u>; ɝ-b<u>ir</u>d; k-<u>c</u>ut, <u>k</u>ite; g-<u>g</u>o; dʒ-<u>j</u>oy; j-<u>y</u>es; ŋ-si<u>ng</u>; ʃ-<u>sh</u>oe; ʧ-<u>ch</u>op; ð-<u>th</u>at; θ-<u>th</u>in; ʒ-mea<u>s</u>ure; (Additional symbols for British RP) e-s<u>e</u>t; ɛə-f<u>air</u>; ə-s<u>u</u>pper; ɜ-b<u>ir</u>d; ɒ-st<u>o</u>p; əʊ-s<u>o</u>, h<u>e</u>ro; o-(followed by l) p<u>o</u>le.

**Simplified Phonics Pronunciation Key: (General American) ee-s<u>ee</u>, happ<u>y</u>; i-s<u>i</u>t; ei-s<u>ay</u>; e-s<u>e</u>t; a-s<u>a</u>t; ah-f<u>a</u>ther; uh-s<u>u</u>n, <u>a</u>bout; aw-s<u>aw</u>; o-s<u>o</u>; oo-sh<u>oo</u>k; oo-s<u>oo</u>n; ow-s<u>ou</u>th; yoo-c<u>u</u>be; ər-b<u>ir</u>d, supper; k-<u>c</u>ut, <u>k</u>ite; g-<u>g</u>o; j-<u>j</u>oy; ng-si<u>ng</u>; kw-<u>qu</u>ick; sh-<u>sh</u>oe; ch-<u>ch</u>op; th-<u>th</u>at; <u>th</u>-<u>th</u>in; zh-mea<u>s</u>ure; (Additional symbols for British RP) ə-b<u>ir</u>d; ə-s<u>u</u>pper; <u>o</u>-st<u>o</u>p; … indicates pronunciation variance too subtle for Simplified Phonics transcription see International Phonetic Alphabet transcription.

◊ British RP pronunciation-see Introduction.

| NAME | INTERNATIONAL PHONETIC ALPHABET* | SIMPLIFIED PHONICS** |
|------|----------------------------------|----------------------|
| Caliban | 'kæ lɪ bæn<br>'kæ lə bæn | ka li ban<br>ka luh ban |
| Carthage | 'kɑr θɪʤ<br>'kɑ θɪʤ ◊ | kahr *th*ij<br>kah *th*ij ◊ |
| Ceres | 'sɪ riz<br>'sɪə riz ◊ | si reez<br>... ◊ |
| Claribel | 'klæ rə bɛl<br>'klæ rə bel ◊ | kla ruh bel<br>... ◊ |
| Dido | 'daɪ do<br>'daɪ dəʊ ◊ | dai do<br>... ◊ |
| Dis | 'dɪs | dis |
| England | 'ɪŋ glənd | ing gluhnd |
| Europe | 'jʊ rəp<br>'jʊə rəp ◊ | y*oo* ruhp<br>... ◊ |
| Ferdinand | 'fɝ də nænd<br>'fɜ dɪ nænd ◊ | fər duh ɴand<br>fə di nand ◊ |
| Francisco | fræn 'sɪs ko<br>fræn 'sɪs kəʊ ◊ | fran sis ko<br>... ◊ |
| Fury | 'fjʊ ri<br>'fjʊə ri ◊ | fy*oo* ree<br>... ◊ |
| Gonzalo | gən 'zɑ lo<br>gɑn 'zɑ lo<br>gɒn 'zɑ ləʊ ◊ | guhn zah lo<br>gahn zah lo<br>gɒn zah lo ◊ |
| Hymen | 'haɪ mən | hai muhn |
| Inde | 'ɪnd<br>'aɪnd | ind<br>aind |
| Indian | 'ɪn diən | in dee uhn |

| NAME | INTERNATIONAL PHONETIC ALPHABET* | SIMPLIFIED PHONICS** |
|------|----------------------------------|----------------------|
| Iris | 'aɪ rɪs | ai ris |
| Italy | 'ɪ tə li | i tuh lee |
| Jack | 'dʒæk | jak |
| Jove | 'dʒoʊv<br>'dʒəʊv ◊ | jov<br>... ◊ |
| Juno | 'dʒu no<br>'dʒu nəʊ ◊ | joo no<br>... ◊ |
| Jupiter | 'dʒu pɪ tɚ<br>'dʒu pɪ tə ◊ | joo pi tər<br>joo pi tə ◊ |
| Kate | 'keɪt | keit |
| Mall/Moll | 'mɑl<br>'mɒl ◊ | mahl<br>mol ◊ |
| Margery | 'mɑr dʒə ri<br>'mɑ dʒə ri ◊ | mahr juh ree<br>mah juh ree ◊ |
| Marian | 'mɛ riən<br>'mɛə riən ◊ | me ree uhn<br>... ◊ |
| Mars | 'mɑrz<br>'mɑz ◊ | mahrz<br>mahz ◊ |
| Mediterranean | mɛ dɪ tə 'reɪ niən<br><br>me dɪ tə 'reɪ niən ◊ | me di tuh rei<br>  nee uhn<br>... ◊ |
| Meg | 'mɛg<br>'meg ◊ | meg<br>... ◊ |
| Milan | mɪ 'lɑn<br>mɪ 'læn<br>'mɪ lən | mi lahn<br>mi lan<br>mi luhn |

| NAME | INTERNATIONAL PHONETIC ALPHABET* | SIMPLIFIED PHONICS** |
|------|-----------------------------------|----------------------|
| Miranda | mə 'ræn də<br>mɪ 'ræn də | muh ran duh<br>mi ran duh |
| Monster | 'mɑn stɚ<br>'mɒn stə ◊ | mahn stər<br>mon stə ◊ |
| Mountain | 'maʊn tɪn | mown tin |
| Naiad | 'naɪ æd<br>'naɪ əd | nai ad<br>nai uhd |
| Naples | 'neɪ pəlz | nei puhlz |
| Neapolitan | niə 'pɑ lɪ tən<br><br>niə 'pɒ lɪ tən ◊ | nee uh pah li tuhn<br><br>nee uh po li tuhn ◊ |
| Neptune | 'nɛp tun<br>'nep tjun ◊ | nep toon<br>nep tyoon ◊ |
| Paphos | 'peɪ fɑs<br>'peɪ fɒs ◊ | pei fahs<br>pei fos ◊ |
| Phoebus | 'fi bəs | fee buhs |
| Phoenix | 'fi nɪks | fee niks |
| Prosper | 'prɑs pɚ<br>'prɒs pə ◊ | prahs pər<br>pros pə ◊ |
| Prospero | 'prɑs pə ro<br>'prɒs pə rəʊ ◊ | prahs puh ro<br>pros puh ro ◊ |
| Prudence | 'pru dəns | proo duhns |
| Sebastian | sə 'bæs ʧən<br>sə 'bæs tiən ◊ | suh bas chuhn<br>suh bas tee uhn ◊ |
| Setebos | 'sɛ tə bas<br>'se tə bɒs ◊ | se tuh bahs<br>se tuh bos ◊ |

291

| NAME | INTERNATIONAL PHONETIC ALPHABET* | SIMPLIFIED PHONICS** |
|------|------|------|
| **Silver** | 'sɪl vɚ<br>'sɪl və ◊ | sil vər<br>sil və ◊ |
| **Stephano** | 'stɛ fə no<br>'ste fə nəʊ ◊ | ste fuh no<br>… ◊ |
| **Sycorax** | 'sɪ kə raks | si kuh raks |
| **Trinculo** | 'trɪŋ kjə lo<br>'ʧrɪŋ kjə lo<br>'trɪŋ kju ləʊ ◊ | tring kyuh lo<br>chring kjuh lo<br>tring kyoo lo ◊ |
| **Tunis** | 'tu nəs<br>'tju nɪs ◊ | too nuhs<br>tyoo nis ◊ |
| **Tyrant** | 'taɪ rənt | tai ruhnt |
| **Venus** | 'vi nəs | vee nuhs |

| NAME | INTERNATIONAL PHONETIC ALPHABET* | SIMPLIFIED PHONICS** |
|------|------|------|
| **Alcibiades** | æl sə 'baɪ ə diz | al suh bai uh deez |
| | æl sɪ 'baɪ ə diz | al si bai uh deez |
| **Amazon** | 'æ mə zɑn | a muh zahn |
| | 'æ mə zən | a muh zuhn |
| **Apemantus/ Apermantus** | æ pɪ 'mæn təs | a pi man tuhs |
| **April** | 'eɪ prəl | ei pruhl |
| **Athenian** | ə 'θi niən | uh *thee* nee uhn |
| **Athens** | 'æ θɪnz | a *thi*nz |
| | 'æ θənz | a *thu*hnz |
| **Byzantium** | bɪ 'zæn tiəm | bi zan tee uhm |
| | bɪ 'zæn ʃiəm | bi zan shee uhm |
| **Caphis** | 'keɪ fɪs | kei fis |
| **Corinth** | 'kɔ rɪnθ | kaw rin*th* |
| | 'kɒ rɪnθ ◊ | k*o* rin*th* ◊ |
| **Cupid** | 'kju pɪd | kyoo pid |
| **Dian** | 'daɪ ən | dai uhn |
| | 'daɪ æn | dai an |
| **Flaminius** | flə 'mɪ niəs | fluh mi nee uhs |
| **Flavius** | 'fleɪ viəs | flei vee uhs |

---

*International Phonetic Alphabet Pronunciation Key: (General American) i-s<u>ee</u>, happ<u>y</u>, Jul<u>i</u>et; ɪ-s<u>i</u>t; eɪ-s<u>ay</u>; ɛ-s<u>e</u>t; æ-s<u>a</u>t; ɑ-f<u>a</u>ther; ʌ-s<u>u</u>n; ə-<u>a</u>bout; ɔ-s<u>aw</u>; oʊ-s<u>o</u>; o-h<u>e</u>ro; ʊ-sh<u>oo</u>k; u-s<u>oo</u>n; aɪ-s<u>igh</u>; ɔɪ-s<u>oy</u>; aʊ-s<u>ou</u>th; ju-c<u>u</u>be; ɚ-s<u>u</u>pp<u>er</u>; ɛr-f<u>air</u>; ɝ-b<u>ir</u>d; k-<u>c</u>ut, <u>k</u>ite; g-<u>g</u>o; ʤ-<u>j</u>oy; j-<u>y</u>es; ŋ-si<u>ng</u>; ʃ-<u>sh</u>oe; tʃ-<u>ch</u>op; ð-<u>th</u>at; θ-<u>th</u>in; ʒ-mea<u>s</u>ure; (Additional symbols for British RP) e-s<u>e</u>t; ɛə-f<u>air</u>; ə-s<u>u</u>pp<u>er</u>; ɜ-b<u>ir</u>d; ɒ-s<u>to</u>p; əʊ-s<u>o</u>, h<u>e</u>r<u>o</u>; o-(followed by l) p<u>o</u>le.

**Simplified Phonics Pronunciation Key: (General American) ee-s<u>ee</u>, happ<u>y</u>; i-s<u>i</u>t; ei-s<u>ay</u>; e-s<u>e</u>t; a-s<u>a</u>t; ah-f<u>a</u>ther; uh-s<u>u</u>n, <u>a</u>bout; aw-s<u>aw</u>; o-s<u>o</u>; *oo*-sh<u>oo</u>k; oo-s<u>oo</u>n; ai-s<u>igh</u>; oy-s<u>oy</u>; ow-s<u>ou</u>th; yoo-c<u>u</u>be; ər-b<u>ir</u>d, s<u>u</u>pp<u>er</u>; k-<u>c</u>ut, <u>k</u>ite; g-<u>g</u>o; j-<u>j</u>oy; ng-si<u>ng</u>; kw-<u>qu</u>ick; sh-<u>sh</u>oe; ch-<u>ch</u>op; th-<u>th</u>at; *th*-<u>th</u>in; zh-mea<u>s</u>ure; (Additional symbols for British RP) ə-b<u>ir</u>d; ə-s<u>u</u>pp<u>er</u>; *o*-s<u>to</u>p; ... indicates pronunciation variance too subtle for Simplified Phonics transcription see International Phonetic Alphabet transcription.

◊ British RP pronunciation-see Introduction.

| NAME | INTERNATIONAL PHONETIC ALPHABET* | SIMPLIFIED PHONICS** |
|------|------|------|
| **Fool** | 'ful | fool |
| **German** | 'ʤɝ mən<br>'ʤɝ mən ◊ | jər muhn<br>jə muhn ◊ |
| **Hortensius** | hɔr 'tɛn siəs<br>hɔ 'ten siəs ◊ | hawr ten see uhs<br>haw ten see uhs ◊ |
| **Hostilius** | hɑ 'stɪ liəs<br>hɒ 'stɪ liəs ◊ | hah sti lee uhs<br>ho sti lee uhs ◊ |
| **Hymen** | 'haɪ mən | hai muhn |
| **Hyperion** | haɪ 'pɪ riən<br>haɪ 'pɪə riən ◊ | hai pi ree uhn<br>… ◊ |
| **Inde** | 'ɪnd<br>'aɪnd | ind<br>aind |
| **Isidore** | 'ɪ zə dɔr<br>'ɪ zə dɔ ◊ | i zuh dawr<br>i zuh daw ◊ |
| **Jack** | 'ʤæk | jak |
| **Jove** | 'ʤoʊv<br>'ʤəʊv ◊ | jov<br>… ◊ |
| **Jupiter** | 'ʤu pɪ tɚ<br>'ʤu pɪ tə ◊ | joo pi tər<br>joo pi tə ◊ |
| **Lacedaemon** | læ sə 'di mən | la suh dee muhn |
| **Lucilius** | lu 'sɪ liəs | loo si lee uhs |
| **Lucius** | 'lu ʃəs<br>'lu siəs | loo shuhs<br>loo see uhs |
| **Lucullus** | lu 'kʌ ləs | loo kuh luhs |
| **Mars** | 'mɑrz<br>'mɑz ◊ | mahrz<br>mahz ◊ |

| NAME | INTERNATIONAL PHONETIC ALPHABET* | SIMPLIFIED PHONICS** |
|------|----------------------------------|----------------------|
| **Mercer** (folio only) | ˈmɝ sɚ<br>ˈmɜ sə ◊ | mər sər<br>mə sə ◊ |
| **Misanthropos** | mɪ ˈsæn θrə pəs | mi san *th*ruh puhs |
| **Neptune** | ˈnɛp tun<br>ˈnep tjun ◊ | nep toon<br>nep tyoon ◊ |
| **Philotus** | fɪ ˈloʊ təs<br>fɪ ˈləʊ təs ◊<br>faɪ ˈləʊ təs ◊ | fi lo tuhs<br>…◊<br>fai lo tuhs ◊ |
| **Phoenix** | ˈfi nɪks | fee niks |
| **Phrynia** | ˈfrɪ niə | fri nee uh |
| **Plutus** | ˈplu təs | ploo tuhs |
| **Sempronius** | sɛm ˈproʊ niəs<br>sem ˈprəʊ niəs ◊ | sem pro nee uhs<br>… ◊ |
| **Servilius** | sɚ ˈvɪ liəs<br>sə ˈvɪ liəs ◊ | sər vi li uhs<br>sə vi li uhs ◊ |
| **Timandra/**<br>**Tymandra** | tɪ ˈmæn drə<br>tɪ ˈmæn dʒrə | ti man druh<br>ti man jruh |
| **Timon** | ˈtaɪ mən | tai muhn |
| **Titus** | ˈtaɪ təs | tai tuhs |
| **Varro** | ˈvæ ɾo<br>ˈvæ ɾəʊ ◊ | va ɾo<br>… ◊ |
| **Ventidius** -folio<br>  **Ventiddius,**<br>  **Ventigius,**<br>  **Ventidgius** | vɛn ˈtɪ diəs<br>vɛn ˈtɪ dʒəs<br>ven ˈtɪ diəs<br>ven ˈtɪ dʒəs | ven ti dee uhs<br>ven ti juhs<br>… ◊<br>… ◊ |

| NAME | INTERNATIONAL PHONETIC ALPHABET* | SIMPLIFIED PHONICS** |
|------|-----------------------------------|----------------------|
| **Aaron** | 'ɛ rən | e ruhn |
| | 'æ rən | a ruhn |
| | 'ɛə rən ◊ | … ◊ |
| **Acheron** | 'æ kə rɑn | a kuh rahn |
| | 'æ kə rən | a kuh ruhn |
| | 'æ kə rɒn ◊ | a kuh ron ◊ |
| **Actaeon** | æk 'ti ən | ak tee uhn |
| **Aemilius/ Emillius** | ɪ 'mi liəs | i mee lee uhs |
| | ɪ 'mil jəs | i meel yuhs |
| **Aeneas** | ɪ 'ni əs | i nee uhs |
| | i 'ni əs | ee nee uhs |
| **Aetna/Etna** | 'ɛt nə | et nuh |
| | 'et nə ◊ | … ◊ |
| **Ajax** | 'eɪ dʒæks | ei jaks |
| **Alarbus** | ə 'lɑr bəs | uh lahr buhs |
| | ə 'lɑ bəs ◊ | uh lah buhs ◊ |
| **Alcides** | æl 'saɪ diz | al sai deez |
| **Andonici** | æn 'drɑ nə saɪ | an drah nuh sai |
| | æn 'drɒ nɪ saɪ ◊ | an dro ni sai ◊ |
| **Andronicus** | æn 'drɑ nə kəs | an drah nuh kuhs |
| | æn 'drɒ nɪ kəs ◊ | an dro ni kuhs ◊ |

---

*International Phonetic Alphabet Pronunciation Key: (General American) i-see, happy, Juliet; ɪ-sit; eɪ-say; ɛ-set; æ-sat; ɑ-father; ʌ-sun; ə-about; ɔ-saw; oʊ-so; o-hero; ʊ-shook; u-soon; aɪ-sigh; ɔɪ-soy; aʊ-south; ju-cube; ə-supper; ɚ-fair; ɝ-bird; k-cut, kite; g-go; dʒ-joy; j-yes; ŋ-sing; ʃ-shoe; tʃ-chop; ð-that; θ-thin; ʒ-measure; (Additional symbols for British RP) e-set; ɛə-fair; ə-supper; ɜ-bird; ɒ-stop; əʊ-so, hero; o-(followed by l) pole.

**Simplified Phonics Pronunciation Key: (General American) ee-see, happy; i-sit; ei-say; e-set; a-sat; ah-father; uh-sun, about; aw-saw; o-so; oo-shook; oo-soon; ai-sigh; oy-soy; ow-south; yoo-cube; ər-bird, supper; k-cut, kite; g-go; j-joy; ng-sing; kw-quick; sh-shoe; ch-chop; th-that; th-thin; zh-measure; (Additional symbols for British RP) ə-bird; ə-supper; o-stop; … indicates pronunciation variance too subtle for Simplified Phonics transcription see International Phonetic Alphabet transcription.

◊ British RP pronunciation-see Introduction.

| NAME | INTERNATIONAL PHONETIC ALPHABET* | SIMPLIFIED PHONICS** |
|------|----------------------------------|----------------------|
| **Apollinem** | ə ˈpɑ lɪ nəm<br>ə ˈpɒ lɪ nəm ◊ | uh pah li nuhm<br>uh po li nuhm ◊ |
| **Apollo** | ə ˈpɑ lo<br>ə ˈpɒ ləʊ ◊ | uh pah lo<br>uh po lo ◊ |
| **April** | ˈeɪ prəl | ei pruhl |
| **Aries** | ˈɛ riz<br>ˈɛə riz ◊ | e reez<br>… ◊ |
| **Astraea** | æ ˈstri ə<br>æs ˈtʃri ə | a stree uh<br>as chree uh |
| **Bassianus** | bæ si ˈeɪ nəs | ba see ei nuhs |
| **Brutus** | ˈbru təs | broo tuhs |
| **Bull** | ˈbʊl | bool |
| **Caesar** | ˈsi zɚ<br>ˈsi zə ◊ | see zər<br>see zə ◊ |
| **Caius** | ˈkai əs<br>ˈkeɪ əs | kai uhs<br>kei uhs |
| **Capitol** | ˈkæ pɪ təl | ka pi tuhl |
| **Caucasus** | ˈkɔ kə səs<br>ˈkɑ kə səs<br>    [gen Am var] | kaw kuh suhs<br>kah kuh suhs<br>    [gen Am var] |
| **Cerberus** | ˈsɚ bə rəs<br>ˈsɜ bə rəs ◊ | sər buh ruhs<br>sə buh ruhs ◊ |
| **Chiron** | ˈkai rɑn<br>ˈkai rən ◊ | kai rahn<br>kai ruhn ◊ |
| **Cimmerian** | sɪ ˈmɪ riən<br>sɪ ˈmɪə riən | si mi ree uhn<br>si miə ree uhn |

297

| NAME | INTERNATIONAL PHONETIC ALPHABET* | SIMPLIFIED PHONICS** |
|---|---|---|
| **Cocytus** | ko 'saɪ təs<br>kəʊ 'saɪ təs ◊ | ko sai tuhs<br>... ◊ |
| **Coriolanus** | kɔ riə 'leɪ nəs | kaw ree uh lei nuhs |
| **Cornelia** | kɔr 'ni liə<br>kɔr nil jə<br>kɔ 'ni liə ◊ | kawr nee lee uh<br>kawr neel yuh<br>kaw nee lee uh ◊ |
| **Cyclops** | 'saɪ klɑps<br>'saɪ klɒps ◊ | sai klahps<br>sai klops ◊ |
| **Demetrius** | dɪ 'mi triəs<br>dɪ 'mi tʃriəs | di mee tree uhs<br>di mee chree uhs |
| **Dian** | 'daɪ ən<br>'daɪ æn | dai uhn<br>dai an |
| **Dido** | 'daɪ do<br>'daɪ dəʊ ◊ | dai do<br>... ◊ |
| **Enceledus** | ɛn 'sɛ lə dəs<br>en 'se lə dəs ◊ | en se luh duhs<br>... ◊ |
| **Goth** | 'gɑθ<br>'gɒθ ◊ | gah*th*<br>*goth* ◊ |
| **Greek** | 'grik | greek |
| **Hector** | 'hɛk tɚ<br>'hek tə ◊ | hek tər<br>hek tə ◊ |
| **Horace** | 'hɔ rəs<br>'hɑ rəs<br>'hɒ rəs ◊ | haw ruhs<br>hah ruhs<br>ho ruhs ◊ |
| **Hymenaeus** | haɪ mə 'ni əs | hai muh nee uhs |
| **Hyperion** | haɪ 'pɪ riən<br>haɪ 'pɪə riən ◊ | hai pi ree uhn<br>hai piə ree uhn ... ◊ |

| NAME | INTERNATIONAL PHONETIC ALPHABET* | SIMPLIFIED PHONICS** |
|------|------|------|
| Jove | 'dʒoʊv<br>'dʒəʊv ◊ | jov<br>… ◊ |
| Jovem | 'dʒoʊ vəm<br>'dʒəʊ vəm ◊ | jo vuhm<br>… ◊ |
| Junius | 'dʒu niəs | joo nee uhs |
| Jupiter | 'dʒu pɪ tɚ<br>'dʒu pɪ tə ◊ | joo pi tər<br>joo pi tə ◊ |
| Laertes | leɪ 'ɛr tiz<br>li 'ɝ tiz<br>leɪ 'ɜ tiz ◊ | lei er teez<br>lee er teez<br>lei ə teez ◊ |
| Lavinia | lə 'vɪ niə | luh vi nee uh |
| Limbo | 'lɪm bo<br>'lɪm bəʊ ◊ | lim bo<br>… ◊ |
| Lucius | 'lu ʃəs<br>'lu ʃiəs | loo shuhs<br>loo shee uhs |
| Lucrece | 'lu kris<br>lu 'kris | loo krees<br>… |
| Marcus | 'mɑr kəs<br>'mɑ kəs ◊ | mahr kuhs<br>mah kuhs ◊ |
| Martem | 'mɑr təm<br>'mɑ təm ◊ | mahr tuhm<br>mah tuhm ◊ |
| Martius | 'mɑr ʃəs<br>'mɑr ʃiəs<br>'mɑ ʃəs ◊<br>'mɑ ʃiəs ◊ | mahr shuhs<br>mahr shee uhs<br>mah shus ◊<br>mah shee uhs ◊ |
| Mauri | 'mɔ ri | maw ree |
| Mercury | 'mɝ kjə ri<br>'mɜ kjʊ ri ◊ | mər kyuh ree<br>mə ky*oo* ree ◊ |

| NAME | INTERNATIONAL PHONETIC ALPHABET* | SIMPLIFIED PHONICS** |
| --- | --- | --- |
| **Moor** | 'mur<br>'mʊr<br>'mʊə ◊ | moor<br>m*oo*r<br>m*oo*ə |
| **Muli** -folio<br>  **Muliteus** | 'mju li | myoo lee |
| **Muliteus** | mju lɪ 'tiəs<br>'mju lɪ tiəs | myoo li tee uhs<br>… |
| **Mutius** | 'mju ʃəs<br>'mju ʃi əs | myoo shuhs<br>myoo shee uhs |
| **Nilus** | 'naɪ ləs | nai luhs |
| **Olympus** | ə 'lɪm pəs<br>o 'lɪm pəs | uh lim puhs<br>o lim puhs |
| **Ovid** | 'ɑ vɪd<br>'ɒ vɪd ◊ | ah vid<br>*o* vid ◊ |
| **Pallas** | 'pæ ləs | pa luhs |
| **Pantheon** | 'pæn θiɑn<br>pæn 'θi ɑn<br>'pæn θiən | pan *th*ee ahn<br>pan *th*ee ahn<br>pan *th*ee uhn |
| **Philomel** | 'fɪ lə mɛl<br>'fɪ lə mel ◊ | fi luh mel<br>… ◊ |
| **Philomela** | fɪ lə 'mi lə | fi luh mee luh |
| **Phoebe** | 'fi bi | fee bee |
| **Pius** | 'paɪ əs | pai uhs |
| **Pluto** | 'plu to<br>'plu təʊ ◊ | ploo to<br>… ◊ |
| **Priam** | 'praɪ əm | prai uhm |

| NAME | INTERNATIONAL PHONETIC ALPHABET* | SIMPLIFIED PHONICS** |
|---|---|---|
| **Progne** | 'prɑg ni<br>'prɒg ni ◊ | prahg nee<br>prog nee ◊ |
| **Prometheus** | pro 'mi θiəs<br>prə 'mi θiəs<br>prəʊ 'mi θjus ◊ | pro mee *thee* uhs<br>pruh mee *thee* uhs<br>pro mee *th*yoos ◊ |
| **Publius** | 'pʌ bliəs | puh blee uhs |
| **Pyramus** | 'pɪ rə məs | pi ruh muhs |
| **Quintus** | 'kwɪn təs | kwin tuhs |
| **Ram** | 'ræm | ram |
| **Roman** | 'roʊ mən<br>'rəʊ mən ◊ | ro muhn<br>… ◊ |
| **Rome** | 'roʊm<br>'rəʊm ◊ | rom<br>… ◊ |
| **Saturn** | 'sæ tɚn<br>'sæ tən ◊ | sa tɘrn<br>sa tən ◊ |
| **Saturnine** | 'sæ tɚ naɪn<br>'sæ tə naɪn ◊ | sa tɘr nain<br>sa tə nain ◊ |
| **Saturninus** | sæ tɚ 'naɪ nəs<br>sæ tə 'naɪ nəs ◊ | sa tɘr nai nuhs<br>sa tə nai nuhs ◊ |
| **Scythia** | 'sɪ ðiə | si thee uh |
| **Semiramus** | sə 'mɪrə mɪs | suh miruh mis |
| **Sempronius** | sɛm 'proʊ niəs<br>sem 'prəʊ niəs ◊ | sem pro nee uhs<br>… ◊ |
| **Sibyl/Sybil** | 'sɪ bəl<br>'sɪ bɪl | si buhl<br>si bil |
| **Sicily** | 'sɪ sə li | si suh lee |

| NAME | INTERNATIONAL PHONETIC ALPHABET* | SIMPLIFIED PHONICS** |
|---|---|---|
| **Sinon** | 'saɪ nən | sai nuhn |
| **Solon** | 'soʊ lən<br>'soʊ lɑn<br>'səʊ lɒn ◊<br>'səʊ lən ◊ | so luhn<br>so lahn<br>so lon ◊<br>... ◊ |
| **[Saint] Stephen** | [seint] 'sti vən<br>[sɪnt] 'sti vən ◊ | [seint] stee vuhn<br>[sint] stee vuhn ◊ |
| **Styga** | 'staɪ gə | stai guh |
| **Styx** | 'stɪks | stiks |
| **Tamora** | 'tæ mə rə<br>'tæm rə | ta muh ruh<br>tam ruh |
| **Tarquin** | 'tɑr kwɪn<br>'tɑ kwɪn ◊ | tahr kwin<br>tah kwin ◊ |
| **Taurus** | 'tɔ rəs<br>'tɑ rəs<br>    [gen Am var] | taw ruhs<br>tah ruhs<br>    [gen Am var] |
| **Tereus** | 'ti rus | tee roos |
| **Thracian** | 'θreɪ ʃən | *th*rei shuhn |
| **Titan** | 'taɪ tən | tai tuhn |
| **Titus** | 'taɪ təs | tai tuhs |
| **Troy** | 'trɔɪ<br>'ʧrɔɪ | troy<br>chroy |
| **Tully** | 'tʌ li | tuh lee |
| **Typhon** | 'taɪ fɑn<br>'taɪ fɒn ◊ | tai fahn<br>tai fon ◊ |

| NAME | INTERNATIONAL PHONETIC ALPHABET* | SIMPLIFIED PHONICS** |
|------|----------------------------------|----------------------|
| **Valentine** | 'væ lən taɪn <br> 'væ lən taɪn ◊ | va luhn tain <br> va luhn tain ◊ |
| **Venus** | 'vi nəs | vee nuhs |
| **Virginius** | və 'dʒɪ niəs <br> və 'dʒɪ niəs ◊ | vər ji nee uhs <br> və ji nee uhs ◊ |
| **Virgo** | 'vɝ go <br> 'vɜ gəʊ ◊ | vər go <br> və go ◊ |
| **Vulcan** | 'vʌl kən | vuhl kuhn |

| NAME | INTERNATIONAL PHONETIC ALPHABET* | SIMPLIFIED PHONICS** |
|------|----------------------------------|----------------------|
| **Achilles** | ə ˈkɪ liz | uh ki leez |
| **Aeneas** | ɪ ˈni əs | i nee uhs |
|  | i ˈni əs | ee nee uhs |
| **Afric** | ˈæ frɪk | a frik |
| **Agamemnon** | æ gə ˈmɛm nən | a guh mem nuhn |
|  | æ gə ˈmɛm nɑn | a guh mem nahn |
|  | æ gə ˈmem nɒn ◊ | a guh mem non ◊ |
| **Ajax** | ˈeɪ dʒæks | ei jaks |
| **Alexander** | æ lɪg ˈzæn dɚ | a lig zan dər |
|  | æ lɪg ˈzɑn də ◊ | a lig zahn də ◊ |
| **Amphimachus** | æm ˈfɪ mə kəs | am fi muh kuhs |
| **Anchises** | æn ˈkaɪ siz | an kai seez |
|  | æŋ ˈkaɪ siz | ang kai seez |
| **Andromache** | æn ˈdrɑ mə ki | an drah muh kee |
|  | æn ˈdʒrɑ mə ki | an jrah muh kee |
|  | æn ˈdrɒ mə ki ◊ | an dro muh kee ◊ |
| **Antenor** | æn ˈti nɔr | an tee nawr |
|  | æn ˈti nɔ ◊ | an tee naw ◊ |
| **Antenorides**<br>-folio | æn tə ˈnɑ rə diz | an tuh nah ruh deez |
| **Antenoridus** | æn tɪ ˈnɒ rə diz ◊ | an ti no ruh deez ◊ |

| NAME | INTERNATIONAL PHONETIC ALPHABET* | SIMPLIFIED PHONICS** |
|------|----------------------------------|----------------------|
| Apollo | ə 'pɑ lo<br>ə 'pɒ ləʊ ◊ | uh pah lo<br>uh po lo ◊ |
| April | 'eɪ prəl | ei pruhl |
| Aquilon | 'æ kwɪ lɑn<br>'æ kwɪ lɒn ◊ | a kwi lahn<br>a kwi lon ◊ |
| Argus | 'ɑr gəs<br>'ɑ gəs ◊ | ahr guhs<br>ah guhs ◊ |
| Ariachne | æ ri 'æk ni | a ree ak nee |
| Aristotle | 'æ rə stɑ təl<br>'æ rə stɒ təl ◊ | a ruh stah tuhl<br>a ruh sto tuhl ◊ |
| Athenian | ə 'θi niən | uh *th*ee nee uhn |
| Athens | 'æ θɪnz<br>'æ θənz | a *th*inz<br>a *th*uhnz |
| Boreas | 'bɔ riəs<br>'bɔ ri æs ◊ | baw ree uhs<br>baw ree as ◊ |
| Brabbler | 'bræ blɚ<br>'bræ blə ◊ | bra blər<br>bra blə ◊ |
| Briareus | braɪ 'ɛ riəs<br>braɪ 'ɛə riəs ◊ | brai e ree uhs<br>... ◊ |
| Caduceus | kə 'du siəs<br>kə 'dju siəs ◊ | kuh doo see uhs<br>kuh dyoo see uhs ◊ |
| Calchas -folio<br>    Calcas, Chalcas,<br>    Calcha | 'kæl kəs | kal kuhs |
| Cancer | 'kæn sɚ<br>'kæn sə ◊ | kan sər<br>kan sə ◊ |

| NAME | INTERNATIONAL PHONETIC ALPHABET* | SIMPLIFIED PHONICS** |
|---|---|---|
| **Cassandra** | kə 'sæn drə | kuh san druh |
| | kə 'sæn ʤrə | kuh san jruh |
| **Cedius** | 'si diəs | see dee uhs |
| **Cerberus** | 'sɝ bə rəs | sər buh ruhs |
| | 'sɜ bə rəs ◊ | sə buh ruhs ◊ |
| **Charon** | 'kɛ rən | ke ruhn |
| | 'kæ rən | ka ruhn |
| | 'kɛə rən ◊ | … ◊ |
| **Chetas** | 'ki təs | kee tuhs |
| **Colossus** | kə 'lɑ səs | kuh lah suhs |
| | kə 'lɒ səs ◊ | kuh lo suhs ◊ |
| **Cressid** | 'krɛ sɪd | kre sid |
| | 'kre sɪd ◊ | … ◊ |
| **Cressida** | 'krɛ sɪ də | kre si duh |
| | 'kre sɪ də ◊ | … ◊ |
| **Cupid** | 'kju pɪd | kyoo pid |
| **Daphne** | 'dæf ni | daf nee |
| **Dardan** | 'dɑr dən | dahr duhn |
| | 'dɑ dən ◊ | dah duhn ◊ |
| **Deiphobus** -folio<br>  **Deiphoebus,**<br>  **Diephoebus,**<br>  **Daephobus** | di 'ɪ fɪ bəs | dee i fi buhs |
| **Diana** | daɪ 'æ nə | dai a nuh |
| **Diomed** | 'daɪ ə məd | dai uh muhd |
| **Diomedes** | daɪ ə 'mi diz | dai uh mee deez |

| NAME | INTERNATIONAL PHONETIC ALPHABET* | SIMPLIFIED PHONICS** |
|------|------|------|
| Doreus | 'dɔ riəs<br>'dɑ riəs<br>  [gen Am var] | daw ree uhs<br>dah ree uhs<br>  [gen Am var] |
| Epistrophus | ɪ 'pɪ strə fəs | i pi stuh fuhs |
| Friday | 'frai deɪ<br>'frai di ◊ | frai dei<br>frai dee ◊ |
| Galathe | 'gæ lə θi | ga luh *thee* |
| Grecian | 'gri ʃən | gri shuhn |
| Greece | 'gris | grees |
| Greek | 'grik | greek |
| Hector | 'hɛk tɚ<br>'hek tə ◊ | hek tər<br>hek tə ◊ |
| Hecuba | 'hɛ kju bə<br>'he kjʊ bə ◊ | he kyoo buh<br>he ky*oo* buh ◊ |
| Helen | 'hɛ lən<br>'hɛ lɪn<br>'he lɪn ◊ | he luhn<br>he lin<br>… ◊ |
| Helenus | 'hɛ lə nəs<br>'hɛ lɪ nəs<br>'he lɪ nəs ◊ | he luh nuhs<br>he li nuhs<br>… ◊ |
| Helias/Ilias | 'hi liəs | hee lee uhs |
| Hyperion | haɪ 'pɪ riən<br>haɪ 'pɪ riən ◊ | hai pi ree uhn<br>hai piə ree uhn … ◊ |
| Ilion | 'ɪ liən<br>'aɪ liən ◊ | i lee uhn<br>ai lee uhn ◊ |
| Illium | 'ɪ liəm<br>'aɪ liəm ◊ | i lee uhm<br>ai lee uhm ◊ |

| NAME | INTERNATIONAL PHONETIC ALPHABET* | SIMPLIFIED PHONICS** |
|---|---|---|
| **India** | 'ɪn diə | in dee uh |
| **Iris** | 'aɪ rɪs | ai ris |
| **Ithaca** | 'ɪ θə kə | i *th*uh kuh |
| **Jove** | 'ʤoʊv<br>'ʤəʊv ◊ | jov<br>... ◊ |
| **Juno** | 'ʤu no<br>'ʤu nəʊ ◊ | joo no<br>... ◊ |
| **Jupiter** | 'ʤu pɪ tə˞<br>'ʤu pɪ tə ◊ | joo pi tər<br>joo pi tə ◊ |
| **Libya** | 'lɪ biə | li bee uh |
| **Margarelon** | mɑr 'gæ rə lən<br>mɑ 'gæ rə lən ◊ | mahr ga ruh luhn<br>mah ga ruh lon ◊ |
| **Mars** | 'mɑrz<br>'mɑz ◊ | mahrz<br>mahz ◊ |
| **May** | 'meɪ | mei |
| **Menalaus** | mɛ nə 'leɪ əs<br>me nə 'leɪ əs ◊ | me nuh lei uhs<br>... ◊ |
| **Menon** | 'mɛ nɑn<br>'mi nɑn<br>'me nɒn ◊<br>'mi nɒn ◊ | me nahn<br>mee nahn<br>me non ◊<br>mee non ◊ |
| **Milo** | 'maɪ lo<br>'maɪ ləʊ ◊ | mai lo<br>... ◊ |
| **Myrmidon** | 'mɝ mə dɑn<br>'mɜ mɪ dən ◊ | mər muh dahn<br>mə muh duhn ◊ |

| NAME | INTERNATIONAL PHONETIC ALPHABET* | SIMPLIFIED PHONICS** |
|------|----------------------------------|----------------------|
| **Neapolitan** | niə ˈpɑ lə tən | nee uh pah luh tuhn |
| | niə ˈpɒ lə tən ◊ | nee uh po luh tuhn ◊ |
| **Nell** | ˈnɛl | nel |
| | ˈnel ◊ | … ◊ |
| **Neoptolemus** | ni ɑp ˈtɑ lə məs | nee ahp tah luh muhs |
| -folio | | |
| **Neoptolymus** | ni ɒp ˈtɒ lə məs ◊ | nee op to luh muhs ◊ |
| **Neptune** | ˈnɛp tun | nep toon |
| | ˈnep tjun ◊ | nep tyoon ◊ |
| **Nestor** | ˈnɛs tɚ | nes tər |
| | ˈnes tə ◊ | nes tə ◊ |
| **Niobe** | ˈnaɪ ə bi | nai uh bee |
| **Olympian** | ə ˈlɪm piən | uh lim pee uhn |
| | o ˈlɪm piən | o lim pee uhn |
| **Olympus** | o ˈlɪm pəs | o lim puhs |
| | ə ˈlɪm pəs | uh lim puhs |
| **Palamedes** | pæ lə ˈmi diz | pa luh mee deez |
| **Pandar** | ˈpæn dɚ | pan dər |
| | ˈpæn də ◊ | pan də ◊ |
| **Pandarus** | ˈpæn də rəs | pan duh ruhs |
| **Paris** | ˈpæ rɪs | pa ris |
| **Patroclus** | pə ˈtrɑ kləs | puh trah kluhs |
| | pə ˈtroʊ kləs | puh tro kluhs |
| | pə ˈtrɒk ləs ◊ | puh tro kluhs ◊ |

| NAME | INTERNATIONAL PHONETIC ALPHABET* | SIMPLIFIED PHONICS** |
|------|----------------------------------|----------------------|
| Perseus | ˈpɝ sus | pər soos |
|  | ˈpɝ siəs | pər see uhs |
|  | ˈpɜ sjus ◊ | pə syoos ◊ |
|  | ˈpɜ siəs ◊ | pə see uhs ◊ |
| Phoebus | ˈfi bəs | fee buhs |
| Phrygia | ˈfrɪ ʤiə | fri jee uh |
| Phrygian | ˈfrɪ ʤiən | fri jee uhn |
| Pluto | ˈplu to | ploo to |
|  | ˈplu təʊ ◊ | … ◊ |
| Plutus | ˈplu təs | ploo tuhs |
| Polixenes/ Polyxenes | pə ˈlɪk sə niz | puh lik suh neez |
| Polydamus | pɑ li ˈdæ məs | pah lee da muhs |
|  | pə ˈlɪ də məs | puh li duh muhs |
|  | pɒ li ˈdæ məs ◊ | po lee da muhs ◊ |
| Polyxena | pə ˈlɪk sə nə | puh lik suh nuh |
|  | pɒ ˈlɪk sə nə ◊ | po lik suh nuh ◊ |
| Priam | ˈpraɪ əm | prai uhm |
| Priamus | ˈpraɪ ə məs | prai uh muhs |
| Proserpina | prə ˈsɝ pɪ nə | pruh sər pi nuh |
|  | prə ˈsɜ pɪ nə ◊ | pruh sə pi nuh ◊ |
| Pyrrhus | ˈpɪ rəs | pi ruhs |
|  | ˈpɪə rəs ◊ | piə ruhs … ◊ |
| Sagittary | ˈsæ ʤɪ tɛ ri | sa ji te ree |
|  | ˈsæ ʤɪ tɛə ri ◊ | … ◊ |
| Sol | ˈsɑl | sahl |
|  | ˈsɒl ◊ | sol ◊ |

310

| NAME | INTERNATIONAL PHONETIC ALPHABET* | SIMPLIFIED PHONICS** |
|------|-----------------------------------|----------------------|
| **Sparta** | 'spɑr tə<br>'spɑ tə ◊ | spahr tuh<br>spah tuh ◊ |
| **Stygian** | 'stɪ ʤiən | sti jee uhn |
| **Styx** | 'stɪks | stiks |
| **Sunday** | 'sʌn deɪ<br>'sʌn di ◊ | suhn dei<br>suhn dee ◊ |
| **Tenedos** | 'tɛ nɪ dɑs<br>'te nɪ dɒs ◊ | te ni dahs<br>te ni dos ◊ |
| **Thetis** | 'θɛ tɪs<br>'θi tɪs<br>'θe tɪs ◊ | *the* tis<br>*thee* tis<br>... ◊ |
| **Thersites** | θɚ 'saɪ tiz<br>θə 'saɪ tiz ◊ | *thər* sai teez<br>*thə* sai teez ◊ |
| **Thoas** -folio<br>   **Thous** | 'θoʊ əs<br>'θoʊ ɔs ◊ | *tho* uhs<br>... ◊ |
| **Timbria/<br>  Tymbria** | 'tɪm briə | tim bree uh |
| **Titan** | 'taɪ tən | tai tuhn |
| **Troilus** | 'ʧrɔɪ ləs<br>'trɔɪ ləs<br>'trəʊɪ ləs ◊ | chroy luhs<br>troy luhs<br>... ◊ |
| **Trojan** -folio<br>  **Trien, Troyan** | 'ʧroʊ ʤən<br>'troʊ ʤən<br>'trəʊ ʤən ◊ | chro juhn<br>tro juhn<br>... ◊ |
| **Troy** | 'trɔɪ<br>'ʧrɔɪ | troy<br>chroy |
| **Troien** | 'trɔɪ ən<br>'ʧrɔɪ ən | troy uhn<br>chroy uhn |

| NAME | INTERNATIONAL PHONETIC ALPHABET* | SIMPLIFIED PHONICS** |
|------|----------------------------------|----------------------|
| **Tymbria** | 'tɪm briə | tim bree uh |
| **Typhon** | 'taɪ fɑn<br>'taɪ fɒn ◊ | tai fahn<br>tai fon ◊ |
| **Ulysses** -folio<br>  **Ulises** | ju 'lɪ siz | yoo li seez |
| **Venus** | 'vi nəs | vee nuhs |
| **Vulcan** | 'vʌl kən | vuhl kuhn |
| **Winchester** | 'wɪn ʧɛ stɚ<br>'wɪn ʧɪ stə ◊ | win che stər<br>win chi stə ◊ |

| NAME | INTERNATIONAL PHONETIC ALPHABET* | SIMPLIFIED PHONICS** |
|---|---|---|
| **Accost** | ə ˈkɔst<br>ə ˈkɒst ◊ | uh kawst<br>uh kost ◊ |
| **Aguecheek** | ˈeɪ gju tʃik | ei gyoo cheek |
| **Agueface** | ˈeɪ gju feɪs | ei gyoo feis |
| **Andrew** | ˈæn dru<br>ˈæn dʒru | an droo<br>an jroo |
| **[Saint] Anne** | [seɪnt] ˈæn<br>[sɪnt] ˈæn ◊ | [seint] an<br>[sint] an ◊ |
| **Antonio** | æn ˈtoʊ nio<br>æn ˈtəʊ niəʊ ◊ | an to nee o<br>… ◊ |
| **Arion** | ə ˈraɪ ən | uh rai uhn |
| **Babylon** | ˈbæ bɪ lən<br>ˈbæ bə lɑn<br>  [gen Am var] | ba bi luhn<br>ba buh lahn<br>  [gen Am var] |
| **Beelzabub/<br>  Belzebub** | bi ˈɛl zə bəb<br>bi ˈel zɪ bəb ◊ | bee el zuh buhb<br>bi el zi buhb ◊ |
| **Belch** | ˈbɛltʃ<br>ˈbeltʃ ◊ | belch<br>… ◊ |
| **[Saint] Bennet** | [seɪnt] ˈbɛ nɪt<br>[sɪnt] ˈbe nɪt ◊ | [seint] be nit<br>[sint] be nit |
| **Brownist** | ˈbraʊ nɪst | brow nist |

---

*International Phonetic Alphabet Pronunciation Key: (General American) i-s<u>ee</u>, happ<u>y</u>, Jul<u>i</u>et;
ɪ-s<u>i</u>t; eɪ-s<u>ay</u>; ɛ-s<u>e</u>t; æ-s<u>a</u>t; ɑ-f<u>a</u>ther; ʌ-s<u>u</u>n; ə-<u>a</u>bout; ɔ-s<u>aw</u>; oʊ-s<u>o</u>; o-h<u>e</u>ro; ʊ-sh<u>oo</u>k; u-s<u>oo</u>n;
aɪ-s<u>igh</u>; ɔɪ-s<u>oy</u>; aʊ-s<u>ou</u>th; ju-c<u>u</u>be; ɚ-s<u>upper</u>; ɛr-f<u>air</u>; ɝ-b<u>ird</u>; k-<u>c</u>ut, <u>k</u>ite; g-<u>g</u>o; dʒ-<u>j</u>oy; j-<u>y</u>es;
ŋ-si<u>ng</u>; ʃ-<u>sh</u>oe; tʃ-<u>ch</u>op; ð-<u>th</u>at; θ-<u>th</u>in; ʒ-mea<u>s</u>ure; (Additional symbols for British RP) e-s<u>e</u>t;
ɛə-f<u>air</u>; ə-s<u>upper</u>; ɜ-b<u>ird</u>; ɒ-st<u>o</u>p; əʊ-s<u>o</u>, h<u>e</u>ro; o-(followed by l) p<u>o</u>le.

**Simplified Phonics Pronunciation Key: (General American) ee-s<u>ee</u>, happ<u>y</u>; i-s<u>i</u>t; ei-s<u>ay</u>;
e-s<u>e</u>t; a-s<u>a</u>t; ah-f<u>a</u>ther; uh-s<u>u</u>n, <u>a</u>bout; aw-s<u>aw</u>; o-s<u>o</u>; <u>oo</u>-sh<u>oo</u>k; oo-s<u>oo</u>n; ai-s<u>igh</u>; oy-s<u>oy</u>;
ow-s<u>ou</u>th; yoo-c<u>u</u>be; ar-b<u>ird</u>, s<u>upper</u>; k-<u>c</u>ut, <u>k</u>ite; g-<u>g</u>o; j-<u>j</u>oy; ng-si<u>ng</u>; kw-<u>qu</u>ick; sh-<u>sh</u>oe;
ch-<u>ch</u>op; th-<u>th</u>at; th-<u>th</u>in; zh-mea<u>s</u>ure; (Additional symbols for British RP) ə-b<u>ird</u>; ə-s<u>upper</u>;
<u>o</u>-st<u>o</u>p; … indicates pronunciation variance too subtle for Simplified Phonics transcription
see International Phonetic Alphabet transcription.

◊ British RP pronunciation-see Introduction.

| NAME | INTERNATIONAL PHONETIC ALPHABET* | SIMPLIFIED PHONICS** |
|------|----------------------------------|----------------------|
| **Candy** | 'kæn di | kan dee |
| **Capilet** | 'kæ pə lɪt | ka puh lit |
| **Castilano** | kæ stɪl 'ja no<br>kæ stɪl 'ja nəʊ ◊ | ka stil yah no<br>... ◊ |
| **Cataian** | kə 'teɪ ən | kuh tei uhn |
| **Cesario** | sə 'zɛ rio<br>sə 'zɑ riəʊ ◊ | suh ze ree o<br>suh zah ree o ◊ |
| **Christian** | 'krɪs tʃən | kris chuhn |
| **Cressida** | 'krɛ sɪ duh<br>'kre sɪ duh ◊ | kre si duh<br>... ◊ |
| **Curio** | 'kju rio<br>'kjʊ riəʊ ◊ | kyoo ree o<br>ky*oo* ree o ◊ |
| **December** | di 'sɛm bɚ<br>dɪ 'sem bə ◊ | dee sem bər<br>di sem bə ◊ |
| **Diana** | daɪ 'æ nə | dai a nuh |
| **Dick** | 'dɪk | dik |
| **Dutch** | 'dʌtʃ | duhch |
| **Egyptian** | i 'dʒɪp ʃən | ee jip shuhn |
| **Elephant** | 'ɛ lɪ fənt<br>'e lɪ fənt ◊ | e li fuhnt<br>... ◊ |
| **Elysium** -folio<br>  **Elizium** | ɪ 'lɪ ziəm<br>ɪ 'lɪ ʒiəm | i li zee uhm<br>i li zhee uhm |
| **England** | 'ɪŋ glənd | ing gluhnd |
| **Eve** | 'iv | eev |

| NAME | INTERNATIONAL PHONETIC ALPHABET* | SIMPLIFIED PHONICS** |
|------|------|------|
| Fabian | ˈfeɪ biən | fei bee uhn |
| Feste | ˈfɛ sti<br>ˈfe sti ◊ | fe stee<br>... ◊ |
| Gobudic/<br>**Gorboduc** folio<br>**Gorbodcake** | ˈgɔr bə dək<br>ˈgɔ bə dək ◊ | gawr buh dek<br>gaw buh duhk ◊ |
| Greek | ˈgrik | greek |
| Illyria | ɪ ˈlɪ riə | i li ree uh |
| India | ˈɪn diə | in dee uh |
| Indies | ˈɪn diz | in deez |
| Jezebel | ˈdʒɛ zə bɛl<br>ˈdʒe zə bel ◊ | je zuh bel<br>... ◊ |
| Jove | ˈdʒoʊv<br>ˈdʒəʊv ◊ | jov<br>... ◊ |
| Lethe | ˈli θi | lee *th*ee |
| Lucrece | ˈlu kris<br>lu ˈkris | loo krees<br>... |
| Mall/Moll | ˈmɑl<br>ˈmɒl ◊ | mahl<br>mol ◊ |
| Malvolio | mæl ˈvoʊ lio<br>mæl ˈvo liəʊ ◊ | mal vo lee o<br>... ◊ |
| Maria | mə ˈri ə<br>mə ˈraɪ ə | muh ree uh<br>muh rai uh |
| Marian | ˈmæ riən | ma ree uhn |
| Mary | ˈmɛ ri<br>ˈmɛə ri ◊ | me ree<br>... ◊ |

315

| NAME | INTERNATIONAL PHONETIC ALPHABET* | SIMPLIFIED PHONICS** |
|------|----------------------------------|----------------------|
| May | 'meɪ | mei |
| Mercury | 'mɚ kjə ri<br>'mɜ kjʊ ri ◊ | mər kyuh ree<br>mə ky*oo* ree ◊ |
| Messaline | 'mɛ sə lin<br>'me sə lin ◊ | me suh leen<br>... ◊ |
| Myrmidon | 'mɚ mə dən<br>'mɚ mə dɑn<br>'mɜ mɪ dən ◊ | mər muh duhn<br>mər muh dahn<br>mə muh duhn ◊ |
| Noah | 'noʊ ə<br>'nəʊ ə ◊ | no uh<br>... ◊ |
| Olivia | o 'lɪ viə<br>ə 'lɪ viə | o li vee uh<br>uh li vee uh |
| Orsino | ɔr 'si no<br>ɔ 'si nəʊ ◊ | awr see no<br>aw see no ◊ |
| Pandarus | 'pæn də rəs | pan duh ruhs |
| Peg | 'pɛg<br>'peg ◊ | peg<br>... ◊ |
| Peg-a-Ramsay | 'pɛ gə 'ræm zi<br>'pe gə 'ræm zi ◊ | pe guh ram zee<br>... ◊ |
| Penthesilia/<br>  Pethesilea | pɛn θɛ sɪ 'leɪ ə<br>pen θe sɪ 'leɪ ə ◊ | pen *th*e si lei uh<br>... ◊ |
| Phoenix | 'fi nɪks | fee niks |
| Phrygia | 'frɪ ʤiə | fri jee uh |
| Pigrogramitus | pɪ gro 'græ mɪ təs<br>pɪ gro 'grɑ mɪ təs<br>pɪ grəʊ 'grɒ mɪ təs ◊ | pi gro gra mi tuhs<br>pi gro grah mi tuhs<br>pi gro gr*o* mi tuhs ◊ |
| Prague | 'prɑg | prahg |

| NAME | INTERNATIONAL PHONETIC ALPHABET* | SIMPLIFIED PHONICS** |
|---|---|---|
| **Pythagorus** | pə ˈθæ gə rəs<br>paɪ ˈθæ gə rəs ◊ | puh *tha* guh ruhs<br>pai *tha* guh ruhs ◊ |
| **Queubus** | ˈkju bəs | kyoo buhs |
| **Quinapulus** | kwɪ ˈnæ pə ləs | kwi na puh luhs |
| **Ramsay** | ˈræm zi | ram zee |
| **Robin** | ˈrɑ bɪn<br>ˈrɒ bɪn ◊ | rah bin<br>r*o* bin ◊ |
| **Roderigo** -folio<br>  **Rodorigo** | rɑ də ˈri go<br>rɒ də ˈri gəʊ ◊ | rah duh ree go<br>r*o* duh ree go ◊ |
| **Roman** | ˈroʊ mən<br>ˈrəʊ mən ◊ | ro muhn<br>… ◊ |
| **Satan** | ˈseɪ tən | sei tuhn |
| **Sebastian** | sə ˈbæs ʧən<br>sə ˈbæs tiən ◊ | suh bas chuhn<br>suh bas tee uhn ◊ |
| **Sophy** | ˈsoʊ fi<br>ˈsəʊ fi ◊ | so fee<br>… ◊ |
| **Sowter** | ˈsu tɚ<br>ˈsaʊ tɚ<br>ˈsu tə ◊<br>ˈsaʊ tə ◊ | soo tər<br>sow tər<br>soo tə ◊<br>sow tə ◊ |
| **Strachy** | ˈstreɪ ʧi | strei chee |
| **Surgeon** | ˈsɝ ʤən<br>ˈsɜ ʤən ◊ | sər juhn<br>sə juhn ◊ |
| **Tartar** | ˈtɑr tɚ<br>ˈtɑ tə ◊ | tahr tər<br>tah tə ◊ |

| NAME | INTERNATIONAL PHONETIC ALPHABET* | SIMPLIFIED PHONICS** |
|------|----------------------------------|----------------------|
| **Taurus** | 'tɔ rəs<br>'tɑ rəs<br>  [gen Am var] | taw ruhs<br>tah ruhs<br>  [gen Am var] |
| **Tiger** | 'taɪ gɚ<br>'taɪ gə ◊ | tai gər<br>tai gə ◊ |
| **Titus** | 'taɪ təs | tai tuhs |
| **Toby** | 'toʊ bi<br>'təʊ bi ◊ | to bee<br>… ◊ |
| **Topas** | 'toʊ pæz<br>'təʊ pæz ◊ | to paz<br>… ◊ |
| **Troilus** | 'tʃrɔɪ ləs<br>'trɔɪ ləs<br>'trəʊɪ ləs ◊ | chroy luhs<br>troy luhs<br>… ◊ |
| **Vapians** | 'veɪ piənz | vei pee uhnz |
| **Vice** | 'vaɪs | vais |
| **Viola** -folio also<br>  **Uiolenta** | 'vaɪ ə lə | vai uh luh |
| **Vox** | 'vɑks<br>'vɒks ◊ | vahks<br>voks ◊ |
| **Vulcan** | 'vʌl kən | vuhl kuhn |
| **Ware** | 'wɛr<br>'wɛə ◊ | wer<br>weə ◊ |

| NAME | INTERNATIONAL PHONETIC ALPHABET* | SIMPLIFIED PHONICS** |
|------|----------------------------------|----------------------|
| **Alphonso** | æl 'fan zo<br>æl 'fan so<br>æl 'fɒn zəʊ ◊ | al fahn zo<br>al fahn so<br>al fon zo ◊ |
| **Antonio** | æn 'toʊ nio<br>æn 'təʊ niəʊ ◊ | an to nee o<br>… ◊ |
| **April** | 'eɪ prəl | ei pruhl |
| **Ariadne** | æ ri 'æd ni | a ree ad nee |
| **Christian** | 'krɪs tʃən | kris chuhn |
| **Crab** | 'kræb | krab |
| **Eglamour** | 'ɛ glə mɔr<br>'e glə mʊə ◊<br>'e glə mɔ ◊ | e gluh mawr<br>e gluh moo ə ◊<br>e gluh maw ◊ |
| **Elysium** -folio<br> **Elizium** | ɪ 'lɪ ziəm<br>ɪ 'lɪ ʒiəm | ɪ li zee uhm<br>i li zhee uhm |
| **Ethiop** | 'i θiap<br>'i θiɒp ◊ | ee *th*ee ahp<br>ee *th*ee op |
| **Ethiope** | 'i θiop<br>'i θiəʊp ◊ | ee *th*ee op<br>… ◊ |
| **Eve** | 'iv | eev |
| **[Saint] Gregory** | [seɪnt] 'grɛ gə ri<br>[sɪnt] 'gre gə ri ◊ | [seint] gre guh ree<br>[sint] gre guh ree ◊ |

*International Phonetic Alphabet Pronunciation Key: (General American) i-s<u>ee</u>, happy, Jul<u>ie</u>t; ɪ-s<u>i</u>t; eɪ-s<u>ay</u>; ɛ-s<u>e</u>t; æ-s<u>a</u>t; ɑ-f<u>a</u>ther; ʌ-s<u>u</u>n; ə-<u>a</u>bout; ɔ-s<u>aw</u>; oʊ-s<u>o</u>; o-h<u>e</u>ro; ʊ-sh<u>oo</u>k; u-s<u>oo</u>n; aɪ-s<u>igh</u>; ɔɪ-s<u>oy</u>; aʊ-s<u>ou</u>th; ju-c<u>u</u>be; ə-supp<u>er</u>; ɛr-f<u>air</u>; ɚ-b<u>ir</u>d; k-<u>c</u>ut, <u>k</u>ite; g-go; dʒ-joy; j-<u>y</u>es; ŋ-si<u>ng</u>; ʃ-<u>sh</u>oe; tʃ-<u>ch</u>op; ð-<u>th</u>at; θ-<u>th</u>in; ʒ-mea<u>s</u>ure; (Additional symbols for British RP) e-s<u>e</u>t; ɛə-f<u>air</u>; ə-supp<u>er</u>; ɜ-b<u>ir</u>d; ɒ-st<u>o</u>p; əʊ-s<u>o</u>, h<u>e</u>ro; o-(followed by l) p<u>o</u>le.

**Simplified Phonics Pronunciation Key: (General American) ee-s<u>ee</u>, happy; i-s<u>i</u>t; ei-s<u>ay</u>; e-s<u>e</u>t; a-s<u>a</u>t; ah-f<u>a</u>ther; uh-s<u>u</u>n, <u>a</u>bout; aw-s<u>aw</u>; o-s<u>o</u>; *oo*-sh<u>oo</u>k; oo-s<u>oo</u>n; ai-s<u>igh</u>; oy-s<u>oy</u>; ow-s<u>ou</u>th; yoo-c<u>u</u>be; ər-b<u>ir</u>d, supp<u>er</u>; k-<u>c</u>ut, <u>k</u>ite; g-go; j-joy; ng-si<u>ng</u>; kw-<u>qu</u>ick; sh-<u>sh</u>oe; ch-<u>ch</u>op; th-<u>th</u>at; *th*-<u>th</u>in; zh-mea<u>s</u>ure; (Additional symbols for British RP) ə-b<u>ir</u>d; ə-supp<u>er</u>; <u>o</u>-st<u>o</u>p; … indicates pronunciation variance too subtle for Simplified Phonics transcription see International Phonetic Alphabet transcription.

◊ British RP pronunciation-see Introduction.

| NAME | INTERNATIONAL PHONETIC ALPHABET* | SIMPLIFIED PHONICS** |
|---|---|---|
| **Hallowmas** | 'hæ lo mæs<br>'hæ ləʊ mæs ◊ | ha lo mas<br>... ◊ |
| **Hebrew** | 'hi bru | hee broo |
| **Hellespont** | 'hɛ ləs pɑnt<br>'he lɪs pɒnt ◊ | he luhs pahnt<br>he lis pont ◊ |
| **Hero** | 'hi ro<br>'hɪə rəʊ ◊ | hee ro<br>... ◊ |
| **Hood** | 'hʊd | hood |
| **Jew** | 'ʤu | joo |
| **Jove** | 'ʤoʊv<br>'ʤəʊv ◊ | jov<br>... ◊ |
| **Julia** | 'ʤu liə<br>'ʤul jə | joo lee uh<br>jool yuh |
| **Launce** | 'lɔns<br>'lɑns<br>'lɒns ◊ | lawns<br>lahns<br>lons ◊ |
| **Laurence** | 'lɔ rəns<br>'lɒ rəns ◊ | law ruhns<br>lo ruhns ◊ |
| **Leander** | li 'æn dɚ<br>li 'æn də ◊ | lee an dər<br>lee an də ◊ |
| **Lucetta** | lu 'sɛ tə<br>lu 'ʧɛ tə<br>lʊ 'se tə ◊ | loo se tuh<br>loo che tuh<br>loo se tuh ◊ |
| **Mantua** | 'mæn ʧuə<br>'mæn tjuə ◊ | man choo uh<br>man tyoo uh ◊ |
| **Merops** | 'mɛ rɑps<br>'me rɒps ◊ | me rahps<br>me rops ◊ |

| NAME | INTERNATIONAL PHONETIC ALPHABET* | SIMPLIFIED PHONICS** |
|---|---|---|
| **Milan** | mɪ 'lɑn<br>mɪ 'læn<br>'mɪ lən | mi lahn<br>mi lan<br>mi luhn |
| **Moses/Moyses** | 'moʊ zɪs<br>'moʊ zɪz<br>'məʊ zɪz ◊ | mo zis<br>mo ziz<br>... ◊ |
| **Nan** | 'næn | nan |
| **[Saint] Nicholas** | [seɪnt] 'nɪ kə ləs<br>[sɪnt] 'nɪ kə ləs ◊ | [seint] ni kuh luhs<br>[sint] ni kuh luhs ◊ |
| **North-gate** | 'nɔrθ 'geɪt<br>'nɔθ 'geɪt ◊ | nawr*th* geit<br>naw*th* geit ◊ |
| **Orpheus** | 'ɔr fiəs<br>'ɔr fjus<br>'ɔ fjus ◊ | awr fee uhs<br>awr fyoos<br>aw fyoos ◊ |
| **Padua** | 'pæ ʤuə<br>'pæ djuə ◊ | pa joo uh<br>pa dyoo uh ◊ |
| **Panthino** | pæn 'θi no<br>pæn 'θi nəʊ ◊ | pan *th*ee no<br>... ◊ |
| **Patrick** | 'pæ trɪk<br>'pæ tʃrɪk | pa trik<br>pa chrik |
| **Pentecost** | 'pɛn tə kɔst<br>'pɛn tə kɑst<br>'pen tə kɒst ◊ | pen tuh kawst<br>pen tuh kahst<br>pen tuh k*o*st ◊ |
| **Phaeton/ Phaethon** | 'feɪ ə tən<br>'feɪ ə θɑn<br>    [gen Am var]<br>'feɪ ə θɒn<br>    [Brit RP var] | fei uh tuhn<br>fei uh *th*ahn<br>    [gen Am var]<br>fei uh *th*on<br>    [Brit RP var] |
| **Proteus** | 'proʊ tiəs<br>'prəʊ tiəs ◊ | pro tee uhs<br>... ◊ |

| NAME | INTERNATIONAL PHONETIC ALPHABET* | SIMPLIFIED PHONICS** |
|------|----------------------------------|----------------------|
| **Robin Hood** | 'rɑ bɪn 'hʊd<br>'rɒ bɪn 'hʊd ◊ | rah bin hood<br>ro bin hood ◊ |
| **Sebastian** | sə 'bæs tʃən<br>sə 'bæs tiən ◊ | suh bas chun<br>suh bas tee uhn ◊ |
| **Sestos** | 'sɛs təs<br>'ses təs ◊ | ses tuhs<br>... ◊ |
| **Silvia** | 'sɪl viə | sil vee uh |
| **Speed** | 'spid | speed |
| **Theseus** | 'θi siəs | *th*ee see uhs |
| **Thurio** | 'θjʊ rio<br>'θʊ rio | *th*yoo ree o<br>*th*oo ree o |
| **Ursula** | 'ɝ sə lə<br>'ɝs lə<br>'ɜ sə lə ◊<br>'ɜs lə ◊ | ər suh luh<br>ərs luh<br>ə suh luh ◊<br>əs luh ◊ |
| **Valentine** | 'væ lən taɪn | va luhn tain |
| **Valentinus** | væ lən 'taɪ nəs | va luhn tai nuhs |
| **Valerius** | və 'lɪ riəs<br>və 'lɪə riəs ◊ | vuh li ree uhs<br>vuh liə ree uhs ... ◊ |
| **Verona** | və 'roʊ nə<br>və 'rəʊ nə ◊ | vuh ro nuh<br>... ◊ |

| NAME | INTERNATIONAL PHONETIC ALPHABET* | SIMPLIFIED PHONICS** |
|---|---|---|
| **Alcides** | æl 'saɪ diz | al sai deez |
| **Alow** | ə 'lu | uh loo |
| | ə 'loʊ | uh lo |
| | ə 'ləʊ ◊ | ... ◊ |
| **Amazonian** | æ mə 'zoʊ niən | a muh zo nee uhn |
| | æ mə 'zəʊ niən ◊ | ... ◊ |
| **Apollo** | ə 'pɑ lo | uh pah lo |
| | ə 'pɒ ləʊ ◊ | uh p*o* lo ◊ |
| **Arcas** | 'ɑr kəs | ahr kuhs |
| | 'ɑ kəs ◊ | ah kuhs ◊ |
| **Arcite** | 'ɑr saɪt | ahr sait |
| | 'ɑ saɪt ◊ | ah sait ◊ |
| **Artesius** | ɑr 'ti ʒiəs | ahr tee zhee uhs |
| | ɑ 'ti ʒiəs ◊ | ah tee zhee uhs ◊ |
| **Athenian** | ə 'θi niən | uh *th*ee nee uhn |
| **Athens** | 'æ θɪnz | a *th*inz |
| | 'æ θənz | a *th*uhnz |
| **Aulis** | 'ɔ lɪs | aw lis |
| **Barbara** | 'bɑr bə rə | bahr buh ruh |
| | 'bɑ bə rə ◊ | bah buh ruh ◊ |

| NAME | INTERNATIONAL PHONETIC ALPHABET* | SIMPLIFIED PHONICS** |
|------|-----------------------------------|----------------------|
| **Barbary** -folio **Barbarie** can also be pronounced as **Barbara** -see above | 'bɑr bə ri<br>'bɑ bə ri ◊ | bahr buh ree<br>bah buh ree ◊ |
| **Bellona** | bə 'loʊ nə<br>bə 'ləʊ nə ◊ | buh lo nuh<br>... ◊ |
| **Capaneus** | kæ pə 'ni əs | ka puh nee uhs |
| **Ceres** | 'sɪ riz<br>'sɪə riz ◊ | si reez<br>... ◊ |
| **Chaucer** | 'tʃɔ sə˞<br>'tʃɑ sə˞<br>'tʃɔ sə ◊ | chaw sər<br>chah sər<br>chaw sə ◊ |
| **Cicely** | 'sɪ sə l i | si suh lee |
| **Creon** | 'kri ɑn<br>'kri ɒn ◊<br>'kri ən ◊ | kree ahn<br>kree on ◊<br>kree uhn ◊ |
| **Daedalus** | 'dɛ də ləs<br>'di də ləs ◊ | de duhl uhs<br>dee duhl uhs ◊ |
| **Dian** | 'daɪ ən<br>'daɪ æn | dai uhn<br>dai an |
| **Dido** | 'daɪ do<br>'daɪ dəʊ ◊ | dai do<br>... ◊ |
| **Dis** | 'dɪs | dis |
| **Elyzium** | ɪ 'lɪ ziəm<br>ɪ 'lɪ ʒiəm | i li zee uhm<br>i li zhee uhm |
| **Emilia** | ɪ 'mi liə<br>ɪ 'mil jə | i mee lee uh<br>i meel yuh |

| NAME | INTERNATIONAL PHONETIC ALPHABET* | SIMPLIFIED PHONICS** |
|---|---|---|
| Emily | 'ɛ mə li <br> 'e mə li ◊ | e muh lee <br> ... ◊ |
| Flavina | flə 'vi nə | fluh vee nuh |
| Friz | 'frɪz | friz |
| Ganymede | 'gæ nə mid <br> 'gæ nɪ mid | ga nuh meed <br> ga ni meed |
| George | 'dʒɔrdʒ <br> 'dʒɔdʒ ◊ | jawrj <br> jawj ◊ |
| Gerrold | 'dʒɛ rəld | je ruhld |
| Giraldo/Girraldo | dʒɪ 'ral do <br> dʒɪ 'ræl do <br> dʒɪ 'ræl dəʊ ◊ | ji rahl do <br> ji ral do <br> ... ◊ |
| Hercules | 'hɝ kjə liz <br> 'hɜ kjʊ liz ◊ | hər kyuh leez <br> hə ky*oo* leez ◊ |
| Hippolyta | hɪ 'pɑ lɪ tə <br> hɪ 'pɒ lɪ tə ◊ | hi pah li tuh <br> hi p*o* li tuh ◊ |
| Hymen | 'haɪ mən | hai muhn |
| Iris | 'aɪ rɪs | ai ris |
| Jove | 'dʒoʊv <br> 'dʒəʊv ◊ | jov <br> ... ◊ |
| Juno | 'dʒu no <br> 'dʒu nəʊ ◊ | joo no <br> ... ◊ |
| Jupiter | 'dʒu pɪ tɚ <br> 'dʒu pɪ tə ◊ | joo pi tər <br> joo pi tə ◊ |
| March | 'mɑrtʃ <br> 'mɑtʃ ◊ | mahrch <br> mahch ◊ |

325

| NAME | INTERNATIONAL PHONETIC ALPHABET* | SIMPLIFIED PHONICS** |
|------|----------------------------------|----------------------|
| **Mars** | 'mɑrz<br>'mɑz ◊ | mahrz<br>mahz ◊ |
| **Maudline** | 'mɔd lɪn | mawd lin |
| **May** | 'meɪ | mei |
| **Meleager** | mɛ li 'eɪ ʤɚ<br>me li 'eɪ ʤə ◊ | me lee ei jər<br>me lee ei jə ◊ |
| **Morr** | 'mɔr<br>'mɔ ◊ | mawr<br>maw ◊ |
| **Morris** | 'mɔ rɪs<br>'mɒ rɪs ◊ | maw ris<br>mo ris ◊ |
| **Nell** | 'nɛl<br>'nel ◊ | nel<br>… ◊ |
| **Neptune** | 'nɛp tun<br>'nep tjun ◊ | nep toon<br>nep tyoon ◊ |
| **Nemean** | 'ni miən<br>nɪ 'mi ən | nee mee uhn<br>ni mee uhn |
| **Palamon** | 'pæ lə mən | pa luh muhn |
| **Pallas** | 'pæ ləs | pa luhs |
| **Parthian** | 'pɑr θiən<br>'pɑ θiən ◊ | pahr *th*ee uhn<br>pah *th*ee uhn ◊ |
| **Pelops** | 'pi lɑps<br>'pi lɒps ◊ | pee lahps<br>pee lops ◊ |
| **Phoebus** | 'fi bəs | fee buhs |
| **Pirithous** | paɪ 'rɪ θo əs<br>paɪ 'rɪ θəʊ əs ◊ | pai ri *th*o uhs<br>… ◊ |

| NAME | INTERNATIONAL PHONETIC ALPHABET* | SIMPLIFIED PHONICS** |
|------|----------------------------------|----------------------|
| **Po** | 'poʊ<br>'pəʊ ◊ | po<br>... ◊ |
| **Proserpine** | 'prɑ sɚ paɪn<br>'prɒ sə paɪn ◊ | prah sər pain<br>pro sə pain ◊ |
| **Pygmies** | 'pɪg miz | pig meez |
| **Robin Hood** | 'rɑ bɪn 'hʊd<br>'rɒ bɪn 'hʊd ◊ | rah bin hood<br>ro bin hood ◊ |
| **Rycas** | 'raɪ kəs | rai kuhs |
| **Sennois** | 'sɛ nɔɪz<br>'se nɔɪz ◊ | se noyz<br>... ◊ |
| **Theban** | 'θi bən | *th*ee buhn |
| **Thebes** | 'θibz | *th*eebz |
| **Timothy** | 'tɪ mə θi | ti muh *th*ee |
| **Trent** | 'ʧrɛnt<br>'trɛnt<br>'trent ◊ | chrent<br>trent<br>... ◊ |
| **Venus** | 'vi nəs | vee nuhs |
| **Ver** | 'vɝ<br>'vɜ ◊ | vər<br>və ◊ |

# Venus and Adonis

| NAME | INTERNATIONAL PHONETIC ALPHABET* | SIMPLIFIED PHONICS** |
|---|---|---|
| **Adon** | 'æ dɑn | a dahn |
| | 'æ don | a don |
| | 'æ dəʊn ◊ | … ◊ |
| **Adonis** | ə 'dɑ nɪs | uh dah nis |
| | ə 'doʊ nɪs | uh do nis |
| | ə 'dəʊ nɪs ◊ | … ◊ |
| **Cupid** | 'kju pɪd | kyoo pid |
| **Cynthia** | 'sɪn θiə | sin *th*ee uh |
| **Cytheria** | sɪ θə 'ri ə | si *th*uh ree uh |
| **Dian** | 'daɪ ən | dai uhn |
| | 'daɪ æn | dai an |
| **Echo** | 'ɛ ko | e ko |
| | 'e kəʊ ◊ | … ◊ |
| **Elysium** | ɪ 'lɪ ziəm | i li zee uhm |
| | ɪ 'lɪ ʒiəm | i li zhee uhm |
| **Henry** | 'hɛn ri | hen ree |
| | 'hen ri ◊ | … ◊ |
| **Jove** | 'dʒoʊv | jov |
| | 'dʒəʊv ◊ | … ◊ |
| **Narcissus** | nɑr 'sɪ səs | nahr si suhs |
| | nɑ 'sɪ səs ◊ | nah si suhs ◊ |

*International Phonetic Alphabet Pronunciation Key: (General American) i-s<u>ee</u>, happ<u>y</u>, Jul<u>ie</u>t; ɪ-s<u>i</u>t; eɪ-s<u>ay</u>; ɛ-s<u>e</u>t; æ-s<u>a</u>t; ɑ-f<u>a</u>ther; ʌ-s<u>u</u>n; ə-<u>a</u>bout; ɔ-s<u>aw</u>; oʊ-s<u>o</u>; o-h<u>e</u>ro; ʊ-sh<u>oo</u>k; u-s<u>oo</u>n; aɪ-s<u>igh</u>; ɔɪ-s<u>oy</u>; aʊ-s<u>ou</u>th; ju-c<u>u</u>be; ə-s<u>u</u>pper; ɛr-f<u>air</u>; ɚ-b<u>ir</u>d; k-<u>c</u>ut, <u>k</u>ite; g-<u>g</u>o; dʒ-<u>j</u>oy; j-<u>y</u>es; ŋ-si<u>ng</u>; ʃ-<u>sh</u>oe; tʃ-<u>ch</u>op; ð-<u>th</u>at; θ-<u>th</u>in; ʒ-mea<u>s</u>ure; (Additional symbols for British RP) e-s<u>e</u>t; ɛə-f<u>air</u>; ə-s<u>u</u>pper; ɜ-b<u>ir</u>d; ɒ-st<u>o</u>p; əʊ-s<u>o</u>, h<u>e</u>ro; o-(followed by l) p<u>o</u>le.

**Simplified Phonics Pronunciation Key: (General American) ee-s<u>ee</u>, happ<u>y</u>; i-s<u>i</u>t; ei-s<u>ay</u>; e-s<u>e</u>t; a-s<u>a</u>t; ah-f<u>a</u>ther; uh-s<u>u</u>n, <u>a</u>bout; aw-s<u>aw</u>; o-s<u>o</u>; oo-sh<u>oo</u>k; oo-s<u>oo</u>n; ai-s<u>igh</u>; oy-s<u>oy</u>; ow-s<u>ou</u>th; yoo-c<u>u</u>be; ər-b<u>ir</u>d; supp<u>er</u>; k-<u>c</u>ut, <u>k</u>ite; g-<u>g</u>o; j-<u>j</u>oy; ng-si<u>ng</u>; kw-<u>qu</u>ick; sh-<u>sh</u>oe; ch-<u>ch</u>op; th-<u>th</u>at; th-<u>th</u>in; zh-mea<u>s</u>ure; (Additional symbols for British RP) ə-b<u>ir</u>d; ə-s<u>u</u>pper; <u>o</u>-st<u>o</u>p; … indicates pronunciation variance too subtle for Simplified Phonics transcription see International Phonetic Alphabet transcription.

◊ British RP pronunciation-see Introduction.

| NAME | INTERNATIONAL PHONETIC ALPHABET* | SIMPLIFIED PHONICS** |
|------|----------------------------------|----------------------|
| **Paphos** | 'peɪ fɑs<br>'peɪ fɒs ◊ | pei fahs<br>pei fos ◊ |
| **Shakespeare** | 'ʃeɪk spir<br>'ʃeɪk spɪə ◊ | sheik speer<br>sheik spiə ◊ |
| **Southampton** | saʊθ 'hæmp tən<br>saʊ 'θæmp tən ◊ | sou*th* hamp tuhn<br>sou *th*amp tuhn ◊ |
| **Tantalus** | 'tæn tə ləs | tan tuh luhs |
| **Titan** | 'taɪ tən | tai tuhn |
| **Titchfield** | 'tɪtʃ fild | tich feeld |
| **Venus** | 'vi nəs | vee nuhs |
| **William** | 'wɪl jəm | wil yuhm |
| **Wroithesley** | 'rɑts li<br>'rɒts li ◊ | rahts lee<br>rots lee ◊ |

| NAME | INTERNATIONAL PHONETIC ALPHABET* | SIMPLIFIED PHONICS** |
|------|----------------------------------|----------------------|
| **Alexander** | æ lıg 'zæn də<br>æ lıg 'zɑn də ◊ | a lig zan dər<br>a lig zahn də ◊ |
| **Antigonus** | æn 'tı gə nəs | an ti guh nuhs |
| **Apollo** | ə 'pɑ lo<br>ə 'pɒ ləʊ ◊ | uh pah lo<br>uh po lo ◊ |
| **April** | 'eı prəl | ei pruhl |
| **Archidamus** | ɑr kı 'deı məs<br>ɑ kı 'deı məs ◊ | ahr ki dei muhs<br>ah ki dei muhs ◊ |
| **Autolycus** | ɔ 'tɑ lı kəs<br>ɔ 'tɒ lı kəs ◊ | aw tah li kuhs<br>aw to li kuhs ◊ |
| **Bohemian** | boʊ 'hi miən<br>bəʊ 'hi miən ◊ | bo hee mee uhn<br>... ◊ |
| **Camillo** | kə 'mı lo<br>kə 'mı ləʊ ◊ | kuh mi lo<br>... ◊ |
| **Cleomenes** -folio<br>**Cleomines** | kli 'ɑ mı niz<br>kli 'ɒ mı niz ◊ | klee ah mi neez<br>klee o mi neez ◊ |
| **Cytherea** | sı θə 'riə | si thuh ree uh |
| **December** | di 'sɛm bə<br>dı 'sem bə ◊ | dee sem bər<br>di sem bə ◊ |
| **Delphos** | 'dɛl fəs<br>'del fəs ◊ | del fuhs<br>... ◊ |

| NAME | INTERNATIONAL PHONETIC ALPHABET* | SIMPLIFIED PHONICS** |
|------|------|------|
| **Deucalion** | du ˈkeɪ liən<br>dju ˈkeɪ liən ◊ | doo kei lee uhn<br>dyoo kei lee uhn ◊ |
| **Dion** | ˈdaɪ ən | dai uhn |
| **Dis** | ˈdɪs | dis |
| **Dorcas** | ˈdɔr kəs<br>ˈdɔ kəs ◊ | dawr kuhs<br>daw kuhs ◊ |
| **Doricles** | ˈdɔ rɪ kliz | daw ri kleez |
| **Emilia** | ɪ ˈmi liə<br>ɪ ˈmil jə | i mee lee yuh<br>i meel yuh |
| **Ethiopian** | i θi ˈoʊ piən<br>i θi ˈəʊ piən ◊ | ee *thee* o pee uhn<br>… ◊ |
| **Europe** | ˈjʊ rəp<br>ˈjʊə rəp ◊ | y*oo* ruhp<br>y*oo*ə ruhp ◊ |
| **Flora** | ˈflɔ rə | flaw ruh |
| **Florizel** | ˈflɔ rə zɛl<br>ˈflɔ rɪ zel ◊ | flaw ruh zel<br>flaw ri zel ◊ |
| **Hermione** | hɚ ˈmaɪ ə ni<br>hə ˈmaɪ ə ni ◊ | hər mai uh nee<br>hə mai uh nee ◊ |
| **Italian** | ɪ ˈtæl jən | i tal yuhn |
| **January** | ˈdʒæn ju ɛ ri<br>ˈdʒæn ju ə ri ◊ | jan yoo e ree<br>jan yuu uh ree ◊ |
| **Jove** | ˈdʒoʊv<br>ˈdʒəʊv ◊ | jov<br>… ◊ |
| **Julio** | ˈdʒu lio<br>ˈdʒu liəʊ ◊ | joo lee o<br>… ◊ |

| NAME | INTERNATIONAL PHONETIC ALPHABET* | SIMPLIFIED PHONICS** |
|---|---|---|
| July | 'dʒu laɪ<br>dʒə 'laɪ | joo lai<br>juh lai |
| Juno | 'dʒu no<br>'dʒu nəʊ ◊ | joo no<br>… ◊ |
| Jupiter | 'dʒu pɪ tɚ<br>'dʒu pɪ tə ◊ | joo pi tər<br>joo pi tə ◊ |
| Leontes | li 'ɑn tiz<br>li 'ɒn tiz ◊ | lee ahn teez<br>lee on teez ◊ |
| Libya/Lybia | 'lɪ biə | li bee uh |
| Mamilius | mə 'mɪ liəs<br>mə 'mɪl jəs | muh mi lee uhs<br>muh mil yuhs |
| March | 'mɑrtʃ<br>'mɑtʃ ◊ | mahrch<br>mahch ◊ |
| Margery | 'mɑr dʒə ri<br>'mɑ dʒə ri | mahr juh ree<br>mah juh ree ◊ |
| Mercury | 'mɝ kjə ri<br>'mɜ kjʊ ri ◊ | mər kyuh ree<br>mə kyoo ree ◊ |
| Mopsa | 'mɑp sə<br>'mɒp sə ◊ | mahp suh<br>mop suh ◊ |
| Neptune | 'nɛp tun<br>'nɛp tjun ◊ | nep toon<br>nep tyoon ◊ |
| Paulina | pɔ 'li nə<br>pɔ 'laɪ nə | paw lee nuh<br>paw lai nuh |
| Perdita | 'pɝ dɪ tə<br>'pɜ dɪ tə ◊ | pər di tuh<br>pə di tuh ◊ |
| Phoebus | 'fi bəs | fee buhs |

| NAME | INTERNATIONAL PHONETIC ALPHABET* | SIMPLIFIED PHONICS** |
|---|---|---|
| Polixenes/ Polyxenes | pə ˈlɪk sə niz | puh lik suh neez |
| Proserpina | pro ˈsɚ pɪ nə<br>prəʊ ˈsɜ pɪ nə ◊ | pro sər pi nuh<br>pro sə pi nuh ◊ |
| Proserpine | ˈprɑ sɚ paɪn<br>ˈprɒ sə paɪn ◊ | prah sər pain<br>pro sə pain ◊ |
| Rogero | ro ˈʤe ro<br>rəʊ ˈʤe rəʊ ◊ | ro je ro<br>… ◊ |
| Romano | ro ˈmɑ no<br>rəʊ ˈmɑ nəʊ ◊ | ro mah no<br>… ◊ |
| Russia | ˈrʌ ʃə | ruh shuh |
| Sicilia | sɪ ˈsɪ liə<br>sɪ ˈsɪl jə | si si lee uh<br>si sil yuh |
| Sicilian | sɪ ˈsɪ liən<br>sɪ ˈsɪl jən | si si lee uhn<br>si sil yuhn |
| Sicily | ˈsɪ sə li | si suh lee |
| Smalus | ˈsmeɪ ləs | smei luhs |
| Smile | ˈsmaɪl | smail |
| Tale-porter | ˈteɪl ˈpɔr tɚ<br>ˈteɪl ˈpɔ tə ◊ | teil pawr tər<br>teil paw tə ◊ |
| Wednesday | ˈwɛnz deɪ<br>ˈwenz di ◊ | wenz dei<br>wenz dee ◊ |
| Whitsun | wɪt sən | wit suhn |

# Detailed explanation
# of the Symbols

*An explanation of the use of International*
*Phonetic Alphabet Symbols*

ACCENTUATION

In order to simplify the transcriptions in this dictionary
the use of diacritical markings is limited to the accent
mark / ' /. Accented syllables are indicated by an accent
mark to the left of the accented syllable, for example, the
accent mark for the name Henry, appears to the left of the
first syllable: /'hɛn ri/.

VOWEL LENGTH

For the purpose of simplification, vowel length, traditionally indicated by the colon symbol /:/, is indicated by
word position only. Longer vowel length is assumed when
the vowel appears in the accented syllable of the word,
shorter vowel length is assumed when the vowel appears
in the unaccented syllable. For example, when the vowel
sound /i/ apppears in a one syllable name, such as, Crete
/'krit/, or, in the accented syllable of a multi-syllable word,
such as, Eden /'i dən/, it is assumed to be of longer length
than when it appears in the unaccented syllable, as in the
name Barbary /'bɑr bɔ ri/ or, when it appears as the weak
element in a diphthong, as in the names Juliet /'ʤu liɛt/
and Claudio /'klɔ dio/.

Whenever possible, the transcription of subsequent syllables in multi-syllable names is begun with a consonant.
This is done in order to avoid glottal shock at the beginning of each new syllable when the name is spoken. For
example, the syllable breaks for names such as Claudio,
and Jessica are given as, /'klɔ dio/, and /'ʤɛ sɪ kə/, rather
than /'klɔd io/, and /'ʤɛs ɪk ə/. In multi-syllabic names
where a two consonant blend occurs between vowel
sounds, such as Antium, the syllable break is made
between the two consonants: /'æn tiəm/, or, before the
first consonant in names such as, Africa: /'æ frɪ kə/ In
names such as Iago, and Thiisa, syllable breaks between
vowels are unavoidable.

## *International Phonetic Alphabet Vowels*

### PURE VOWELS

**Note:** The term 'Pure Vowel' refers to all vowels which are composed of a
single sound, as opposed to the term 'Diphthong,' which refers to vowels
which are composed of two vowels sounds. For example, / i /, / ɑ /, and
/ u /, are pure vowels, and, / aɪ /, / ɔɪ /, and / aʊ /, are diphthongs.

### / i /

**Note:** Because / i / is used in both accented and unaccented syllables,
length is determined by word position (see ACCENTUATION, above).

The 'long E' sound, / i / occurs as:

• the accented vowel in names such as Crete, and Creon.

• the weak, final syllable in names such as Albany,
Barbary, Stanley, Dizie. Older dictionaries express this
weakly positioned vowel as a 'short I,' rather than a 'long
E,' (Kokeritz, Kenyon and Knott, Jones ), however, current
trends indicate the raising of this vowel, (Wells, 1990).

• the weak element in a diphthong in names such as
Juliet, Amiens, Ariel, Romeo.

• the beginning of a triphthong in names such as Bentii.

## / ɪ /

The 'short I' sound, / ɪ / occurs as:

• the accented vowel in names such as, R<u>i</u>chard, W<u>i</u>ll, N<u>y</u>m, and S<u>y</u>ria.

• the unaccented vowel in names such as, Cress<u>i</u>da, and Yor<u>i</u>k.

## / ε /

**Note:** This symbol appears in 'general American' transcription only. In 'British RP' transcription / e / is used in place of / ε /. The reason for this variance in symbols is twofold; 1) There is, arguably, a difference in the pronunciation of the 'short E' vowel in American and British speech, although, this difference is negligable. 2) The current transcription style for this vowel in British lexicons favors the use of / e / (Wells, Jones), with the notable exception of the Oxford English Dictionary, which in the style of U.S. dictionaries uses / ε /. Authorities on U.S. pronunciation have traditionally used / ε / (Kenyon and Knott, Wells, 1982).

The 'short E' sound, / ε / occurs as:

• the accented vowel in 'general American' transcription of names such as, N<u>e</u>ll, H<u>e</u>nry, and <u>E</u>dward.

• the unaccented vowel in 'general American' transcription of names such as, B<u>e</u>nvolio, and M<u>e</u>diterranean.

## / e /

The 'short E' sound, / e / occurs as:

• the accented vowel in 'British RP' transcription of names such as, N<u>e</u>ll, H<u>e</u>nry, and <u>E</u>dward.

• the unaccented vowel in 'British RP' transcription of names such as B<u>e</u>nvolio, and M<u>e</u>diterranean.

## / æ /

**Note:** The following names are pronounced with the 'short a'/ æ /in 'general American' speech and the 'broad a' / ɑ / in 'British RP' speech: Alex<u>a</u>nder, Alex<u>a</u>ndria, Beregom<u>a</u>sk, Bl<u>a</u>nch, Bullc<u>a</u>lf, C<u>a</u>stle, C<u>a</u>stor, Falst<u>a</u>ff, Fl<u>a</u>nders, Fr<u>a</u>nce, Fr<u>a</u>nces, Fr<u>a</u>ncis, H<u>a</u>lfcan, H<u>a</u>lfmoon, Hopd<u>a</u>nce, Oldc<u>a</u>stle. For example, the name Blanch is transcribed/ 'blæntʃ /for U.S. speech, and / 'blɑntʃ / for British RP speech. Such names are said to belong to a spelling-based category of words known in the American Theater as the 'ask list' (Skinner). The practice in the U.S. of lowering / æ / to / ɑ / in words of this type, as a compromise with British RP pronunciation is now losing currency (Wells,1990, Colaianni,

Mufson, Knight). Names such as M<u>a</u>b, <u>A</u>tlas, Aj<u>a</u>x, and Rosencr<u>a</u>ntz, are pronounced with / æ / in both 'general American,' and British RP.'

The 'short a' sound, / æ / occurs as:

• the accented vowel in names such as M<u>a</u>b, and <u>A</u>tlas.

• the accented vowel in names such as, Fr<u>a</u>nce, and Falst<u>a</u>ff in 'general American' transcriptions only (see note, above).

• the unaccented vowel in names such as, Aj<u>a</u>x, and Rosencr<u>a</u>ntz.

/ ʌ /

**Note:** / ʌ / only occurs in the accented position of a word; for example, it occurs in one-syllable words such as j<u>u</u>mp, and multi-syllable words such as, <u>u</u>mpire. The symbol for the same sound in unaccented syllables is / ə /, as in the words <u>a</u>gain, and comp<u>a</u>ny.

/ ʌ / occurs as:

• the accented vowel in names such as, Sn<u>u</u>g, D<u>u</u>ncan, and Montg<u>o</u>mery.

/ ə /

**Note:** In both 'general American' and 'British RP' speech / ə / represents the neutral, unaccented vowel in words such as, <u>a</u>gain, and comp<u>a</u>ny. In 'British RP' it also represents the non-rhotic unaccented vowel in words such as fath<u>er</u> and opp<u>or</u>tune (see 'R, And Its Relationship To Vowels,' below).

The 'schwa' or, 'neutral vowel,'/ ə / occurs as:

• the unaccented syllable in names such as, Abr<u>a</u>ham, Octavi<u>a</u>, Pand<u>o</u>lph, and P<u>u</u>blicola.

• the non-rhotic, unaccented vowel in 'British RP' tran-scription of names such as, Mortim<u>er</u>.

/ ɑ /

**Note:** The vowel spelled with O in such words as, h<u>o</u>t, and p<u>o</u>nd, or with WA, in words such as, w<u>a</u>sh, and w<u>a</u>nt, is pronounced with the 'broad a' sound / ɑ / in 'general American' speech and the 'short o' sound / ɒ / in 'British RP' speech.

**Note:** The following names are pronounced with the 'short a' / æ / in 'general American' speech and the 'broad a' / ɑ / in 'British RP' speech: Alex<u>a</u>nder, Alex<u>a</u>ndria, Beregom<u>a</u>sk, Bl<u>a</u>nch, Bullc<u>a</u>lf, C<u>a</u>stle, C<u>a</u>stor, Falst<u>a</u>ff, Fl<u>a</u>nders, Fr<u>a</u>nce, Fr<u>a</u>nce, Fr<u>a</u>nces, Fr<u>a</u>ncis, H<u>a</u>lfcan, H<u>a</u>lfmoon,

Hopdance, Oldcastle. For example, the name Blanch is transcribed / ˈblæntʃ / for U.S. speech, and / ˈblɑntʃ / for British RP speech.

The 'broad a' sound,/ ɑ / occurs as:

• the accented vowel in names such as, Adriano, Iago, Prague, and Solanio.

• the accented vowel in 'general American' transcriptions of names such as, Doll, Apollo, and Washes.

• the accented vowel in 'British RP' transcription of names such as France, and Falstaff (see note above).

• the accented vowel preceding R in 'British RP' transcription of names such as Arden, (see R, And Its Relationship To Vowels, below).

• the unaccented vowel in 'general American' transcriptions of names such as, Aesop, and Constantitinople.

• a variant for the accented vowel in 'general American' transcriptions of names such as, Gaunt, Audrey, Cawdor, and Waterford.

• a variant for the unaccented vowel in 'general American' transcription of names such as, Cadwal.

## / ɒ /

**Note:** The vowel spelled with O in such words as, hot, and pond, and WA, in words such as wash, and want, is pronounced with the 'broad a' sound / ɑ / in 'general American' speech and the 'short o' sound / ɒ / in 'British RP' speech.

The 'short O' sound, / ɒ / occurs as:

• the accented vowel in 'British RP' transcription of names such as, Doll, Apollo, and Washes.

• the unaccented vowel in 'British RP' transcription of names such as, Aesop, and Constantinople.

## / ɔ /

/ ɔ / occurs as:

• the accented vowel in such names as, Gaunt, Audrey, Cawdor, Waterton, and Dorset, (see / ɑ /, above, for 'general American' variant pronunciation).

• the unaccented vowel in names such as Cadw<u>a</u>l (see / ɑ /, above, for 'general American' variant pronunciation).

## / o /

**Note:** The 'pure vowel' / o /, is used in 'general American' transcription to express the 'long O' sound in unaccented positions; in accented positions it is transcribed as the diphthong, / oʊ / (see / oʊ /, below). In 'British RP' speech the 'long O' sound is transcribed as the diphthong / əʊ /, in both accented and unaccented positions (see / əʊ /, below), except in the case of OL spellings, when it is transcribed as the pure vowel / o / (see below).

/ o / occurs as:

• the unaccented vowel in 'general American' transcription of names such as, Apoll<u>o</u>, and Ech<u>o</u>.

• the accented vowel in 'British RP' transcription of names spelled with OL, such as, P<u>o</u>land, and C<u>o</u>ldspur.

## / ʊ /

/ ʊ / occurs as:

• the accented vowel in names such as, B<u>u</u>tcher, and G<u>oo</u>dman.

• the unaccented vowel in names such as Bolingbr<u>o</u>ke, and Ringw<u>oo</u>d.

## / u /

The 'long u' sound, / u /, occurs as:

• the accented vowel in names such as, J<u>u</u>le, Sm<u>oo</u>th, Ber<u>ow</u>ne, L<u>ew</u>is, and Petr<u>u</u>chio.

• the unaccented vowel in names such as, Andr<u>ew</u>, Joshu<u>a</u>, and Halfm<u>oo</u>n.

### DIPHTHONGS

**Note:** The term 'Diphthong' refers to vowels which are composed of two vowel sounds, as opposed to 'Pure Vowel,' which refers to vowels which are composed of a single vowel sound. For example, / aɪ /, / ɔɪ /, and / aʊ /, are diphthongs, and / i /, / ɑ /, and / u /, are pure vowels.

## / eɪ /

The 'long A' sound, / eɪ / occurs as:

• the accented vowel in such names as, P<u>a</u>ge, C<u>ai</u>n, P<u>ei</u>phos, and Mele<u>a</u>ger.

• the unaccented vowel in names such as, <u>A</u>driana, and Gallow<u>ay</u>.

## / aɪ /

The 'long I' sound, / aɪ / occurs as:

• the accented vowel in names such as, Sm<u>i</u>le, <u>I</u>ras, and C<u>y</u>prus.

• the unaccented vowel in names such as, Rosal<u>i</u>ne, and Bent<u>ii</u>.

## / aʊ /

/ aʊ / occurs as:

• the accented vowel in names such as, G<u>ow</u>er, and S<u>ou</u>ndpost.

• the unaccented vowel in names such as, S<u>ou</u>thampton.

## / oʊ /

**Note:** In 'general American' speech, the 'long O' sound is transcribed as the diphthong, / oʊ /, in accented positions, and the 'pure vowel' / o/, in unaccented positions (see / o / above). In 'British RP' speech the 'long O' sound is transcribed as / əʊ /, in both accented and unaccented positions, (see / əʊ / below), except in the case of OL spellings, when it is transcribed with the pure vowel / o /, (see / o / above).

The 'long O' sound, / oʊ / occurs as:

• the accented vowel in 'general American' transcription of names such as, J<u>oa</u>n, <u>Oa</u>tcake, R<u>o</u>mco, P<u>o</u>land, and C<u>o</u>ldspur.

## / əʊ /

**Note:** In 'British RP' speech the 'long O' sound is transcribed as / əʊ /, in both accented and unaccented positions, except in the case of OL spellings, when it is transcribed as the pure vowel / o / (see above). In 'general American' speech, the 'long O' sound is transcribed as the diphthong, / oʊ /, (see above), in accented positions, and the 'pure vowel' / o /, (see above), in unaccented positions.

/ əʊ / occurs as:

• the accented vowel in 'British RP' transcription of names such as, Jo<u>a</u>n, <u>O</u>atcake, and R<u>o</u>meo.

• the unaccented vowel in 'British RP' transcription of names such as, Apoll<u>o</u>, and Ech<u>o</u>.

/ ɔɪ /

/ ɔɪ / occurs as:

• the accented vowel in names such as, P<u>oi</u>nes, le R<u>oy</u>, Fr<u>oi</u>ssart.

• the unaccented vowel in names such as, Montj<u>oy</u>, and Charl<u>ois</u>.

/ ju /

Note: The 'liquid U' sound, / ju / occurs in both 'general American,' and 'British RP' pronunciation in words such as cute, and few. However, there are many words pronounced with / u / in 'general American,' which are pronounced with / ju / in 'British RP'. These words adhere to the following rule of spelling: words spelled with U or, EW preceded by D, N, T, and ST, such as Duke, news, tune, and stew, and formerly S, L, and TH, such as, suit, lute, and enthusiasm, are pronounced with / u / in 'general American' and / ju / in 'British RP'. The practice of pronouncing such words with / ju / in the U.S. is presently losing currency (Wells, 1990, Colaianni, Mufson, Knight).

The 'liquid U' sound, / ju / occurs as:

• the accented vowel in names such as, H<u>ugh</u>, and C<u>u</u>pid.

• the unaccented vowel in names such as, Emman<u>u</u>el, and Bartholom<u>ew</u>.

• the accented vowel in 'British RP' transcription of names such as, Brun<u>du</u>sium, N<u>u</u>ma, and T<u>ew</u>ksbury, as well as H<u>ugh</u>, and C<u>u</u>pid.

• the unaccented vowel in 'British RP' transcription of names such as, D<u>u</u>main, Mant<u>u</u>a, and Orph<u>eu</u>s, as well as Emman<u>u</u>el, and Bartholom<u>ew</u>.

## / iə /

/ iə / occurs as:

• the unaccented diphthong in names such as, Act<u>iu</u>m, Bor<u>ea</u>s, Fab<u>ia</u>n, Lib<u>ya</u>, Prometh<u>eu</u>s, Cor<u>io</u>lanus and Jul<u>ie</u>t (variant).

## / io /

/ io / occurs as:

• the unaccented diphthong in 'general American' transcription of names such as, Anton<u>io</u>, and Rom<u>eo</u>.

## / iəʊ /

/ iəʊ / occurs as:

• the unaccented diphthong in 'British RP' transcription of names such as, Anton<u>io</u>, and Rom<u>eo</u>.

## / iɛ /

/ iɛ / occurs as:

• the unaccented diphthong in a variant 'general American' transcription of the name Jul<u>ie</u>t.

## / ie /

/ ie / occurs as:

• the unaccented diphthong in a variant 'British RP' transcription of the name Jul<u>ie</u>t.

### R, AND ITS RELATIONSHIP TO VOWELS

## / ɚ /

/ ɚ / occurs as:

• the unaccented 'r-colored' vowel in 'general American' transcription of names such as, Mortim<u>er</u>, Cast<u>or</u>, Rich<u>ar</u>d, and B<u>er</u>nardo. For example, / ˈmɔr tɪ mɚ /.

# / ə /

/ ə / occurs as:

• the unaccented, non-rhotic vowel in 'British RP' transcription of names such as, Mortimer, Castor, Richard, and Bernardo. For example, / 'mɔ tɪ mə/.

# / ɝ /

/ ɝ / occurs as:

• the accented 'r-colored' vowel in 'general American' transcriptions of names such as, Mercury, and Birnum. For example,/ 'mɝ kjə ri/.

# / ɜ /

/ ɜ / occurs as:

• the accented, non-rhotic vowel in 'British RP' transcription of names such as, Mercury, and Birnum. For example,/ 'mɜ kjʊ ri/.

# / ɪr /

/ ɪr / occurs as:

• the 'r-colored' vowel in 'general American' transcription of names such as, Pierce and Lackbeard. For example, / 'pɪrs /.

# / ɪə /

/ ɪə / occurs as:

• the accented, non-rhotic vowel in 'British RP' transcription of names such as Pierce, Lackbeard.

# / ɛr /

/ ɛr / occurs as:

• the 'r-colored' vowel in 'general American' transcription of names such as, Ariel, Clare, and Ligarius. For example, / 'ɛ riəl /.

## / ɛə /

/ ɛə /occurs as:

• the diphthong preceding R in 'British RP' transcription of names such as, A̲riel, Cla̲re, and Liga̲rius. For example, / ˈɛə riəl /.

## / ɑr /

/ ɑr / occurs as:

• the 'r-colored' vowel in 'general American' transcriptions of names such as A̲rden, and Ca̲rthage. For example, / ˈɑr dən/.

• for 'British RP' pronunciation of names such as, A̲rden, and Ca̲rthage, see / ɑ / above.

## / ɔr /

/ ɔr / occurs as:

• the 'r-colored' vowel in 'general American' transcription of names such as, Mo̲re, and Do̲rset. For example,/ ˈmɔr/.

• for 'British RP' pronunciation of names such as, Mo̲re, and Do̲rset, see/ ɔ /above.

## / ʊr /

/ ʊr /occurs as:

• the 'r-colored' vowel in 'general American' transcriptions of names such as, Mo̲o̲rditch, and Su̲recard. For example, / ˈmʊr dɪtʃ /.

## / ʊə /

/ ʊə / occurs as:

• the accented vowel in 'British RP' transcription of names such as Mo̲o̲rditch, and Su̲recard. For example, / ˈmʊə dɪtʃ /.

# International Phonetic Alphabet Pronunciation Key

The following two charts outline 'general American' and 'British RP' use of the International Phonetic symbols in this dictionary. Shakespeare's names are used as key words in these charts. The first chart outlines the use of phonetic symbols in the 'general American' transcriptions. The second chart provides additional symbols used in 'British RP' transcription which differ from those used for 'general American'.

## 'General American' Pronunciation Key
## Using International Phonetic Alphabet

| PHONETIC SYMBOL | 'GENERAL AMERICAN' PRONUNCIATION KEY USING INTERNATIONAL PHONETIC ALPHABET |
|---|---|
| **Vowels** | **Alphabet** |
| i | Crete /ˈkrit/ |
| ɪ | Will /ˈwɪl/ |
| ɛ | Nell /ˈnɛl/ (gen Am only) |
| æ | Mab /ˈmæb/ |
| ɑ | Prague /ˈprɑg/ |
|  | Doll /ˈdɑl/ (gen Am only) |
| ʌ | Snug /ˈsnʌg/ |
| ə | Abraham /ˈeɪ brə hæm/ |
| ɝ | Mercury /ˈmɝ kjə ri/ (gen Am only) |
| ɚ | Mortimer /ˈmɔr tɪ mɚ/ (gen Am only) |
| ɔ | Gaunt /ˈgɔnt/ |
| o | Apollo /ə ˈpɑ lo/ (gen Am only) |
| ʊ | Butcher /ˈbʊ tʃɚ/ |
| u | Smooth /ˈsmuð/ |

## Diphthongs

| | |
|---|---|
| eɪ | Page /ˈpeɪʤ/ |
| aɪ | Iras /ˈaɪ rəs/ |
| aʊ | Gower /ˈgaʊ ɚ/ |
| ɔɪ | Poines /ˈpɔɪnz/ |
| ju | Hugh /ˈhju/ |

## Unaccented diphthongs containing /i /

| | |
|---|---|
| iə | Actium /ˈæk tiəm/ |
| io | Antonio /æn ˈtoʊ nio/ |
| iɛ | Juliet /ˈʤu liɛt/ |

## Consonants

| | |
|---|---|
| b | Bates /ˈbeɪts/ |
| p | Paul /ˈpɔl/ |
| d | Dis /ˈdɪs/ |
| t | Tib /ˈtɪb/ |
| g | Gam /ˈgæm/ |
| k | Car /ˈkɑr/ |
| | Kate /ˈkeɪt/ |
| v | Vice /ˈvaɪs/ |
| f | Fife /ˈfaɪf/ |
| z | Friz /ˈfrɪz/ |
| s | Say /ˈseɪ/ |
| ʒ | Artesius /ɑr ˈti ʒəs/ |
| ʃ | Shaw /ˈʃɔ/ |
| ð | Netherlands /ˈnɛ ðɚ ləndz/ |
| θ | Thebes /ˈθibz/ |
| ʤ | Jove /ˈʤoʊv/ |
| ʧ | Charles /ˈʧɑrlz/ |
| h | Hal /ˈhæl/ |
| j | York /ˈjɔrk/ |
| l | Luce /ˈlus/ |

| m | Mab /'mæb/ |
| n | Nym /'nɪm/ |
| ŋ | Fang /fæŋ/ |
| r | Rose /'roʊz/ |
| w | Wall /'wɔl/ |

## Additional International Phonetic symbols for 'British RP' Pronunciation

PHONETIC SYMBOL   ADDITIONAL INTERNATIONAL PHONETIC SYMBOLS FOR 'BRITISH RP' PRONUNCIATION

### Vowels — Pronunciation

| e | Nell /'nel/ |
| ɒ | Doll /'dɒl/ |
| ɜ | Mercury /'mɜ kjʊ ri/ |
| ə (neutral vowel) followed by r | Mortimer /'mɔ tɪ mə/ |

### Diphthongs

| ju | Tunis /'tju nɪs/ |
| ɪə | Pierce /'pɪəs/ |
| eə | Ariel /'eə ri əl/ |
| ʊə | Moorditch /'mʊə dɪtʃ/ |
| iəʊ | Antonio /æn 'təʊ niəʊ/ |
| ie | Juliet /'ʤu liet/ |

## *Explanation of the Simplified Phonics symbols*

ACCENTUATION

No accent marks are used in the Simplified Phonics Alphabet transcription. To determine the accented syllable, refer to the International Phonetic Alphabet transcription in the center column of the dictionary. (See Accentuation, above).

See syllable division explanation above.

## ee

The 'long E' sound, **ee**, occurs as:

• the accented vowel in names such as Crete and Creon.

• the weak, final vowel in names such as Albany, Barabary, Stanley, and Dizie.

• the weak element in a diphthong in names such as Juliet, Amiens, Ariel, and Romeo.

• the first element in a triphthong in names such as, Bentii.

## i

The 'short I' sound, i, occurs as:

• the accented vowel in names such as Richard, Will, Nym, and Syria.

• the unaccented vowel in names such as, Cressida, and Yorick.

## e

**Note:** In the Simplified Phonics Alphabet transcription, the **e** symbol represents both 'general American,' and 'British RP' pronunciation of the 'short e' sound.

The 'short E' sound, **e** occurs as:

• the accented vowel in names such as, Nell, Henry, and Edward.

• the unaccented vowel in names such as Benvolio, and Mediterranean.

## a

**Note:** The following names are pronounced with the 'short A' sound, **a** in U. S. speech and the 'broad A' sound, **ah** in British RP speech: Alexander, Alexandria, Beregomask, Blanch, Bullcalf, Castle, Castor, Falstaff, Flanders, France, Frances, Francis, Halfcan, Half-moon,

Hopdance, Oldcastle. For example, the name Blanch is transcribed, blanch, for 'general American,' and, blahnch, for 'British RP'. Such names are said to belong to a spelling-based category of words known in the American Theater as the 'ask list' (Skinner). The practice in the U.S. of lowering a in words of this type to an 'intermediate A' as a compromise with 'British RP' pronunciation is now losing currency (Wells,1990, Colaianni, Mufson, Knight). Names such as Mab, Atlas, Ajax, and Rosencrantz, are pronounced with a in both 'general American,' and 'British RP'.

The 'short A' sound, **a**, occurs as:

• the accented vowel in names such as Mab, and Atlas.

• the accented vowel in names such as, France, and Falstaff, in 'general American' transcriptions only, (see note).

• the unaccented vowel in names such as, Ajax, and Rosencratz.

## uh

**uh** occurs as:

• the accented vowel in names such as, Snug, Duncan, and Montgomery.

• the unaccented vowel in names such as Abraham, Octavia, Pandulph, and Publicola.

## ah

**Note:** The vowel spelled with O, in words such as, hot, and pond, and WA, in words such as, wash, and want, is pronounced with the 'broad a' sound, **ah**, in 'general American' speech and the 'short o' sound **o** (see below), in 'British RP' speech.

**Note:** The following names are pronounced with the 'short A' sound, **a** in 'general American' speech and the 'broad A' sound, **ah** in 'British RP' speech: Alexander, Alexandria, Beregomask, Blanch, Bullcalf, Castle, Castor, Falstaff, Flanders, France, Frances, Francis, Halfcan, Half-moon, Hopdance, Oldcastle. For example, the name Blanch is transcribed, blanch, for 'general American,' and, blahnch, for 'British RP'.

The 'broad A' sound, **ah**, occurs as:

• the accented vowel in names such as, Adriano, Iago, Prague, Solanio, and Arden.

• the accented vowel in 'general American' transcriptions of names such as, Doll, Apollo, and Washes.

• the accented vowel in 'British RP' transcriptions of names such as, France, and Falstaff (see note).

• the unaccented vowel in 'general American' transcriptions of names such as, Aesop, and Constantinople.

• a variant pronunciation for the accented vowel in 'general American' transcription of names such as, Gaunt, Audrey, Cawdor, and Waterford (see also, **aw**, below).

• a variant pronunciation for the unaccented vowel in 'general American' transcription of names such as, Cadwal.

## *o*

**Note:** The vowel spelled with O, in words such as, hot, and pond, is pronounced with the 'broad a' sound, **ah**, in 'general American' speech and the 'short o' sound *o*, in 'British RP' speech.

The 'short o' sound, italicized *o*, occurs as:

• the accented vowel in 'British RP' transcriptions of names such as, Doll, Apollo, and Washes.

• the unaccented vowel in 'British RP' transcriptions of names such as, Aesop, and Constantinople.

## **aw**

**aw** occurs as:

• the accented vowel in names such as, Gaunt, Audrey, Cawdor, Waterton, and Dorset (see **ah** above for 'general American' variant pronunciation).

## *oo*

italicized *oo* occurs as:

• the accented vowel in names such as, Butcher, and Goodman.

• the unaccented vowel in names such as Bolingbroke, and Ringwood.

## oo

The 'long U' sound, **oo** occurs as:

• the accented vowel in names such as, J<u>u</u>le, Sm<u>oo</u>th, Ber<u>ow</u>ne, L<u>ewi</u>s, and Petr<u>u</u>chio.

• the unaccented vowel in names such as, Andr<u>ew</u>, Joshu<u>a</u>, and Halfm<u>oo</u>n.

DIPHTHONGS:

## ei

The 'long A' sound, **ei**, occurs as:

• the accented vowel in names such as, P<u>a</u>ge, C<u>ai</u>n, P<u>ei</u>phon, and Mele<u>a</u>ger.

• the unaccented vowel in names such as, <u>A</u>driana, and Gallow<u>ay</u>.

## ai

The 'long I' sound, **ai**, occurs as:

• the accented vowel in names such as, Sm<u>i</u>le, <u>I</u>ras, and C<u>y</u>prus.

• the unaccented vowel in names such as, Rosal<u>i</u>ne, and Bent<u>ii</u>.

## ow

**ow** occurs as:

• the accented vowel in names such as, G<u>ow</u>er, and S<u>ou</u>ndpost.

• the unaccented vowel in names such as, S<u>ou</u>thampton.

## o

**Note:** In Simplified Phonics transcription, the single character, **o** represents both 'general American,' and 'British RP' pronunciation of the 'long O' diphthong.

The 'long o' sound, **o**, occurs as:

• the accented vowel in names such, J<u>oa</u>n, <u>Oa</u>tcake, R<u>o</u>meo, P<u>o</u>land, and C<u>o</u>ldspur.

• the unaccented vowel in names such as, Apoll<u>o</u>, and Ech<u>o</u>.

## oy

**oy** occurs as:

• the accented vowel in names such as, P<u>oi</u>nes, le R<u>oy</u>, and Fr<u>oi</u>ssart.

• the unaccented vowel in names such as, Montj<u>oy</u>, and Charl<u>ois</u>.

## yoo

**Note:** The 'liquid U' sound, **yoo**, occurs in both 'British RP' and 'general American' pronunciation of words such as cute, and few. However, many words pronounced with **oo** in 'general American,' are pronounced with **yoo** in 'British RP'. 'Liquid U' words can be identified by the following rule of spelling: words spelled with U, or, EW, preceded by D, N, T, and ST, such as Duke, news, tune, and stew, and, formerly S, L, and TH, such as, suit, lute, and enthusiasm, are pronounced with **oo** in 'general American' and **yoo** in 'British RP'. The practice of pronouncing such words with **yoo** in the U.S. is presently losing currency (Wells, 1990, Colaianni, Mufson, and Knight).

The 'liquid U' sound, **yoo**, occurs as:

• the accented vowel in names such as, H<u>ug</u>h, and C<u>u</u>pid.

• the unaccented vowel in names such as, Emman<u>ue</u>l, and Bartholom<u>ew</u>.

• the accented vowel in 'British RP' transcription of names such as, Brund<u>u</u>sium, N<u>u</u>ma, and T<u>ew</u>ksbury, as well as H<u>ug</u>h, and C<u>u</u>pid.

• the unaccented vowel in 'British RP' transcription of names such as, D<u>u</u>main, Mant<u>ua</u>, and Orph<u>eu</u>s, as well as Emman<u>ue</u>l, and Bartholom<u>ew</u>.

## ər

ər occurs as:

• the accented, 'r-colored' vowel in 'general American' transcription of names such as, M<u>er</u>cury, amd B<u>ir</u>num.

• the unaccented 'r colored' vowel in 'general American' transcription of names such as, Mortim<u>er</u>, Cast<u>or</u>, Rich<u>ar</u>d, and B<u>er</u>nardo.

## *ə*

italicized *ə* occurs as:

• the accented vowel in 'British RP' transcription of names such as, M<u>er</u>cury, amd B<u>ir</u>num.

## ə

ə occurs as:

• the unaccented vowel in 'British RP' taranscription of names such as, Mortim<u>er</u>, Cast<u>or</u>, Rich<u>ar</u>d, and B<u>er</u>nardo.

## ir

ir occurs as:

• the 'r-colored' vowel in 'general American' transcription of names such as, P<u>ie</u>rce and Lackb<u>ear</u>d.

## iə

iə occurs as:

• the accented vowel in 'British RP' transcription of names such as, P<u>ie</u>rce and Lackb<u>ear</u>d.

## er

er occurs as:

• the 'r-colored' vowel in 'general American' transcription of names such as <u>A</u>riel, Cl<u>are</u>, and Lig<u>ar</u>ius.

## eə

eə occurs as:

• the accented vowel in 'British RP' transcription of names such as, <u>A</u>riel, Cl<u>a</u>re and Lig<u>a</u>rius.

## ahr

ahr occurs as:

• the 'r-colored' vowel in 'general American' transcription of names such as, <u>Ar</u>den, and C<u>ar</u>thage.

• for 'British RP' pronunciation of names such as, <u>Ar</u>den, and C<u>ar</u>thage, see **ah**, above.

## awr

awr occurs as:

• the 'r-colored' vowel in 'general American' transcription of names such as M<u>ore</u>, and D<u>or</u>set.

• for 'British RP' pronunciation of names such as, More, and Dorset, see **aw**, above.

## oor

oor occurs as:

• the 'r-colored' vowel in 'general American' transcription of names such as, M<u>oor</u>ditch, and S<u>ur</u>card.

## *ooə*

*ooə* occurs as:

• the accented vowel in 'British RP' transcription of names such as, M<u>oo</u>rditch, and S<u>ur</u>ecard.

# Simplified Phonics Alphabet Pronunciation Key

The following two charts outline 'general American' and 'British RP' use of the Simplified Phonics symbols in this dictionary. Shakespeare's names are used as key words in these charts. The first chart outlines the use of Simplified Phonics symbols in 'general American' transcription. The second chart provides additional Simplified Phonics symbols used in 'British RP' transcription which differ from those used for 'general American'.

'General American' Pronunciation Key
Using Simplified Phonics Symbols

| SIMPLIFIED PHONICS SYMBOL | 'GENERAL AMERICAN' PRONUNCIATION KEY USING SIMPLIFIED PHONICS SYMBOLS |
|---|---|
| **Vowels** | **Symbols** |
| ee | Crete – kreet |
| | Barbary – bahr buh ree |
| i | Will – wil |
| e | Nell – nel |
| a | Mab – mab |
| ah | Prague – prahg |
| | Doll – dahl |
| uh | Snug – snuhg |
| | Abr*a*ham – ei bruh ham |
| ər | Mercury – mər kyuh ree |
| | Mortim*er* – mawr ti m*ər* |
| aw | Gaunt – gawnt |
| *oo* | Butcher – b*oo* chər |
| oo | Smooth – smooth |

## Diphthongs

| ei | Page – peij |
|----|-------------|
| ai | Iras – ai ruhs |
| ow | Gower – gow ər |
| oy | Poines – poynz |
| o | Joan – jon |
| | Apoll<u>o</u> – uh pah lo |
| yoo | Hugh – hyoo |

## Unaccented diphthongs containing ee

| ee uh | Act<u>iu</u>m – ak tee uhm |
|-------|---------------------------|
| ee o | Anton<u>io</u> – an to nee o |
| ee e | Jul<u>ie</u>t – joo lee et |

## Consonants

| b | <u>B</u>ates – beits |
|---|----------------------|
| p | <u>P</u>aul – pawl |
| d | <u>D</u>is – dis |
| t | <u>T</u>ib – tib |
| g | <u>G</u>am – gam |
| k | <u>C</u>ar – kahr |
| | <u>K</u>ate – keit |
| v | <u>V</u>ice – vais |
| f | <u>F</u>ife – faif |
| z | Fri<u>z</u> – friz |
| s | <u>S</u>ay – sei |
| zh | Arte<u>s</u>ius – ahr tee zhuhs |
| sh | <u>Sh</u>aw – shaw |
| th | Ne<u>th</u>erlands – ne thər luhndz |
| *th* | <u>Th</u>ebes – *th*eebz |
| j | <u>J</u>ove – jov |
| ch | <u>Ch</u>arles – chahrlz |
| h | <u>H</u>al – hal |

| y | <u>Y</u>ork – yawrk |
|---|---|
| l | <u>L</u>uce – loos |
| m | <u>M</u>ab – mab |
| n | <u>N</u>ym – nim |
| ng | Fa<u>ng</u> – fang |
| r | <u>R</u>ose – roz |
| w | <u>W</u>all – wawl |

## Additional Simplified Phonics Symbols for 'British RP' Pronunciation

| SIMPLIFIED PHONICS SYMBOL | ADDITIONAL SIMPLIFIED PHONICS SYMBOLS FOR 'BRITISH RP' PRONUNCIATION |
|---|---|

### Vowels

| *o* | Doll – d*o*l |
|---|---|
| ə | M<u>er</u>cury – mə ky*oo* r*ee* |
| ə | Mortim<u>er</u> – maw ti mə |

### Diphthongs

| yoo | T<u>u</u>nis – tyoo nis |
|---|---|
| iə | Pierce – piəs |
| eə | Snare – sneə |
| *oo*ə | M<u>oo</u>rditch – m*oo*ə dich |

# Bibliography

BARNHART, Clarence L. *The New Century Cyclopedia of Names*. New York: Appleton-Century-Crofts, 1954.

BARTLETT, John. *A Complete Concordance ... of Shakespeare*. New York: St Martin's Press, 1966.

BOLLARD, James K. *Pronouncing Dictionary of Proper Names*. Detroit, Michigan: Omnigraphics, 1993.

CERCIGNANI, Fausto. *Shakespeare's Works and Elizabethan Pronunciation*. New York: Clarendon Press: Oxford University Press, 1981.

COLAIANNI, Louis. *The Joy of Phonetics and Accents*. New York: Drama Book Publishers, 1994.

DARNTON, John. "The English Are Talking Funny Again." *New York Times* Volume CXLIII, Number 49,552, December 21, 1992.

EZARD, John. "New Yorkers Catch Up On Accent That Would Send Henry Higgins Back To His Phonetics Laboratory." *The Guardian,* London, December 22, 1993.

FURNESS, Mrs Horace Howard. *A Concordance to Shakespeare's Poems*. Philadelphia: Lippincott, 1875.

HOBBS, Robert L. *Teach Yourself Transatlantic*. Palo Alto, California: Mayfield Publishing Company, 1986.

IRVINE, Theodora. *A Pronouncing Dictionary of Shakespearean Proper Names*. New York: Barnes and Noble, 1944.

JONES, Daniel. *Everyman's English Pronouncing Dictionary*. GIMSON, A.C., editor. Cambridge: Cambridge

University Press, 1991.

KENYON, John Samuel, and KNOTT, Thomas Albert. *A Pronouncing Dictionary of American English.* Springfield, Massachusetts: G & C Merriam Company, 1953.

KNIGHT, Dudley. "William Tilly And 'Good Speech'." Voice and Speech Trainers Association Volume 6, Number 1, 1992.

KOKERITZ, Helge. *Shakespeare's Names: A Pronouncing Dictionary.* New Haven: Yale University Press, 1959.

LANE-PLESCIA, Gillian. *South African For The Actor.* Chicago: Act One Books, 1994.

LINKLATER, Kristin. *Freeing the Natural Voice.* New York: Drama Book Publishers, 1976.

MORIARTY, John. *Diction.* Boston: E.C. Schirmer Music Company, 1975.

MUFSON, Dan. "Falling Standard." *Theater,* Yale School of Drama/Yale Rep Volume 25, Number 1, 1994.

SCHMIDT, Alexander. *Shakespeare Lexicon.* New York: Arno Press, 1980.

SHAKESPEARE, William, and FLETCHER, John. *The Two Noble Kinsmen.* New York: Penguin Books, 1977.

SHAKESPEARE, William. *The Complete Works.*

SKINNER, Edith. *Speak With Distinction.* New York: Applause, 1990.

SPEVAK, Marvin. *The Harvard Concordance to Shakespeare.* Cambridge, Massachusetts: Belknap Press of Harvard University Press, 1973.

WELLS, J.C. *Longman's Pronunciation Dictionary.* London: Longman Group UK Limited, 1995.

WELLS, J.C. *Accents of English.* Cambridge: Cambridge University Press, 1982.